'Accounting in China has experienced significant reforms as the opening and growing of China's economy has become one of the most critical stories on the world stage during the past four decades. The book includes sixteen new scholarly papers on conceptual and empirical issues related to the contemporary accounting and auditing issues in China. It offers a collective and innovative perspective that should benefit scholars and practitioners.'

– **Heibatollah Sami**, *Professor of Accounting, Lehigh University, US*

THE ROUTLEDGE COMPANION TO ACCOUNTING IN CHINA

There is increasing interest in accounting issues in China. Despite a relatively short history, China's stock market is the world's second largest. This growth has been accompanied by increasing demand for accounting information alongside reforms of accounting and auditing rules, as international investors have paid increasing attention to investment opportunities in this dynamic and energetic country with a large population and economic growth potentials. Despite this, at present there are few books which offer students, academics and practitioners a comprehensive guide to current accounting issues in China.

The Routledge Companion to Accounting in China fills this important gap in the literature. The volume is organized in six thematic sections which cover capital market and corporate finance, financial accounting, managerial accounting, auditing, taxation and internal controls. The structure is intended to reflect the increasing diversity of contemporary accounting issues in China, including a balanced overview of current knowledge, identifying issues and discussing relevant debates.

This book is a prestigious reference work which offers students, academics and practitioners an introduction to current accounting issues in the emerging market of China.

Haiyan Zhou is a professor at the University of Texas Rio Grande Valley, US. Professor Zhou obtained a Ph.D. in accounting from Temple University and has been teaching both undergraduate and graduate accounting and auditing courses. Professor Zhou serves as Editor-in-Chief of *Asian Review Accounting*, and as an editorial board member of the *Journal of International Accounting, Auditing and Taxation*.

ROUTLEDGE COMPANIONS IN BUSINESS, MANAGEMENT AND ACCOUNTING

Routledge Companions in Business, Management and Accounting are prestige reference works providing an overview of a whole subject area or sub-discipline. These books survey the state of the discipline including emerging and cutting edge areas. Providing a comprehensive, up to date, definitive work of reference, Routledge Companions can be cited as an authoritative source on the subject.

A key aspect of these Routledge Companions is their international scope and relevance. Edited by an array of highly regarded scholars, these volumes also benefit from teams of contributors which reflect an international range of perspectives.

Individually, Routledge Companions in Business, Management and Accounting provide an impactful one-stop-shop resource for each theme covered. Collectively, they represent a comprehensive learning and research resource for researchers, postgraduate students and practitioners.

Published titles in this series include

The Routledge Companion to European Business
Edited by Gabriele Suder, Monica Riviere and Johan Lindeque

The Routledge Companion to Management Buyouts
Edited by Mike Wright, Kevin Amess, Nick Bacon and Donald Siegel

The Routledge Companion to Co-opetition Strategies
Edited by Anne-Sophie Fernandez, Paul Chiambaretto,
Frédéric Le Roy and Wojciech Czakon

The Routledge Companion to Reward Management
Edited by Stephen J. Perkins

The Routledge Companion to Accounting in China
Edited by Haiyan Zhou

For more information about this series, please visit: www.routledge.com/Routledge-Companions-in-Business-Management-and-Accounting/book-series/RCBMA

THE ROUTLEDGE COMPANION TO ACCOUNTING IN CHINA

Edited by Haiyan Zhou

Routledge
Taylor & Francis Group

LONDON AND NEW YORK

First published 2019
by Routledge

2 Park Square, Milton Park, Abingdon, Oxfordshire OX14 4RN
52 Vanderbilt Avenue, New York, NY 10017

Routledge is an imprint of the Taylor & Francis Group, an informa business

First issued in paperback 2020

British Library Cataloguing-in-Publication Data
A catalogue record for this book is available from the British Library

Library of Congress Cataloging-in-Publication Data
Names: Zhou, Haiyan, editor.
Title: The Routledge companion to accounting in China / edited by Haiyan Zhou.
Description: Abingdon, Oxon ; New York, NY : Routledge, 2019. | Series:
Routledge companions in business, management and accounting | Includes
bibliographical references and index.
Identifiers: LCCN 2018021993 | ISBN 9781138678538 (hardback) | ISBN
9781315558899 (ebook)
Subjects: LCSH: Accounting—China.
Classification: LCC HF5616.C5 R68 2019 | DDC 657.0951—dc23
LC record available at https://lccn.loc.gov/2018021993

ISBN: 978-1-138-67853-8 (hbk)
ISBN: 978-0-367-65610-2 (pbk)

Typeset in Bembo
by Apex CoVantage, LLC

CONTENTS

Contents

CONTRIBUTOR BIOGRAPHIES

Qiang Cao is an associate professor of finance and economics at Central University of Finance and Economics. Dr. Cao completed his Ph.D. with Prof. Hanwen Chen at Xiamen University in China in July 2009. He has published one academic monograph and 15 papers in journals such as *Journal of Industrial Engineering and Management* (EI), *Accounting Research* (China) and *Journal of Central University of Finance & Economics* (China). His current research interests are economics of auditing, financial reporting and risk management. In particular, he is interested in studying whether audit firms' mergers improves financial reporting comparability, which factors determine the possibility and level of the improvement of financial reporting comparability and whether and how local culture influence financial reporting behavior.

Hanwen Chen is Distinguished Professor of Accounting at University of International Business and Economics. He used to be a professor and doctoral faculty member at Xiamen University. He has served on Boards of Directors of Xiamen International Bank Co., Ltd., Dalian Wanda Commercial Properties Co. Ltd. and Xiamen Overseas Chinese Electronic Co. Ltd. He is a Chair Professor of China Business Executives Academy, Dalian, Co-Editor-in-Chief of the *China Journal of Accounting Research* (CJAS) – the top Chinese professional accounting publication – an editorial board member of *Auditing Research*– the top Chinese professional auditing publication. Being one of the top Chinese accountants recognized by the Ministry of Finance, he also serves as a judge on the Fujian Senior Auditor Review Committee and the Fujian Senior Accountant Review Committee, Standing Director of China Audit Society, and Vice Chairman of Fujian Internal Auditing Association, the Fujian Auditing Society, and the Xiamen Municipal Accounting Society.

Songsheng Chen is a full professor and chair in the Department of Accounting, Beijing Institute of Technology. He holds a B.S. and M.S. in accounting from the School of Accounting of Jiangxi University of Finance and Economics, and a Ph.D. from Renmin University of China. He is the author or co-author of approximately 40 journal articles, including publications in *Journal of Information Systems*, *Journal of Business Research*, *Journal of Emerging Technology in Accounting*, *Journal of International Accounting Research*, *Asia-Pacific Journal of Accounting and Economics* and *Journal of International Accounting Research*. He also visited Karlsruhe Institute of Technology (Germany), the University of South Carolina (the United States) and the National University of Singapore, as a senior visiting scholar. He was a member of the American Accounting Association and China Institute of Internal Auditors. He also was a member of Education Branch of China Auditing Society, where he served as deputy secretary general. He is a member of the councils of China Accounting Review and China Auditing Review.

Wang Dong is an associate professor in the Department of Finance and Accounting, School of Management, Zhejiang University. He is also a research associate at the Center for China's Governmental Auditing Research. He obtained his Ph.D. in accounting from Xiamen University. He holds a CPA (Certified Public Accountant, non-practicing) and a CIA (Certified Internal Auditor). His research interests include auditing, internal control and corporate finance. He has published his research in journals including *European Accounting Review, Review of Quantitative Finance and Accounting, Journal of Business Ethics, Asia-Pacific Journal of Accounting and Economics, Journal of Financial Research* (in Chinese) and *Auditing Research* (in Chinese). He currently serves as an independent director and audit committee chair on several publicly listed companies and provides consulting service on internal control to public companies.

Wei Gao is a graduate student in accounting at the School of Management, Xiamen University. Wei Gao's research interest is in management accounting.

Na Gong is Associate Professor and director of financial management of the School of Accounting at Shanghai Lixin University of Accounting and Finance. She got her bachelor's degree, master's degree and doctorate degree in management from Jilin University. She teaches financial management, management accounting, case study of financial management, case study in management accounting and financial analysis. Her research interests are equity incentive and private enterprise governance. She has published several related papers in top journals in China. She has also received many grants, including a grant from the MOE (Ministry of Education in China) Project of Humanities and Social Sciences.

Huiting Guo is Associate Professor at the School of Economic Management, Chang'an University, China. Her research interest includes capital market, corporate analysis and evaluation, and accounting information disclosure in China. She has published ten research papers in Chinese journals such as *Management Science, Hua Dong Economic and Management, Journal of Shan Xi Finance and Economics University, Statistic and Information Forum*, the *Journal of Applied Business Research* and *International Journal of Global Environmental Issues*. She has presented her research work at the International Symposium on Empirical Accounting Research in 2014 and 2017. She was a visiting scholar at Massey University, New Zealand in 2016.

Xiaomei Guo is Professor of Accounting at the School of Management, Xiamen University and Director of the Study Center of Management Accounting at Xiamen University. She obtained her Ph.D. in Management (accounting) from Xiamen University. She is also a member of CICPA and CGMA. She serves as a consultant in management accounting for the Finance Department of Fujian Province, and she is a member of the Northeast Asia Management Accounting Leaders Think Tank, CGMA100. She was visiting scholar to Ivey Business School of Western University, Canada in 2017 and was visiting scholar to Saint Mary's University in 2000. She has been teaching in Xiamen University since 1995 and working as a part time CPA in a CPA firm for many years. She is actively engaged with practice and has been a consultant for several enterprises. Her research interests are in management accounting, especially in corporate governance and risk management, management controls and environmental accounting. Her major publications include many articles and books, such as *Collection of Cases in Management Accounting Practice*, *On Environmental Management Accounting Practice* and *On Management Accounting Principles*.

Nanwei Hu is Associate Professor at China University of Mining and Technology (Beijing). Dr. Hu completed her Ph.D. with Prof. Hanwen Chen at Xiamen University in China in July 2009. She has published two academic monographs and a dozen articles in journal such as *Journal of Industrial Engineering and Management* (EI), *Accounting Research* (China) and *Journal of Central University of Finance & Economics* (China). Her current research interests include topics on the impact of client importance on audit quality, corporate disclosure policy, corporate earning management, tax aggressiveness and tax avoidance in China.

Zhiying Hu is Associate Professor in the Department of Accounting and Finance, Donglinks School of Economics and Management, University of Science and Technology, Beijing. She obtained her Ph.D. degree in accounting from the Research Institute for Fiscal Science, Ministry of Finance. She is a member of CICPA (Certified Public Accountants, non-practicing). Her current research interests include topics on venture capital, merger and acquisition, management gender and business groups. She has published papers in *China Journal of Accounting Research*, *Accounting Research* (in Chinese), *Nankai Management Review* (in Chinese), *China Accounting Review* (in Chinese), *Auditing Research* (in Chinese) and *Journal of Financial Research* (in Chinese). Her work has been presented at annual meetings of the American Accounting Association. She used to work as a senior manager in Grant Thornton International Ltd and as an accountant in Alstom (China) Investment Inc.

Guiru Hua is Associate Professor in the Department of Accounting at the East China University of Science and Technology and a visiting scholar at University of Texas, Rio Grande Valley. He has published extensively in top finance and accounting journals in China, such as the *Financial Research*, *Accounting Research* and *Managerial Accounting Research*.

Haiyan Jiang is Associate Professor of Accounting at Waikato Management School, University of Waikato in New Zealand. She specializes in international accounting research topics, such as accounting information quality, capital markets, governance issues in accounting and auditing. She has published in *Journal of International Accounting Research*, *The British Accounting Review*, *The International Journal of Accounting*, *Journal of Contemporary Accounting and Economics* and other peer reviewed journals. She frequently presents her work at leading international conferences, such as American Accounting Association annual conferences, European Accounting Association Annual Congress and Accounting and Finance Association Australian and New Zealand annual conferences. Haiyan collaborates with Chinese scholars intensively in recent years and has growing engagements with the Chinese academic community. She has been working on topics including related party transactions and political connection, which are the prominent factors shaping managers' financial reporting incentives in China. She also focuses on the effect of changing regulations and the unique institutional settings of China on corporate reporting, information quality and auditing. She serves on the editorial board of *Journal of International Accounting, Auditing and Taxation*.

Xiankun Jin is currently a Ph. D. student in Accounting at the Business School, Sun Yat-sen University. His research interests mainly lie in executive compensation, China's anti-corruption campaign and monitoring systems in Chinese State-owned enterprises.

Yun Ke has been Assistant Professor in the Department of Accounting, Goodman School of Business, Brock University since 2014. He received his Ph.D. in accounting from the University of British Columbia in 2015 and his MBA from Washington University in St. Louis in 2009. His current research interests include financial analysis, social capital and trust, internal control and financial reporting. He has published his research in *Journal of Business Ethics*. His work has been presented in annual meetings of the American Accounting Association and the Canadian Academic Accounting Association. Before starting the accounting Ph.D. program, he worked as a securities analyst.

Jiangna Li is currently a lecturer at Rongzhi College of Chongqing Technology and Business University. She received her M.A. in corporate finance from Northeast Normal University and B.A. in marketing from Beijing University of Chinese Medicine. Her professional experience includes being a securities analyst at Huatai Securities in China. She has both the securities qualification certificate and the fund qualification certificate. Her research interests include financial statement analysis, corporate finance and earnings forecast. She teaches investment theory, corporate finance and securities analysis. She has published one co-authored book and several papers in *Study & Exploration* and *Research on Financial and Economic Issues*. She also presented her research work at annual conferences such as the International Conference on Financial Risk and Corporate Finance Management, and the International Conference on Education, Management and Social Science (ICEMSS 2013).

Feng Liu serves as Minjiang Chair Professor of Accounting at Xiamen University, and Doctoral Mentor of Accounting, at Xiamen University. In the past, Professor Liu served as Director of the Modern Accounting and Finance Center and Associate Dean of School of Management and Doctoral Adviser of the Accounting Department at Sun Yat-sen University. He has been an Independent Director for many enterprises. He earned his Ph.D. of Accounting in Xiamen University in 1994. His research interest covers accounting standards, auditing, merger and acquisition, and board of director. His major publications include many articles and books. He frequently presents his work at leading international conferences such as *American Accounting Association annual conferences*. He is the co-founding editor of *China Journal of Accounting Research*, and currently serves as the chief editor of *Contemporary Accounting Review* (in Chinese). He serves also on the editorial board of *Asia Review of Accounting*.

Qingqing Liu is a Ph.D. candidate at Beijing Institute of Technology. Her research interests are auditing, analysts forecast and corporate governance. She has published a paper in *Auditing Research* (in Chinese), which also received the Best Paper Reward in the Academic Forum of Accounting Society of China (Auditing Panel Session). She was a co-author of The Frontier Research Report on the discipline of accounting and auditing in 2016, which was published by Economy & Management Publishing House (China). Her papers were presented in the 2016 and 2017 Annual Meeting of the American Accounting Association, the 2017 Annual Meeting of the Canadian Accounting Association, as well as the 2018 Annual Congress of the European Accounting Association.

Tongtong Liu is currently studying as a postgraduate in the Department of Accounting and Finance, Donglinks School of Economics and Management, University of Science and Technology, Beijing. She obtained her bachelor's degree in accounting from the School of Economics and Management at Yanshan University. She is a recipient of the National Endeavor Scholarship and the First-Class Scholarship. She used to serve as a junior accountant in accounting and consulting firms and provided auditing service and consulting service on management for public companies.

Xu Lou is Lecturer in Accounting at Zhengzhou University of Aeronautics. She currently is responsible for teaching ACCA management accounting and CIMA affairs. She graduated with a Master of Science in Finance (MsF) from the University of Tulsa in 2014. She earned a dual degree from Wuhan University in English Literature and Finance. Her research area is corporate governance and financial management. She is also interested in effectiveness and efficiency of accounting education, in particular, ACCA Student Study Patterns. She has published in *Public Finance* and *Management Accounting*.

Xiaohui Qu is Professor of Accounting at Xiamen University and the founder and chief editor of *Contemporary Accounting Review* (CSSCI, in Chinese). Professor Qu holds a Ph.D. from Xiamen University and is the first female Ph.D. in accounting in China. She was appointed to Dean of the Institute for Financial and Accounting Studies in 2010, Minjiang Professor at Xiamen University in 2006 and Chair Professor and Director of the Center for Accounting Studies at Xiamen University, effective in 2000. Prof. Qu has published research papers in domestic and international journals, as well as monographs and textbooks on a range of accounting and finance topics. The awards she has received include a Fulbright Research Scholar Award, 12 Ministry and provincial Social Science Research Awards and two best paper awards from the Accounting Society of China. She was honored as National Distinguished Woman designated by the All-China Federation of Trade Union, Academic Expert for the 21st Century designated by The Ministry of Education, China's Outstanding Social Scientist (2007) and a recipient of a government special allowance for the outstanding contributions to higher education by the State Council of China. She is the expert in assessment on China-Foreign joint-education programs invited by the Ministry of Education and the Advisory Expert of China Accounting Standards Committee. She initiated the Master of Professional Accounting as a national professional education program and has served as a member on the Nationwide MPAcc Teaching Steering Committee and the panel chief of teaching affairs. She served as a member of directors for China's Academic Degree & Graduate Education Society from 1995 to 2001 and has been on the panel of experts for project application assessment of the National Social Science Fund since 2000. She has served in the Chinese Accounting Professors Association as the president-elect, current & previous in 2004–2007 and as the director for the Committee of Accounting Theory for the Accounting Society of China since 2008 and a member of the Social Science Committee of MOE since 2007. She has been the editorial advisor of *Accounting Education: An International Journal* (printed in UK) since 1995 and a member of the editorial boards of *China Accounting and Finance Review* (bilingual), *China Accounting Review* (Chinese), *China Journal of Accounting Research* (English) and *Frontiers of Business Research in China* (English). She was the Chair of the Editorial Board for the *Journal of China Accounting Research & Education* (Chinese) from 2006 to 2009. She has served as member of the Board of Directors for several listed companies since 2009.

Grant Samkin is Professor in the Department of Accounting at the University of Waikato, and Professor in the Department of Financial Accounting at the University of South Africa. His research interests include narrative or non-financial reporting (including corporate social responsibility, sustainability and intellectual capital issues), education and accounting history. His research in accounting links three the broad themes of sustainability, history and education. Exploring these linkages helps academics to take a critical view of the role accounting plays in society. His recent work involves the development of a reporting and evaluation framework that can be used as an assessment tool and reporting guide by organizations whose operations impact on biodiversity. Other work involves a review of the development in governance in Africa.

Huanda Shi is a postgraduate student in the Department of Accounting at the East China University of Science and Technology. His research interests are in the area of investor sentiment and corporate finance. His working paper on tax preference, invest sentiment and M&A is accepted to be published. He has made several academic presentations His presentation on how investor sentiment drives M&A won the second prize for literature review at the business school in 2016, and his presentation on tax preference, invest sentiment and M&A at Donghua University won the third prize in 2017. He also worked as an intern in the credit card division for the Bank of China.

Yi Wang is a teaching assistant at the Accounting School at Zhengzhou University of Aeronautics, and a Ph.D. Candidate in the Business School at the University of International Business and Economics. She graduated from Shanghai International Studies University in 2012 and obtained a Bachelor of Administration (Accounting Major) degree and a Bachelor of Arts (English Major) degree. Yi pursued her graduate studies at the Robert. H. Smith Business School at the University of Maryland, where she earned a Master of Science in Accounting degree in 2013. She has taught financial accounting courses under the framework of US GAAP and IFRS, such as financial statement analysis, financial reporting (F7 of ACCA) and advanced accounting. Her research areas include microfinance, accounting information and capital market.

Deren Xie is Professor of Accounting at the School of Economics and Management, Tsinghua University. He received his Ph.D. in accounting from Xiamen University in June 1998. He had been a visiting scholar at MIT and Tulane University in 2009 and 2002, respectively. He focuses on the interdisciplinary study on accounting, new institutional economics and theory of the firm, the setting of accounting standards, corporate governance and executive incentives, and regulation of the CPA industry. He has published more than 40 papers in China's top accounting, finance, management and economics journals and three books since 1994. Many viewpoints of his papers have important contributions to both the theory and practice. As a result, he is among the accounting scholars with highest citation rate in China and has a very high reputation in the academia and is recognized as one of the outstanding accounting scholars by the Ministry of Finance of China. He has been the member of the 1st Advisory Council of Chinese Accounting Standards for Business Enterprises of the Ministry of Finance since 2016, and the member of the 17th Issuance Examination Committee of China Securities Regulatory Commission since 2017. He has also served on the board of directors of some top companies in China.

Yu Xin is Professor of Accounting at Sun Yat-sen University. He graduated from Hong Kong Polytechnic University with Ph.D. in Finance (2003). He joined Sun Yat-sen University in 2003, where he has served as the Head of the Department of Finance and Investment (2009–2012), and the Associate Dean of the Business School (2013–2015). His research areas are corporate governance and corporate finance. His publications appear in *Journal of Financial and Quantitative Analysis, Journal of Futures Markets, China Accounting and Finance Review, China Journal of Accounting Research* and Chinese journals such as *Economic Research Journal, Management World, Nankai Business Review, Journal of World Economy, China Industrial Economics, Accounting Research, Journal of Financial Research* and so on. He received research grants from the National Social Science Found of China (one Key Research Project) and the National Natural Science Foundation of China (three projects). He got best paper awards from the 2011 CICF and the 2010 China Finance Conference, from the Ministry of Education of China (2009), and from the Guangdong Planning Office of Philosophy and Social Science (2006, 2008, 2012).

Liquan Xing is Research Fellow at Shanghai Stock Exchange. He holds a Ph.D. in Accounting from Xiamen University. His research and practice interests are mainly in corporate governance, product market competition and earnings management.

Liping Xu is Professor of Accounting at the Business School, Sun Yat-sen University. She joined Sun Yat-sen University in 2004. She graduated from Hong Kong Polytechnic University with Ph.D. in Finance (2004). Her research areas are financial accounting and corporate finance. Her publications appear in *Journal of Financial and Quantitative Analysis, Journal of Corporate Finance, Journal of Banking and Finance, China Accounting and Finance Review, China Journal of Accounting Research*, and Chinese journals such as *Economic Research Journal, Management World, Nankai Business Review, The Journal of World Economy, Accounting Research* and so on. She has received research grants the National Natural Science Foundation of China (three projects). She received best paper awards from the 2011 CICF and the 2010 China Finance Conference, from the Ministry of Education of China (2009) and from the Guangdong Planning Office of Philosophy and Social Science (2006, 2008, 2012).

Fan Ye, a lecturer of Xiamen National Accounting Institute, holds B.A., M.A. and PH.D. from the Accounting Department of Xiamen University. He is a Certified Public Accountant (CPA) of P.R. China. His main research interest is in auditing, financial fraud and capital structure in China. He has published articles in academic journals such as Accounting Research (in Chinese).

Xiaoxiao Yu, a clerk of People's Bank of China Xiamen Central Sub-branch engaged in the field of accounting, payment and settlement, earned a bachelor degree in accounting from Dongbei University of Finance and Economics and a master degree in accounting from Xiamen University.

Liqun Yuan, CGMA, Deputy CEO of Midea Holdings Limited company, ex-CFO of Midea Group. She was in charge of the financial management, risk management and cash management of the group. She actively led her finance team to implement new concepts of cost management to support the shift of strategy of the company. Her research and practice interests are mainly in finance topics such as financial management, capital operation, business strategy and information management.

Tao Zeng is Associate Professor at Lazaridis School of Business and Economics, Wilfrid Laurier University. She received her Ph.D. from Queen's University in Canada. She has many publications in the fields of economics, management, accounting and taxation. Her articles have been published in a variety of academic journals such as *Asian Review of Accounting, Canadian Journal of Administrative Sciences, Review of Accounting and Finance, Journal of Financial Economic Policy, Canadian Tax Journal, Journal of Financial Economic Policy, Accounting Perspectives, Social Responsibility Journal*, etc. Her research interests include theoretical and empirical study of corporate governance and ownership structures, corporate tax, personal tax planning and capital market. She is Associate Editor of the *Journal of Economic and Administrative Sciences.*

Gongfu Zhang is Professor and Associate Dean in the Accounting School at Zhengzhou University of Aeronautics. He obtained his Ph.D. from Jinan University in 2008. He is a member of the editorial advisory board of *Asian Review of Accounting*, director of the *Committee of China Accounting Review* and Accounting Associate of Henan Province, and an anonymous peer reviewer for *Accounting Research of China, Nankai Management Review* and *Theory and Practice of Finance and Economics*. His research interests are in empirical corporate finance, corporate governance and behavior corporate finance. He has published more than 30 articles and three academic monographs.

Guohua Zhang, Professor and Director of the Center for Accounting Studies, Hairbin University of Commerce and an adjunct professor at Xiamen University,. Current research interests: fair value accounting and international convergence of accounting standards. Her recent publication is Xiaohui Qu & Guohua Zhang. 2015. Value-Relevance of Earnings and Book Value over the Institutional Transition in China: The Suitability of Fair Value Accounting in this Emerging Market, *International Journal of Accounting*, 50(2) June: 195–223.

Xiaohui Zhang is a postgraduate of Zhengzhou University of Aeronautics. Her research interests are in corporate governance and enterprise investment. She has published several articles in relevant journals.

Dengjin Zheng is Assistant Professor at the School of Accountancy, Central University of Finance and Economics. He received a Ph.D. in accounting from Tsinghua University in June 2017. He had been a research assistant at the School of Accountancy, Singapore Management University from July 2016 to April 2017. His primary research interests are in accounting and capital markets, corporate governance and corporate finance. He has published 13 papers in English or Chinese journals such as *Journal of Accounting and Public Policy* (in English) and *Management World* (in Chinese). Some of the published papers are about the Chinese Accounting Standards, such as the development cost accounting policy. He also achieved some academic honors and awards, i.e. Excellent Doctoral Dissertation of Tsinghua University and National Scholarships of Ministry of Education. He primarily teaches financial accounting and corporate finance.

Lulu Zheng completed her B.S. and M.S. Degree with Prof. Nanwei Hu at China University of Mining and Technology (Beijing) in July 2012 and 2015 respectively. She is working at Zhe Jiang Zhengeng Fuxing Fuel Co., Ltd. as an accountant.

Tingyong Zhong is currently Associate Professor and Dean of MPAcc at Rongzhi College of Chongqing Technology and Business University. He received his Ph.D. in Economics, M.A. in Corporate Management and B.A. in Human Resource Management from Northeast Normal University. His research interests include financial statement analysis, corporate finance and cost stickiness. He has published two co-authored book and more than a dozen papers in academic journals, including *Management World*, *Taxation and Economy*, and *Research on Financial and Economic Issues*. He also receives grants from Jilin Planning Office of Philosophy and Social Science and Chongqing Education Committee.

Haiyan Zhou is Professor of Accounting at the University of Texas–Rio Grande Valley, and its former institute University of Texas–Pan American (UTPA). Prof. Zhou obtained a Ph.D. in accounting from Temple University. Prof. Zhou has been teaching both undergraduate and graduate accounting and auditing courses. Prof. Zhou serves as editor-in-chief of *Asian Review Accounting*, and as an editorial board member of *International Accounting, Auditing and Taxation*. Some of her research appeared in top accounting and auditing journals, such as *Journal of Contemporary Accounting and Economics, Auditing: a Journal of Theory and Practice, Journal of Accounting, Auditing, and Finance, Journal of Accounting and Public Policy, International Journal of Accounting, Journal of International Accounting, Auditing and Taxation, and Journal of International Financial Management and Accounting*.

PREFACE

The idea for writing this book came from a perception that, although several books have been written on accounting in China, none has been updated to reflect recent developments. The intention is, therefore, to provide a rich collection of essays that would address the new emerging accounting issues in China and from different perspectives, and would, hopefully, provide a basis of reference for those who are interested in the current accounting issues in the emerging market of China.

The contributors are mostly academics from China, Australia, Canada and the USA, with many of them serving on boards of publicly listed firms. One would expect that the book therefore presents a variety of styles. Each chapter is independent and should be treated as such. In this book, we cover areas of corporate finance, financial accounting, managerial accounting, tax, auditing and internal control. When a specific topic is presented, it is inevitable that there might be some duplication in the introductions, in particular those discussions on institutional settings. No attempt is made to moderate that because the view was that the eliminating of the background information and cross-refereeing the readers to other chapters would disrupt the information flow in the chapter and would potentially affect the readability of the chapter. Therefore, it is suggested that the book be regarded as a book of reference or a collection of manuscripts on the recent developments in accounting in China, and not necessarily a textbook. It is not expected that readers are to read the chapters in a sequence.

It is a courtesy to remind readers to be aware that the views expressed in the chapters of the book are those of the individual authors and should not be taken as representation of the views of any institutions with which the contributors are affiliated. Similarly, the views should not be taken as representing the view of the publisher.

ACKNOWLEDGEMENTS

Teamwork is the fuel that make unusual achievements happen. I sincerely agree with this unknown quote. This book is a collective effort of many scholars, and I would like to take this opportunity to express my gratitude to all the contributors, for taking time off their busy schedules to write up their manuscripts and make this book available in a timely manner. I am grateful to many colleagues for their helpful comments and suggestions, especially Dr. Guiru Hua, Dr. Stephen Owusu-Ansah and Professor Gongfu Zhang. My thanks are also extended to Matthew Ranscombe, Sinead Waldron and Terry Clague at Routledge for commissioning this book and nursing it through to completion, and to Emily Shi and Elizabeth Shi for invaluable help with sub-editing the material.

INTRODUCTION TO ACCOUNTING IN CHINA

Haiyan Zhou

There is increasing interest in accounting issues in the emerging market of China. In the early 1990s two national stock exchanges were established in the mainland of China – Shanghai Stock Exchange and Shenzhen Stock Exchange. They surpassed Tokyo Stock Exchange in Japan as the world's second largest stock market several times in the last decade amid growing investor confidence in the growing Chinese economy. Meanwhile, the demand for accounting disclosure has been a hot topic, accompanied by a series of accounting reforms. These reforms include the first set of accounting standards implemented in 1996 and the first set of auditing standards in 1997, followed by more standards and revisions in the recent decades. The accounting reforms are mainly modeled after international practices, especially the International Accounting Standards (IASs), which later was renamed the International Financial Reporting Standards (IFRSs).

These reforms can be traced back to the economic reform and opening-up policy implemented in China in late 1978, when the government and accounting professionals gradually reintroduced accounting theory and practice of western countries. Before 1978, China used the format of accounting regulation of the former Soviet Union, which was based on planned economy. During this period, the Chinese accounting regulation was known as an accounting system rather than accounting standards. Since 1978, China has reformed its economy from a planned economy into a planned-market economy and a market economy, and accounting regulation has been changed accordingly. Along with the reforms of China's economy and the notable development of stock markets, the accounting profession has undergone rapid development in China. In 1980s, public accounting practice barely resumed as a result of privatization of State-owned enterprises and the separation of government from enterprises (Xiang, 1998). At present, there are more than 7400 accounting firms, over 8.5 million CPAs and nearly 30 million employees in China (Wang and Dou, 2015).

The capital markets in China have unique features, such as weak institutional environment and unique government ownership (Zhou and Hua, 2017). These features also influence the acconting and auditing practices in China. Compared with developed markets in western countries, the legal framework for CPAs are relatively ineffective and insufficient, and litigation risk is low. In addition, unlike the developed countries, many publicly listed firms show high level government ownership. Consequently, the accounting issues in China are inevitably affected by institutional environment, and many accounting reforms are driven by the government, such as the disaffiliation program during 1997–1998 (Gul et al. 2009), and mergers and acquisions of CPA firms during 1999–2006 (Chan and Wu, 2011). Therefore, when reviewing the development of accounting standards and practices in China, researchers need to be aware of the influence of weak institutional environment and unique government ownership on its current accounting pratices, as well as the role of government-driven accounting and auditing reforms in the development of public accounting service.

Several books on accounting issues in China focus on the early reforms around the 1990s when the IASs were introduced to the emerging market for the first time. For instance, Ji (2001) focused on the development of accounting and auditing systems in China around this period. There also existed a collection by Blake and Gao (1995) on perspectives on accounting and finance issues in China in the early 1990s. Although most reforms occurred after China's entry into the World Trade Organization (WTO) in 2001, to date there are very few books on current accounting issues in China. Therefore, a high demand exists for a comprehensive survey of the subject area up to date. To fill this important gap in the literature, thus, this book attempts to provide a prestigious reference work which offers students, researchers, and practitioners an introduction to current accounting issues in the emerging market of China.

The volume is organized into six thematic sections. The sections cover capital market and corporate finance, financial accounting, managerial accounting, auditing, taxation and internal control. The structure is intended to reflect the increasing diversity of contemporary research on accounting issues in China. Each chapter would provide a balanced overview of the current knowledge, key issues and relevant debates. Authors are also expected to reflect on where the research agenda is likely to advance in the future. The style of the chapters is analytical and engaging. The chapters cover established and emerging themes, and as such, they necessarily vary in length. The contents of each chapter are briefly introduced in the following sections.

Capital market and corporate finance

As a transition economy, the institutional background of China is quite different from developed countries, in which State-owned enterprises (SOEs) play substantial roles in the economy and the government still plays an important role in intervening corporate practices through government planning and many other indirect macroeconomic controls. For instance, Zhang, Wang, Lou and Zhang (Chapter 1) investigate the institutional background, practice and academic research of investment in China and argue that investment practice in Chinese enterprises currently is characterized by rapid growth of enterprise investment and a low-return on investment. Chinese scholars have conducted both theoretical and empirical researches on enterprise investment efficiency, determinants and economic consequences of corporate investment. These studies find that corporate investment efficiency in China is generally low, demonstrating either under- or over-investment. Such inefficient investment impairs corporate value. Moreover, government intervention, political connections, agency problem, information asymmetry as well as market competition could directly or indirectly influence corporate investment decision.

The unique institutional background also makes China an interesting setting to examine the effect of irrational market on corporate activities. Most of the research in modern corporate finance is based on the supposition of "the rational economic man" and "the effective market". However, in practice, the imperfect arbitrage results in ineffective market and mispricing, rational managers could perceive and exploit the mispricing when they make corporate decisions such as financial policy and real invest policy. Likewise, the enterprise managers frequently display the psychological characteristics which deviate with the most superior decision-making. Hua and Shi (Chapter 2) focus on related literature on the effect of irrational market on corporate finance in China, as well as the studies on managerial biases and the relevant effectiveness. The realization of efficient market requires the effective operation of a complete set of macro and micro mechanisms. They argue that the lack of macro- and micro-efficient market mechanisms and Confucian culture results in China's inefficient stock market and irrational management. China's capital market system has seen huge changes since the establishment of the Shanghai and Shenzhen Exchanges in 1990. However, restrictions on short sales in China led to imperfect arbitrage and a lack of micro-efficient market mechanisms, and misguided regulation by the China Securities Regulatory Commission (CSRS) and poor law enforcement cause the lack and ineffectiveness of macro-efficient market mechanisms. Over the past decade, many empirical studies have focused on the efficiency of China's stock market and found evidence supporting the notion that China's stock market is inefficient or weak-form efficient. In addition, due to Confucian culture and a lack of effective external monitoring and disciplining mechanisms, managers possess almost absolute power and authority, which makes them more overconfident and irrational than their peers in other countries.

The emerging market of China also features imbalanced economic development in different regions. Hu and Liu (Chapter 3) discuss the impact of firm location on corporate finance in China. Because the choice of payment methods can directly influence large shareholder control rights and capital structures of acquirer firms, it is interesting to study how acquirer firm's location influence the choice of payment methods in M&A. They find that the rural acquirer firms with longer distance away from urban prefer to use equity payment, but the preference is moderated by acquirer firm's large shareholder control, financial constraints, property right and information asymmetry.

Financial accounting

Accounting laws and regulations in China have been set and developed by a number of government agencies such as the National People's Congress, the State Council, the Ministry of Finance (MOF) and the China Securities Regulatory Commission (CSRC) when it comes to listed company information disclosures. According to the *Accounting Act* by the National People's Congress, the MOF is responsible for most of the accounting affairs in China, including setting up Chinese Accounting Standards (CAS) for business enterprises and government sector. Hence, the CAS is a formal legal regulation and a mandatory standard set. The current CAS for business enterprises has been highly convergent with International Financial Reporting Standards (IFRS). Xie and Zheng (Chapter 4) focus on the accounting standard issues in China. They discuss in details the development of CAS, the current situation of CAS, the Basic Standard, the differences between current CAS and IFRS, and the future of CAS.

Converging with the International Financial Reporting Standards (IFRS), the development of the fair value accounting (FVA) standard in China has attracted much debate as in other countries. The most important change for the accounting profession is the development of new accounting standards. In 1992, the Accounting Standard for Business Enterprise (ASBE) was issued for the first time based on the International Accounting Standards (IASs), which serves market-oriented economies. It took 14 years for China to totally convert the centrally planned economy oriented Chinese accounting system into a market-oriented accounting system. However, it took a longer time to adopt FVA into Chinese Accounting Standards (CASs), as ASBE Basic Standard 1992 did not include FVA due to the underdevelopment of capital market. Qu and Zhang (Chapter 5) introduce the development of fair value accounting in China in the past decades. Based on the most important accounting regulations related to FVA, they state that the development of FVA in China has gone through the following six periods: infancy period (1984–1992), introduction period (1993–1997), period of limited adoption (1998–1999), period of suspension and wide discussion period (2000–2006), period of wide adoption (2007–2014) and IFRS 13 adoption period (2014–present).

Earnings management issues prevail in the emerging markets and has attracted much attention of many researchers. Among many factors, product market competition has an important impact on accrued earnings management, as well as earnings management through real activities. Earnings management via real activities could affect a company's current and future cash flows and therefore affect the long-term value of the company. With constant improvement in accounting standards and regulations, accrual earnings management space available to managers is increasingly narrowing, so to achieve performance goals managers tend to increase real activities earnings management. Xing, Chen and Zhou (Chapter 6) investigate the relationship between market competition and earnings quality in the emerging market of China. Using a sample of observations from the Chinese public companies for the period of 2007–2012, they find that firms confronted with more product market competition are associated with more earnings management. In addition, when a firm is ranked at a higher competitive position in the industry with stronger pricing power, it is more likely to commit real earnings management and less likely to commit earnings management via accruals.

Managerial accounting

Along with financial accounting, managerial accounting in China also has experienced significant changes over time. Among many managerial accounting topics, a few areas are covered including cost accounting, executive compensations and digitalization in financial practice and business strategy. For instance, Zhong and Li (Chapter 7) investigate the relationship between corporate strategy and cost stickiness under different managerial expectations. Using data from listed companies from 2002 to 2015, they find that the cost stickiness of differentiation strategy is higher than those choosing low-cost strategy, and optimistic expectations can increase cost stickiness while pessimistic expectations will reduce cost stickiness. Finally, management expectation can adjust the relationship between corporate strategy and cost stickiness. When management expectation is optimistic, cost stickiness is higher with differentiation strategy than those with low-cost strategy. When management expectation is pessimistic, cost stickiness is higher with low-cost strategy than those with differentiation strategy.

The executive compensation is also a frequently visited topic in managerial accounting. The government still plays an important role in deciding the corporate executive compensation plans, especially in SOEs. In different stages of the reforms, the level of executive cash compensation was rather low earlier, but it grows rapidly recently. Gong (Chapter 8) investigates the institutional background, practice and academic research of executive compensation in China. She argues that the level of economic development, capital structure, corporate governance and social network are believed to influence the level of cash compensation of top management. Although the history of stock options in China is less than one decade, an increasing number of companies published the executive equity incentive plans during 2006–2016. The literature has found that the stock option plan influences corporate financing behavior, investment behavior, R&D decision as well as dividend payment behavior. Gong (Chapter 8) also discusses the executive compensation gap of listed companies, especially the compensation gap of SOEs, compensation dispersion of top management team and compensation differences between executives and employees.

The practice of using equity incentive plans started in China relatively late, which only can be traced back to 2006. About 30% of listed firms had proposed equity incentive plans by the end of 2016, which are mainly stock options and restricted stocks. Xu, Jin and Xin (Chapter 9) survey equity-based compensation in Chinese listed firms to provide a general picture on the institutional background, the evolution, the contract design and the economic consequences of equity incentive plans in China. They argue that regulation and institutional factors shape the development of equity-based compensation in China. The salient features include, but are not limited to, a relatively short valid period of five years, the dominant use of accounting measures as performance hurdles, the regulated grant prices and the dividend protective exercise price. Simple tests on the contract design support the managerial power hypothesis of contracting. State-controlled listed firms subject to more regulation, issue less and conservative equity incentive plans. Firms are found to manage earnings to lower the grant prices and to overcome performance hurdles. Firms with equity-based compensations distribute more cash and stock dividends to lower the exercise prices. Even so, studies still find incentive effect of equity-based compensation in terms of improving operating efficiency and firm performance.

Digitalization has forced many firms to revisit their strategies and business models to be sustainable in a complex dynamic business environment. In the digitalized world, it is recognized that the traditional way of thinking about strategy is limited in the amorphous, unbounded and fluid business network. How should strategy be redesigned, and in particular, how can the accountants help to support the strategy? To answer this question, Guo, Yuan and Gao (Chapter 10) present a case study on Midea, one of the top five electrical appliance manufacturers in the world. They argue that the digitalization changes the nature of products, the process of value chain and thus it has significant implications on how firms attain and sustain competitive advantage. Midea has changed its strategy since 2011 and has built a new business model incorporating the philosophy of internet and digitalization. During that process, its finance function was redesigned and innovated, including efficiency management and finance platform. In particular, the authors discuss the financial practices, construct a process model of the shift strategy and explore the link between the financial practice and the strategy. The case cast some lights on management accounting practices that function in the digital economy and provide some actionable model for the practitioners.

Auditing

Two major forces have driven the development of independent auditing in emerging markets: cross-listings and foreign investments. Since the implementation of economic reform and opening-up policy in 1978, an increasing number of Chinese firms have chosen to list on domestic and overseas stocks exchanges. Meanwhile, an increasing number of foreign companies have established their branches or have joint ventures with local firms in China. As investors need reliable accounting information to make their business decisions, they require firms to have independent auditors. It is important for investors to understand the role of independent audit, especially for the international investors. Chen and Liu (Chapter 11) discuss the development of independent auditing, evolution of Independent Auditing Standards, educations of CPAs, accounting firms and the development of independent audit market.

The independent audit market has experienced significant changes in terms of regulations and practices. Liu, Ye and Yu (Chapter 12) introduce audit reports, opinions, audit fees and the regulatory environment in China. They discuss some distinctive features of the market that may affect audit quality and audit fees and find that Chinese audit firms have expanded their size quickly because of regulatory intervention but their market concentration is still low. Individual auditors pay more attention to their clients and to personal risk. Engagement risk mainly arises from changes of organizational form and penalties and sanctions imposed by the CSRC. The policy of mandatory rotation has been adopted, China issued a series of rules and regulations for the rotation of the partners in-charge. As to the rotation of accounting firms, China only made rotation requirements for the central enterprises. Finally, they also discuss the research framework and give some directions for future China-related auditing research.

Tax

The tax system has been significantly changed in China over time, including the recent corporate income tax reform in 2008 and new income tax accounting methods in 2006. Zeng (Chapter 13) reviews the tax system and its development in China and examines corporate reactions to the 2008 corporate tax reform and the effects of corporate governance and ownership structure on tax aggressiveness. In addition, Zeng (Chapter 13) examines inter-temporal income shifting as well as the impact of ownership structures on income shifting during the 2008 corporate tax rate reduction. It shows that firms shift income to the low-tax periods, which is mainly in operating income. It also shows that corporate ownership structures, including large shareholders and state ownership, are important factors in connection with both total and operating income shifting.

The Ministry of Finance issued the new China accounting standards on February 15, 2006 (CAS2006), which requires listed companies to use the balance sheet liability method for the income tax accounting. It gives scholars an opportunity to investigate the earnings management of listed companies from the perspective of income tax. Hu, Cao, Zheng and Zhong (Chapter 14) investigate the relationship between income tax planning and earnings management in the publicly companies under the balance sheet liability method and find that when engaging in earnings management, companies will trade off conforming and nonconforming earnings management from the perspective of income tax cost. When companies have motivations to turn losses into gains and to avoid penalties associated with fraud being found, companies prefer to employ more conforming earnings management strategies.

Internal control

As Chinese economy grows enormously, and Chinese companies expands rapidly, corporate internal control becomes more important. To improve corporate management expertise and promote sustainable economic growth, Chinese government and its agencies actively promote the development of internal control. The implementation of internal control has many innovative and distinct Chinese characteristics, which are largely different from those in the USA. The research on internal control in China emerged recently. Dong and Ke (Chapter 15) introduce internal control institution in China, including framework and practices, and review the related literature on corporate Internal control.

The strength of a firm's internal control could also affect auditor's judgment on client cash flow management. Jiang, Guo and Samkin (Chapter 16) find that the association between auditors' modified opinion and cash flow management is conditional on the strength of firms' internal control. Auditors are more likely to issue modified audit opinions on cash flow irregularities in client firms with weak internal control systems. They also find that cash flow management is only positively related to modified audit opinions in firms with weak internal control systems. In client firms with weak internal controls, big auditors are more likely to issue modified audit opinions on clients with high risk of cash flow management when compared to small auditors. In addition, in firms with weak internal controls, auditors are more likely to issue modified audit opinions for State-owned enterprises (SOEs) than they do in non-SOEs.

References

Blake, J. and S. Gao. 1995. *Perspectives on Accounting and Finance Issues in China*. London: Routledge.

Chan, K. H. and D. Wu. 2011. Aggregate Quasi Rents and Auditor Independence: Evidence From Audit Firm Mergers in China. *Contemporary Accounting Research* 28 (1): 175–213.

Gul, F., H. Sami, and H. Zhou. 2009. Auditor Disaffiliation Program in China and Auditor Independence. *Auditing: A Journal of Practice & Theory* 28 (1): 29–51.

Ji, X. D. 2001. *Development of Accounting and Auditing Systems in China*. London: Routledge.

Wang, C. and H. Dou. 2015. Does the Transformation of Accounting Firms' Organizational Form Improve Audit Quality? Evidence From China. *China Journal of Accounting Research* 8 (4): 279–293.

Xiang, B. 1998. Institutional Factors Influencing China's Accounting Reforms and Standards. *Accounting Horizons* 12 (2): 105–119.

Zhou, H. and G. Hua. 2017. Institutional Environment, Auditing Reforms and Independent Auditing in China. In *Accounting in Asia*. Z. Lin (Ed.). London: Routledge.

PART I

Capital market and corporate finance

1

CORPORATE INVESTMENT IN CHINA

Background, practice and research

Gongfu Zhang, Yi Wang, Xu Lou, Xiaohui Zhang[1]

1. Introduction

Investment decision is one of the vital financial decisions that enterprises face. As the main motivation of firm growth and the fundamental of future cash flow, investment determines a firm's operational risks, profitability and capital market evaluations of its operating performance and future prospects. Corporate investment is also crucial to economic growth. Since the economic reform, the Chinese economy grows at an average 10% annual increase in GDP for the last 30 years. The contribution of investment to economy reaches an average 40%, up to 87.6%. Yet there are many problems in the sharp rise in enterprise investment, such as the inefficiency of investment, severe government intervention and defects in investment decision-making. Among those, enterprise investment inefficiency might be the ultimate problem. Research shows that the average return on capital investment of Chinese listed companies is merely 2.6% during 1999–2004, far lower than the cost of capital (Xin et al., 2007b).

Despite of the crucial role investment plays in Chinese economy, academics in China have barely started to conduct studies on enterprise investment. The theoretical research on investment emerged in the 1950s in western countries, while it only attracted academic attention in China since 1993, when the Chinese government formally established socialist market economy. Before 1993, the average number of papers with the word "investment" in their titles is 670 per year. From 1994 to 2015, this number increased to 7265 per year. The research on Chinese enterprise investment has made great progress and become one of the popular topics in corporate finance. Chinese academics conducted both theoretical and practical researches on enterprise investment efficiency, determinants and economic consequences of enterprise investment.

Different from the market economy in developed countries, China had a highly centralized planned economy from 1949 to 1978. In the planned economy, government had the overall control of whether enterprises invested, what they invested in and how much to invest, not the enterprises themselves. Enterprise investment was funded according to fiscal budget, and investment income was returned to government. Enterprise had no autonomy in financing activities and income distribution. In 1978, Chinese economic reform took place and the government gradually delegated the investment authority. Enterprise investment funding changed from fiscal budgeting to government loans, and the major profit was allowed to be retained in enterprises and used for reinvestment. Till 2003, project organization and management authority was entirely separated from government agencies. Enterprise investment activities had finally become enterprise behavior instead of governmental behavior. State-owned enterprises (SOEs) had become the investment subject. In July 2004, the State Council of China issued *Decision on Investment System Reform*. This renovated the project approval system, gave enterprise true autonomy on investment, simplified the reviewing procedures, expanded the investment decision-making scope in large enterprises and increased the financing resources available to enterprise.

Influenced by a series of investment system reforms, investing practices of Chinese enterprises currently demonstrate five main characteristics. First, enterprise investment activities are limited by government interference. Second, investment decisions are mainly made by major shareholders. Third, the growth of enterprise investment is rapid. Fourth, return on investment (ROI) is disappointing. Finally, investment tools are diversified.

To provide an insight into Chinese enterprise investment research, this chapter covers three main fields regarding enterprise investment in China: institutional background, investment practice and investment research. The rest of sections in this chapter are arranged as follows: the second section discusses the institutional background of Chinese enterprises investment; the third section introduces the Chinese enterprise investment practice; the fourth section covers the literature review of Chinese enterprises investment and the fifth section explores the challenges in Chinese enterprise investment research.

2. Institutional background of corporate investment in China

The year 1978 has witnessed a series of significant political and economic changes in China under the reform and opening policy. Thus we identify two different periods – the period of traditional investment approach and the period with investment reform.

2.1 *Traditional investment approach*

China implemented a strict planned economic system from the year 1949 to 1978, when the government controlled and regulated production, distribution and prices. The typical characteristics of Chinese investment system during this period can be summarized below.

First, authorities of determining investment projects were highly centralized (Ying, 1999). The domination of central government was emphasized in making investment decisions and assigning investment tasks. The investment directions and projects were determined by domestic and international situations, as well as the national development planning. For instance, during the early 1950s to 1960s, the restoration of infrastructures was significant and most investments were concentrated on projects like water conservancy and railroad transportation.

Second, the appropriation of funds used for investments was highly centralized (Cao and Wang, 2000). National investment plan, project plan and allocation plan were set annually, and related amount was distributed once a year based on the planning without any consideration for real conditions.

Third, in contrast to the highly centralized decision-making process and funds appropriation, the management responsibilities of investment system were arbitrarily separated. The planning, approval and monitoring of funds arrangement as well as labor management were responsibilities of different levels of government departments and professional institutions, which ignored the inherent relationship among various factors of investment and was likely to cause information asymmetry, thus hindering the implementation of investment projects (Cao and Wang, 2000).

Fourth, accountabilities of investment projects were not clarified. As introduced above, due to both the planning-based funds appropriation and the arbitrary division of investment management, no particular person or department would bear responsibilities when any failure occurred.

It could not be denied that traditional investment approach contributed to the recovery of national economy during the early period when the industry base was weak and economic structure was imbalance (Ying, 1999). However, as the economy developed, the centralized and rigid system became barriers to investment and removed incentives from producers.

2.2 Investment reform

Although not explicitly put forward, it was generally believed that the investment reform began from the year 1979 along with the reform and opening in China. Since then, the investment system reform could be divided into four phases (Zhang, 2015).

2.2.1 Pilot reform (1979–1983)

The main theme of pilot reform is the delegation of more decision power to State-owned enterprises. Since July 1979, the State Council has issued a series of documents, allowing State-owned enterprises to retain and decide how to use profits they earned. State-owned enterprises were no longer required to deliver all their profits to government and government only charged part of their profits in the form of taxes. Meanwhile, the Construction Council proposed to restore economic responsibility and introduce contracts; pilot projects were conducted in architecture business, allowing fees directly paid from the investment income instead of budget; bank loans began to replace fiscal appropriation and gradually became the major investment sources of fixed asset investment; and foreign capital was accepted in domestic investment in special economic zones such as Shenzhen, Zhuhai, Shantou and Xiamen (Tian, 2008).

2.2.2 Comprehensive development (1984–1991)

During 1984–1991, *Provisions on the Reform of Planning*, and *Interim Provisions on the Reform of the Construction Industry and the Basic Construction Management* signaled the beginning of comprehensive development (Tian, 2008). Economic responsibility system was re-emphasized, "loan instead of project appropriation" reform was further implemented, and foreign capital was accepted in 14 more coastal cities in China. The State Council began to implement preferential policies in foreign-funded enterprises with locations, taxes, credited loans and production and management autonomy. Besides, the State Council began to simplify administrative proceeding and delegate approval authority of investment projects, and improve management of investment projects through establishment of evaluation and review system.

2.2.3 Innovation and further development (1992–2003)

To establish market-oriented economy, corporate mainly focused on clarifying responsibilities of investment subjects, reforming investment and financing modes and improving risk management. Owner's reasonability and legal person reasonability were clarified. Investment projects were divided into three categories – competitive investment projects, fundamental investment projects and public welfare investment projects. Investment and financing methods were determined respectively for different categories of investment projects.

2.2.4   Systematic reform (after 2004)

In July 2004, the State Council issued *Decision of the State Council on the Reform of Investment System* (The State Council of China, 2004), which proposed further improvement in investment projects. Accordingly, government agencies proposed regulations in recent years. In July 2016, *Opinions of the CPC Central Committee and State Council on Deepening the Reform of Investment and Financing System* (The CPC Central Committee and State Council of China, 2016) was issued. These reforms include:

> First, the roles of firms and government in investment are clearly defined. Firms started to take active roles in investment decisions and risk management. In contrast, the scope of government investment is strictly limited to areas where market cannot allocate resources effectively, such as social service, public infrastructure, and national securities and so on.
>
> Second, the regulations are to optimize investment management by government. Previously, government performed its functions in investment management mainly through establishing strict and complicated investment approval procedures. However, with the recognition of firms' primary role in investment activities, government gradually changes its functions in investment management, and now emphasizes on providing services to facilitate corporation investments.
>
> Third, the regulations are to encourage diverse financing methods and reduced financing barriers of investment projects. The government issues related policies, to promote financing instruments and transform national savings into effective investments.
>
> Fourth, the regulation are to synergize investment system reform with other aspects of economic reform in China, such as reform of State-owned enterprises, the supply-side reform (promoting more effective resources allocation through the adjustment of economic structure) and the fiscal and tax reform (establishing a scientific fiscal system that suits the current economic condition and the current capabilities of national governance).

2.3   The characteristics of current investment and financing system in China

The current investment system, include investment subjects, respective authorities and responsibilities of investment activities participants, sources and usage of investment funds, the motivation and restraint system, as well as related macro-control mechanism. The main characteristics of current investment and financing system in China are summarized in table 1.1.

With years of investment reforms, the investment system becomes more market-oriented. However, compared with developed countries such as the United States and the United Kingdom, government inferences exist within current investment and financing practice.

First, although nowadays the government does not directly decide corporate investments, it indirectly guides corporate investments through national planning. In China, a national strategic plan is prepared every five years dating back to1953, and the 13th five-year plan was issued early 2016. To ensure the realization of the five-year plan, the government issues series of corresponding regulations as well as sub-plans. Documents like development plans for specific industries always indicate areas where investments are encouraged and where preference policies can be provided. Government plans can limit corporate independence in making investment decisions.

Second, firms in China can be categorized as State-owned enterprises, mixed ownership enterprises and private firms. As a shareholder of State-owned or mixed ownership enterprises,

Table 1.1 Characteristics of current investment system in China

Contents	Description
Investment Subjects	Investment subjects under current Chinese investment practice include corporations, individuals and various levels of governments. Governments were undeniably primary investment subjects during early years of China. After years' of investment reform, it is recognized through related documents that corporations are in primary position among all types of investment subjects.
Division of Authorities and Responsibilities	Investment subjects who make investments should have authorities to make investment decisions. Investment subjects who benefit from investment returns should also assume responsibilities to control and manage the investment projects and bear related risks. For corporate investments, corporations should propose investment projects and analyze feasibilities of investment alternatives using scientific tools and decisions should be made internally through established procedures. However, for certain corporate investments that concern areas like national security, public interests and strategic resources exploitation, corporations need to submit documents like project proposal, feasibility report and commencement report of construction work and apply for government approval. Moreover, government also plays roles in in-process and post monitoring of investment projects.
Sources and Usage of Investment Funds	Diversified financing sources are encouraged. Corporations are allowed to raise funds through variety of ways including issuing stock, borrowing from banks and other financial institutions, making use of bonds and other forms of financial instruments. Currently, the government is also promoting a creative financing method for infrastructure constructions. The method is called Public-Private Partnership (PPP for short), under which private funds and public funds are combined, allowing governments and private corporations to cooperate in public services investment projects.
Motivation and Restraint Mechanism	From the micro perspective, investment activities are motivated and restraint by investment alternatives' potential returns and risks, as well as the corporate governance system. From the macro perspective, investment activities are generally motivated through government's industry development policies, simplified government approval procedures, tax and other fiscal preferences and unblock financing channels; investment activities are regulated through system of related laws and regulations, governmental and social monitoring, capital contribution requirements and responsibilities to repay liabilities.
Investment Related Macro-control Mechanism	Current investment related macro-controls in China take an indirect format instead of direct. The government controls investment activities mainly through the following ways: 1 Issuing industry standards as well as industry development plans in accordance to overall national development plans to guide and encourage private investments; 2 Issuing laws and regulations to regulate investment subjects' activities; 3 Implementing fiscal policies, creating stable and continuously growing economic environments; 4 Adjusting aggregate demand and supply of capital through monetary policies such as money supply and benchmark interest rate.

the government may intervene in investment decisions and management process (Zhang, 2015). The government does not directly intervene in investment decisions of private corporations, but still requires them to submit project applications in order to put investment projects on record.

Third, private firms can freely invest into areas that are not explicitly prohibited by laws or regulations. However, currently State-owned enterprises still dominate or even monopolize most industries in China, which means that private corporations may face fierce competitions against State-owned enterprises in many industries (Xiao, 2012). State-owned enterprises may control more resources and gain protections from governments.

Fourth, compared with developed countries, types of financial instruments and financial resources are limited in China (Meng and Ma, 2004). Corporations obtain capital mainly through bank loans. However, major domestic banks are government-owned. Though recently the government has deregulated deposit and loan interest rates, those government-backed banks may over-react to monetary policies and make loan too easily or difficultly as they adjust their loan policies mainly based on information provided by government instead of the market condition. Moreover, the government background of most banks may motivate them to provide preference policies to State-owned enterprises, thus making financing activities of private corporations more difficult.

Last but not least, an important character of investment systems in developed countries is the existence of various effective intermediate institutions like accounting firms, law firms and industry associations (Meng and Ma, 2004). The intermediate institutions provide independent and objective services to improve information transparency, provide professional consultation to corporations and improve the monitoring of investment projects. However, many intermediate institutions in China were primarily established by government. Although now they are separated from government, their close relationships with government in the past still exist thus influence their independence and objectivity in providing related services (Xiao, 2012).

3.   Corporate investment practice in China

Due to institutional backgrounds, the investment practice in China departed from that in western countries in many areas such as enterprise autonomy in decision-making, investment decision-making authority, investment growth, investment return and decision tools.

3.1   *Enterprise autonomy in decision-making*

Many studies show severe government intervention in China. According to the *China Enterprise Manager Questionnaire Report in 2013* released by Chinese Entrepreneur Survey, 11% of managers believed local government intervention was the number one problem. The percentage was 6.4% in 2012, indicating the number almost doubled within one year. The World Bank Report (2007) reported that the average time firms spent on dealing with tax agents, police officers, environmental protection agency and labor and social security was 61 days. In addition, the decisions made by firms are heavily influenced by local governments. As increasing investment helps to create employment opportunities and GDP, which thus improve local social stability, and helps the local government in performance evaluation and promotion, local government is highly motivated to intervene with the market. Second, before the release of *Decision of the State Council on the Reform of Investment System*, investment projects solely relied on government approval. Such a process enabled local government to intervene with the market, who could support or obstruct the investment of enterprises based on its own benefits.

3.2   *Investment decision-making authority*

Public companies propose the plans to the general meeting of shareholders, board of directors, chairman and general manager for approval. Companies where general meeting of shareholders approve project accounts for more than 10% of net assets are categorized as companies with strict investment control, while companies where general meeting of shareholders only need to approve projects more than 50% of net assets are categorized as companies with loose investment control. According to survey by Shanghai Stock Exchange in 2004, among 208 sample companies, major shareholders from 158 firms strictly control the power of board in decision-making (76% of the sample). A survey made by Shenzhen Stock Exchange showed similar results. Major shareholders from 78% of the companies strictly controlled such power.[2] Those findings show the decision-making process in Chinese public companies are heavily influenced by major shareholders. Such a practice could help restraining over-investment, but on the other hand, it also could lead to low efficiency.

3.3   Investment growth

Because of policy incentives and government intervention, managers in Chinese enterprises had a strong preference for investment, leading to a trend of investment rapid growth. Figure 1.1 demonstrates the trend between 2007 and 2015, based on the data from the National Bureau of Statistics. From 2007 to 2015, the investment growth rates of domestic enterprises all exceeded 10%. However, the curve was downward sloping, meaning that investment growth rates of domestic enterprises were declining except for the year 2009. The growth rates varied among different types of companies. Compared with domestic enterprises, the growth rates of foreign enterprises were much lower. The growth rates of private sector were higher than those of State-owned enterprises despite in 2009. The abnormal investment growth of State-owned enterprise was very much likely to be the result of China's "four-trillion-bail-out" in 2008 to deal with the financial crisis. The main beneficiaries in this policy were State-owned companies rather than others.

3.4   Investment return

Companies are motivated to maximize their profits to assure that their rate of return should be at least higher than the cost of capital. Figure 1.2 shows the EBIT and after-tax cost of one-year short-term debt (K) for the same period during 1994–2013.[3] Among all the 26,342 observations,

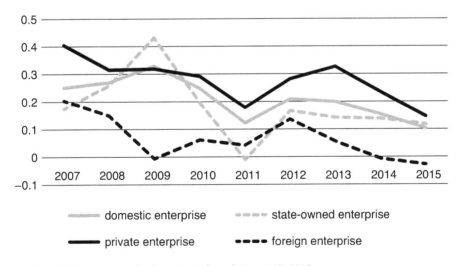

Figure 1.1   The investment in fixed assets in China during 2007–2015

Note: The growth rate was calculated based on the number in previous year.

Source: National Bureau of Statistics.

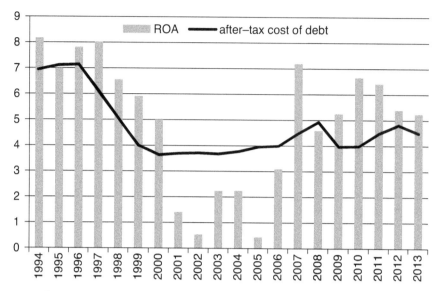

Figure 1.2   The comparison between EBIT and after-tax cost of debt during 1994–2013

Note: The poly line stands for EBIT while the bar stands for cost of debt. If the company's net profit is positive, the after-tax cost of debt is calculated as the firm's one-year lending rate multiply by (1–33%) for the year before 2008 and (1–25%) for the year after 2008, respectively. Otherwise, the cost of debt equals to its one-year lending rate in the same period. Interest rate data was retrieved from www.pbc.gov.cn.

9,278 had lower ROA compared with K, which indicates approximately 35.22% of companies failed to cover their debts with their profits. Figure 1.2 explicitly showed that EBIT was declining during 1994 to 2005. In 2006, EBIT started to increase. In 1995, 2001, 2002, 2003, 2004, 2005, 2006 and 2008, the average of listed companies' EBIT was lower than that of their cost of debt.

3.5   Investment decision tools

To make reasonable decisions, companies are expected to establish effective investment decision-making procedures, and to employ appropriate decision approaches. Due to the lack of appropriate decision-making procedures, China listed companies often made decisions based on past experience in new situations. Firms thus would fail to make consistent policies and consider the long-term goals.

Theoretically, taking the time value of money into consideration was supposed to give more reasonable decisions than not, 74.93% and 75.61% of CFOs always or almost always used NPV and IRR to evaluate projects (Graham and Harvey, 2001). However, the survey in China yields different results. In 2002, Nanjing University conducted a survey on 77 firms. At that time, 62.2% of firms valued ROI as the most important index when making decisions. 41.9% believed payback period provided the most reliable solution to whether the project should be accepted. Only a small percentage thought NPV, profitability index and IRR were important when making decisions. Chow et al. (2007) conducted a survey among the CFOs from 337 listed companies in seven provinces. It was found the most popular decision method was payback period. Qi and Li (2007) concluded that firms favored payback period method to make valuation. In addition, they found that publicly listed and large companies were more likely to use payback periods rather than private and small companies. Such findings contradicted with Graham and Harvey (2001) because they didn't agree with scale effect. Li et al. (2007) also revealed that although NPV was one of the important decision-making tools in their 167 sample companies, it was far less likely to become the most important one.

What's more, the majority of the sample companies employed cost of debt as the discount rate. Qi and Li (2007), including Li et al. (2007), found that companies preferred the interest rates of bank loans as discount rates when making decisions. Nanjing University (2002) came to similar conclusion. These results indicate that enterprises could accept negative NPV projects, leading to over-investment.

However, on the most important risks in decision-making, scholars couldn't reach an agreement. Qi and Li (2007) believed that China firms took financial risks as the top risk. Product life cycle, government policy and technology risks came as the following. Firms didn't take interest rate fluctuation and inflation risks into consideration. However, Li et al. (2007) drew a different conclusion. Investigating 167 listed companies, they found companies kept a close eye on risks regarding interest rate, commodity price, term structure of interest risk, GDP and economic cycle but not unpredicted inflation and financial risks. To examine whether company characteristics play a role, Qi and Li (2007) found that large companies took financial risks and interest rates risks more frequently than small companies, that publicly listed companies took financial risks, technology risks and product life cycle risks more frequently than private companies, and that State-owned enterprises were more likely to take interest rate risks into consideration. It was not explained by scholars why companies with less financing constraints and with economies of scale paid more attention to financial risks and interest rates risks than those without. Such kinds of research would be interesting and demand more attention.

Managers in China believed non-financial indicators should play vital roles in decision-making. According to Fremgen (1973), 97% of US firms adopted strategies which were financially unacceptable, but could fulfill certain non-financial objectives. Similarly, Chinese companies which solely relied on financial indicators in decision-making only made up 1.6%, indicating Chinese firms took non-financial indicators into consideration (Qi and Li, 2007). According to Li et al. (2007), Chinese firms also regarded product sales forecast and product market competition as the most important factors when making decisions. Those factors even came before financial indicators such as IRR, required rate of return and net present value. Public companies preferred to use financial indicators and both more frequently than the private companies. Big companies were in favor of both kinds of methods while small companies would like to use non-financial indicators.

4. Corporate investment research in China

In China, most studies employed western models and data from publicly listed companies of China to investigate investment decisions. These papers can be classified into three categories: investment efficiency, determinants of investment and the relationship between firm investment and performance.

4.1 *Measurement of enterprise investment efficiency*

There are two approaches Chinese academics use to measure investment efficiency: inefficient investment approach and ROI approach. The former contains three models: Investment-cash flow sensitivity model (FHP model) (Fazzari et al., 1988), cash flow and investment relationship model (Vogt, 1994) and residual valuation model (Richardson, 2006). The latter includes two models:

Mueller and Reardon (1993)'s market value based model and Baumol et al. (1970)'s accounting earning based model.

Feng (1999) was the first to use Fazzari et al. (1988) model measuring investment efficiency in China. Using observations on 135 public companies from manufacturing industry during 1995–1997, he found that asymmetric information led to investment-cash flow sensitivity in firms with low dividend payout and without government sponsorship. Many researches used a similar model and drew similar conclusions. However, results are mixed regarding how firm type plays a role in investment-cash flow sensitivity. For example, when discussing financing constraints in SOEs and private enterprises, based on data from all the companies listed on SSE and SZSE during the period of 1996–1999, Zheng et al. (2001) found that under-investment were more common in firms with high proportion of State-owned shares; while based on data from all manufacturing companies listed in SSE and SZSE from 1998 to 2004, Zhu et al. (2006) found that the existing soft budget constraints distorted financing constraints of State-owned companies rather than private companies. Western researchers showed that small businesses were more vulnerable to financing constraints caused by asymmetric information; while Chinese academics failed to find similar results. Quan et al. (2004) documented that large companies generally had under-investment issues. Tang and Guo (2007) found that financing constraints caused investment-cash flow sensitivity existed in small businesses.

Vogt (1994)'s model was widely used in China. For example, He and Ding (2001) and Zhang and Lv (2009) found that the cash flow/investment relationship was negative, which indicated investment-cash flow sensitivity in Chinese firms originated from the agency problem between management and shareholders.

Richardson (2006)'s residual model was also favorable in China. Wei and Liu (2007), Xin et al. (2007a) and Zhang and Song (2009) adopted the model to evaluate the degree of firm investment efficiency. Empirical results showed that the average optimal investment rate was 24.4% on net fixed assets at the beginning of the year, 39.26% of the companies over-invest while 60.74% under-invest (Zhang and Song, 2009).

Other than inefficient investment measurement model, Chinese scholars also used ROI as indicator of investment efficiency. Xin et al. (2007b) calculated the return on capital investment of Chinese listed companies during 1999–2004 based on the models of Mueller and Reardon (1993) and Baumol et al. (1970). The rate of return was only 2.6%, which was far less than the corporate cost of capital. Xu and Zhou (2009) estimated the investment efficiency from 2000 to 2008 and found that the investment returns were merely half of their investment cost.

4.2 Determinants of corporate investment

Chinese scholars have also shown strong interest in the factors that influence corporate investment. Current researches showed that government intervention, political connection, agency problem, asymmetric information and market competition were the factors that affected investment decisions in Chinese enterprises directly or indirectly.

4.2.1 Government intervention

Since Chinese economic reform, the appraisal and promotion of local officials are mainly based on local GDP. Hence, local government has a strong incentive to intervene in corporate investment to achieve their goals of economic growth. Over-investment caused by government interference was a common problem in State-owned listed companies (Xin et al., 2007a; Cheng et al., 2008; Tang et al., 2010). Local government intervention would aggravate the over-investment of companies with free cash flow (Zhang, 2011).The mechanism of government intervention on enterprise investment was also explored (Huang and Li, 2014). As employees' skill was specific to industries or firms, the government's goal of maintaining employment provided implicit promise for the permanent contracts to employees. This prevented labor intensive companies from ceasing in time when an industry recession took place. As a result, over-investment came in place as a balance (Huang and Li,2014).

4.2.2   Political connection

Top executives with political connection are prevalent in China. Research shows that during 1999 to 2009, 51.7% of 260 listed private-owned companies had political connection (Yu et al., 2012). However, empirical evidences on the impact of political connections on investment efficiency in Chinese firms were mixed. Some showed that firms with political relations tended to over-invest as they were more easily to obtain debt financing from banks at lower cost (Zhang et al., 2010; Zhang et al., 2011). Others took political relation as the "helping hand", which meant that firms could alleviate financing constraints by utilizing political relations to gain more investment opportunities and favorable bank loans (Cheng and Geng, 2013).

4.2.3   Agency problem

Investment is one of the main sources of firm value creation, while it can also be manipulated by managers for their personal interests. The agency conflict between managers and shareholders directly affect corporate investment. Some over-investment problems in China were caused by the abuse of firm resources by managers; others were resulted from managerial overconfidence (Li, 2014). A significant and negative correlation was found between agency cost and investment efficiency in central government controlled SOEs, local government controlled SOEs and private companies (Luo, 2014). Evidence showed a positive relationship between the two types of agency costs and over-investment. Financial development could weaken the positive correlation between the first type of agency cost and the corporate over-investment (Yang and Liu, 2014)

One of the vital functions of corporate governance is to alleviate or restrain the agency problem. Learning from the western, Chinese firm established two-tier corporate governance mechanism with both board of directors (BOD) and board of supervisors. The size of BOD plays a role in corporate investment as well. When a firm has free cash flow surplus, large BOD could deteriorate the over-investment based on free cash flow by managerial overconfidence (Wang and Xue, 2014).

China imported independent director system in 2001. In 2003, the proportion of independent directors on BOD has reached one-third. However, the literature demonstrated that independent directors had not played an effective role in restraining over-investment. For instance, Liu et al. (2012) found that independent directors could mitigate under-investment caused by tunneling behavior of major shareholders. However, the link between independent directors and over-investment due to agency problem remained unclear. Wang and Xue (2014) had similar conclusion that, regardless of the availability of free cash flow, an increase in board independence could not reduce investment inefficiency caused by overconfident managers.

The executive incentive system was introduced late in China. Till the end of the 20th century, remuneration system was rarely developed in Chinese listed companies. For instance, although on average the percentage of CEO shareholding increases from 1999 to 2015, nearly half of the CEOs did not hold any stock share. Due to the absence of effective nominal reward system, executives' competence and diligence were hardly covered by their salaries or stock options, which encouraged them to seek other formats of compensations. Accepting investment projects with negative NPV for personal gain was one of them, which resulted in over-investment (Xin et al., 2007a).

4.2.4   *Information asymmetry*

At the stage of economic transition, information asymmetry is prevailing in China. Chinese scholars have conducted theoretical and empirical researches on several perspectives, such as investment-cash flow sensitivity and the effect of information disclosure on capital cost. It was found that even without information asymmetry, the unique equity arrangement in China including market segmentation[4] and low proportion of private/tradable shares would end in over-investment with equity financing. Due to information asymmetry and market segment, the over-investment under equity financing in Chinese listed companies was higher than their peers in developed stock market only (Pan and Jin, 2003). Qu et al. (2011) used probability of informed based trading (PIN) to measure information asymmetry, as one of financial constraints. Their results showed that information asymmetry could lower firm investment but increase investment-cash flow sensitivity. They also showed a nonlinear relationship between financial constraint and investment-cash flow sensitivity.

Financial constraint caused by asymmetric information also has a direct impact on corporate investment activities. Lian and Su (2009) estimated the investment efficiency of Chinese listed firms by using the heteroscedastic stochastic frontier model. They concluded that the investment efficiency of Chinese listed companies declined by 20–30% due to the financial constraints, with average efficiency of 72%. Empirical evidences also indicated that financial constraint had suppressed corporate investment (Li et al., 2007). Monetary policy shocks in recent years deteriorated the difference in financial constraints between SOEs and non-SOEs. Government grant went to the SOEs while credit resources of non-SOEs got crowded out, which led to continuous decline in investment efficiency of non-SOEs (Yu et al., 2014).

4.2.5   *Product market competition*

Product market competition is one of the external governance elements. Product market competition could restrain corporate over-investment activities (Zhang, 2009; Liu and Li, 2013). However, the mechanisms could be different. Zhang (2009) found that when product market competition increase, major shareholders would increase ownership, enhanced corporate governance and self-disciplined tunneling behavior to suppress the managerial over-investment behavior effectively. Liu and Li (2013) found that EVA evaluation system could lower the over-investment in central government controlled SOEs and such an effect is more significant in higher-competition industries.

4.3   *Enterprise investment and performance*

Investment does not always increase firm value as inefficient investment would reduce corporate performance (Jiang, 2011). Inside investment, mergers and acquisitions (M&A) investment and total investment in firms with overconfident managers were generally higher than those with rational managers. However, these investments could reduce corporate performance (Ye and Wang, 2013). Liu (2009) believed that diversified investment would damage company value. Zhang (2014)'s paper disclosed that the relationship between under-investment and corporate performance was linked to the market competition corporate facing. Under-investment could improve corporate performance when industry net operating income margin was over 13%. When it went under 13%, under-investment impaired corporate performance.

5. Summary and further research prospects

This chapter investigates the institutional background, practice and academic research of investment in China. As a transition country, the institutional background of China is quite different from developed countries. The primary role of top management in State-owned enterprises in making investments has not been completely established, and the government still plays an important role in intervening corporate investments through government planning and many other indirect macroeconomic controls. Investment practice in Chinese enterprises currently is characterized with the rapid growth of enterprise investment and the low-return on investment. Chinese scholars have conducted both theoretical and empirical researches on enterprise investment efficiency, determinants and economic consequences of corporate investment. These studies find that corporate investment efficiency in China is generally low, demonstrating either under- or over-investment. Such inefficient investment impairs corporate value. Moreover, government intervention, political connections, agency problem, information asymmetry as well as market competition could directly or indirectly influence corporate investment decisions.

Based on current corporate investment practices and research in China, we expect future research on corporate investment theories and policies will be characterized with continuous development of new research perspectives, introduction of new methodology, and the extension of research objects to unlisted companies.

5.1 Several possible future research perspectives

The main strand of research on corporate investment would continuously focus on determinants of investment behavior, but should be conducted from different perspectives, including cyclical fluctuation of macro economy, economic policies adjustments, changes of investment system and the comparison of government, shareholders and management's influence on corporate investment.

Cyclical fluctuation of macro economy and corporate investment

The financial crisis in 2008 generates studies about its influences on corporate investment. For instance, Duchin et al. (2010) and Zhang (2010) analyzed the effect of financial crisis on corporate investment in the United States and in China respectively. Since the beginning of large-scale industrial construction in 1953, GDP growth rate fluctuation of China has experienced 10 cycles, indicating that cyclical fluctuation is one of laws of China's economic development. Therefore, corporate investment behavior under different economic cycles is worth studying.

Economic policies adjustments and corporate investment

According to Rajan and Zingales (1998), regulations could influence macroeconomic performance only through their influences on micro organization behaviors. Thus it is particularly important to study the effect of external regulations on firm behavior and firm performance in institutional transition countries like China. Currently, macro-control has become major resolutions for market failure, and various economic policies were issued after the financial crisis in 2008. It is meaningful to analyze whether these kinds of polices influenced corporate investment and their underlying mechanism.

Investment system changes and corporate investment

As introduced above, China has experienced significant changes in investment system since the reform and opening-up in 1978. Whether the investment system reform reduced government intervention, delegated more investment power to firms and improved corporate investment efficiency is an open question.

Governments, majority shareholder, managements and their influences on corporate investment

Various literatures studied the respective influences of management, majority shareholders and government intervention on corporate investment, but very few made comparisons among them. If influences of these three kinds of stakeholders are analyzed simultaneously, which one eventually determines corporate investment behavior? In different industries or different types of firms, are their influences significantly different?

5.2   New methodology used in corporate investment research

As for the research methods, empirical study and normative study are widely used in existing literatures, while experimental study and case study are rarely adopted and could be used in future research.

Experimental study

In China, a few corporate finance related researches have adopted experimental study method, for example, Liu and Liu (2004) analyzed the influence of decision-making responsibility, decision-making procedure rationality and accountability mechanism on escalation of commitment through experiments. However, experimental study is seldom used in corporate investment researches currently. Actually, this kind of methodology could be used to study topics such as the influence of management incentive on corporate investment behavior, management investment myopia, emotional factors in the process of investment decision and the application of behavioral investment theory in Chinese firms.

Case Study

Case study has been widely used in corporate governance related researches but is seldom used in studies about corporate investment theories and policies. Most existing investment related literatures focus on outcomes of investment decision using large volume of open data, ignoring the process of investment decision-making and construction of investment project. Obviously, the case study method is more appropriate to investigate issues such as investment feasibility analysis, the decision-making method selection, the board of directors' voting behavior, the construction process of investment projects and the project operation after construction.

5.3   Investment behaviors of unlisted companies

Most literatures use listed companies as samples to investigate corporate investment for the availability of data. However, the low proportion of listed companies to total firms (about 3000 listed companies out of 10 million total firms in China) indicates that representativeness of sample may be questionable. The conclusion drawn from listed companies may not be applicable to unlisted firms since unlisted firms are always characterized with relatively poorer corporate governance, fewer external regulations and smaller size. Thus, it is necessary to conduct investment researches for unlisted firms, with information obtained from the National Bureau of Statistics, survey, field research and other possible routes.

Notes

1 We are grateful to Xueting Wang for providing English translation help.
2 He, W. E. 2003. *The Survey on the Effectiveness of Corporate Governance*. Shenzhen Stock Exchange.
3 Since it was difficult to evaluate the cost of equity, and the short-term debt made up the majority of the total debts, which was about 80%, in China, this chapter made a comparison between EBIT and the cost of short-term debt.
4 Prior to 2005, many Chinese listed companies had both tradable shares and non-tradable shares. The rights and responsibilities regarding these shares were different, as well as the prices, which is called market segmentation.

References

Baumol, W. J., Heim, P., Malkiel, B.G., and Quandt, R.E., 1970, 'Earnings Retention, New Capital and the Growth of the Firm', *Review of Economics and Statistics*, 52, pp. 345–355.

Cao, H. J., and Wang, S. J., 2000, 'The Formation, Development and Reform of Chinese Investment Management System', *Eastern Forum (In Chinese)*, 3, pp. 65–71.

Cheng, A., and Geng, Q., 2013, 'Political Connection, Financial Constraints and Overinvestment', *Shanghai Finance(In Chinese)*, 12, pp. 64–69.

Cheng, Z., Xia, X., and Yu, M., 2008, 'Government Intervention, Pyramid Structure and Investment in Local SOEs', *Management World (In Chinese)*, 9, pp. 37–47.

Chow, C. W., Duh, R., and Xiao, J.Z., 2007, 'Management Accounting Practices in the People's Republic of China', In Chapman, C.S., Hopwood, A.G., and Shields, M.D., ed. *Handbooks of Management Accounting Research*, Oxford, Elsevier, pp. 923–967.

Duchin, R., Ozbas, O., and Sensoy, B.A., 2010, 'Costly External Finance, Corporate Investment, and the Subprime Mortgage Credit Crisis', *Journal of Financial Economics*, 97 (3), pp. 418–435.

Fazzari, S., Hubbard, G., and Peterson, B., 1988, 'Financing Constraints and Corporate Investment', *Brookings Papers on Economic Activity*, 1, pp. 141–195.

Feng, W., 1999, 'Internal Cash Flow and Corporate Investment: Evidence From Chinese Listed Companies', *Economic Science (In Chinese)*, 1.

Fremgen, J.M., 1973, 'Capital Budgeting Practices: A Survey', *Management Accounting*, 54 (11), pp. 19–25.

Graham, J.R., and Harvey, C.R., 2001, 'The Theory and Practice of Corporate Finance: Evidence From the Field', *Journal of Financial Economics*, 60 (2–3), pp. 187–243.

He, J., and Ding, J., 2001, 'Empirical Analysis of Investment Decision in Listed Companies', *Securities Market Herald (In Chinese)*, 9, pp. 44–47.

He, W.E., 2003. *The Survey on the Effectiveness of Corporate Governance (In Chinese)*. Shenzhen Stock Exchange.

Huang, J., and Li, Z., 2014, 'Government Intervention, Employment and Over-investment', *Journal of Financial Research (In Chinese)*, 8, pp. 118–130.

Jiang, D., 2011, 'Overinvestment and Corporate Value', *Management World (In Chinese)*, 208 (1), pp. 174–175.

Li, Y., 2014, 'Agency Problem or Overconfidence? Reason for Enterprise Overinvestment', *The Journal of World Economy (In Chinese)*, 12, pp. 95–117.

Li, Y., Xiong, D.H., Zhang, Z., and Liu, L., 2007, 'Corporate Financial Theory and Behavior: Based on 167 Listed Companies in China', *Management World (In Chinese)*, 11, pp. 108–118.

Lian, J., and Su, Z., 2009, 'Financial Constraints, Uncertainty and Firms' Investment Efficiency', *Management Review (In Chinese)*, 1, pp. 19–26.

Liu, F., and Li, Q., 2013, 'Market Competition, EVA Evaluation and Corporate Over-investment', *Accounting Research (In Chinese)*, 2, pp. 54–62.

Liu, H., Wu, L., and Wang, Y., 2012, 'SOE Restructuring, Board Independence and Investment Efficiency', *Journal of Financial Research (In Chinese)*, 9, pp. 127–140.

Liu, J., 2009, 'Diversified Investment, Agency Problem and Corporate Performance', *Journal of Financial Research (In Chinese)*, 9, pp. 127–140.

Liu, Z.Y., and Liu, C., 2004, 'Interpretation of Escalation of Commitment Based on an Experiment Research: Self-Justification Theory or Prospect Theory?', *China Accounting Review (In Chinese)*, 2 (2), pp. 249–257.

Luo, M., 2014, 'Property Right, Agent Cost and Investment Efficiency: Evidence From Chinese Listed Companies', *China Soft Science (In Chinese)*, 7, pp. 172–184.

Meng, Y., and Ma, X.Y., 2004, 'Analysis of Investment and Financing Systems of Developed Countries', *Economy and Management (In Chinese)*, 1, pp. 89–91.

Mueller, D.C., and Reardon, E.A., 1993, 'Rates of Return on Corporate Investment', *Southern Economic Journal*, 60 (2), pp. 430–453.

Nanjing University, 2002, *The Accounting Investigation of Chinese Firms*, Dalian, Dongbei University of Finance and Economics Press (In Chinese).

Pan, M., and Jin, Y., 2003, 'Asymmetric Information, Equity Structure Design and Overinvestment of Chinese Listed Enterprises', *Journal of Financial Research (In Chinese)*, 1.

Qi, Y.F., and Li, L., 2007, *The Operation and Management of Investment and Financing in China's Enterprises-a Study based on Questionnaire and Public Data*, Beijing, Economic Science Press (In Chinese).

Qu, W., Xie, Y., and Ye, Y., 2011, 'Information Asymmetry and Investment-Cash Flow Sensitivity: An Empirical Research Based on Market Microstructure Theory', *Economic Research Journal (In Chinese)*, 6.

Quan, L., Jiang, X., and Chen, J., 2004, 'An Empirical Study of the Impact of Cash Flow on Investment Decision Under Different Firm Size', *Journal of Shanghai Jiaotong University (In Chinese)*, 3.

Rajan, R.G., and Zingales, L., 1998, 'Financial Dependence and Growth', *American Economic Review*, 88 (3), pp. 559–586.

Richardson, S., 2006, 'Over-Investment of Free Cash Flow', *Review of Accounting Studies*, 11, pp. 159–189.

Shanghai Stock Exchange Research Center, 2004, *Corporate Governance Report in China (2004): The Independence and Effectiveness of Board of Directors*, Shanghai, Fudan Press (In Chinese).

Tang, X., and Guo, J., 2007, 'Empirical Study of Investment Behavior Based on Hypothesis of Free Cash Flow Agency Cost', *Securities Market Herald (In Chinese)*, 4.

Tang, X., Zhou, X., and Ma, R., 2010, 'Government Intervention, GDP Growth and Local SOE Overinvestment', *Journal of Financial Research (In Chinese)*, 8.

Tian, J.H., 2008, '30 Year's Investment System Reform in China', *Review of Economic Research (In Chinese)*, 51, pp. 3–10.

The CPC Central Committee and State Council of China, 2016, *Opinions of the CPC Central Committee and State Council on Deepening the Reform of Investment and Financing System (In Chinese)*. Available from: www.gov.cn/zhengce/2016-07/18/content_5092501.htm. [Accessed: 29th May 2018].

The State Council of China, 2004, *Decision of the State Council on the Reform of Investment System (In Chinese)*. Available from: www.gov.cn/zwgk/2005-08/12/content_21939.htm. [Accessed: 29th May, 2018].

Vogt, S.C., 1994, 'The Cash Flow/Investment Relationship: Evidence From Us Manufacturing Firms', *Financial Management*, 23 (2), pp. 3–20.

Wang, Y., and Xue, L., 2014, 'Board Governance, Managerial Overconfidence and Investment Efficiency', *Review of Investment Studies (In Chinese)*, 3, 93–106.

Wei, M., and Liu, J., 2007, 'SOE Dividend, Governance Element and Overinvestment', *Management World (In Chinese)*, 4.

World Bank, 2007, *Government Governance, Investment Climate and Harmonious Society: Competence of 120 Cities in China Improvement*, Beijing, China Financial and Economic Publishing House (In Chinese).

Xiao, F.J., 2012, 'China's Investment and Fund-raising System: Historic Change and Key Points of Current Reform', *Journal of Central University of Finance & Economics (In Chinese)*, 6, pp. 23–28.

Xin, Q., Lin, B., and Wang, Y., 2007a, 'Government Control, Executive Compensation and Capital Investment', *Economic Research Journal (In Chinese)*, 8.

Xin, Q., Lin, B., and Yang, D., 2007b, 'Return to Capital Investment and Its Determinants in China: Evidence From Listed Companies', *China Economic Quarterly (In Chinese)*, 4.

Xu, Y., and Zhou, W., 2009, 'Measurement of Investment Efficiency Under Different Capital Structures and Ownership Arrangements: An Empirical Evidence From Chinese Listed Companies', *China Industrial Economics (In Chinese)*, 11, pp. 131–140.

Yang, H., and Liu, G., 2014, 'Financial Development, Agency Cost and Overinvestment', *Macroeconomics (In Chinese)*, 1, pp. 61–74.

Ye, L., and Wang, Y., 2013, 'Managerial Overconfidence, Investment and Enterprise Performance: Empirical Evidence From Chinese A-share Listed Companies', *Journal of Shanxi University of Finance and Economics (In Chinese)*, 35 (1), pp. 116–124.

Ying, W. J., 1999, 'The Retrospect and Prospect of Investment System Reform in China', *Journal of Finance and Economics (In Chinese)*, 10, pp. 53–59.

Yu, K., Li, Z., Zhang, X., and Xu, J., 2014, 'Investment Efficiency Puzzle: Financial Constraint Hypothesis and Monetary Policy Shock', *Economic Research Journal (In Chinese)*, 5, pp. 106–120.

Yu, W., Wang, M., and Jin, X., 2012, 'Political Connection and Financing Constraints: Information Effect and Resource Effect', *Economic Research Journal (In Chinese)*, 9, pp. 125–139.

Zhang, C., and Lv, W., 2009, 'Disclosure, Information Intermediary and Over-investment', *Accounting Research (In Chinese)*, 1, pp. 60–65.

Zhang, G.F., 2009, 'Product Market Competition, Largest Shareholder and Over-investment: Evidence From Shanghai and Shenzhen Industrial Listed Companies', *East China Economic Management (In Chinese)*, 7, pp. 68–75.

Zhang, G.F., 2010, 'Impact of Financial Crisis, Cash Reserve and Corporate Investment – Empirical Data From Chinese Listed Companies', *Economic Survey (In Chinese)*, 3, pp. 78–82.

Zhang, G.F., 2011, 'Government Intervention, Political Connections and Corporate Inefficient Investment: Empirical Research by the Panel Data From Listed Company of China', *The Theory and Practice of Finance and Economics (In Chinese)*, 3, pp. 24–30.

Zhang, G.F., 2015, *Research on Enterprise Investment Behavior Under Government Intervention*, Beijing, Tsinghua University Press (In Chinese).

Zhang, G.F., and Song, X., 2009, 'Measuring Inefficient Investment by Listed Companies in China: Overinvestment or Underinvestment?', *Accounting Research (In Chinese)*, 5, pp. 69–77.

Zhang, H.H., 2014, 'Inefficiency Investment and Corporate Performance Under the Market Competition: Evidence From Listed Companies of China', *Systems Engineering (In Chinese)*, 5, pp. 9–18.

Zhang, M., Zhang, S., Wang, C., and Shen, H., 2010, 'Political Connection and Distribution Efficiency of Credit Resources: Empirical Evidence From Chinese Private Listed Companies', *Management World (In Chinese)*, 11.

Zhang, Z., Zeng, M., and Liu, Y., 2011, 'Political Relations, Debt Financing and Enterprise Investment: Empirical Evidence From Listed Companies of China', *China Soft Science (In Chinese)*, 5, pp. 106–121.

Zheng, J., He, X., and Wang, H., 2001, 'Financing Constraints on Investment in Listed Companies: Empirical Evidence From Equity Structure', *Journal of Financial Research (In Chinese)*, 11.

Zhu, H., He, X., and Chen, X., 2006, 'Financial Development, Softbudget Constraints, and Firm Investment', *Accounting Research (In Chinese)*, 10, pp. 64–71.

2

IRRATIONAL MARKETS, MANAGERIAL BIASES AND CORPORATE FINANCE

A review of capital markets in China

Guiru Hua, Huanda Shi[1]

1. Introduction

The majority of research in modern corporate finance is based on the supposition of "the rational economic man" and "the effective market". However, in practice, the imperfect arbitrage results in ineffective market and mispricing, rational managers could perceive and exploit the mispricing when they make corporate decisions such as financial policy and real invest policy. Likewise, the enterprise managers frequently display the psychological characteristics which deviate with the most superior decision-making. Research in behavioral corporate finance replaces the traditional rationality assumptions with behavioral foundations that are more evidence-driven (Baker and Wurgler, 2013).

The realization of efficient markets requires the effective operation of a complete set of macro and micro mechanisms. China's stock market has seen huge changes since the establishment of the Shanghai and Shenzhen Exchanges in 1990. However, restrictions on short sales in China lead to imperfect arbitrage and lack of micro-efficient market mechanisms, and misguided regulation by the China Securities Regulatory Commission (CSRS) and poor quality of law enforcement cause the lack and ineffectiveness of macro-efficient market mechanisms. Over the past decade, many empirical studies have focused on the efficiency of China's stock market and find evidence supporting the notion that China's stock market is inefficient or weak-form efficient.

In China, due to Confucian culture and lack of effective external monitoring and disciplining mechanisms, the enterprise managers possess almost the absolute power and authority. Chinese managers are likely to be more overconfident and irrational than their peers in other countries.

Therefore, the lack of macro- and micro-efficient market mechanisms and Confucian culture results in China's inefficient stock market and irrational manager. The emerging markets in China provide unique settings to investigate the impact of inefficient market and managerial biases on corporate finance.

The remainder of the paper is organized as follows. Section 2 discusses related literature on the effect of irrational markets on corporate finance in China. Section 3 discusses the studies on managerial biases and the relevant effectiveness. Section 4 concludes the paper.

2. The effect of irrational markets on corporate finance

2.1 Real investment policy

Based on the rational economic man hypothesis, the traditional financial theory systematically studies the influence of the investment behavior on the stock price, and has achieved fruitful results, but paid little attention to the investor sentiment caused by the stock price shock may impact on corporate investment behavior. Especially since 2008, the global financial tsunami triggered by the subprime mortgage crisis has exacerbated the fluctuation of investor sentiment in the Chinese capital market, and the trend has gradually spread to the real economy. On the basis of the hypothesis of the "inefficient market", China's financial research on corporate investment behavior has undergone a directional change, starting to regard the shock of securities assets price as the cause of changes in corporate investment behavior, with particular attention to the real impact of stock mispricing caused by investor sentiment on corporate investment behavior. In this section, we discussed the research on three important questions as follows.

2.1.1 How inefficient stock market affects corporate investment?

Based on the assumption of irrational investors and the rational manager, the existing literature regarded the investment behavior of enterprises as a rational reaction of managers to the mispricing of securities market, and tested and confirmed two displays of investor sentiment on corporate investment.

The first type of inefficient market-driven investment was tested by Baker et al. (2003, "equity financing channel"), which confirmed that investor sentiment affected the cost of equity financing, and it affected corporate investment. The second was found by Polk and Sapienza (2009, "Rationally catering channel"), which argued that rational managers would increase corporate investment in order to cater to investor sentiment and boost the mispricing. However, in practice, bounded rationality of investors and managers often coexists (Shleifer, 2003; Baker et al., 2006). To be close to the more real capital market, using a sample of all listed companies in China from 2000 to 2006, Liu and Hua (2009) thoroughly abandon the "perfectly rational hypothesis" and incorporate limited rational investors and mangers into the same framework. They found that investor sentiment may have an indirect effect on corporate investment by shaping managerial optimism or pessimism. Such findings showed that there existed a "third road" along which investor sentiment affects corporate investment in China' capital market, i.e., the "intermediate effect channel of managerial optimism".

Is there another way that the investor sentiment can influence the corporate investment besides the "equity financing channel", "Catering channel" and "managerial optimism channel"? Using a sample of all listed companies in China from 2002 to 2010, Huang and Liu(2014) expanded the investor sentiment effect on investment level to the layer of "credit financing", studying whether investor sentiment can affect credit financing level and the inner mechanism of the effect. Based on the co-directional variation of investor sentiment and credit financing, this paper had more findings in the partial media pathway in which investor sentiment affected corporate investment level through credit financing.

2.1.2 What are the economic consequences of the effect of inefficient market on corporate investment?

Most of the existing literature ignored the economic consequences of the effect of inefficient market on corporate investment (Baker and Wurgler, 2013). For example, while Chang et al. (2007, Dong et al. (2007) and Polk and Sapienza (2009) confirmed that investor sentiment had a positive influence on corporate investment behavior, it does not take into account the economic consequences on resource allocation efficiency. Only a small amount of literature argued that the inefficient market-driven investment will distort the resource allocation. Chirinko and Schaller (2001) simply believed that investment sentiment affected the investment behavior of enterprises, which would lead to the distortion and inefficiency of resource allocation.

However, as Baker and Wurgler (2013) pointed out, although inefficient market affects corporate investment, it is not necessary to lead to inefficient allocation of resources. For example, if there is under-investment due to agency or asymmetric information, bubbles may bring investment closer to the efficient level-or overshoot (Baker and Wurgler, 2013).

Based on the above logic framework, Hua et al. (2010) use a sample of all listed companies in China from 1993 to 2010 and find that investor sentiment has a positive effect on over-investment and a negative effect on under-investment. Furthermore, the findings show that the effect of investor sentiment on performance of the firm is manifested in a process of "positive effect – negative effect – gradual decline". It suggests that investor sentiment has a two-sided economic effect on resource allocation efficiency.

2.1.3 Institutional environment and the relationship between investor sentiment and corporate investment

THE PROPERTY OF ENTERPRISES

There are differences in the motives and behaviors of the controlling shareholders who have different control attributes in China (Liu and Jin, 2013). In the case of the State-owned nature of the controlling shareholder of a listed company, the manager is often designated by the government because of the absence of final ownership. Moreover, managers of State-owned enterprise pay more attention to the political future, rather than pay (Wu and Huang, 2010). The motivation of managers to meet market sentiment is weak in State-owned enterprises because they are insensitive to stock price.

This is supported by the empirical data from China. For example, Luo (2013), Zhang and Yang (2015) find investor sentiment has positive effect on over-investment and negative effect on under-investment, and the effects on private companies are larger than those on State-owned companies.

MAJOR SHAREHOLDERS

It has been found that most companies in China have a concentrated ownership structure, and the agency conflict between controlling shareholders and minority shareholders has replaced the owner-manager conflict and become the focus of corporate governance researches. Due to concentrated ownership structure, the controlling shareholders are motivated to maximize their own interests. They also have the ability to exploit market sentiment to influence the company's investment decisions, such as exacerbating excessive investment or encroaching on the company's cash assets.

Luo (2013) and Liu and Jin. (2013) address such a question. Using a sample of all listed companies in China from 1993 to 2010, they find that investor sentiment has significant negative effect on corporate under-investment behavior, and has significant positive effect on corporate over-investment behavior. Furthermore, the findings show that the correlation between investor sentiment and over-investment is stronger in case of controlling shareholder with high share proportion, but the correlation between investor sentiment and under-investment is weaker when the share proportion is high.

2.2   *Financial policy*

The simple theoretical framework suggests that long-horizon managers may reduce the overall cost of capital paid by their ongoing investors by issuing overpriced securities and repurchasing underpriced securities. Next, we survey the evidence on the extent to which market timing affects IPO, SEO, debt issues and capital structure in China.

In recent years, with the rise of behavioral finance, the financing theory has also been integrated into the behavioral finance, so a new financing theory called market timing theory, has emerged. Timing theory suggests that managers always choose to issue more equity financing when the stock price is overvalued, and choose repurchase rights or issue debt financing when the stock price is undervalued, so as to take advantage of the low-cost advantage of equity financing caused by stock price fluctuation.

2.2.1   *IPO*

Stein (1996 studied firms' investment and financing behavior in the case of ineffective market, proposing the Market Timing Hypothesis of corporate finance. Stein's theoretical model shows that in the non-efficient market, management can not only create value for shareholders through the use of positive NPV programs, but also use market inefficiencies to rationalize financing to create value.

The phenomena of high initial IPO return and poor long-term return are popular in China's stock market and it is known as "IPO puzzle" in academic. In recent years, people try to provide explanations to the IPO puzzle in China's stock market from the perspective of individual investors' irrational biases. For instance, Yu et al. (2015) construct a buy-sell imbalance (BSI) index, using initial IPO from the investors' trading data, to represent investor sentiment to study these IPO phenomena in China and find that investors' sentiment and disagreement have significant positive impacts on the initial returns, and when the disagreement is big, the impact of sentiment is more serious. Meanwhile, sentiment has significant positive impact on the long-term abnormal return, but disagreement has no such impact. Duan et al. (2015) analyze the formation mechanism of the IPO first-day excess return from two aspects including first market underpricing and secondary market overpricing and find that there is no deliberate underpricing and the price efficiency reaches 99.9%. Meanwhile, the mood indicator of investors significantly correlated with IPO overpricing rate, which means the mood factors of investors lead to certain price bubble. However, when investors become more rational toward new shares, share price returns to the normal level. Tian et al. (2016) find that the irrational component of individual investor sentiment negatively influence long-run performance and rational component of institutional investor sentiment affect positively in China's growth enterprise market. By constructing proxy variables to measure investors' irrational behavior, Xie et al. (2016) also verifies the influence of investor sentiment on IPO premium.

2.2.2   *SEO*

Due to the lower degree of marketization in China, the government and regulatory authorities play a decisive role in the capital market. Whether listed companies could have timing behavior in SEO is regulated by authorities, meanwhile, in terms of the number of implementation or the amount raised, SEO has already become the main means of refinancing, while share allotment is shrinking (Xu and Hu, 2012). In this context, it is worth discussing whether investors' sentiment affects SEO timing behavior of Chinese listed companies.

From the perspectives of corporate internal governance and external markets, Cui and He. (2016) simultaneously investigates how opportunism of big shareholders and investor sentiment influence the discount of SEO and thereby affect the wealth transfer among shareholders. The result shows that the opportunism of big shareholders may promote big shareholders to gain wealth transfer by high discount rate, and investor sentiment may strengthen the extent of this wealth transfer. Compared to other investors, big shareholders show a stronger motivation for wealth transfer when they participate in SEO, and the higher investor sentiment, the higher the degree of wealth transfer.

2.2.3   Debt issues

With the rapid development of China's securities market, listed companies tend to diversify the financing, such as corporate bonds, convertible bonds and separable convertible bonds. From 2006 to 2016, the issuance of bonds has been increasing. Xuand Yang. (2013) studies the impact of investor sentiment in stock markets on bond issue costs in China. Based on the joint action mechanism between stock markets and bond markets, the overoptimistic sentiment from stock markets would spread to bond markets, or the rational investors would hedge through bonds to avoid the bubble risk, both of which would inflate the demand for bonds and consequently decrease bond issue costs. Their empirical results show that higher investor sentiment in stock markets results in lower bond issue costs. The effect is more significant with regard to firms with higher credit ratings, better accounting performance and controlled by governments and bonds with a convertible option, thereby supporting the hypothesis of rational arbitrage.

Does investor sentiment affect bank loans in China? Huang and Liu (2013) find that accompanied with the high investor sentiment, more bank loans are allocated to small private listed companies, which alleviates these companies' financing constraints and increases the allocation efficiency of credit resources. Furthermore, they show that the allocation efficiency of market-driven credit is reduced. Over-investment companies exacerbate over-investment with bank loans allocated. The bank loans received in the high investor sentiment reduces the enterprise's subsequent operating performance significantly.

2.2.4   Capital structure

Capital structure is related to firm market value, and the relation between capital structure and firm value is systematically discussed by the theory of time marketing (Baker and Wurgler, 2002; Alti, 2006; Kayhan and Titman, 2007). In this spirit, Chen and Zhao (2005 and Hovakimian (2006) find evidence that market timing behavior affects the capital structure in developed capital market.

According to the cross-section data of Chinese listed companies, Li (2006) examined the effectiveness of time marketing theory. The results of their study showed that current difference of horizontal cross-section has great influence on capital structure, however, the aggregate change of market–book ratio has almost no explanation on capital structure. Such results demonstrated that the financing behavior of Chinese listed companies has a short-term tendency. Similarly, Lu and Gao(2012) use the Tobit model to predict the firms target capital structure and find the evidence of the market timing behavior in China, but it has only lasted for three years.

2.3   Dividend policy

Why do public corporate pay dividend? The traditional theory such as tax theory, information model and agent hypothesis, cannot explain the "dividend puzzle" drastically and profoundly. Recently, an explanation of dividend brought forward called catering theory from behavior corporate finance. It is said that the reason why corporate pay dividends is: to raise the stock price. Rational managers will cater to shareholder's changing demands for dividends.

Huang and Shen(2007) started with the re-examination of catering theory and find that the catering theory can explain Chinese public corporate dividend policy. Managers cater to large shareholders' demands instead of whole shareholders. The demands of small and middle shareholders are ignored. The aim of corporate has departed from value maximization.

2.4 Earning management

Ball and Brown (1968) are the first to find evidence that the market had mispriced earnings news and the stock has not responded adequately to the earnings announcement window and that the stock price continued to move in the direction of earnings changes after the earnings announcement. Furthermore, consistent with catering, managers with "short horizons" are especially likely to manage earnings. Bergstresser and Philippon (2006), Sloan (1996) and Teoh et al. (1998) support the views on the effect of the irrational market on earning management in US.

However, in China, the relation between investor sentiment and earning management usually is affected by institutional environment (e.g. internal control, institutional holdings). For instance, Zhang et al. (2014) find that for companies with low internal control quality, stock market responses to earnings news are more likely to be influenced by investor sentiment, with high (low) investor sentiment increasing earnings response coefficients of good (bad) news. The results also show that high internal control quality not only can inhibit the improvement effect of investor sentiment on earnings response coefficients, but it can also have a safe harbor effect. In addition, they find that the above phenomenon is more evident for small companies and non-state owned companies.

Taking the listed companies in China from 2007 to 2011 as a sample, Lu and Yao (2016) examines the influences of institutional holdings on the relation between investor sentiment and earning management. Results indicate that the magnitude of mispricing of the accruals is relatively high (low) during periods of high (low) sentiment. The impacts of institutional overall ownership on the relationship between investor sentiment and the accrual anomaly differ at different time windows, institutional overall ownership strengthens the positive impacts of investor sentiment on the accrual anomaly in the short run, but it alleviates the positive impacts of investor sentiment on the accrual anomaly in the long run.

3. Managerial biases and the relevant effectiveness

3.1 Investment policy

3.1.1 Real investment

With the development of cognitive psychology and the emergence of a series of financial scandals such as Enron and WorldCom, the assumption of "rational individuals" is broken through and the effect of managerial overconfidence on over-investment has become the focus of behavioral finance research. Malmendier and Tate(2005) first find that overconfident managers are more likely to carry out investment activities that hurt corporate value than rational CEOs.

China's economy has suffered from the serious overcapacity since 2008, and corporate over-investment may be the main reason for overcapacity. However, will managerial overconfidence lead to over-investment and reduce corporate performance? From the perspective of managerial overconfidence, Ma et al. (2012), Li et al. (2014), and Cha and Guo (2014) find that managerial overconfidence is one of the important reasons for excessive investment behavior in China, and with the increase of overconfidence level, the investment amount that managers make in the private enterprise will continue to expand.

However, how to control the inefficiency of investment brought by managerial overconfidence effectively has been a very hot topic in China. The literature document that political connection, cash holding, corporate governance and accounting conservatism affect the influence of managerial biases on real investment.

For instance, Hu and Zhou (2012) find that the manager with the background as government officers is more easily to be overconfident than those with background as representatives of the CNNPC or CPPCC, and managers overconfidence promote investment excessively. From the perspective of cash holding, Li et al. (2014) study the relationship between managers' overconfidence of Chinese listed companies and over-investment and find that corporate sufficient cash flow will promote managers' over-investment. Zhang et al. (2014) test the restriction effect of governance mechanisms and find that independent board, splitting of CEO and Chairman, and creditor and the government's interference can play the restraining role, while the industry competition cannot. Therefore, the results show that higher levels of company governance weaken overconfident managers' tendency toward over-investment. Furthermore, Hu and Zhou (2013) argue that accounting conservatism could restrict managers' irrationality and its effectiveness on excess investment in China.

Therefore, in order to suppress investment inefficiency caused by managerial overconfidence, it's highly suggested to consider the impact of political and monetary policy, corporate governance and accounting conservatism.

3.1.2   Merger and acquisition

In China, Li et al. (2016) find that there is a significant positive correlation between management overconfidence and M & A decision. However, what's the economic consequences of M&A leaded by managerial overconfidence? Managers' overconfidence significantly reduce the company's financial performance and market performance (Xie et al., 2012; Zhang et al., 2014; Song and Dai, 2015). Furthermore, Li et al. (2015) point out that overconfidence managers may lose desire to search for the information because of illusion of control, and consequently may neglect the value of information advantages and cause the hidden loss in M&A decision.

How does China's institutional environment affect the relationship between overconfidence of managers and M&A?

Managers in State-owned listed companies are more prone to overconfidence to promote M&A than executives in private listed companies (Ge and Shan, 2015). Moreover, Sun et al. (2016) find that the binding force of informal rules is significantly related to CEO overconfidence and it will influence the relationship between overconfidence and M&A behaviors. Even though M&A is popular over the whole country, in regions with stronger religious force, CEO has less influence on companies' M&A behaviors.

3.1.3   Enterprise innovation

Innovation helps companies to gain competitive advantages and realize sustainable growth and performance. It belongs to investment activities of enterprises, but it is different from general investment, since its result is full of uncertainty, and innovation involves great expenditure. As a whole, it is not surprised that the level of enterprise innovation is very low in China.

Overconfident CEOs pay too much trust on their own judgment and the reliability of private information, and tend to overestimate future earnings and underestimate risk (Bernardo and Welch, 2001). Using a sample of Chinese listed firms during the period from 2000 to 2012, Yi et al. (2015) find that overconfident top executives in large firms obtain greater innovation success than that of overconfident top executives in small firms. In non-financial expansion firms, the relationship between overconfident top executives and innovation performance is significantly positive. In contrast, this positive relationship is not significant anymore for financial expansion firms. So firm size and debt will moderate the relationship significantly between overconfidence and innovation.

In addition, when enterprises are exposed to high uncertain environment, managers will reduce R&D, but overconfident ones who are more adventurous weaken the negative correlation between them. Lin et al. (2014) test the positive correlation between R&D investment and firm value, and find that overconfident managers can promote enterprises' R&D investment and improve firm value under the uncertain environment in China.

3.2 Financial policy

3.2.1 Equity finance

There is a growing body of evidence that managerial biases affect financing patterns. In China' listed companies, it gives first priority to short-term debt financing, with equity financing in second place. The companies with overconfident managers prefer long-term liabilities financing to internal financing. However, the companies with non-overconfident managers do quite the opposite (Liu et al., 2012).

In China, managerial overconfidence has a negative effect on accounting information opacity and equity capital cost (Luo et al., 2013). Moreover, the more overconfident the managers are, the worse the market performance after the overall listing will be (Yu et al., 2015).

3.2.2 Debt Finance

Xie and Huang (2013) find that managerial overconfidence is prevalent in China' listed companies, overconfident managers are more inclined to debt finance. The higher degree of managerial overconfidence the companies have, the higher financial leverage will be chosen, and the short-term liabilities will be preferred (Dai et al., 2015).

In addition, Zhu et al. (2014) also argue that managers with overconfidence behavior affect debt maturity decisions. In detail, overconfident managers often choose higher debt ratio, but they also tend to use short-term debt financing.

3.2.3 Capital structure

Managerial overconfidence is not conducive to the capital structure decision-making of listed companies. In China' listed companies, Shen (2013) find that manager overconfidence will reduce the speed of adjustment of the capital structure, and increase the bias from the target capital structure.

Moreover, Companies with large scale and high growth opportunity have large structure dynamic adjustment; the greater actual capital structure deviate from target leverage, the smaller structure dynamic adjustment is. Overconfident managers will choose lower structure dynamic adjustment, but in companies with large scale, high growth opportunity and low deviation, managerial overconfidence slows down structure dynamic adjustment to a lesser extent (Shen, 2013).

4.   Summary and conclusions

In this paper, we review the development of behavioral corporate finance in China. Based on the assumptions of inefficient markets and smart managers, it is documented that China's stock market is inefficient or weak-form efficient, investor sentiment and securities mispricing had an important role in investment, financing and other corporate decisions. Based on the assumptions of irrational managers and efficient capital markets, Chinese managers are likely to be more overconfident and irrational than their peers in other countries, are more optimistic about future cash flow and risk in place than outside investors and managerial overconfidence and optimism can have an important effect on corporate finance, such as investment, financial policy and capital structure.

The capital market and manager have a much higher effect on corporate finance following the accomplishment of stock split reform. In order to improve the efficiency of resource allocation and develop the real economy, Chinese government has gradually adopted and implemented a series of reforms, such as financial system reform and reform of the personnel system reform of the State-owned Enterprises. To what extent should the foregoing reforms improve the efficiency of capital market and depress investor sentiment and correct managerial biases? Will the improvement of China's inefficient stock market and irrational manager has a positive influence on corporate finance? The emerging markets in China provide unique settings to investigate a number of exciting and important research questions.

Note

1 Guiru Hua acknowledges financial support from the Fundamental Research Funds for the Central Universities (No. 222201422010), the National Natural Science Foundation of China (No. 71302042; 71472096), National Natural Science Foundation of Shanghai (No. 13ZR1411100) and China scholarship council (No. 201506745030). Any remaining error is the responsibility of the authors.

References

Alti, A. (2006). How Persistent Is the Impact of Market Timing on Capital Structure? *Journal of Finance*, 61(4), 1681–1710.

Baker, M., Stein, J., & Wurgler, J. (2003). When Does the Market Matter? Stock Prices and the Investment of Equity-Dependent Firms. *Quarterly Journal of Economics*, 118, 969–1006.

Baker, M., Taliaferro, R., & Wurgler, J. (2006). Predicting Returns with Managerial Decision Variables: Is There a Small-Sample Bias? *Journal of Finance*, 61(4), 1711–1730.

Baker, M., & Wurgler, J. (2002). Market Timing and Capital Structure. *Journal of Finance*, 57(1), 1–32.

Baker, M., & Wurgler, J. (2013). Behavioral Corporate Finance: An Updated Survey. *Handbook of the Economics of Finance*, edited by G.M. Constantinides, M. Harris and R. Stulz. Elsevier Science B.V.

Ball, R., & Brown, P. (1968). An Empirical Evaluation of Accounting Income Numbers. *Journal of Accounting Research*, 6(2), 159–178.

Bergstresser, D., & Philippon, T. (2006). CEO Incentives and Earnings Management. *Journal of Financial Economics*, 80, 511–529.

Bernardo, A. E., & Welch, I. (2001). On the Evolution of Overconfidence and Entrepreneurs. *Journal of Economics & Management Strategy*, 10(3), 301–330.

Chen, L., & Zhao, J. (2005). *Profitability, Mean Reversion of Leverage Ratios, and Capital Structure Choices*. Working Paper, Washington University.

Chirinko, R. S., & Schaller, H. (1995). Why Does Liquidity Matter in Investment Equations? *Journal of Money Credit & Banking*, 27(2), 527–548.

Chirinko, R. S., & Schaller, H. (2001). Business fixed investment and "bubbles": The Japanese Case. *American Economic Review*, 91(3), 663–680.

Cui, X. L., & He, J. (2016). The Effect of Investor Sentiment on the Wealth Transfer in Private Placement— a Perspective of Discount Rate of Private Placement. *Journal of Shanxi University of Finance & Economics*, 38(11), 35–46 (in Chinese).

Dai, W. (2015). Managerial Overconfidence and Financial Preference: Evidence of the Real Estate Listed Companies. *Journal of Wuhan University of Technology*, 28(1), 100–106.

Dong, M., Hirshleifer, D. A., & Teoh, S. H. (2007). Stock Market Misvaluation and Corporate Investment. *Siew Hong Teoh*, 25(12), 3645–3683.

Duan, Y. L., Wang, S. J., Yang, W. W., Business, S. O., University, N., & School, I. B. (2015). Research on IPO First-Day Excess Return and the Long-Term Performance Based on the Mood of the Investors. *Journal of Yunnan University of Finance & Economics*, 31(6), 90–101 (in Chinese).

Ge, H. L., & Shan, Z. (2015). Impact of Managerial Overconfidence on M&A Decisions in China's Listed Companies—Empirical Research Based on Comparative Perspective Between State-Owned Enterprises and Private Companies. *Journal of Beijing Technology & Business University*, 30(5), 82–91 (in Chinese).

Guo-Liu, H. U., & Zhou, S. (2012). Political Association, Overconfidence and Non-Efficient Investments. *Theory & Practice of Finance & Economics*, 33(6), 37–42 (in Chinese).

Hovakimian, A. (2006). Are Observed Capital Structures Determined by Equity Market Timing? *Journal of Financial & Quantitative Analysis*, 41(1), 221–243.

Hu, G. L., & Zhou, S. (2013). Accounting Conservatism, Managers' Overconfidence and Excessive Investment. *Journal of Southeast University*, 15(2), 50–55 (in Chinese).

Hua, G. R., Liu, Z. Y., & Xu, Q. (2010). Investor Sentiment, Corporate Investment and Resource Allocation Efficiency. *Accounting Research*, 11, 49–55 (in Chinese).

Huang, H. B., & Liu, Z. Y. (2013). The Impact of Investor Sentiment and Credit Scale on the Allocation Efficiency of Credit Resources. *Systems Engineering*, 31(4), 1–12 (in Chinese).

Huang, H. B., & Liu, Z. (2014). Investor Sentiment, Credit Financing and Corporate Investment Level. *Securities Market Herald*, 7, 28–34, 39 (in Chinese).

Huang, J. A., & Shen, Y. (2007). To Whom Do Public Corporate Dividend Policies Cater?–an Empirical Evidence from Chinese Public Corporations. *Accounting Research*, 20(8), 36–43 (in Chinese).

Kayhan, A., & Titman, S. (2007). Firms' Histories and Their Capital Structures. *Journal of Financial Economics*, 83(1), 1–32.

Li, G. C. (2006) Capital Structure and Market Timing: Evidence from Cross-Section Data of Chinese Listed Companies. *Journal of Central University of Finance & Economics*, 8, 22–28 (in Chinese).

Li, J. (2016). Ownership Concentration, Management Overconfidence and Enterprise M&A Decision. *Finance Forum*, 9, 45–56 (in Chinese).

Li, L., Guan, Y., Gu, C., School, B., & University, N. (2014). Study on Impact of Governance Supervision Mechanism on Overinvestment of China's Listed Companies: The Applicability of Agent Theory. *Management Review*, 26(5), 139–148 (in Chinese).

Li, S. M., Huang, C., & Shi, X. X. (2015). Impact of Information Advantage on M&A—Perspective from Social Network. *China Industrial Economics*, 11, 141–155 (in Chinese).

Lin, H. T., & Wang, M. L. (2014). Managerial Overconfidence, Uncertainty and Corporate Innovation. *Economic Management Journal*, 11, 94–102 (in Chinese).

Liu, Z. Y., & Hua, G. R. (2009). A Review and Prospect of Researches on Investor Sentiment and Corporate Investment Behavior. *Foreign Economies and Management*, 31(6), 45–51 (in Chinese).

Liu, Z. Y., & Jin, G. H. (2013). Investor Sentiment and Corporate Investment Efficiency: An Empirical Study on the Moderating Effects of Shareholding Ratio and Rights Separation. *Management Review*, 25(5), 82–91 (in Chinese).

Liu, Z. Y., Tian, H. E., School, B., & University, C. S. (2016). The Empirical Evidence for Institutional Investor's Influence on the Variability of China's Stock Market. *Theory & Practice of Finance & Economics*, 37(1), 64–69 (in Chinese).

Lu, B., & Gao, B. Y. (2012). Market Timing and Target Capital Structure: Evidence from Chinese Stock Markets. *South China Journal of Economics*, 30(1), 39–46 (in Chinese).

Lu, P., & Yao, H. X. (2016). Institutional Ownership, Investor Sentiment and Accrual Anomaly. *Management Review*, 28(11), 3–15 (in Chinese).

Luo, J., Li, Y., & Management, S. O. (2013). Effect of Managerial Overconfidence on Equity Capital Cost: From Perspective of Information Transparency. *Technology Economics*, 32(12), 111–117 (in Chinese).

Luo, Q. (2013). Ownership Properties, Investor Sentiment and Corporate Inefficient Investment. *Finance & Trade Research*, 24(4), 148–156 (in Chinese).

Ma, R., Li, Y., Yang, Y., & Zhang, W. (2012). Managerial Overconfidence, Over-Investment and Corporate Governance Mechanism: Evidence from Chinese Listed Companies. *Securities Market Herald*, 6, 38–43 (in Chinese).

Malmendier, U., & Tate, G. (2005). CEO Overconfidence and Corporate Investment. *Journal of Finance*, 60, 2661–2700.

Polk, C., & Sapienza, P. (2009). The Stock Market and Corporate Investment: A Test of Catering Theory. *Review of Financial Studies*, 22(1), 187–217.

Shen, Y. (2013). Managerial Overconfidence and Dynamic Adjustment of Capital Structure-Based on Panel Data Analysis. *Shanghai Journal of Economics*, 10, 35–48 (in Chinese).

Shleifer, A., & Vishny, R. W. (2003). Stock Market Driven Acquisitions. *Journal of Financial Economics*, 70(3), 295–311.

Sloan, R. (1996). Do Stock Prices Fully Reflect Information in Accruals and Cash Flows About Future Earnings? *The Accounting Review*, 71, 289–316.

Song, S. Q., & Dai, S. J. (2015). Managerial Overconfidence, M&A Type and M&A Performance. *Macroeconomic Research*, 5, 139–149 (in Chinese).

Stein, J. C. (1996). Rational Capital Budgeting in an Irrational World. *Journal of Business*, 69, 429–455.

Sun, Y., Guo, M., & Han, J. (2016). Informal Rules, Overconfidence and the Enterprise Mergers and Acquisitions. *Zhejiang Social Sciences*, 1, 36–44+156–157 (in Chinese).

Teoh, S. H., Welch, I., & Wong, T. J. (1998). Earnings Management and the Long-Run Market Performance of Initial Public Offerings. *Journal of Finance*, 53, 1935–1974.

Tian, L., Liu, C., & Huang Fu, Y. T. (2016). Study on Investor Sentiment and IPOs' Long-Run Performance—Evidence from China's Growth Enterprise Market. *Journal of Hebei University of Economics and Business*, 37(4), 84–91 (in Chinese).

Wu, R. X., & Huang, J. B. (2010). Could the Managerial Cognitive Bias Only Bring Negative Effect?—a Review of the Existing Research Paradigm About Managerial Overconfidence. *Economic Management Journal*, 9, 172–179 (in Chinese).

Xie, L. H., Liu, S. C., & Qiu, W. H. (2012). The Impact of Manager's Over-Confidence on M&A Performances—an Analytical and Empirical Research Based on Group Decision Making Perspective. *Journal of Applied Statistics & Management*, 4, 531–535 (in Chinese).

Xie, Z. L., & Huang, H. (2013). Research on the Influence of Managerial Overconfidence on Corporate Financing Decision-Making. *Public Finance Research*, 12, 80–83 (in Chinese).

Xu, H. P., & Yang, G. C. (2013). The Cross-Market Impacts of Investor Sentiment in Stock Markets: On the Effect of Investor Sentiment on Bond Issue Costs. *Journal of Finance & Economics*, 2, 47–57 (in Chinese).

Xu, L., & Hu, A. G. (2012). Heterogeneous Beliefs, Investor Sentiment, and Corporate SEO Preferences. *Economy Science*, 34(5), 81–91 (in Chinese).

Yi, J., Zhang, X., & Wang, H. C. (2015). Firm Heterogeneity, Top Executives' Overconfidence, and Corporate Innovation Performance. *Nankai Business Review*, 18(6), 101–112 (in Chinese).

Yu, H. H., Li, X. D., & Geng, Z. Y. (2015). Investor Sentiment, Disagreement and IPO Puzzle in China's Stock Market. *Journal of Management Sciences in China*, 3, 78–89 (in Chinese).

Yu, J., Yang, X. C., & Ni, Z. Q. (2015). Managerial Overconfidence, Overall Listing by Private Placement and Value of the Listed Company. *Journal of Xinjiang University*, 43(6), 13–20 (in Chinese).

Zha, B., & Guo, J. E. (2014). Overconfident Manager's Investment Decisions and Compensation Contracts Under the Behavior of Project Value Anticipation. *Soft Science*, 28(9), 2661–2700 (in Chinese).

Zhang, Q. C., & Yang, D. C. (2015). Monetary Policy, Investor Sentiment and Corporate Investment Behavior. *Journal of Central University of Finance & Economics*, 12, 57–68 (in Chinese).

Zhang, X., Zhang, L., Business, S. O., & University, C. S. (2014). Impact of Corporate Merger and Acquisition on Financial Risk: Empirical Study from Perspective of Managerial Overconfidence. *Technology Economics*, 33(3), 90–96 (in Chinese).

Zhu, G. Y., Ai-Qin, X. I., & Ding, J. X. (2014). Empirical Research on Effects of the Irrational Performance of Managers in Corporate Finance Decisions. *Journal of Guizhou University of Finance & Economics*, 4, 63–69 (in Chinese).

3

THE INFLUENCE OF FIRM LOCATION ON THE CHOICE OF PAYMENT METHODS IN MERGER AND ACQUISITION

Zhiying Hu, Tongtong Liu

1. Introduction

Merger and acquisition (M&A) is the important topic in capital market, which has attracted interest from academic scholars. In recent years, an increasing number of firms participate in M&A and the size of transactions increase rapidly, which indicates that M&A has become more important in resources allocation. There have been studies on M&A and focusing the choice of M&A payment method (Amaro de Matos and Mergulhão, 2012; Nikolaos et al., 2014). Normally, acquirer firms pay by issuing shares or by cash which is financed by debt. If the size of M&A is enormous, payment method may affect the acquirer' ownership structure, financial leverage, control right, risk-taking, taxes and the decision of cash-holdings for both the acquirer and target firms (Faccio and Masulis, 2005). In this sense, payment method choice is an important financial decision in the M&A process. However, it is unclear how managers made decisions on M&A payment.

The geographical factors imply the potential information superiority, political resources, social relationship and business environment and hence have profound impacts on a company's behavior. The literature documents the impact of geographical factors on financial behavior and the related economic consequences. For instance, some studies examine the effects of geographical factors in corporate investment (Kang and Kim, 2008; Cai and Jiang, 2013), financing activities (Arena and Dewally, 2012), dividend policy (John et al., 2011), liquidity management (Almazan et al., 2007), corporate governance (Francis et al., 2007; Knyazeva et al., 2010) and firm performance (Kim et al., 2012). Further, Koutmos et al. (2014) find that the geographical location of acquirer firms significantly affected the payment method of M&A in the US compared to other developed countries. Regional development in China is unbalanced; the geographical difference exists not only between urban and rural areas, but also between eastern and western regions. As a transition economy, the problem of information asymmetry is serious in China because of the imperfect institutions. Under this circumstance, informal institutions such as political resources and social ties are often used to deal with business problem under policy uncertainty. That suggests a rich potential economic information, political resources and social ties implied in geographical factors would lead more significant impact on corporate behavior.

To achieve this aim, we examine M&A transactions of acquirer firms listed in the A-share market between 2009 and 2013. We find that acquirer firms located in the remote rural areas are more likely to choose stock payment compared with those located in the urban areas. Furthermore, we study the influences of geographical factors on M&A payment methods from the aspects of large shareholder's control rights, financing constraints, property rights and information asymmetry, and we find that the probability of stock payment for the acquirer firms located in the remote rural areas will be reduced when the large shareholder's control right is between 20% and 60%, when the acquirer firms have less severe financial constraints, when the acquirer firms are State-owned and when information asymmetry risk is low.

Our study has the following contributions: first, although the impact of geographical location on corporate finance has attracted wide interests, few studies examine this topic in the emerging market of China. We document that in the emerging market geographical factors play critical roles in the M&A payment method. Second, this essay can also enrich the M&A payment method choice literature by the further exploration of the influential mechanism from the aspects of large shareholders control rights, financing constraints, property rights and information asymmetry.

The rest of the essay is organized as follows: the second part is a literature review and hypothesis development, the third part is research design and sample selection, the fourth part is empirical results, the fifth part is additional research and the sixth part concludes this paper.

2. Literature review and hypothesis development

Undoubtedly, significant difference between urban and rural areas may affect the financial behavior of companies. On one hand, compared with the remote rural areas, there are more professional institutional investors and securities analysts, richer political resources and social ties in the urban areas (Coval and Moskowitz, 1999; Loughran and Schultz, 2005). As a result, firms located in or near the urban areas have a lesser degree of information asymmetry, especially soft information that requires close observation (Loughran, 2008), lower cost of equity capital (Kim et al., 2012) and more political resources, thus it is easier for them to access debt financing, particularly bank loans (Arena and Dewally, 2012). On the other hand, it costs much higher for the firms located in the remote rural areas to access information and resources because of the undeveloped transportation, so they are often at information disadvantages when making financial decisions (Loughran, 2008; Koutmos et al., 2014).

In recent years, the impact of geographic location on financial behavior and the related economic consequences has attracted much academic interest. For example, Kedia et al. (2005), Kang and Kim (2008) and Cai et al. (2014) find that the positive returns due to geographical proximity will be reduced when the acquirer firms are located in remote rural areas, and further when there are traffic disadvantages between the acquirer and target firms. Meanwhile, firms located in urban areas are more likely to become target firms, and the probability of success is also higher. In addition, Arena and Dewally (2012) find that firms in rural areas face higher financing costs and receive fewer loans from banks. John et al. (2011) find that the agency problem is more severe for the firms located in remote areas because of a lack of observability of management action, so they are willing to pay a relatively higher cash dividend to alleviate conflicts. Furthermore, Almazan et al. (2007) find that firms located in industrial concentration areas tend to reserve excess cash for the future M&A. Additionally, some scholars find that the location of corporate headquarters often affected a CEO's power and the composition of the board of directors (Francis et al., 2007; Knyazeva et al., 2010). Finally, political geography will have a combined effect on the firm's stock returns, and firms located in the region with high PAI (Political Alignment Index) have significantly better returns than those located in the region with low PAI (Kim et al., 2012).

M&A is an important corporate behavior that attracts widespread attention from academic scholars. The M&A literature has covered motives, payment method choices, accounting methods, earnings management, tax policies and economic consequences. The payment method choice in the M&A process becomes a research focus because it can directly impact acquirers' cash flow and capital structure. Typical payment methods include cash, stock and cash-stock mixed payment.

Compared to full stock payment, full cash payment can reduce free cash flow and thus reduce agency costs of equity (Jensen, 1986). Acquirer firms will choose stock payment when their share price is overvalued. Stock payment in this situation will lead to adverse selection (Shleifer and Vishny, 2003), thus cash payment can lead to higher yields for both acquirer and target firms (Travlos, 1987). And even when stock payment can bring short-term excess returns, it will damage the value of shareholders in the long-term (Song et al., 2008). Moreover, cash payment can also avoid the equity dilution of the acquirer firms. Based on the asymmetric information theory, early researchers argued that management has a negative attitude toward stock payment in order to avoid the dilution of the company's control, and they prefer cash payment (Amihud et al.,1990; Martin,1996; Ghosh and Ruland, 1998). However, cash payment is subject to several restrictions. First, cash payment requires a large amount of cash, which is difficult for acquirer firms with financing constraints and high investment opportunities to obtain (Faccio and Masulis, 2005). Second, cash payment preference is also influenced by the information accessed by acquirer firms. That means that if acquirer firms consider themselves at the information disadvantage, one-time cash payment may lead to excessive premiums. Therefore in order to avoid this situation, the acquirer firms would tend to choose stock payment (Hansen, 1987).

Large amounts of soft information are involved in the M&A process (Coff, 1999). Unlike hard information, soft information is more difficult to encode and transmit. Therefore soft information communication, such as valuation of knowledge-based assets and management skills, requires close interaction between the acquirer and the target firms (Cai et al., 2014). In this sense, geographical locations are important to both acquirer and target companies. A firm's physical location determines convenience of traffic, which will affect the transmission of soft information (Cai et al., 2014) and the means to acquire information. It is more convenient for the acquirer firms located in the urban area to obtain information and to have a more comprehensive and profound understanding of the target companies, thus achieving a more accurate valuation of target firms and paying less excessive premiums due to information asymmetry. Therefore, the acquirer firms located in the urban area prefer cash payment.

Moreover, economic information, political resources, social ties and business environment are also implied in the geographical location of the acquirer firms, which directly affect the firms' debt financing and influence the choice of M&A payment method. In general, the acquirer firms located in the urban area are more capable of debt financing because of the richer political resources and social ties, so they prefer cash payment in enjoying excess return. In line with this, Koutmos et al. (2014) find that compared to unban acquirer firms, the acquirer firms located in the rural area are more likely to choose full stock payment.

Similar to other developing countries, regional development in China is more unbalanced compared with other developed countries. Such difference exists not only between urban and rural areas, but also between eastern and western regions. The level of transportation development is highly unbalanced, and the transportation of most areas still under development (Cao et al., 2007). In addition, as a transition economy, asymmetry information problem is more serious due to the imperfect institutions, where political resources and social ties are used to deal with policy uncertainty circumstance. Geographical factors will affect the choice of M&A

payment methods more significantly in such settings than the developed countries. We propose the following hypothesis:

Hypothesis 1: In the process of M&A, acquirer firms located in central city or close to central city are more likely to choose cash payment.

3. Research design and sample

3.1 Research design

We establish model (1) to test our hypotheses:

$$Logit(CASH\_PAY) = \alpha_0 + \alpha_1 NOCENTER(DISTANCE) + \sum_c \alpha_c CONTROLS + \varepsilon \quad (1)$$

CASH_PAY is a dummy variable, which equals one if it is the full cash payment, otherwise it equals zero. We use two ways to measure the geographical location of acquirer firms, the first measure is NOCENTER, which takes one if the acquirer firms are not located in the central city, and takes zero otherwise. We adopt this measure based on the literature. For instance, Loughran and Schultz (2005) and John et al. (2011) take the top ten cities in the United States as the center city, Cai and Jiang (2013) take the top 20 cities in China as the center city, which is ranked by *China Economic and Social Development Research Center* based on economic competitiveness in 2011. Similarly, we take the 17 cities as the center city, which are the top 20 cities excluding Hong Kong, Macao and Taipei, ranked by *China Economic and Social Development Research Center* based on economic competitiveness in 2013. These cities include Shanghai, Shenzhen, Beijing, Guangzhou, Suzhou, Qingdao, Ningbo, Wuxi, Hangzhou, Dalian, Nanjing, Foshan, Chongqing, Chengdu, Tianjin, Wuhan and Xiamen. Distance measures the remoteness of a company's location, measured as the distance to a central city. The formula is shown as follow.

$$DISTANCE = R \star ar \cos[\cos w_1 \cos w_2 \cos(j_1 - j_2) + \sin w_1 \sin w_2] \quad (2)$$

R is the radius of the Earth, and we take 6371 km in this formula; j_1 and j_2 are the longitude of X and Y cities; ω_1 and ω_2 are the latitudes of X and Y cities. Chinese domestic cities are all with east longitude and north latitude, so their *distance* values are all positive. Therefore if the coefficient of noncenter (distance) is significantly negative, our hypothesis will be supported.

In addition, we include some control variables in this model according to prior literatures: (1) large shareholders' Control right (*CONTORL*). Acquirer firms are likely to generate new shareholders after M&A if they choose stock payment, and which will dilute the control of a large shareholder, so the control of shareholders will influence the choice of payment methods (Faccio and Masulis, 2005; Su et al., 2009); (2) financial leverage (*DEBTRATIO*). Acquirer firms with relatively high debt to assets ratio are more likely to choose stock payment (Faccio and Masulis, 2005); (3) firm size (*ASSET*). As firm size may affect the ability of financing, thus having impact on the choice of the methods of payment (Faccio and Masulis, 2005); (4) ratio of tangible assets (*TANGIBLE*). The proportion of tangible assets will affect the ability of borrowing (Hovakimian et al., 2004), therefore influencing the choice of the methods of payment; (5) returns on total net assets (*ROATTM*), which is the ratio of net income to total assets in the last four quarters. The company's profitability will also affect the choice of the methods of payment through the ability of financing; (6) cash ratio (*CURRENTRATI*). With the higher cash and cash equivalent

Table 3.1 Variable definitions

Type	Variable	Definitions
Dependent Variable	CASH_PAY	It equals to 1 if there is full cash payment, otherwise 0.
Independent Variable	NONCENTER	It equals to 1 if a company's location is not in the below cities, otherwise equals 0. We define 17 cities as center cities, which are the top 20 cities excluding Hong Kong, Macao and Taipei, ranked *by China Economic and Social Development Research Center* based on economic competitiveness in 2013.
	DISTANCE	a measure on distance between the location of acquirer firm and the nearest central city, using Equation (2)
	CONTROL	shareholding proportion of the actual controller of t-1 year
Control Variables	DEBTRATIO	the ratio of total liabilities to total assets
	ASSET	total assets
	TANGIBLE	the ratio of total intangible assets to total assets
	ROATTM	the ratio of net income to total assets
	CURRENTRATIO	the ratio of the cash and cash equivalents to total assets
	INDUSTRY	a dummy variable on industry code of the acquirer firm based on CSRC definition
	YEAR	a dummy variable of transaction year

to assets ratio, acquirer firms will be more capable to choose cash payment. Variable definitions are presented in Table 3.1.

3.2 Sample

We use M&A transactions whose acquirer firms were listed in A-share market between 2009 and 2013 as the initial sample. We obtain M&A transaction information from the CSMAR (*China Stock Market Accounting Research*) database. First we get 32,996 transactions of acquirer firms who are public firms. Then we delete: (1) failed transactions; (2) transactions described as bankruptcy acquisitions, divestitures, privatization, leveraged buyouts, repurchases, restructurings and anti-takeovers; (3) transactions missing necessary payment data in the CSMAR Database; (4) transactions that choose assets payment, debt payment or mixed payment; (5) transactions missing financial information of parent firm in the CSMAR database; (6) firms issuing B shares. When several target firms are involved at the same time, we combine all these transactions together as one sample. When a branch office participate in M&A, we treat it as its headquarters. Our final sample includes 5060 transactions.

We obtain center city data from the *Development Research 2013* issued by the China Economic and Social Development Research Center. Cities' location data are obtained from *National Geometrics Center of China*.

Table 3.2 reports the yearly distribution of sample firms. The results show that although cash payment accounts for the vast majority, the proportion of stock payment increased year by year,

Table 3.2 The year distribution of sample firms

	2009	*2010*	*2011*	*2012*	*2013*	*Total*
Cash	723	911	994	973	927	4528
%	14.29	18.01	19.65	19.23	18.32	89.50
Stock	132	104	67	83	145	531
%	2.61	1.12	0.81	1.15	2.37	10.50
Total	855	1015	1061	1056	1072	5059
%	16.90	20.06	20.97	20.87	21.19	100.00

especially in 2013, in which the proportion of stock payment reached 2.37%. In total, cash payment accounted for 89.5% and stock payment accounted for 10.5%.

4. Empirical test

4.1 Univariate test

In order to observe the difference between the sample firms located in the non-central and central city, we divide the sample into two groups according to whether they choose cash payment. In Table 3.3, 47.81% sample firms are located in non-central city, in which 47.21% choose full cash payment, 52.91% choose stock payment. The t-statistic of their difference is 2.4894, which is significant at the 5% level. It indicate that the proportion of firms choosing cash payment in central cities is significantly higher than those in non-central cities. Second, the result of distance to central city (*DISTANCE*) shows that the average distance between acquirer firms choosing cash payment and central city is 160.27, which is significantly lower than those choosing stock payment at the 1% level. This indicates that listed firms located far from center city are more likely to use their stocks to pay in M&A.

4.2 Multiple regression analysis

4.2.1 Descriptive statistics

Table 3.4 provides the result of descriptive statistics for the control variables. The return on total assets (*ROATTM*) of the cash payment group is 0.07, performing significantly better than 0.04 of the non-cash payment group at the level of less than 1%. In addition, the tangible asset ratio of the cash payment group (*TANGIBLE*) is 0.955, which is slightly higher than 0.93 in the stock payment group. The average assets size (*ASSET*) of the cash payment group is 3.25 billion RMB, which is significantly higher than that of the stock payment group (1.16 billion) at the 1% level. The cash ratio (*CURRENTRATIO*) of the cash payment group is 1.74%, also significantly higher than 1.55% of the non-cash payment group. The asset-liability ratio (*DEBTRATIO*) of cash payment group is 42%, which is significantly much lower than 88% of the non-cash payment group at the 1% level. In sum, the financial position of cash payment group seems better than the stock payment group, e.g. higher profitability and more cash flow. Meanwhile, the cash payment group also has better financing capability and faced with lower financing constraints because they usually have bigger size, higher tangible assets ratio and lower debt ratio. In addition, firms with higher large shareholder control are more likely to choose cash payment with the concern of control dilution.

Table 3.3 Univariate test

	Total (5059)		Stock payment (531)		Cash payment (4528)		t-Statistics
	Mean	Standard deviation	Mean	Standard deviation	Mean	Standard deviation	
noncenter	0.4781	0.4995	0.5291	0.0216	0.4721	0.0074	−2.4894★★
distance	167.12	4.2846	225.51	14.9014	160.27	4.4462	−4.6768★★★

★★★,★★, and ★ indicate statistical significance at the 1%, 5%, and 10% levels, respectively.

Table 3.4 Descriptive statistics of control variables

	N	All samples		Stock payment		Cash payment		t-Statistics
		Mean	Standard deviation	Mean	Standard deviation	Mean	Standard deviation	
ROATTM	4887	0.06	0.0027	0.04	0.0215	0.07	0.0014	2.6826★★★
TANGIBLE	4887	0.950	0.0011	0.93	0.0046	0.955	0.0010	1.4370
CURRENT RATIO	4887	1.55	3.44	0.82	8.96	1.74	3.70	3.0056★★★
ASSET	4887	3.16E+10	6.50E+09	1.16E+10	2.24E+09	3.25E+10	7.28E+09	1.1740
DEBTRATIO	4887	0.56	0.0423	0.88	0.3858	0.42	0.0058	−5.8128★★★
CONTROL	4847	39.22	17.45	35.54	17.75	39.66	17.36	5.1209★★★

★★★,★★, and ★ indicate statistical significance at the 1%, 5%, and 10% levels, respectively.

4.2.2   Correlation analysis

Table 3.5 reports the Pearson correlation coefficient of independent variables. Consistent with the result of descriptive statistics, Table 3.5 shows that the remote firms are associated with higher return on assets, tangible assets ratio, cash ratio, assets size, large shareholder control and lower debt ratio. The largest correlation coefficient between all variables is between *DEBTRATIO* and *ROATTM*, which is −0.5679.

4.2.3   Regression results

The regression results are shown in columns 2 and 3 of Table 3.6. The coefficient of *NON-CENTER (DISTANCE)* is −0.0855(−0.000493), significant at the 10% (1%) level, which confirms our Hypothesis 1. In addition, the coefficient of *TANGIBLE, CURRENTRATIO, ROATTM* are significantly positive, while the coefficient of *DEBERATIO* is significantly negative at the 1% level. This suggests there is a stronger financing capacity and more abundant cash reserve for acquirer firms with better performance, more adequate cash flow, higher tangible assets ratio and lower levels of debt. They tend to choose cash payment in M&A and enjoy the higher stock return that cash payment has brought. At the same time, as expected, *Control* is also positive at the 1% level, which suggests that acquirer firms are less likely to choose stock payment when their equity is more concentrated.

Table 3.5 Correlation analysis between variables

	NONCENTER	DISTANCE	ROATTM	TANGIBLE	CURRENT RATIO	ASSET	DEBTRATIO	CONTROL
NONCENTER	1							
DISTANCE	0.5699	1						
ROATTM	-0.0143	-0.0051	1					
TANGIBLE	-0.0849	-0.0082	0.0209	1				
CURRENT RATIO	-0.0603	-0.003	-0.0124	-0.0563	1			
ASSET	-0.0450	-0.0129	-0.014	0.0354	0.0387	1		
DEBTRATIO	0.0194	-0.007	-0.5679	-0.0042	-0.007	0.0063	1	
CONTROL	-0.0883	-0.0762	0.0451	0.0370	0.0523	0.0018	-0.0505	1

Table 3.6 Regression results

	CASH_PAY (Competitiveness)	CASH_PAY (Competitiveness)	CASH_PAY (GDP)	CASH_PAY (GDP)
DISTANCE	−0.000493★★★ (−3.85)		−0.000458★★★(−3.51)	
NONCENTER		−0.0855★ (−1.67)		−0.164★★★ (−3.21)
ROATTM	1.468★★★ (3.12)	0.500★★ (2.83)	1.398★★★ (3.00)	0.503★★★ (2.84)
TANGIBLE	0.919★★ (1.57)	−0.854★★★ (−2.70)	1.432★★ (2.64)	−0.875★★★ (−2.76)
ASSET	1.19e-12 (1.08)	3.51e-13 (0.84)	1.22e-12 (1.10)	3.40e-13 (0.83)
CURRENT RATIO	0.0487★★ (2.13)	0.0255★★★ (2.74)	0.0489★★ (2.13)	0.0242★★ (2.61)
DEBTRATIO	−0.356★★★ (−3.79)	−0.200★★★ (−4.36)	−0.353★★★ (−3.75)	−0.198★★★(−4.32)
CONTROL	0.0103★★★ (3.66)	0.00555★★★ (3.82)	0.0105★★★ (3.73)	0.00543★★★ (3.74)
_CONS	1.367★★ (2.30)	1.915★★★ (5.90)	0.872 (1.57)	1.967★★★ (6.06)
INDUSTRY	control	control	control	control
YEAR	control	control	control	control
N	4847	4847	4847	4847
LR chi^2	176.03	164.97	175.22	172.49
P	0.0000	0.0000	0.0000	0.0000

★★★,★★, and ★ indicate statistical significance at the 1%, 5%, and 10% levels, respectively.

4.2.4   Robustness tests

As robustness tests, we use GDP rankings to select top 20 cities and redefine NONCENTER. We repeat the logistic regression. The results are shown in Columns 4 and 5 of Table 3.6. The results qualitatively remain the same. The coefficient of NONCENTER (DISTANCE) is −0.164 (−0.000458) and significant at the 1% (1%) level. Therefore, Hypothesis 1 is supported.

5.   Additional analyses

Geographical location leads to different transportation conditions, information availability, political resources and social ties, which would make a difference in acquirer firms' financing capacity and impact information asymmetry between two sides in M&A. When an acquirer firm is located in a rural area, it will more likely be faced with financial constraints and information disadvantage, and they will choose stock payment in M&A. Meanwhile, according to Faccio and Masulis (2005), M&A payment method is significantly influenced by factors such as large shareholder's control right, financing capacity and information asymmetry as well. We further investigate whether and how location and other factors interact to affect the choice of M&A payment methods.

5.1   The impact of large shareholder's control right

Acquirer firms prefer to pay cash when they are perceived to be under the threat of control dilution, and a large shareholder's control rights could affect the choice of payment method. For instance, Faccio and Masulis (2005) find that firms are more likely to pay cash when the control is between 20% and 60%. Therefore, we divide the whole sample into two subsamples according to whether the control right is between 20% and 60%. We include the interaction term

CONTROL*NONCENTER (DISTANCE) in Model (1) and run the regression. The results are presented in Columns 2–5 of Table 3.7.

Table 3.7 shows that the coefficient of *DISTANCE* is significantly −0.00113 at the level of less than 1% for firms with shareholder control right between 20% and 60%. The coefficient of *CONTROL*NONCENTER* is 0.0000211 and significant at the 5% level. In the group with shareholder control less than 20% or greater than 60%, the coefficient of *CONTROL*DISTANCE* is −0.00000435 and not significant. The regression results show a similar pattern. In the sub-sample with shareholder control right between 20% and 60%, the coefficient of *NONCENTER* is −0.00000435 and significant at 1%, and the coefficient of *CONTROL*NONCENTER* is 0.0144 which is significant at 1%. However the coefficient of interaction is not significant in the sub-sample, with control right larger than 60% or less than 20%. Thus, when shareholder control rights are between 20% and 60%, the increase in control reduces the likelihood of using stock payment. It suggests that the concern of control dilution intermediates the effect of geographic location on the payment method choice of M&A.

5.2 The impact of financing capacity

Firm's financing capacity is also an important factor affecting the payment method choice of M&A. With better financing, the acquirer firms are more inclined to pay cash (Travlos, 1987). Usually firm asset size is used to proxy for financing capability. To test the impact of the company's financing capacity on the effect of geographical location on payment method choice of M&A, we include the interaction terms *ASSET*DISTANCE* and *ASSET*NONCENTER* in the Model (1) and repeat the regression. The regression results are reported in Table 3.7 Columns 6 and 7, which show that the coefficient is −0.153(−0.000392), significantly negative at 1%. (1%) level and the coefficient of the interaction term is 1.21E-11(2.32E-14) with the significance level of 1% (5%). Therefore, we believe that firm size will increase financing capability, which in turn will decrease the probability of remotely located acquirer companies' choice of stock payment.

5.3 The nature of the property rights

As State-owned enterprises obtain more political and economic resources, they would have a lower level of likelihood to use stock payment in remote areas. In order to test this, we include *STATE*, the interaction terms *STATE*DISTANCE* and *STATE*NONCENTER* in the Model (1), in which *STATE* is a dummy variable indicating whether the firm is a State-owned enterprise. Then we run the regression of Model (1). Columns 8 and 9 of Table 3.7 show that the coefficient of *DIATANCE (NONCENTER)* is −0.000390(−0.186), which is significantly negative at the 1% (5%) level, and the coefficient of *State*distance (STATE*NONCENTER)* is 0.000255(0.201), which is significant and positive at the 10% (10%) level. So we can reach the conclusion that property rights would reduce the probability of acquirer firms choosing stock payment in remote areas. This means that the advantages of State-owned enterprises would increase their probability of cash payment in M&A, even if they were located in remote areas.

5.4 Analyst following

Based on the game theory, Hansen (1987) proves that the capacity of accessing information will have an impact on the preferences of cash payment for the acquirer firms. The acquirer firms tend to choose stock payment in order to avoid excessive premiums caused by cash payment

Table 3.7 The impact of control, financing constraints, nature of the property rights and analyst tracking

	Control right				Financial capacity		Property right		Analyst following	
	20%=< Control<=60% (DISTANCE)	Control>60% or Control< 20% (NONCENTER)	20%=< Control<=60% (DISTANCE)	Control>60% or Control< 20% (NONCENTEER)	(NONCENTER)	(DISTANCE)	(NONCENTER)	(DISTANCE)	(NONCENTER)	(DISTANCE)
DISTANCE	-0.00113*** (-3.32)	-0.000208 (-0.91)				-0.000392*** (-4.60)		-0.000390*** (-3.52)		-0.000387*** (-4.20)
CONTROL*DISTANCE	0.0000211** (2.49)	-0.00000435 (-0.60)								
NONCENTER			-0.642*** (-3.01)	-0.144 (-0.93)	-0.153*** (-2.76)		-0.186** (-2.45)		-0.165** (-2.63)	
CONTROL*NONCENTER			0.0144*** (2.71)	0.00182 (0.52)						
ASSET*NONCENTER					1.21e-11*** (2.90)					
ASSET*DISTANCE						2.32e-14** (2.47)				
STATE*NONCENTER							0.201* (1.88)			
STATE							-0.180** (-2.31)	-0.120* (-1.92)		
STATE*DISTANCE								0.000255* (1.70)		
ANALYST*NONCENTER									0.00624** (2.35)	

(Continued)

Table 3.7 (Continued)

	Control right				Financial capacity		Property right		Analyst following	
	20%=< Control<=60% (DISTANCE)	Control>60% or Control< 20% (NONCENTER)	20%=< Control<=60% (DISTANCE)	Control>60% or Control< 20% (NONCENTEER)	(NONCENTER)	(DISTANCE)	(NONCENTER)	(DISTANCE)	(NONCENTER)	(DIATANCE)
ANALYST									0.00427**	0.00537***
									(2.52)	(3.58)
ANALYST* DISTANCE										0.0000966**
										(1.97)
ROAHTM	1.233***	-0.0581	1.246***	-0.0513	0.512***	0.487***	0.384**	0.364**	0.382**	0.372**
	(4.46)	(-0.24)	(4.51)	(-0.21)	(2.89)	(2.76)	(2.16)	(2.05)	(2.17)	(2.12)
CONTROL	-0.00155	0.00656***	-0.00520	0.00523**	0.00515***	0.00520***	0.00559***	0.00526***	0.00462***	0.00455***
	(-0.50)	(3.04)	(-1.37)	(2.13)	(3.52)	(3.56)	(3.57)	(3.37)	(3.15)	(3.10)
TANGIBLE	-0.465	-1.874**	-0.446	-1.882**	-0.877***	-0.869***	-0.906***	-0.887***	-0.776**	-0.785**
	(-1.30)	(-2.60)	(-1.25)	(-2.61)	(-2.76)	(-2.73)	(-2.77)	(-2.71)	(-2.45)	(-2.47)
ASSET	1.23e-11***	-2.17e-13	1.26e-11***	-1.86e-13	1.77e-13	2.03e-13	4.18e-13	4.45e-13	9.84e-14	9.10e-14
	(3.87)	(-0.58)	(3.95)	(-0.49)	(0.58)	(0.59)	(0.81)	(0.84)	(0.55)	(0.55)
DEBTRATIO	-0.312***	-0.165**	-0.326***	-0.167**	-0.204***	-0.202***	-0.175***	-0.175***	-0.188***	-0.188***
	(-3.55)	(-2.62)	(-3.70)	(-2.65)	(-4.45)	(-4.40)	(-3.81)	(-3.80)	(-4.13)	(-4.13)
CURRENTRATIO	0.0193	0.0444**	0.0199	0.0444*	0.0275**	0.0257**	0.0379*	0.0367*	0.0268**	0.0259**
	(1.83)	(2.02)	(1.88)	(2.00)	(2.93)	(2.76)	(2.36)	(2.30)	(2.86)	(2.77)
_CONS	1.699***	3.256***	1.813***	3.250***	1.962***	1.972***	2.024***	2.013***	1.768***	1.788***
	(4.47)	(4.47)	(4.66)	(4.44)	(6.03)	(6.07)	(5.98)	(5.98)	(5.41)	(5.48)
INDUSTRY	control	control	control	control	control	control	control	control	control	control
YEAR	control	control	control	control	control	control	control	control	control	control
PSEUDO R^2	0.0754	0.0684	0.0718	0.0649	0.0528	0.0551	0.0463	0.0488	0.0599	0.0627
LR CHI2	181.95	62.23	173.16	59.06	175.51	183.05	134.52	141.87	199.25	280.5
N	3612	1235	3612	1235	4847	4847	3974	3974	4847	4847

***, **, and * indicate statistical significance at the 1%, 5%, and 10% levels, respectively.

when they think they are at an information disadvantage. Koutmos et al. (2014) suggest that the acquirer firms located in remote areas may find themselves in an information disadvantage due to difficulty in obtaining detailed information of M&A, making it difficult to value the target firms correctly. However, stock payment has contingent price characteristics which link the interests of two parties in M&A and avoid the risk of excessive premium caused by cash payment, so it is often chosen by acquirer firms located in remotely rural areas. But they did not directly test this argument in their paper.

In general, firms followed by more analysts should be higher-quality firms and have more bargaining power (Fan and Wang, 2010; Wang and Zhao, 2014). Therefore, if acquirer firms located in the remote areas are followed by more analysts, they should be in a more favorable position in the M&A negotiations, which may reduce the difficulty of obtaining information. At the same time, analyst following also helps discover the value of target firms in M&A (Xu and Tang, 2010). Therefore, we use the number of analysts following as a proxy to measure whether the acquirer firms is at the information disadvantage. So we include *analyst*, the interaction terms *analyst* *distance (*analyst**noncenter) in Model (1) and then repeat the regression of Model (1). The regression results are shown in Columns 9 and 10 of Table 3.7, which show that the coefficient of *distance* (*noncenter*) is −0.000387(−0.165) and significantly negative at the 1% (5%) level, and the coefficient of *analyst**distance (*analyst**noncenter) is 0.00000966(0.00624) and significantly positive at the 5% (5%) level. Thus, as expected, with more analysts following, acquirer firms are less likely to be at an information disadvantage in M&A negotiations, thus reducing the likelihood of stock payment by firms located in remote areas.

6. Conclusions

M&A is an everlasting topic in capital market. Since the payment method choice of M&A directly affects the financial position and shareholder control rights, it has attracted interest from academic scholars. Based on the argument that geographical location implies potential information asymmetry and financing capacity, we analyze the impact of geographical location on payment methods of M&A. We use M&A transactions whose acquirer firms were listed in the A-share market between 2009 and 2013, and we identify geographical location of acquirer firms as center cities if they are located in the top 20 cities excluding Hong Kong, Macao and Taipei, ranked by *China Economic and Social Development Research Center* based on economic competitiveness in 2013. After controlling for the influences of firm performance, assets size, financial leverage, control rights, cash flow and tangible assets ratio, we draw the following conclusions:

(1) The acquirer firms located in the central city or close to the central city prefer cash payment, while those located in the non-central cities or farther away from the central cities have more preference for stock payment. In addition, after replacing the central city according to the GDP rankings, the results remain unchanged.

(2) Shareholder control right, financing capacity, property right and information asymmetry will further influence the effect of geographic location on payment method choice. First, when the control of shareholders is between 20% and 60%, concentrated control will reduce the preference of stock payments of acquirer firms located in the remote area to avoid control right dilution. Second, the increase in financing capacity will also reduce the preferences of stock payments for acquirer firms located in remotely rural areas. Third, because State-owned enterprises have more political and economic resources, the preferences for stock payment will reduce when they are located in remote areas. Finally, as firms followed by more analysts should be higher-quality and have more bargaining power, and analyst

following also helps in discovering the value of the target companies, there will be lower preference of stock payment when they are located in remote areas.

Overall, we find the empirical evidence that the geographic location affects company's financing in the emerging market of China. However, the study can be expanded further. First, by including geographical location of target firms, we can also study the impact of target firms' location, the distance between acquirer and target firms and the interaction between the physical location of the target and the acquirer firms on payment method choice of M&A. Second, in the case of mixed payment methods, we did not study the influence of geographic location on the proportion of cash payment. Future study could follow this line to provide further insights on the impact of geographic location on M&A payment methods.

References

Almazan, A., De Motta, A., Titman, S., and Uysal, V., 2007, *Financial Structure, Liquidity, and Firm Locations (No. w13660)*, National Bureau of Economic Research.

Amaro de Matos, J., and Mergulhão, J., 2012, *Directors' Network and the Method of Payment in Mergers and Acquisitions Nova School of Business and Economics*, Working paper. Available at SSRN: https://ssrn.com/abstract=2154497 or http://dx.doi.org/10.2139/ssrn.2154497

Amihud, Y., Lev, B., and Travlos Nickolaos, G., 1990, Corporate control and the choice of investment financing: The case of corporate acquisitions, *The Journal of Finance* 45, 603–616.

Arena Matteo, P., and Dewally, M., 2012, Firm location and corporate debt, *Journal of Banking and Finance* 36, 1079–1092.

Cai, Q., and Jiang, Y., 2013, Does the company's geographic position influence its cash dividend policy? *Finance and Economics Research* 7, 38–48 (in Chinese).

Cai, Y., Tian, X., and Han, X., 2014, *Locations, Proximity, and M&A*, Transactions Santa Clara University, Working paper.

Cao, X., Zhang, L., Xue, D., and Wang, D., 2007, The variation of level of urban transport development, *Journal of Geography* 10, 1034–1040 (in Chinese).

Coval, J., and Moskowitz, T., 1999, Home Bias at home: Local equity preference in domestic portfolios, *Journal of Finance* 54, 2045–2073.

Coff, R., 1999, How buyers cope with uncertainty when acquirer firms in knowledge-intensive industries: Caveat emptor, *Organization Science* 10, 144–161.

Faccio, M., and Masulis, R.W., 2005, The choice of payment method in European mergers and acquisitions, *The Journal of Finance* 60, 1345–1388.

Fan, Z., and Wang, J., 2010, Securities analyst following: Determinants and economic consequences, *Journal of Shanghai Lixin Accounting Institute* 1, 61–69 (in Chinese).

Francis, B., Hasan, I., John, K., and Waismann, M., 2007, *Geography and CEO Pay, Rensselaer Polytechnic Institute*, New York University and Fordham University, Working paper.

Ghosh, A., and Ruland, W., 1998, Managerial ownership, the method of payment for acquisitions, and executive job retention, *Journal of Finance* 2, 785–798. Hansen, R.G., 1987, A theory for the choice of exchange medium in mergers and acquisitions, *Journal of Business* 60, 75–95.

Hovakimian, A., Hovakimian, G., and Tehranian, H., 2004, Determinants of target capital structure: The case of dual debt and equity issues, Determinants of target capital structure: The case of dual debt and equity issues, *Journal of Financial Economics*, 517–540.

Jensen, M.C., 1986, Agency costs of free cash flow, corporate finance and takeovers, *American Economic Review* 76, 323–329.

John, K., Knyazeva, A., and Knyazeva, D., 2011, Does geography matter? Firm location and corporate payout policy, *Journal of Financial Economics* 101, 533–551.

Kang, J.K., and Kim, J.M., 2008, The geography of block acquisitions, *Journal of Finance* 63, 2817–2858.

Kedia, S., Panchapagesan, V., and Uysalvahap, B., 2005, *Geography and Acquirer Firms Returns*, Working paper. Available at SSRN: https://ssrn.com/abstract=871513 or http://dx.doi.org/10.2139/ssrn.871513

Kim, C. (Francis), Pantzalis, C., and Park, J.C., 2012, Political geography and stock returns: The value and risk implications of proximity to political power, *Journal of Financial Economics* 106, 196–228.

Knyazeva, A., Knyazeva, D., and Masulis, R., 2010, *Local Director Talent and Board Composition*, University of Rochester and University of New South Wales, Working paper.

Koutmos, D., Song, W., and Zhou, S., 2014, Firm location and the method of payment in mergers and acquisitions, *Applied Economics Letters* 21, 317–324.

Loughran, T., 2008, The impact of firm location on equity issuance, *Financial Management*, 1–21.

Loughran, T., and Schultz, P., 2005, Liquidity: Urban versus rural firms, *Journal of Financial Economics* 78, 341–374.

Martin, K. J., 1996, The method of payment in corporate acquisitions, investment opportunities, and management ownership, *The Journal of Finance* 51, 1227–1246.

Nikolaos, K., Dimitris, P., and Travlos, N.G., 2014, Credit ratings and the choice of payment method in mergers and acquisitions, *Journal of Corporate Finance* 25, 474–493.

Shleifer, A., and Vishny, R.W., 2003, Stock market driven acquisitions, *Journal of Financial Economics* 70, 295–311.

Song, X., Zhang, Q., and Chu, Y., 2008, An empirical study on the performance of merger and acquisition in Chinese listed companies, *China Industrial Economy* 7, 111–120 (in Chinese).

Su, W., Li, X., and Li, Y., 2009, Corporate control, information asymmetry and M & A payment, *Collected Essays on Finance and Economics* 5, 67–73.

Travlos, N.G., 1987, Corporate takeover bids, methods of payment, and bidding firms' stock returns, *Journal of Finance*, 4, 943–963.

Wang, S., and Lan, Z., 2014, IPO-based securities analyst following factors, *Journal of Guangxi University* (Philosophy and Social Science Edition) 5, 6–10 (in Chinese).

Xu, X., and Tang, Q., 2010, Analyst following and enterprise R & D activities, *Financial Studies*, 12, 173–189 (in Chinese).

PART II

Financial accounting

4

ACCOUNTING STANDARDS IN CHINA

Deren Xie, Dengjin Zheng

1. Introduction

Accounting laws and regulations in the People's Republic of China (hereafter, China) have been set and developed by a number of government agencies such as the National People's Congress, the State Council, the Ministry of Finance (MOF) and the China Securities Regulatory Commission (CSRC) when it comes to listed company information disclosures. According to the supreme accounting law (*Accounting Act*), which was set by the National People's Congress, the MOF is responsible for most of the accounting affairs in China. As a result, the MOF is responsible for the setting of the China Accounting Standards (CAS) for business enterprises and government sector.[1] Hence, the CAS is a formal legal regulation and a mandatory standard system. It is well-known that the CAS for business enterprises has been highly convergent with International Financial Reporting Standards (IFRS). In this chapter, we will focus on the accounting standard issues in China. The chapter includes four sections among which Section 1 describes the development of CAS, Section 2 introduces the current situation of CAS, Section 3 summarizes the Basic Standard and identifies the main differences between current CAS and IFRS and the last section concludes the chapter and discusses the future of CAS.

2. The development history of the CAS

In this section, we focus on the development of CAS after 1978. There was no concept of accounting standards before 1978, and the accounting systems imitated from the former Soviet Union were served for the planned economy in China. In December 1978, the third Plenary Session of the eleventh Central Committee of the Communist Party of China announced a decision of immense importance – to implement the policy of reform and opening. To adapt to the market-oriented economic reforms, China began to discuss, introduce and set accounting standards. Since then CAS has already experienced immense changes.

2.1 The Enlightenment period of CAS

To attract foreign capital investments and conform to the requirements of Sino-foreign joint ventures economy, *The Accounting Act of the PRC* and *The Accounting Regulations of the PRC for the Joint*

Ventures Using Chinese and Foreign Investment were both first promulgated in 1985. *The Accounting Act* meant that China began to rebuild the legalization of accounting. The *Accounting Act* was revised twice in 1993 and 1999, respectively, to meet the needs of within the development of the Chinese socialist market economy. It is always the highest authority on accounting in China and empowers the MOF to administer accounting affairs and to establish uniform accounting regulations and systems. *The Accounting Regulations of the PRC for the Joint Ventures Using Chinese and Foreign Investment*[2] includes 17 chapters and adopted the general accounting principles, accounting subjects, accounting methods and accounting statements in market economy (Cai, 1985). Although there was some difference between the accounting regulations of China and International Accounting Standards (IAS) issued by International Accounting Standards Committee (IASC),[3] it was an important beginning to accounting convergence with IAS for China (Liu, 2007). Besides, the MOF had set up a department for discussing and drawing up accounting standards since 1988. Overall, the Chinese government made the necessary practice preparations for the promulgation of new accounting standards.

Meanwhile, many accounting scholars in China also started to introduce the conceptual framework for modern financial accounting, discussing the concept of accounting standards and how to establish accounting standards in China. Wang and Lin (1985) discussed the difference among accounting assumptions, accounting principles, accounting standards and accounting systems. In their opinions, accounting principles are based on accounting postulates, while accounting standards are based on accounting principles and provide the guidance for accounting systems. Xie (1987) proposed that a united accounting standard was urgent, which should be applied to all firms and would be good for reporting management stewardship to shareholders. Yang (1989) and Ge (1989) were both prefer to use an accounting standard instead of an accounting principle, because an accounting standard could reflect the nature of accounting better and be of idiomatic usage in most countries. The accounting standard that was the standard of all accounting treatments, the guidance of specific accounting systems, should obey *The Accounting Act of the PRC* and be in accord with China's political and economic environment (Ge, 1989; Yang, 1989). Scholars suggested that accounting standards could be classified into basic standards and specific standards; a basic standard must include accounting assumptions, general principles, accounting elements and accounting reports, which is the guidance of specific standards and contains the basic rules of accounting recognition, measurement, recording and reporting (Ge, 1992; Jiang, 1992; Lou and Zhang, 1992; Yan, 1992). It was worthwhile to note that the accounting standard in China was different with IAS because the former was promulgated by the Chinese government with a legal effect (Ge, 1989; Yang, 1989; Lou and Zhang, 1992). Overall, accounting scholars' studies regarding accounting standard had provided an important theoretical basis and preparation for the setting of the CAS.

2.2   The initiation and harmonization period of the CAS: 1992–2002

There is no doubt that the establishment of Shanghai and Shenzhen securities exchanges in 1991 and Deng Xiaoping's speeches in 1992 promoted the initiation of the CAS. *The Accounting Standard for Business Enterprises (Basic Standard)* was officially promulgated by the MOF on November 11, 1992, and took effect on July 1, 1993. This *Basic Standard* for business enterprise contains ten chapters with 66 articles, including general provisions, general principles, assets, liabilities, owners' equity, revenue, expenses, profit and loss, financial reports and supplementary provisions, which serves as the conceptual framework of accounting in China. Ge (1993) argued that the *Basic Standard* in 1992 was of historic importance for China and had three features: (1) The *Basic Standard* was formulated to meet the needs of developing a socialist market economy in China, to standardize accounting practice and to ensure the quality of accounting information, and to be applicable to all enterprises established within the territory of China. (2) The *Basic Standard* should suite the actual conditions of China. (3) The *Basic Standard* should be accorded with the convention of international accounting as much as possible. However, the *Basic Standard* should be further improved on in regards to coverage, selectivity and objectivity of financial reporting (Ge, 1993). The *Basic Standard* in 1992 was not sufficiently rigorous and did not form a system of the basic concepts of the standard (Xie, 1995).

After setting and issuing the *Basic Standard* in 1992, the MOF continued to develop a body of CAS that was broadly in line with IAS or IFRS.[4] Before the drafts of 30 specific standards were completed in 1996, the MOF had organized many conferences about how to set specific standards. After completing due processes on each specific standard, the MOF formally issued the first specific standard in 1997 and other sixteen specific standards were released year by year till 2002. Table 4.1 presents the name, the effective date, and the application scope of each specific accounting standard from 1997 to 2002 (hereafter, CAS 2002).

The following were the main differences between CAS 2002 and IAS/IFRS in the corresponding period: (1) some accounting policies were not allowed under CAS 2002 but allowed

Table 4.1 Specific Accounting Standards of CAS-2002

No.	Name of Specific Standards	Effective Date	Application Scope
1	Disclosure of Related Party Relationships and Transactions	January 1, 1997	Listed companies
2	Cash Flow Statements (minor revision in 2001)	January 1, 1998	All firms
3	Events Occurring After the Balance Sheet Date (minor revision in 2003)	January 1, 1998	Listed companies
4	Debt Restructuring(revised significantly in 2001)	January 1, 1999	All firms
5	Revenue (minor revision in 2001)	January 1, 1999	Listed companies
6	Investments (minor revision in 2001)	January 1, 1999	Joint Stock Limited companies (it applied to listed companies only before 01/01/2001)
7	Construction Contracts	January 1, 1999	Listed enterprises
8	Changes in Accounting Policies and Estimates and Corrections of Accounting Errors (minor revision in 2001)	1 January 1, 1999	All firms (it applied to listed companies only before 01/01/2001)
9	Non-monetary Transactions (revised significantly in 2001)	January 1, 2000	All firms
10	Contingencies	July 1, 2000	All firms
11	Intangible Assets	January 1, 2001	Joint Stock Limited companies s
12	Borrowing Costs	January 1, 2001	All firms
13	Leases	January 1, 2001	All firms
14	Interim Financial Reporting	January 1, 2002	Listed companies
15	Inventories	January 1, 2002	Joint Stock Limited companies
16	Fixed Assets	January 1, 2002	Joint Stock Limited companies

under IAS/IFRS. For instance, property, plant and equipment could be measured at cost or at revalued amounts under IAS/IFRS whereas CAS 2002 required cost basis. (2) A few accounting standards such as accounting for hyperinflation were not included in CAS 2002 because of their limited applications in China. (3) In light of the practical circumstances of Chinese enterprises, the MOF had not adopted certain accounting conventions applied in the IAS/IFRS, notably the pervasive use of fair value. (4) Some accounting standards are still under consideration of MOF – which the MOF was planning to issue. The MOF had an ongoing program to issue standards that would deal with the areas specifically addressed by IAS/IFRS. The MOF's objective was to establish a set of accounting standards that could both adapt to China's circumstances and harmonize with the IAS/IFRS in an orderly manner.

Meanwhile, because specific accounting standards were principle-based and primarily applicable to the Joint Stock Limited Enterprises, China also constructed accounting systems with specific accounting treatments in practice for all enterprises, which were based on *The Accounting Act* and *Basic Standard*[5] and in accord with China's real conditions (Huang and Liu, 2001; Liu, 2001). The MOF developed 13 industry-specific accounting systems, first in 1993 for all enterprises in different industry, such as those for agriculture, communication and transportation. Accounting systems were also applied to different types of unlisted financial institutions. However, with the development of China's socialist market economy, the industry-specific accounting systems were difficult to adapt in business practice. In 1999, *The Accounting Act* was revised by the Standing Committee of National People's Congress, and it mentioned the importance of using a unified accounting system as the standard to judge illegal accounting activities. The State Council of PRC also issued *Financial Accounting and Reporting Rules for Business Enterprises (FARR)* in 2000, and many definitions and concepts included in *Basic Standard* were revised or updated by *FARR*.[6] *FARR* also emphasized to use a unified accounting system to guide actual accounting behaviors for all enterprises. In January 2001, the MOF adopted a comprehensive *Accounting System for Business Enterprises (Accounting System)*,[7] which contained 14 chapters with 106 articles, including general provisions, assets, liabilities, owners' equity, revenue, costs and expenses, profit and profit appropriation, non-monetary transactions, foreign currency transactions, accounting adjustments, contingencies, related party relationships and transactions, financial reports and supplementary provisions. This was an important supplement of CAS 2002 and serves as the detailed operational guidance of CAS 2002. *Accounting System* was based, in part, on the experience of the MOF in implementing the *Accounting System for Joint Stock Limited Enterprises* and, in part, on the existing individual accounting standards issued in the past few years. Other than enterprises in banking, insurance and small enterprises,[8] all joint-stock limited companies were required to follow the *Accounting System* since January 1, 2001, and the MOF extended the applicability of the *Accounting System* to all enterprises on January 1, 2003. In addition, if a parent company adopts the *Accounting System*, the parent should require all of its subsidiaries to adopt the *Accounting System* as well. The MOF used the *Accounting System* to unify the accounting treatment of different industries and enterprises, which enhanced the accounting comparability and was also conducive to the convergence of the CAS with IFRS (Gai, 2001; Zhang, 2001).

In summary, China initiated the CAS development and made great progress during 1992–2002 as the result of the Chinese economy's marketization, internationalization and the development of capital market. Although China joined the IASC in 1998 and the CAS tried to primarily harmonize with the IAS, it had two distinctive features at that time: (1) the conceptual framework for financial accounting, which existed as the *Basic Standard*, was an important part of accounting standards and had the legal effect. (2) The principle-based CAS was co-existed with the rule-based accounting systems (including general accounting system and industrial accounting systems).

2.3   Evolution of CAS during 2003–2013: from harmonization to convergence

After becoming a formal member of the World Trade Organization (WTO) in December 2001, China's international trade grew rapidly and had to face more and more anti-dumping cases at the same time. Among complaints about these cases, one of the reasons why Chinese economy was not recognized as a complete market economy was that there were many important differences between CAS and international accounting practices. In order to help Chinese firms to deal with the anti-dumping cases and accelerate the internationalization of China's capital market, the Chinese government decided not only to harmonize CAS with IAS/IFRS but also to converge with IAS/IFRS. From the perspective of the MOF, the convergence was substantial, complete, continuous and interactive. As a result, after the issuance of the 16 specific accounting standards, the MOF and accounting scholars kept working to achieve convergence of CAS with IFRS. In 2005, the MOF published the revision of *Basic Standard* and 22 exposure drafts of *Specific Standards*. In the same year, the MOF and the IASB signed *The Joint Statement of Secretary-General of the China Accounting Standards Committee and the Chairman of the International Accounting Standards Board*. In the joint statement, China stated that CAS should have the same effects as IFRS, and the way to converge with IFRS should be decided by China. The China Accounting Standards Committee (CASC) and IASB acknowledged that the differences between CAS and IFRS still existed at the moment on a limited number of matters, and both parties identified a number of accounting issues under China's unique circumstances and environments. Both parties also agreed to work to eliminate those difference as quickly as possible, which could strengthen the communication and cooperation between the two parties and achieve the complete convergence of CAS with IFRS quickly.

On February 15, 2006, the MOF announced its great achievement regarding accounting standards convergence to the world by officially issuing the new and integrated set of CAS, which included one *Basic Standard* and 38 *Specific Standards* (hereafter, CAS 2007) and their application guidance.[9] These standards took effect for all firms (including listed companies) on January 1, 2007, and the *Accounting System for Business Enterprises* of 2001 was dismissed. CAS 2007 meant that China preliminarily completed the task about the establishment of CAS and achieved the substantial convergence with IFRS (Ge, 2006; Liu, 2007; Fu, 2007), which was also acknowledged by IASB. The MOF evaluated the implementation of CAS 2007 based on listed companies' annual report and issued one report every year from 2007 to 2010. These evaluation reports show that most listed firms could adopt CAS 2007 strictly and CAS 2007 had important positive effect on the rapid development of China's national economy.

In order to provide a general guideline on the convergence of CAS with IFRS, the MOF issued the exposure draft of *Continuous Convergence Roadmap between CAS and IFRS* (*Continuous Convergence Roadmap*) in 2009 and officially issued and adopted the *Continuous Convergence Roadmap* in 2010. The *Continuous Convergence Roadmap* meant that CAS would keep pace with IFRS under China's unique environments and indicated the direction and schedule of the convergence.

As the result of CAS's significant and complete convergence with IFRS in 2006, CAS and Hong Kong Accounting Standards (HKAS) have been officially recognized as equivalent since 2007. Starting in December 2012, the Chinese companies whose shares listed in the Hong Kong Exchange were able to prepare financial statements by using CAS. The European Union and China signed a joint statement in 2010 that CAS and European accounting standards would be equivalent in 2011. Besides, in order to reduce the transaction costs, it is important to make CAS equivalent to accounting standards of other countries or regions. China is continuing to have more cooperation and conferences with the United States of America, Japan, South Korea and other Asian countries, Oceanian Countries, etc.[10]

3.   Continuous and complete convergence of CAS: 2014–2017

Over the last ten years, the IASB has made many big changes to IFRS in order to deal with the issues arising from the 2008 Financial Crisis and adapt to the post-financial crisis environment. To keep continuous convergence of IFRS and keep the stability of CAS at the same time, the MOF substantially revised some specific standards of CAS 2007 by issuing serial *Accounting Standard Interpretation*. In 2012, the MOF issued revision drafts of some existing standards and exposure drafts of some new standards.

In 2014, the MOF formally revised five specific standards (CAS No.2, 9, 30, 33, 37) and issued three new specific standards (CAS No.39, 40, 41).[11] At the same time, the MOF revised the definition of *Fair Value* in the *Basic Standard* in order to accord with CAS No. 39, which adopts the newest definition of *Fair Value* in IFRS. In December 2015, the MOF issued the revised draft of CAS No.14 (*Revenue*).

During the first seven months of 2017, the MOF had formally revised CAS Nos. 14, 22, 23, 24, 37 and issued a new standard – CAS No. 42. The new edition of CAS No. 14 (*Revenue*) is not only a revision of the former CAS No. 14 but also substitutes CAS No. 15 (*Construction Contracts*). The revised CAS No. 14 will take effect on January 1, 2018 for those listed companies whose shares are traded both in China and foreign exchanges. At the same time, it will take effective on January 1, 2020 for other listed companies whose shares are only traded in Chinese capital market, and on January 1, 2021 for non-listed companies who adopt CAS. All these firms are encouraged to voluntarily adopt CAS No. 14 in 2017. The revised CAS No. 14 is completely converged with IFRS No. 15 and uses the control transfer model to substitute the risk-reward transfer model to recognize revenues. As a result, till the end of July 2017, CAS comprises *Basic Standard*, forty-one *Specific Standards* and related application guidance.[12] Compared with CAS 2007, the current CAS is more principle-based, adopts more fair value measurement and focuses more on reporting and disclosure. Just like IFRS, there are three types of Specific Standards of CAS, including general standards (*G*), industry-specific standards (*I*), and reporting and disclosure standards (*R*). Table 4.2 presents the name of the latest CAS in 2017, the corresponding name of the latest IFRS in 2016 and the type of accounting standard. Table 4.2 shows that the *Basic Standard* of CAS and the 41 Specific standards of CAS are basically corresponding with the conceptual framework for financial reporting, 40 specific standard and interpretations of IFRS, respectively, which indicates that the current CAS is completely convergent with IFRS.[13]

4.   Basic standard and the main differences between CAS and IFRS

4.1   Basic standard: China's conceptual framework for financial accounting

As mentioned in Section 1, the content of the basic standard is same as the conceptual framework for financial accounting, but its position is higher than the similar conceptual framework in IFRS or US GAAP because it is a formal part of CAS and direct the setting of specific standards. To grasp the basic spirit of CAS, one shall read the basic standard carefully.

The *Basic Standard* revised in 2014 comprises eleven chapters with fifty articles, including general provisions, qualitative requirements of accounting information, assets, liabilities, owners' equity, revenue, expenses, profit, accounting measurement, financial reports and supplementary provisions, which is in accordance with *The Accounting Act of the PRC* and other relevant laws and regulations. It is formulated to prescribe the recognition, measurement and reporting activities of enterprises for accounting purposes and to ensure the quality of accounting information. It plays a core role in CAS.

Table 4.2 The Current CAS in 2017

No. & Name of CAS	Type	No. & Name of IFRS
Basic Standard		The Conceptual Framework for Financial Reporting
CAS 1 Inventories	G	IAS 2 Inventories
CAS 2 Long-term Equity Investments	G	IAS 27 Separate Financial Statements
		IAS 28 Investments in Associates and Joint Ventures
		IAS 39 Financial Instruments: Recognition and Measurement
		IFRS 9 Financial Instruments
		IFRS 11 Joint Arrangements
CAS 3 Investment Property	G	IAS 40 Investment Property
CAS 4 Fixed Assets	G	IAS 16 Property, Plant and Equipment
CAS 5 Biological Assets	I	IAS 41 Agriculture
CAS 6 Intangible Assets	G	IAS 38 Intangible Assets
CAS 7 Exchange of Non-monetary Assets	G	IAS 16 Property, Plant and Equipment
		IAS 38 Intangible Assets
		IAS 40 Investment Property
		IFRS 15 Revenue from Contracts with Customers
CAS 8 Impairment of Assets	G	IAS 36 Impairment of Assets
CAS 9 Employee Compensation	G	IAS 19 Employee Benefits
CAS 10 Enterprise Annuity Fund	G	IAS 26 Accounting and Reporting by Retirement Benefit Plans
CAS 11 Share-based Payments	G	IFRS 2 Share-based Payment
CAS 12 Debt Restructuring	G	IAS 39 Financial Instruments: Recognition and Measurement
		IFRS 9 Financial Instruments
CAS 13 Contingencies	G	IAS 37 Provisions, Contingent Liabilities and Contingent Assets
CAS 14 Revenue	G	IFRS 15 Revenue from Contracts with Customers
CAS 15 Construction Contracts(invalid after 01/01/ 2018)	G	IFRS 15 Revenue from Contracts with Customers
CAS 16 Government Grants	G	IAS 20 Accounting for Government Grants and Disclosure of Government Assistance
CAS 17 Borrowing Costs	G	IAS 23 Borrowing Costs
CAS 18 Income Taxes	G	IAS 12 Income Taxes
CAS 19 Foreign Currency Translation	G	IAS 21 The Effects of Changes in Foreign Exchange Rates
		IAS 29 Financial Reporting in Hyperinflationary Economies
CAS 20 Business Combinations	G	IFRS 3 Business Combinations
CAS 21 Leases	G	IFRS 16 Leases
CAS 22 Recognition and Measurement of Financial Instruments	G	IAS 39 Financial Instruments: Recognition and Measurement
		IFRS 9 Financial Instruments
CAS 23 Transfer of Financial Assets	G	IAS 39 Financial Instruments: Recognition and Measurement
		IFRS 9 Financial Instruments

(*Continued*)

Table 4.2 (Continued)

No. & Name of CAS	Type	No. & Name of IFRS
CAS 24 Hedging	G	IAS 39 Financial Instruments: Recognition and Measurement
		IFRS 9 Financial Instruments
CAS 25 Original Insurance Contracts	I	IFRS 4 Insurance Contracts
CAS 26 Reinsurance Contracts	I	IFRS 4 Insurance Contracts
CAS 27 Exploitation of Petroleum and Natural Gas	I	IFRS 6 Exploration for and Evaluation of Mineral Resources
CAS 28 Changes in Accounting Policies and Accounting Estimates, and Error Correction	G	IAS 8 Accounting Policies, Changes in Accounting Estimates and Errors
CAS 29 Events after the Balance Sheet Date	G	IAS 10 Events after the Reporting Period
CAS 30 Presentation of Financial Statements	R	IAS 1 Presentation of Financial Statements
CAS 31 Cash Flow Statements	R	IAS 7 Statement of Cash Flows
CAS 32 Interim Financial Report	R	IAS 34 Interim Financial Reporting
CAS 33 Consolidated Financial Statements	R	IAS 27 Separate Financial Statements
		IFRS 10 Consolidated Financial Statements
CAS 34 Earnings Per Share	R	IAS 33 Earnings per Share
CAS 35 Segment Reporting	R	IFRS 8 Operating Segments
CAS 36 Related Party Disclosures	R	IAS 24 Related Party Disclosures
CAS 37 Presentation of Financial Instruments	R	IAS 32 Financial Instruments: Presentation
		IFRS 7 Financial Instruments: Disclosures
		IFRS 9 Financial Instruments
CAS 38 First-time Adoption of Accounting Standards for Enterprises	G	IFRS 1 First-time Adoption of International Financial Reporting Standards
CAS 39 Fair Value Measurement	G	IFRS 13 Fair Value Measurement
CAS 40 Joint Arrangements	G	IFRS 11 Joint Arrangements
CAS 41 Disclosure of Interests in Other Entities	R	IFRS 12 Disclosure of Interests in Other Entities
CAS 42 Non-current Assets Held for Sale, Disposal Groups and Discontinued Operations	G	IFRS 5 Non-current Assets Held for Sale and Discontinued Operations
Application Guidance and Interpretations of CASs		Interpretations of IFRS

Chapter one, the general provisions, points out that CAS shall apply to firms operated within PRC, and the objective of financial reports is to provide accounting information of the firm to the users of the financial reports, which show the results of the management's stewardship and assists users of financial reports to make economic decisions. Recognition, measurement and reporting for accounting purposes shall be based on the accrual basis and the transactions or events that an enterprise itself have occurred, and measured by monetary unit. An enterprise shall be assumed to be a going concern, close the accounts and prepare financial reports for each separate accounting period, and apply the double entry method.

The qualitative characteristics of accounting information are discussed in Chapter two. The most important qualitative characteristic in the first article requires that an enterprise should faithfully represent the accounting elements and other relevant information to satisfy recognition and measurement requirements, and ensure the accounting information is true, reliable and complete. It also requires that accounting information provided by an enterprise shall be relevant, clear and understandable, comparable and important for the users to make economic decisions. Besides, an enterprise shall recognize, measure and report transactions or events based on their substance, and not merely based on their legal form, which is the "substance over form" principle. Finally, it also requires an enterprise shall prudently and timely recognize, measure and report transactions or events occurred.

The six accounting elements are in Chapter three to Chapter eight, including assets, liabilities, owners' equity, revenue, expenses and profit. The accounting measurement is in Chapter 9. The accounting measurement bases mainly comprise historical cost, replacement cost, net realizable value, present value and fair value. An enterprise shall generally adopt historical cost as the measurement basis for accounting elements. If the accounting elements are measured at replacement cost, net realizable value, present value or fair value, the enterprise shall ensure such amounts can be obtained and reliably measured.

The financial report is in Chapter Ten. Financial report includes financial statements and notes and other information or data that shall be disclosed in a financial report. Financial statements shall at least comprise a balance sheet, an income statement and a cash flow statement. A small enterprise is not required to provide a cash flow statement.

Although the Basic Standard has been revised for several times, it falls behind specific standards to some extent. For example, it does not define the comprehensive income and other comprehensive income which have been used in specific standards. It is also expected to update the definition about "control" in order to direct the specific standards regarding business combinations, revenue and consolidated financial statements, etc. At the same time, there are differences between the basic accounting elements' definition between the *Basic Standard* and some specific standards. Naturally, the *Basic Standard* needs to be updated to converge with the IASB's conceptual framework for financial reporting.

4.2   The main differences between CAS and IFRS

Although the current CAS is substantially convergent with IFRS, there are still some differences between CAS and IFRS because of the differences in the economic and law environment.

As a whole, there are four types of differences between CAS and IFRS: (1) there are differences regarding conceptual framework and basic concepts. (2) As to the same transactions or events, there is different accounting policy choice space. (3) As to the same or similar specific standard, there is different scope of application. (4) There is a certain time lag between the adoption of CAS and IFRS, especially when IFRS allow certain amendments of accounting standards being adopted in advance before the real effective date.

In details, there are some specific differences between CAS and IFRS.

(1) As mentioned before, there are many significant differences between the *Basic Standard* of CAS and the conceptual framework for financial reporting of IFRS. Accounting elements (financial statement elements) in IFRS include assets, liabilities, equity, income and expenses, while accounting elements in CAS include assets, liabilities, owners' equity, revenue, expenses and profit. IFRS does not regulate the specific fiscal year-end, while CAS requires it to be December 31. Assets (liabilities) either are not classified or are classified

into current and noncurrent in IFRS, while assets (liabilities) must be classified into current and noncurrent in CAS. Expenses in the income statement can be classified by their nature or by their function in IFRS, while they are only classified by their function in CAS and encouraged to be disclosed in the footnotes of income statements by their nature.

(2) The accounting for inventory. There are not regulations on allocation of fixed overhead under subnormal production capacity in CAS, while IFRS requires that allocation of fixed overhead into processing cost is based on normal production capacity.

(3) The accounting for investment properties. CAS gives a clear scope of investment properties, while IFRS does not clearly define the scope.[14] In CAS, an enterprise shall make a follow-up measurement to the investment real estate by using the historical cost approach on the balance sheet date. When well-established evidence shows that the fair value of an investment real estate can be obtained in a continuous and reliable way, a follow-up measurement may be made to the investment real estate by using the fair value measurement. Even though the fair value measurement is reliably available, firms could choose historical cost approach. However, an enterprise can choose the historical cost approach or the fair value approach in IFRS.

(4) Accounting policy choice space. In order to increase the information comparability, CAS reduces the discretion of the accounting policy choices, while the space of some accounting policy choices is bigger in IFRS. For example, IFRS accepts both the revaluations method and the cost method for the subsequent measurement of fixed asset and intangible assets. However, CAS only adopts cost method for the subsequent measurement of fixed assets and intangible assets.

(5) The accounting treatment of impairments on the fixed assets and intangible assets. In CAS, once any impairment on the fixed assets and intangible assets has been recognized, the impairment could not be reversed in the future accounting periods, even if their value can be recovered in the subsequent period. However, IFRS allows the reversal of impairment of fixed assets and intangible assets, except for goodwill.

(6) The accounting treatment of the share-based payment. Although CAS 11 *Share-based Payment* is similar with IFRS 2 *Share-based Payment*, there is not share-based payment for exchanging goods in CAS. Besides, the scope of share-based payment in CAS is just about the enterprises itself, while it also includes parent firm or enterprises under the same business group in IFRS. Finally, the share-based payments shall be classified into equity-settled share-based payments and cash-settled share-based payments in CAS, while share-based payment with cash option is also covered in IFRS.

(7) The accounting treatment of debt restructuring and exchange of non-monetary assets. Debt restructuring and exchange of non-monetary assets are regulated directly by two specific standards in CAS, while IFRS regulates the accounting treatment of debt restructuring and exchange of non-monetary assets in several specific standards.

(8) The accounting treatment of the business combinations under common control. CAS 20 *Business Combinations* has unequivocal rules about how to account for business combinations under common control, while IFRS 3 *Business Combinations* excludes business combinations under common control from its application scope. CAS requires firms to use the historical acquisition method (that is, accounting measurement would be based on the book value of the acquiree's net assets from the perspective of the ultimate controller's consolidated financial statements) to do the accounting for business combinations under common control and restate the comparative financial statements, while different methods are acceptable in practice under IFRS, such as the pooling of interest method, the acquisition method and the carry over method.

(9) Parent-only financial statements and the accounting for the long-term equity investments. CAS requires that firms should prepare and disclose parent-only financial statements and consolidated financial statements at the same time, but IFRS does not require firms to disclose parent-only financial statements. As a result, IFRS does not set the specific rule regarding the accounting treatment method of long-term equity investments in the subsidiaries in the parent-only financial statements, According to IAS 27, firms can choose to use either the equity method, or cost method, or fair value method to account for investments in subsidiaries. On the contrary, CAS has clearly required firms to use cost method to do the accounting for long-term equity investments in the subsidiaries in the parent-only financial statements in the CAS 2 and transfer to equity method in order to prepare consolidated financial statements. Furthermore, there are some differences in the accounting treatments of the transactions regarding long-term equity investments in the subsidiaries at the parent-only financial statements level and consolidated financial statements level.

(10) The difference on the accounting for government grants. In CAS, the government subsidies pertinent to assets shall be recognized as deferred income, equally distributed and included in the income statement within the useful lives of the relevant assets. But the government subsidies measured at their nominal amounts shall be directly included in the current profits and losses. In 2017, the revised CAS 16 *Government Grants* requires an enterprise shall disclose government subsidies alone in the other income item in the income statement. However, in IFRS, government grants shall be recognized in profit or loss on a systematic basis over the periods in which the entity recognizes as expenses the related costs for which the grants are intended to compensate.

(11) The difference on the accounting for borrowing costs. In CAS, where the borrowing costs incurred to an enterprise can be directly attributable to the acquisition and construction or production of assets eligible for capitalization, it shall be capitalized and recorded into the costs of relevant assets. Other borrowing costs shall be recognized as expenses on the basis of the actual amount incurred, and shall be recorded into the current profits and losses. The term "assets eligible for capitalization" mainly refer to the fixed assets, investment real estate and some kind of inventories whose acquisition and construction or production may take quite a long time to get ready for its intended use or for sale. However, in IFRS, an entity shall capitalize borrowing costs that are directly attributable to the acquisition, construction or production of a qualifying asset as part of the cost of that asset. But when it comes to qualifying inventories, firms could choose to expense the related borrowing cost.

(12) The difference on IAS 29 Financial Reporting in Hyperinflationary Economies. This IAS is not independently set in CAS, and it is embodied in CAS in several other specific standards, e.g. CAS 19 Foreign Currency Translation and Application Guidance of CAS 19.

Overall, most standards of the CAS are convergent with IFRS and the differences between CAS and IFRS are much less than ever before as the result of the joint efforts of the MOF of China and IASB. Besides the above differences, there are some small and unimportant differences between the CAS and IFRS, which have little economic impacts.

5. Conclusion and the future development of the CAS

The CAS becomes more and more integrated after 1992 when the first accounting standard for business enterprises was promulgated, and is highly convergent with IFRS now. China has made great progress in the accounting standards development and international convergence, and the CAS has provided important and successful support for China's economic growth.

The current CAS contains one *Basic Standard*, 41 *Specific Standards* and 41 application guidance up to 2017, which has significantly enhanced the quality and transparency of financial reporting in China and finally improves the healthy and orderly development of China's capital market. However, in order to keep pace with the economic development of China, the CAS still needs to be improved. The following are the future areas of CAS which need more work in our views.

First, with the deep involvement of China in the globalization, it is undisputed to further promote the complete convergence of the CAS with IFRS. More than 100 countries and regions now require the use of IFRS for all firms or for publicly listed companies. The post-adoption analysis has shown that IFRS has substantially increased the quality and consistency of financial reporting within adopting jurisdictions. The MOF of China and IASB both note the importance of continuing international support for the goal of achieving a single set of high quality, global accounting standards and reaffirming the goal of complete convergence, as demonstrated recently by the September 2015 Statement of the Financial Stability Board. In the bilateral meeting on the occasion of the trustees in October 2015, the MOF reaffirmed China's continued commitment toward the goal of complete convergence with IFRS, and both parties would establish a joint working group to explore ways and steps to improve the use of IFRS within China. This objective is also compatible with China's reforms and openness policy. In our view, in the foreseeable future, the most important task of convergence to the MOF is to do serious research on the basic concepts for financial accounting and reporting and revise the *Basic Standard* in order to provide a high quality conceptual basis for specific standards-setting and revising, and the revision should be converged with the Conceptual Framework for Financial Reporting issued by the IASB in March 2018.

Besides, the MOF shall enhance continuous cooperation with IASB. China has involved and needs to continuously involve the IASB, various advisory bodies and consultative working groups in the setting of IFRS. The MOF shall establish some special task forces to study the international standards and CAS, whose research findings will be conductive to the convergence and improvement of both IFRS and CAS. In 2016, the MOF founded a new council, the *Advisory Council of Chinese Accounting Standards for Business Enterprises*, to help improve the quality of the CAS. We believe that China will not only follow the IFRS but also lead the IFRS development in some accounting areas to some extent in the foreseeable future. China could be expected to play a more important role in the international convergence of accounting standards.

Second, China shall unify the accounting standards for both the publicly held companies and the private companies. Of course, the accounting standards would include the CAS for big companies and small-size companies. The unification of accounting standards will help to improve the accounting information quality and help the development of venture capital market and securities market. It will also help improve the macro-control of China's economy.

In the future, the MOF should improve the writing style of the CAS (that is, in more plain Chinese) in order to enhance understandability of CAS. Besides, the MOF should prepare more operable application guidance for the accounting standards regarding business combination, consolidated financial statements, financial instruments, goodwill impairment test, fair value measurement and revenue recognition.

Last but not least, the MOF should reinforce coordination between the CAS and other China's laws and regulations. The CAS itself is just a part of Chinese accounting regulation system. As discussed before, The *Accounting Act* is the supreme accounting regulation in China, it requires CAS to help reflect the management's stewardship and provides the basis for profit distribution. CAS should abide by the *Accounting Act*. The *Company Act* also has some general rules on the financial accounting and reporting for all firms including private and public firms. The *Securities Act* regulates the disclosure rule of accounting information for firms who publicly issue bonds and shares. The CSRC is responsible for setting the specific disclosure rules for listed firms. Consequently, CAS should coordinate with the *Company Act* and the *Securities Act* and other regulations at the same time. Unfortunately, maybe because the development of CAS is faster than the modification of laws, there are some conflicts or inharmoniousness between CAS and the related laws and regulations. Consequently, it is important for the MOF to pay more attention to and strengthen the coordination between CAS and related laws and regulations.

Notes

1 This chapter focuses on the accounting standards for business enterprises. As to government accounting standards, the MOF set government accounting system before 2015. In 2015, the MOF issued "The Government Accounting Standards: Basic Standard". In 2016, the MOF issued four specific government accounting standards: Inventory (GAS No.1), Investment (GAS No.2), Fixed Assets (GAS No.3), Intangible Assets (GAS No.4). In 2017, the MOF issued GAS No.5- Infrastructure and GAS N0.6- Government Reserves (updated to July 2017).
2 It was renamed into *the Accounting System of the PRC for the Foreign Investment* in 1992 and was abolished in 2001.
3 The major difference was whether the accounting regulations accepted or denied the conservatism principle. The accounting regulations of China denied the conservatism principle, while IASC admitted it (Ge, Lin and Wei, 1988). For example, there was no provision for bad debt in the accounting regulations of China at that time.
4 The International Accounting Standards Committee (IASC), formed in 1973, was the first international standards-setting body. It was reorganized in 2001 and became an independent international standard setter, the International Accounting Standards Board (IASB). Since then, International Accounting Standards (IAS) is renamed by the international financial reporting standards issued by the IASB.
5 Article 3 of *Basic Standard* issued in 1992 states that enterprises are required to comply with this Standard.
6 *FARR* focuses on financial accounting and reporting matters such as bookkeeping, preparation of financial statements and reporting practices. *FARR* applies to all enterprises other than very small ones that do not raise funds externally.
7 www.casc.org.cn/2016/0503/131875.shtml.
8 On January 1, 2002, a new separate *Accounting System for Financial Institutions* issued by the MOF in 2001 was officially applied to financial institutions. On January 1, 2005, the *Accounting System for Financial Institutions* issued by the MOF in 2004 was officially applied to small enterprises. As to the small-size firms, the MOF issued the *Accounting System for Small-size Business Enterprises* in 2004, which was substituted by *Accounting Standards for Small-size Business Enterprises* issued by the MOF in 2011 (effective date is 1 January, 2013).
9 We will introduce the latest version of CAS (2017), which includes one basic standard and 41 specific standards, in section 2.
10 For example, China has joined two accounting standards cooperative forces: (1) Northeastern Asia standard-setters conference including Japan, South Korea, Hong Kong, Macau and Mainland China. (2) Asian-Oceanian Standard-Setters Group (AOSSG), including 26 Asian and Oceanian countries and regions.
11 See Table 2.
12 Besides, there are also 12 interpretations of CAS developed till 2017.
13 The consolidated text of IFRS includes 16 IFRS Standards and 25 IAS Standards. In January 2014, the IASB firstly adopted IFRS No. 14 Regulatory Deferral Accounts on rate-regulated activities. However, the rate-regulated activities are not mentioned in CAS.
14 These standards shall apply to the following investment real estates: (1) the right to use any land which has already been rented; (2) the right to use any land which is held and prepared for transfer after appreciation; and (3) the right to use any building which has already been rented.

References

Cai, H. An Important Regulation on Foreign-Related Economic Work: A Brief Introduction to the Sino-Foreign Joint Venture Accounting System. *Accounting Research*, 1985 (3): 23–28.

Fu, L. Review and Thinking on Chinese Enterprises Accounting Reform. *Accounting Research*, 2007 (12): 23–28+96.

Ge, J. Discussions on the Basic Characteristics of China's Accounting Standards for Business Enterprises. *Accounting Research*, 1993 (1): 7–9.

Ge, J. How to Use International Experience for Setting Chinese Accounting Standards. *Accounting Research*, 1992 (2): 16–19+2.

Ge, J. Several Questions on the Setting of Financial Accounting Standards for Business Enterprises in China. *Accounting Research*, 1989 (2): 16–21.

Ge, J. A Standard With the Combination of Innovation and Convergence: Comments on the "Accounting Standard for Business Enterprises: Basic Standard". *Accounting Research*, 2006 (3): 3–6+95.

Ge, J., Lin, Z., and Wei, M. Accounting System for Firms With Foreign Investments and Conservatism Principle. *Accounting Research*, 1988 (5): 19–22.

Huang, S., and Liu, W. Important Measures to Enhance Accounting Information Quality: Understanding the *Accounting System for Business Enterprises. Accounting Research*, 2001 (2): 3–8+65.

IFRS Foundation of the IASB. *IFRS (Red Book)*, 2016. Available from: www.iasplus.com/en/news/2016/03/red-book.

Jiang, G. The Preliminary Practice of Setting Chinese Accounting Standards. *Accounting Research*, 1992 (2): 26–30+39.

Liu, Y. The Chinese Characteristics and Harmonization With International Practices of *Accounting System for Business Enterprises. Accounting Research*, 2001 (3): 3–8+65.

Liu, Y. On Chinese Accounting Standards System: Framework, Convergence and Equivalence. *Accounting Research*, 2007 (3): 2–8.

Lou, E., and Zhang, W. Comparative Research on Chinese Accounting Standards. *Accounting Research*, 1992 (2): 5–15.

MOF of China. Accounting Standard for Business Enterprises: Basic Standard, 1992, 2001, 2006, 2016, Economic Science Press.

MOF of China. *Accounting System for Business Enterprises*, 2001, Economic Science Press.

MOF of China. *China Accounting Standard*, 2006, 2014, 2016, 2017, Economic Science Press.

MOF of China. *Continuous Convergence Roadmap Between CAS and IFRS* (Continuous Convergence Roadmap), 2010. Available from: http://kjs.mof.gov.cn/zhengwuxinxi/zhengcefabu/201004/t20100419_288013.html.

MOF of China and the IASB. *The Joint Statement of Secretary-General of the China Accounting Standards Committee and the Chairman of the International Accounting Standards Board*, 2005. Available from: http://upload.news.esnai.com/news/200511171233686198.pdf.

Wang, W., and Lin, D. A Study on Several Concepts in Accounting Theory. *Accounting Research*, 1985 (3): 42–44.

Xie, D. A Discussion on the Setting of Chinese Accounting Standards. *Accounting Research*, 1995 (10): 23–25.

Xie, Z. A Systematic Conceiving About Accounting System. *Accounting Research*, 1987 (3): 9–12.

Yan, D. A Study on the Chinese Accounting Standards Model and Structure. *Accounting Research*, 1992 (2): 20–25.

Yang, J. Some Questions on the Accounting Standards. *Accounting Research*, 1989 (2): 2–5.

Zhang, H. On the Necessity of Setting Unified Accounting System: From the Perspective of Setting Objectives. *Accounting Research*, 2001 (3): 9–13.

5

FAIR VALUE ACCOUNTING IN CHINA

Xiaohui Qu, Guohua Zhang

1. Introduction

There are 140 out of 150 jurisdictions (93%) that have made a public commitment to IFRS Standards as the single set of global accounting standards (IASB, 2017) around the world. The debate on the adaptability of fair value accounting (FVA) around the world, especially in emerging markets, has never stopped. In this chapter, we introduce the development of fair value accounting in China in the past decades.

With the economic reform and opening-up policy implemented in China in late 1978, the government and accounting professionals gradually reintroduced the accounting theory and practice of western countries. Before 1978, China used the accounting regulations of the former Soviet Union, which is based on a planned economy. During this period, the Chinese accounting regulation was called an accounting system rather than accounting standards. Since 1978, China has reformed its economy from a planned economy into a planned-market economy and market economy, and accounting regulation has been changed accordingly. The accounting reforms are mainly modeled after international practice especially the International Accounting Standards (IASs), which later on was renamed as International Financial Reporting Standards (IFRSs). Most reforms occurred after China's entry into the World Trade Organization (WTO) in 2001.

The most important change for the accounting profession is the development of new accounting standards. In 1992, Accounting Standard for Business Enterprise (ASBE) was issued for the first time. The ASBEs were based on the International Accounting Standards (IASs), which serves a market-oriented economy. It took 14 years for China to totally convert the centrally planned economy oriented Chinese accounting system into a market-oriented accounting system. However, it took longer time to adopt FVA into Chinese Accounting Standards (CASs). ASBE – Basic Standard 1993 did not include FVA due to the underdevelopment of market environment. Based on the most important accounting regulations related to FVA, the development of FVA in China has gone through the following six periods: infancy period (1984–1992), introduction period (1993–1997), period of limited adoption (1998–1999), period of suspension and wide discussion period (2000–2006), period of wide adoption (2007–2014) and IFRS 13 adoption period (2014 – present).

2. Infancy period (1984–1992)

Accompanied by the massive introduction of western accounting theory and practice, especially the IASs into China after 1978, the term of fair value was also introduced. At the infancy stage, fair value appeared in Chinese academic journals several times, but there was no definition or explanation. The earliest appearance of fair value in Chinese academic literature was 1984, when Chen and Xiang (1984) introduced western fixed assets evaluation theory in their paper published in *Accounting Research*, the top Chinese academic journal in accounting. The study introduced the current input value of fixed assets includes replacement cost, evaluation value and fair value, but there was no further explanation on the meaning of fair value. Two years later, Tang (1986) introduced US GAAP into China and compared US GAAP with Chinese accounting standards (CASs), in which fair value was recognized as a difference between the two different accounting standards. Three years later, when Lin (1989) introduced the new progress of international accounting harmonization, the fair value appeared again. Fair value was listed as a requirement or priority method to one of the issues discussed by the IASC. Although the systematically reformed CASs in 1992 followed the tradition of IASs, fair value measurement was not adopted at that time due to the lack of fully understanding of fair value and underdevelopment of institutional settings.

3. Introduction period (1993–1997)

The wide introduction of fair value in China started in 1994. In 1992, the Ministry of Finance (MOF) issued ASBE – Basic Accounting Standard, which took effective on July 1, 1993. This is similar to the conceptual framework for financial reporting of the Financial Accounting Standards Board (FASB) in the US and the Preparation and Presentation of Financial Statements of the International Accounting Standards Board (IASB).

Right after the Basic Accounting Standard was issued, the accounting regulations for 13 industries respectively were issued one after another in 1993 and promptly implemented by companies. These accounting regulations for 13 industries were soon replaced by 16 specific accounting standards, which were issued one after another from 1997 through 2001.

The IASs and its new progress have attracted extensive attention in Chinese academia and among standard-setters, since China decided to harmonize its accounting standards with the IASs. In 1994, for the first time, the definition of fair value was introduced to China in the translated version of *IAS22 Business Combination*, in which fair value was defined as the amount for which an asset could be exchanged or a liability settled between knowledgeable, willing parties in an arm's length transaction (Zhu and Shen, 1994). In 1995, in the translated version of *IAS 32 Financial Instrument: Disclosure and Presentation*, not only the concept of fair value was defined, but also market value. In IAS 32, market value was defined as the amount obtainable from the sale, or payable on the acquisition of a financial instrument in an active market (Zhu and Shen, 1995). This new progress and the innovation of financial instruments brought wide attention in China. Ge and Chen (1995) discussed the impact of financial instrument innovation on financial accounting and proposed that not only accounting elements need to be redefined, but the recognition criteria, measurement basis and the presentation of financial reports need to be reconsidered as well. They inferred that historical cost should not be the only measurement attribute. The possible development tendency was that both historical cost and fair value would coexist for quite long time. As to the origin of fair value, Ge (2002) proposed "from the measurement attributes, one of the related basic assumptions is that market price and cost or fair value and cost. This assumption is not a new idea but today's reaffirmation of Moonitz's views expressed forty years ago".

In 1995, the MOF issued a series of exposure drafts of *Accounting Standards for Business Enterprises* (ASBE). For the first time the concept of fair value was officially defined in several Eds, and the concept is exactly the translation of IASs' definition. Soon after, FVA was introduced into several specific accounting standards as well. During this period, fair value was allowed to be used in the evaluations of non-monetary transactions such as fixed assets, intangible assets, donated assets, and mortgage etc. in the ED of Chinese ASBE *Fixed Assets, Intangible Assets, Owner's Equity* and *Basic transactions in Bank*. In 1996, Meng (1996) proposed how to evaluate non-monetary transactions by using fair value.

4. Period of limited adoption (1998–1999)

In 1998, FVA, for the first time, officially appeared in accounting regulations in the ASBE – *Debt Restructuring* – in which the concept of fair value was defined as the amount for which an asset could be exchanged, or a liability could be settled, between willing parties in an arm's length transaction. In the same year, FVA was also adopted into the new ASBE *Investment* and ASBE *Non-Monetary Transactions*.

5. Period of suspension and wide discussion (2000–2006)

However, the initial application of FVA was soon prohibited in the 2000 revision of ASBE, as it was found that fair value was widely employed by business enterprises to manipulate profit (Yang, 2008). During the period of FVA application, debates among scholars and practitioners had been increasing. Ge and Ye (2010) pointed out that mixed measurement model will produce "two misclassifications": misclassification between the assets and liabilities transformed according to the real value of invested capital or assuming the obligations (the assets or liabilities measured by historical cost) and the assets or liabilities measured according to expected estimates of the price (the assets and liabilities measured with fair value); misclassification between the realized recognizable actual gains or losses and unrealized recognizable gains or losses.

6. Period of widely adoption period (2007–2013)

The ASBE 2006 is substantially convergent with the IFRS. In ASBE 2006, fair value was aggressively re-introduced, and the adoption scope of FVA was also greatly extended. Among the 38 specific standards issued in 2006, 25 specific standards require or allow the direct or indirect use of fair value measurement; 17 specific standards require the use of fair value in the initial measurement of assets and liabilities; eight specific standards require its use in subsequent measurement of assets and liabilities; 11 specific standards require its use in asset impairment testing; and 17 specific standards require a disclosure of fair value in accounting measurement and financial reporting, as well as the allocation of lump-sum cost based on fair value of acquired assets (Peng and Bewley, 2010).

Based on ASBE 2006, FVA is more or less applied in 17 specific standards, most of which are appropriate for all industrial sectors, while only a few are applicable to some specific industrial sectors and give management options to use FVA or historical cost accounting, such as ASBE 5 – *Biological Assets*, and ASBE 27 – *Extraction of Oil and Natural Gas*. Qu and Zhang (2015) select the four industrial sectors (financial sector, real estate sector, mining sector, and farming–forestry–fishery sector) that were most likely to apply fair value measurement for the valuation of assets and liabilities.

Ge (2009) believe that FVA has two main characteristics, i.e. mark-to-market and so-called market price is reporting date (current) market quotes or other estimated price. He pointed out that the most important impact of the main characteristics of FVA is on the estimation and revaluation or subsequence measurement, the two steps of that companies try to avoid, which affect the essence of financial accounting information.[1]

7. Adoption of IFRS 13 (2014–present)

On January 26, 2014, the MOF (2014a) issued the *Notice of the Issuance of ASBE No.39 – Fair Value Measurement*, which said

> in order to meet the needs of the development of the socialist market economy, standardize the fair value measurement and disclosure of enterprises, improve the quality of accounting information, according to the ASBE – *Basic Standard*, MOF sets the ASBE No. 39 – Fair Value Measurement, which is hereby printed and distributed, will implement in all of enterprises implementing ASBE since July 1, 2014, and encourage the overseas listed companies perform ahead of time.

The CAS39 Fair Value Measurement regulated the factors should be considered for fair value measurement, such as the premise and assumptions, valuation techniques, the input value order, the hierarchy of the fair value and the disclosure of the fair value of the fair value measurement for the disclosure of related assets or liabilities.

It is well-known that the CASs were converged with IFRS in 2006 and the converged accounting standards were put into practice on January 1, 2017. After the convergence, the CASs did not converge step by step with IFRS. However, in 2014, MOF revised five specific accounting standards, and newly issued three accounting standards including the ASBE No. 39 Fair Value Measurement. To be consistent with the ASBE No. 39 (CAS 39), the Basic Standard was also revised with changes in the definition of fair value.

The MOF issued the Decision to amend the ASBE – Basic Standard in the form of the Minister Command (MOF, 2014b) on July 23, 2014, which was effective on date of issurance. The purpose is to "meet the actual needs of the development of enterprises and capital markets in China, realize the continuous convergence of accounting standards with International Financial Reporting Standards". According to the decision of the Ministry of Finance, the fifth item of the article forty-two of the ASBE – Basic Standard shall be amended to:

> Fair value. Under the fair value measurement, assets and liabilities are measured as the price that would be received to sell an asset or paid to transfer a liability in an orderly transaction between market participants at the measurement date . This decision comes into force as of the date of promulgation.

The ASBE – Basic Standard was amended accordingly.

Before this amendment, the fair value definition in the ASBE – Basic Standard (MOF, 2006) was: under fair value measurement, assets and liabilities are calculated according to the amount the parties that are familiar with the situation are willing to undertake asset exchange or the amount of debt repayment in a fair transaction.[2]. This definition was also in accordance with that of the IAS. This Minister Command highlights the actual needs of the development of enterprises and capital markets in China, but it seems that the continuous convergence of accounting standards with IFRS is more important or dominated. After comparing the CAS 39 with the IFRS 13, it is obviously that there are too many common contexts, from the title to the definition, main contents, exceptions and techniques, etc. (See Table 5.1). Therefore, it is believed that the accounting standards setter of China, the MOF, adopts the IFRS 13 Fair Value Measurement.

Table 5.1 The Comparison between IFRS 13 and CAS 39

Item	IFRS 13	CAS 39	Notes
Title	*Fair Value Measurement*	*Fair Value Measurement*	*Same*
Main function	Fair Value Measurement (a) defines fair value; (b) sets out in a single IFRS a framework for measuring fair value; and (c) requires disclosures about fair value measurements.	Fair Value Measurement defines fair value; sets out in a single standard a framework for measuring fair value; and requires disclosures about fair value measurement.	Same
Definition of fair value	This IFRS defines fair value as the price that would be received to sell an asset or paid to transfer a liability in an orderly transaction between market participants at the measurement date. Para.9	Fair vale refers to the price that would be received to sell an asset or paid to transfer a liability in an orderly transaction between market participants at the measurement date. Article2	Same
Scope	This IFRS applies when another IFRS requires or permits fair value measurements or disclosures about fair value measurements (and measurements, such as fair value less costs to sell, based on fair value or disclosures about those measurements), except as specified in paragraphs 6 and 7, para.5	This standard applies when another IFRS requires or permits fair value measurements or disclosures about fair value measurements, except as specified in article 4 and 5. Article3.	Same
Exception1	The measurement and disclosure requirements of this IFRS do not apply to the following: (a) share-based payment transactions within the scope of IFRS 2 Share-based Payment; (b) leasing transactions within the scope of IAS 17 Leases; and (c) measurements that have some similarities to fair value but are not fair value, such as net realizable value in IAS 2 Inventories or value in use in IAS 36 Impairment of Assets. para.6	The measurement and disclosure requirements of this IFRS do not apply to the following: (1) similar to other measurement attributes of fair value measurement and disclosure, such as the ASBE No. 1 – Inventories specification of net realizable value, ASBE No. 8 – Asset Impairment, the specification of the expected the present value of future cash flow, one for each of the ASBE No. 1 – Inventories and ASBE No. 8 – Asset Impairment. (2) the measurement and disclosure of shares payment business shall apply to the ASBE No. 11 – Share-based Payment. (3) the measurement and disclosure of the leasing business shall apply to the ASBE No. 21 – Leases. Article 4	Same

(*Continued*)

Table 5.1 (Continued)

Item	IFRS 13	CAS 39	Notes
Title	*Fair Value Measurement*	*Fair Value Measurement*	Same
Exception2	The disclosures required by this IFRS are not required for the following: (a) plan assets measured at fair value in accordance with IAS 19 Employee Benefits; (b) retirement benefit plan investments measured at fair value in accordance with IAS 26 Accounting and Reporting by Retirement Benefit Plans; and (c) assets for which recoverable amount is fair value less costs of disposal in accordance with IAS 36. para. 7	The following disclosures shall apply to other relevant accounting standards: (1) the disclosure of the assets which recoverable amounts determined in a net amount after subtracting the disposal costs from the fair value, apply ASBE No. 8 – Impairment of Assets; (2) disclosure of the assets of the welfare plan after the employee's departure from the fair value measurement, apply ASBE No. 9 – Employee Compensation; (3) disclosure of investment by enterprise annuity fund measured with fair value, apply ASBE No. 10 – Enterprise Annuity Fund. Article 5	Almost exactly the same
Chapters	INTRODUCTION OBJECTIVE SCOPE MEASUREMENT (Definition of fair value; The asset or liability; The transaction; Market participants; The price; Application to non-financial assets; Application to liabilities and an entity's own equity instruments; Application to financial assets and financial liabilities with offsetting; positions in market risks or counterparty credit risk; Fair value at initial recognition; Valuation techniques; Inputs to valuation techniques; Fair value hierarchy) DISCLOSURE APPENDICES (A Defined terms; B Application guidance; C Effective date and transition; D Amendments to other IFRSs)	1 General provisions 2 Related assets or liabilities 3 Orderly transactions and markets 4 Market participants 5 Initial measurement of fair value 6 Valuation techniques 7 Fair value hierarchy 8 Fair value measurement of non-financial assets 9 Fair value measurement of liabilities and enterprise's own equity instruments 10 Fair value measurement of financial assets and financial liabilities their market risk or credit risk may be offset 11 Fair value disclosure 12 Connection provisions 13 Supplementary provisions	
Approaches of fair value measurement	Example	Approaches of fair value measurement: Elements need to determine for FVM; Use evaluation technique; Assumptions, input values, and fair value hierarchy; The cohesion of fair value measurement criteria; Existing problems	

Item	IFRS 13	CAS 39	Notes
Title	*Fair Value Measurement*	*Fair Value Measurement*	*Same*
Elements need to determine for FVM	Example	Elements need to determine for FVM: Assets or liabilities measured at fair value; Orderly trading and markets; Market participants; Appropriate valuation techniques; The input values; Fair value hierarchy	
Use evaluation technique:	Example	Use evaluation technique: Companies that measure assets or liabilities at fair value should adopt valuation techniques that are applicable in the current situation and have sufficient available data and other information to support them. The purpose of using valuation techniques is to estimate the price that market participants sell an asset or transfer a liability in an orderly transaction under the current market conditions on the measurement date.	
Evaluation technique	Example	Valuation techniques mainly include market approach, income approach and cost approach	same
Market approach	Appendix A Defined terms A559	Market approach: A valuation technique that uses prices and other relevant information generated by market transactions involving identical or comparable (similar) assets, liabilities or a group of assets and liabilities, such as a business.	same
Income approach	Appendix A Defined terms A559	Income approach: Valuation techniques that convert future amounts (e.g. cash flows or income and expenses) to a single current (i.e. discounted) amount. The fair value measurement is determined on the basis of the value indicated by current market expectations about those future amounts.	same

(Continued)

Table 5.1 (Continued)

Item	IFRS 13	CAS 39	Notes
Title	Fair Value Measurement	Fair Value Measurement	Same
Cost approach	Appendix A Defined terms A560	Cost approach: A valuation technique that reflects the amount that would be required currently to replace the service capacity of an asset (often referred to as current replacement cost).	same
Active market	IFRS13 A559	Active market: A market in which transactions for the asset or liability take place with sufficient frequency and volume to provide pricing information on an ongoing basis.	Same
Assumption	IFRS13 IN9	Assumption: When measuring fair value, an entity uses the assumptions that market participants would use when pricing the asset or liability under current market conditions, including assumptions about risk.	same
Inputs	IFRS13 A559	Inputs: The assumptions that market participants would use when pricing the asset or liability. Inputs may be observable or unobservable.	Same
Observable inputs	IFRS13 A560	Observable inputs: Inputs that are developed using market data, such as publicly available information about actual events or transactions, and that reflect the assumptions that market participants would use when pricing the asset or liability.	Almost same
Unobservable inputs	IFRS13 A560	Unobservable inputs: Inputs for which market data are not available and that are developed using the best information available about the assumptions that market participants would use when pricing the asset or liability.	Same
Inputs: Priority	IFRS13 para.3	When a price for an identical asset or liability is not observable, an entity measures fair value using another valuation technique that maximizes the use of relevant observable inputs and minimizes the use of unobservable inputs.	Same

Item	IFRS 13	CAS 39	Notes
Title	*Fair Value Measurement*	*Fair Value Measurement*	*Same*
Inputs: Priority	IFRS13 para.72	The fair value hierarchy gives the highest priority to quoted prices (unadjusted) in active markets for identical assets or liabilities (Level 1 inputs) and the lowest priority to unobservable inputs (*Level 3 inputs*).	
Inputs: Priority	IFRS13 para.67	Valuation techniques used to measure fair value shall maximize the use of relevant observable inputs and minimize the use of unobservable inputs.	Same
Fair value hierarchy	IFRS13 para.72 IFRS13 A559 IFRS13 para.81 & A559 IFRS13 A559	To increase consistency and comparability in fair value measurements and related disclosures, this IFRS establishes a fair value hierarchy that categorizes into three levels (see paragraphs 76–90) the inputs to valuation techniques used to measure fair value. Level 1: Inputs are quoted prices (unadjusted) in active markets for identical assets or liabilities that the entity can access at the measurement date. Level 2: Inputs are inputs other than quoted prices included within Level 1 that are observable for the asset or liability, either directly or indirectly. (1) quoted prices for similar assets or liabilities in active markets. (2) quoted prices for identical or similar assets or liabilities in markets that are not active. (3) inputs other than quoted prices that are observable for the asset or liability, for example: (4) *market-corroborated inputs.* Level 3: Inputs are unobservable inputs for the asset or liability.	Same

(*Continued*)

Table 5.1 (Continued)

Item	IFRS 13	CAS 39	Notes
Title	*Fair Value Measurement*	*Fair Value Measurement*	*Same*
Priority to Inputs	IFRS13 para. 3	The priorities order of inputs: When a price for an identical asset or liability is not observable, an entity measures fair value using another valuation technique that maximizes the use of relevant *observable inputs and minimizes the use of unobservable inputs.*	
Issue	IASB issued on May 12, 2011 IFRS 13 Fair Value Measurement	MOF issued on January 26, 2014 ASBE 39 Fire Value Measurement.	
Effective	The IFRS 13 is to be applied for annual periods beginning on or after January 1, 2013. Earlier application is permitted.	Starting July 1, 2014	
Implementation		It will be implemented in all enterprises that implement Accounting Standards for Business Enterprises, and encourage enterprises listed abroad to implement ahead of time.	Same
Connection	Applying the future application method from the beginning of the year adapting the IFRS 13.	Not require the retrospect adjustment for the previous fair value measurement that is not consistent with standard 39 Fair Value Measurement. No need to make the retrospect adjustment for the previous information is not consistent with the requirement of Standard 39 Fair Value Measurement.	

8. Conclusions

China, as one of emerging economies, has substantially converged her accounting standards with IFRSs since 2006. The new set of accounting standards has extensively adopted FVA which derived from IFRS. However, as IFRS was created in response to the needs of developed rather than emerging economies (Peng and Bewley, 2010), it takes long time to develop FVA in China. Empirical studies suggest that the publicly listed firms have some reservations in adopting FVA, and the institutional setting and economic environment is not ready yet for a full adoption of FVA in China (Qu and Zhang, 2015). Based on the most important accounting regulations related to FVA, the development of FVA in China has gone through the following six periods: infancy period (1984–1992), introduction period (1993–1997), period of limited adoption (1998–1999), period of suspension and wide discussion period (2000–2006), period of wide adoption (2007–2014) and IFRS 13 adoption period (2014 – present). Future studies need to investigate whether the new standard has met the needs of the development of the market, standardize the fair value measurement and disclosure of enterprises and improve the quality of accounting information.

Notes

1 Ge, J.S. (2009) 'Research on Fair Value Accounting: The Essential Characteristics of Financial Accounting', *Accounting Research (in Chinese)*, 5: 6–13, p. 10.
2 MOF (2006) Accounting Standards for Business Enterprises – Basic Standard. *Accounting Standards for Business Enterprises 2006*, Beijing: Economic Science Press (in Chinese), p. 6.

References

Chen, J.C. and Xiang, X.P. (1984) 'Introduction to Western Fixed Assets Evaluation Theory', *Accounting Research (in Chinese)*, 1: 49–52.p. 52.

Ge, J.S. (2002) 'Rethinking the Basic Assumptions of Financial Accounting', *Accounting Research (in Chinese)*, 1: 5–10, p. 9.

Ge, J.S. (2009) 'Research on Fair Value Accounting: The Essential Characteristics of Financial Accounting', *Accounting Research (in Chinese)*, 5: 6–13, p. 10.

Ge, J.S. and Chen, J.S. (1995) 'A Brief Discussion on the Impact of Financial Instrument Innovation on Financial Accounting', *Accounting Research (in Chinese)*, 8: 1–8.

Ge, J.S. and Ye, F.Y. (2010) 'The New Exploration on Double Measurements in Financial Statements: A Hypothetical Example of Our Suggestions', *Journal of Xiamen University (A Quarterly for Studies in Arts & Social Sciences) (in Chinese)*, 1: 38–45, p. 13.

IASB (2011) 'IFRS13 – Fair Value Measurement', *IFRS Red Book 2014*: A533–A579.

IASB (2017). 'Use of IFRS Standards by Jurisdiction', www.ifrs.org/use-around-the-world/use-of-ifrs-standards-by-jurisdiction/. December 3, 2017.

Lin, Z.J. (1989) 'New Development of International Accounting Harmonization', *Accounting Research (in Chinese)*, 10: 49–52.

Meng, F.L. (1996) 'Comments on "Accounting Standards for Business Enterprises No. X-Non-monetary Transactions" (Exposure Draft)', *Accounting Research (in Chinese)*, 8: 22–24.

MOF (2006) 'Accounting Standards for Business Enterprises – Basic Standard', *Accounting Standards for Business Enterprises 2006*, Beijing: Economic Science Press, 2006:1–10.

MOF (2014a) 'Accounting Standards for Business Enterprises No. 39 – Fair Value Measurement', http://kjs.mof.gov.cn/zhengwuxinxi/zhengcefabu/201401/P020140128564739706439.pdf. December 1, 2017.

MOF (2014b) 'The Decision to Amend the Accounting Standards for Business Enterprise – Basic Standard', www.casc.org.cn/2015/1228/125324.shtml. December 1, 2017.

Peng, S. and Bewley, K. (2010) 'Adaptability to Fair Value Accounting in an Emerging Economy, A Case Study of China's IFRS Convergence', *Accounting, Auditing & Accountability Journal*, 23(8): 982–1011.

Qu, X.H. and Zhang, G.H. (2015) 'Value-relevance of Earnings and Book Value Over the Institutional Transition in China: The Suitability of Fair Value Accounting in This Emerging Market', *The International Journal of Accounting*, 50: 195–223.

Tang, Y.W. (1986) 'American Generally Accepted Accounting Standards', *Shanghai Accounting (in Chinese)*, 1: 31–35.

Yang, M. (2008) 'Review and Enlightenment of the Application of Fair-value Accounting in China', *Accountant's Friends (in Chinese)*, 3: 94–95.

Zhu, H.L. and Shen, X.N. (1994) 'International Accounting Standards 22 Business Combination', *Accounting Research (in Chinese)*, 6: 43–52.

Zhu, H.L. and Shen, X.N. (1995) 'International Accounting Standards 32 Financial Instrument: Disclosure and Presentation', *Accounting Research (in Chinese)*, 12: 32–37.

6

PRODUCT MARKET COMPETITION AND EARNINGS QUALITY

Liquan Xing, Hanwen Chen, Haiyan Zhou

1. Introduction

In recent years, a series of studies show that product market competition has an important impact on accrual-based earnings management (Hou and Robinson 2006; Tinaikar and Xue 2009; Bagnoli and Watts 2010). The literature finds that besides accrual-based earnings management, company executives may also manipulate earnings through real activities (Fudenberg and Tirole 1995; Healy and Wahlen 1999; Dechow and Skinner 2000; Gunny 2005; Roychowdhury 2006; Zang 2012). Earnings management via real activities could affect the company's current and future cash flows, and therefore affect the long-term value of the company. With constant improvement of accounting standards and regulations, accrual earnings management opportunities available for managers are continuously reduced in order to achieve performance goals, the manager tends to increase real activities earnings management (Cohen et al. 2008). For instance, Cohen and Zarowin (2010) find that in addition to accrual earnings management, managers will adjust profit prior to the issuance of secondary offerings using real earnings management.

In the literature on accrual earnings management and product market competition, the literature has documented mixed results. For sample, Karuna et al. (2012) also document a positive relationship between product market competition and earnings management, both through accruals and real activities in US listed companies. Tian (2012) finds that increased product market competition could reduce the company's accrual earnings management in China. Given the managers become more inclined to employ real earnings management (Cohen et al. 2008), in order to understand real earnings management of activities in the emerging market, we first investigate the relationship between product market competition and earnings management, both through accruals and real activities in the emerging market.

Using observations on the listed companies from China during the period of 2007–2012, we find that product market competition and competitive position have a significant impact on accrual earnings management and real activity earnings management. In particular, firms in the industries confronted with higher competitions are associated with higher accrual earnings management. Firms with lower competition status in the industry are associated with higher degree of real activities earnings management, that is, lower operating cash flow, higher abnormal production costs and lower abnormal discretionary expenses.

These studies have implications for investors in the emerging markets. Our findings on the link between product market competition and earnings management could help investors obtain better understanding of earnings management activities and estimating firms' values.

The remainder of the paper is organized as follows. Section 2 reviews the relevant literature and develops research hypotheses. Section 3 discusses the sample selection and research design. Section 4 presents the empirical results and discusses various sensitivity tests. Section 5, the final section concludes the paper.

2.   Theory, literature and hypotheses development

2.1   *Product market competition and earnings management*

In order to increase executive compensation (Bergstresser and Philippon 2006, etc.), avoid reporting losses (Burgstahler and Dichev 1997), or to achieve specific performance goal (DeGeorge et al. 1999), managers will manipulate accruals to meet their earnings goals. In addition to accrual earnings management, managers may also manipulate earnings through real activities (Fudenberg and Tirole 1995; Healy and Wahlen 1999; Dechow and Skinner 2000; Gunny 2005; Burgstahler and Eames 2006; Roychowdhury 2006).

Accrual earnings management refers to managers make accounting choices based on the methods available under GAAP in reporting financial performance, although company's actual cash flow is not affected. Earnings management in real activity refers to managers implement specific financial activities, timing and restructure the business, investment and financing plans. Different from accrual earnings management, real activities earnings management will have a real impact on current and future cash flows of the company.

Accrual earnings management has low cost, but it is easy to be detected by regulators and auditors to detect with accounting guidelines and regulations becoming more rigorous, managers have limited room to perform accrual earnings management. In contrast to real activity earnings management which involves higher cost to shareholders, it is not easy to be detected. When the space for accrual earnings management becomes increasingly narrow, management tends to use real activity earnings management to achieve expected performance goal (Cohen et al. 2008). Graham et al. (2005) find that 80% managers interviewed think that they will reduce the cost of research and development, advertising and maintenance to meet earnings target, while about 50% think they will postpone new projects to achieve specific performance target, even if this practice will reduce firm value. Cohen et al. (2008) find that after the enactment of Sarbanes-Oxley, US firms shift from accrual earnings management to real activity earnings management.

Roychowdhury (2006) finds that managers will use a variety of methods to use sales discount to temporarily boost sales, reduce excessive production costs to improve profit margins, lower the cost of goods sold to meet the expected financial performance and avoid reporting losses. Yang et al. (2010) find that managers use both accrual and real activity earnings management to reach performance goals. Cohen and Zarowin (2010) find that real activities earning management can reduce earnings more significantly than accrual earnings management.

Bagnoli and Watts (2001) argue that when facing more market competition, managers have more motivations to exercise earnings management. Because of cost consideration, managers tend to choose accrual earnings management; due to confidentiality concerns, managers tend to select real activities earnings management. Raith (2003) and Gaspar and Massa (2006) argue that as product market competition makes firms face higher business risks, risk-averse managers would become more conservative, postpone or even abandon investment projects which are likely to generate cash flow in the future. Due to product market competition, managers will focus on short-term horizons to influence the market and to boost short-term performance.

Current literature shows that product market competition affect company executive's remuneration and career. On one hand, product market competition would affect firm's profitability and thus influence management remuneration (Schmidt 1997; Raith 2003; Cunat and Guadalupe 2005, 2009a; Beiner et al. 2011). On the other hand, product market competition will arise managers' career concerns, which also have important implications on their decision makings (Fama 1980; Narayanan 1985; Nagar1999; Hou and Robinson 2006; Hermalin and Weisbach 2012;).

Cunat and Guadalupe (2005) find that the higher the product market competition, the more would be the incentive section of total executive pays. Cunat and Guadalupe (2005, 2009a) and Beiner et al. (2011) show that after reaching a certain level of competition in the product market, CEO pay-performance sensitivity increases with product market competition. Tian (2012) shows that lower industry concentration and more product market competition are associated with higher sensitivity of executive compensation to firm performance in Chinese firms.

Parrino (1997) finds that the more homogenous the companies in the industry, the more competitive the product market would be, and the more easily would the CEOs with poor performance identified. Also CEO turnover and the likelihood of hiring a new CEO in the industry increase with product market competition. Defond and Park (1999) find that firms in competitive industries would replace CEOs more frequently, and it is more likely relevant to accounting performance and CEO turnover. Karuna et al. (2012) find that in a more competitive market, investor supervises more closely on managers, which would increase managers' career concerns. With relative performance evaluation (RPE) is widely used, managers at competitive industry concerns more seriously about career.

Narayanan (1985) finds that managers who care about reputation have incentives to sacrifice long-term value of shareholders to improve short-term performance. Shleifer (2004) argues that competition will push firms to choose aggressive earnings management behavior. Competition could motivate managers manipulates earnings to increase stock prices. High stock prices can reduce capital cost of capital, enable managers to exercise stock options and motivate managers to perform excellent work, thus keeping firm's competitive status.

Increased competition will not only reduce profits in the current period, but also would put companies at a higher level of liquidity risk in the future (Hou and Robinson 2006). This would bring more oversight from board and more managers' turnover, thus reduce the agency cost of firms. If earnings management is available as an effective tool to distort earnings, increased product market competition would encourage managers to do so to mislead stakeholders. Hermalin and Weisbach (2012) find that managers' career concerns encourage CEOs to manipulate financial disclosure to the capital markets. Tinaikar and Xue (2009) find that when industries are confronted with earnings management of the firms in these sectors will increase. Competition will reduce a company's profitability and motivate management to distort the results of operations via earnings management to protect their private interests (Bagnoli and Watts 2010). Increased competition will encourage managers to focus on short-term goal to improve a company's prospects, thus enhance or maintain a competitive advantage (Christie et al. 2003). Fresard and Valta (2013) find that competition will cause companies to reduce capital expenditures and research cost, increase cash holdings and shares equity and reduce debt.

From a financing perspective, product market competition would reduce the company's market power and profit margins, thereby making it more difficult to gain access to external financing. Those companies in financing need would have an incentive to manipulate earning to compete for external resources. Linck et al. (2013) propose that the adoption of earning management can alleviate the financial constraints and provide access to external finance, so as to reduce investment costs of capital and increase firm value.

When the operating environment is complicated and manager's behaviors are less visible, managers who are facing intense competition would have greater motivations in decision-making and thus have more opportunities to manage earnings (Christie et al. 2003).

In sum, managers could be motivated to manage earnings to, avoid reporting losses and/or to achieve specific performance benchmark in certain circumstances. Product market competition increases the managers' pay-performance sensitivity, enhance managers' career concerns, thereby affect managers' earnings management behaviors. Thus, we propose the following hypothesis.

Hypothesis 1: Firms with more competitive products would be more likely to commit earnings management than their counterparts.

The effect of product market competition in the industry varies from company to company. Most industries have one or more recognized as the market leader(s) which have (has) a higher competitive position in the industry and can establish market price. As other companies could act more as a follower of the leader(s), they can only profit from the difference between marginal cost and market price, and thus confronted with more competition. As a buffering mechanism, firms with more pricing power have the ability to pass on the price volatility to customers and thereby reduce cash flow volatility, and reduce the need for accrual earnings management. Those firms at a pricing disadvantage have a strong motivation to manipulate earning to meet market expectations. In addition, firms may also manipulate earnings to maintain a competitive advantage. Datta et al. (2013) find that companies with less pricing power would have higher accrual levels and the industry product market competition would increase accruals within the industry. However, few studies examine the relationship between competitive advantages and real earnings management.

The literature show that firms with higher competitive position of listed companies in the industry has the higher pay-performance sensitivity. In addition, firms with more pricing power could pass the pressure of price volatility to customers to reduce cash flow volatility. From this perspective a higher competitive position could provide stronger motivations for managers to conduct earnings management via real operation activities. In sum, if a firm has a higher competitive position in the industry, it is less likely to do accrual earnings management and more likely to do real earnings management. Hence, we propose the following hypotheses:

Hypothesis 2a: Firms with more advantage are less likely to conduct accrual earnings management.
Hypothesis 2b: Firms with more advantage are more likely to conduct earnings management.

3. Research design

Earnings management model

Following the earnings management literature (Roychowdhury 2006; Cohen 2008; Cohen and Zarowin 2010), we perform an OLS regression of the following model:

$$\begin{aligned}
EM_{i,t} = {} & \beta_0 + \beta_1\, PMC_{i,t} + \beta_2\, SIZE_{i,t} + \beta_3\, INAR_{i,t} + \beta_4\, LEV_{i,t} + \beta_5\, ROA_{i,t} \\
& + \beta_6\, BIG4_{i,t} + \beta_7\, ANALYST_{i,t} + \beta_8\, M/B_{i,t} + \beta_9\, SMROE_{i,t} + \beta_{10}\, SOE_{i,t} \\
& + \beta_{11}\, SHRCR1_{i,t} + \beta_{12}\, MSHR_{i,t} + \beta_{13}\, IDR_{i,t} + \beta_{14}\, CEOCHG_{i,t} \\
& + \sum\nolimits_{j=8}^{12} \beta_{15j}\, YearDummies_j + \varepsilon_{i,t}
\end{aligned} \tag{1}$$

EM represents accrual earnings management variables (DA and |DA|) and real activity variables on earnings management (EM, AbProd, AbCFO and AbDisx). We use the modified Jones model (Bartov et al. 2000) to estimate discretionary accruals (DA and |DA|).

$$\frac{TA_{it}}{Assets_{i,t-1}} = a_1 \frac{1}{Assets_{i,t-1}} + a_2 \frac{\Delta REV_{it}}{Assets_{i,t-1}} + a_3 \frac{PPE_{it}}{Assets_{i,t-1}} + \varepsilon_{it} \qquad (2)$$

Where $Assets_{i,t-1}$ is total assets of firm i at the end of year t–1; REV_{it} is annual changes in revenues of firm i at the end of year t, and PPE_{it} is book value of property, plant and equipment of firm i at the end of year t. We run the regressions by industry and year, which yield coefficients for the following model to calculate non-discretionary accruals.

$$\frac{NDA_{it}}{Assets_{i,t-1}} = a_1 \frac{1}{Assets_{i,t-1}} + a_2 \frac{\Delta REV_{it} - \Delta REC_{it}}{Assets_{i,t-1}} + a_3 \frac{PPE_{it}}{Assets_{i,t-1}} \qquad (3)$$

Where ΔREV_{it} is changes in net receivables of firm i in year t;, and other variables are defined as. The discretionary accruals are thus calculated as the difference between the total accruals and non-discretionary accruals.

Following Roychowdhury (2006) and Cohen and Zarowin (2010), we estimate real activity earnings management using three measures: abnormal operating cash flow (AbCFO), abnormal production costs (AbProd) and abnormal discretionary fee (AbDisx). Abnormal operating cash flow (AbCFO) usually is caused by a company's price discounts and loose credit policies to promote product. Promotions can increase gross profit temporality, but it will lead abnormal operating cash flows (AbCFO) to decline. Abnormal production costs (AbProd) is caused by the abnormal manufacturing activities which can reduce the cost per unit of output, improve profit margins, thus increase company profits in the current period, but extraordinary production will increase other manufacturing cost and inventory cost, which finally lead to unusual production costs (AbProd) on the high side. Abnormal discretionary cost (AbDisx) is caused by the cut-off of research and development (R&D), selling and administration expenses in order to increase net income. It will also lead to higher net cash flow for the current period.

$$\frac{CFO_{it}}{Assets_{i,t-1}} = b_1 \frac{1}{Assets_{i,t-1}} + b_2 \frac{SALES_{it}}{Assets_{i,t-1}} + b_3 \frac{\Delta SALES_{it}}{Assets_{i,t-1}} + \varepsilon_{it} \qquad (4)$$

$$\frac{Prod_{it}}{Assets_{i,t-1}} = c_1 \frac{1}{Assets_{i,t-1}} + c_2 \frac{SALES_{it}}{Assets_{i,t-1}} + c_3 \frac{\Delta SALES_{it}}{Assets_{i,t-1}} + c_4 \frac{\Delta SALES_{i,t-1}}{Assets_{i,t-1}} + \varepsilon_{it} \qquad (5)$$

$$\frac{DISX_{it}}{Assets_{i,t-1}} = d_1 \frac{1}{Assets_{i,t-1}} + d_2 \frac{\Delta SALES_{i,t-1}}{Assets_{i,t-1}} + \varepsilon_{it} \qquad (6)$$

We use regression equations above estimate regression coefficients, and estimate normal levels of operating cash flow (CFO). Abnormal production costs (AbProd) and discretionary expenses (AbDisx), respectively. Then we calculate abnormal operating cash flows (AbCFO), abnormal production costs (AbProd) and abnormal discretionary expenses. Firms could manage up earnings through abnormal low operating cash flow (AbCFO), abnormal high production costs (AbProd), and abnormal low unexpected costs (AbDisx). Following Zang (2012), we also use an integrated measure as an index, to measure real activity earnings management (REM), which is calculated as REM = AbProd – AbCFO – AbDisx. A higher value of REM suggests a higher level of real activity earnings management.

PMC represents product market competition variables (HHI, CR4, and PCM). Herfindal – Hirschman Index (HHI) is the sum of the squared percentage of revenues of the client firm among the total revenues of all public companies each year, which is $HHI = \sum_{i=1}^{N} \left(S_i \middle/ S \right)^2$, with N is the number of listed companies in the industry, Si is the revenues for an individual firm and S is the total revenues of all public companies within the same industry. When HHI becomes close to 0, it indicates more intense competition within the industry. When HHI becomes close to 1, it indicates that the industry is controlled by a few large companies. CR4 is the operating income of the top four firms among the industry based on revenue. A larger CR4 value means a higher industry concentration and less intense competition within the industry. Lerner index (PCM) is also called as price cost margins, which measures a firm's competitive position (pricing power) in the industry. We refer to the Peress (2010) method to estimate Lerner index as net operating income divided by sales. A higher value of PCM indicates more product pricing power and a higher competitive advantage of a company.

Following earnings management literature (Roychowdhury 2006; Cohen 2008; Cohen and Zarowin 2010), we also include the following control variables. Firm size (SIZE), measured as the natural log of total assets, can have impacts on real earnings management activities. The inventory and receivables (INAR) can provide managers greater opportunities to lower cost of goods sold and manipulate sales (Roychowdhury 2006). Larger INAR values indicate higher real earnings management activities. Financial leverage (LEV), the ratio of total liabilities to total assets at the end of the end, is to control for the effects of financial needs on earnings management behavior. Generally, a higher level of indebtedness suggests a stronger motivation of earnings management. Firm profitability (ROA) and return on assets, is to control for the effects of profitability on earnings management, as a stronger profitability indicates less need for earnings management. BIG4 is a dummy variable which is coded as one if a firm is audited by the international Big 4 CPA firms and zero otherwise. Big 4 accounting firms can provide high quality audits, and thus they are more likely to deter and detect earnings management. ANALYST is measured as logarithm of (1+M), with M is the number of financial analysts issuing at least one earnings forecast for a firm during the year. More analysts following would arise more attentions about earnings management, thus helping deter or detect earnings management. We use book to market ratio to control for firm growth as real earnings management will detract firms from creating the long-term value, and firms with better growth prospects should not use active earnings management. MARGIN is a dummy for firms with small positive earnings, coded as one if a firm has ROE (return on equity) of 0–1% and zero otherwise. In firms with small earnings, there is a high likelihood that firms manage up their earnings to avoid reporting a loss. In addition, corporate governance features, such as ultimate controlling stakeholders (SOE), ownership percentage of the largest shareholder (SHRCR1), share percentage owned by managers (MSHR), share percentage owned by independent directors on the board (IDR) and CEO changes (CEOCHG), can affect earnings management and thus are included in our model as well.

Sample selection

The data used in this paper is selected from CSMAR database. We collect the observations on all publicly listed companies during 2006-2012. As change variables are used in our study, our paper focus on the observations during 2007-2012. The sample selection process is as follows: (1) delete observations on financial companies; (2) delete observations on ST listed companies; (3) delete observations on companies with negative net book value; (4) remove the observations in the industry with less than 10 observations during the observed years (wood and furniture industry); (5) delete the observations with missing data. Following this screening process, the resulted final sample is 9123 firm-year observations. In order to remove the impact of outliers on the empirical results, we truncate the data at 1% and 99%.

4. Empirical results

Descriptive statistics

The sample distribution by year is shown in Panel A of Table 6.1. The number of observations in Year 2007 is 1241, and shows an increasing trend over the subsequent years. In Year 2012, the number of observations is 2013. The sample distribution by industry is shown in Panel B of Table 6.1. There are more observations from machines, machinery and instrument industry than others while communication and cultural industry shows the lowest number of observations.

Table 6.1 Sample selection and distribution

Panel A: Sample distribution by year

Year	2007	2008	2009	2010	2011	2012	total
N	1241	1340	1410	1482	1637	2013	9123

Panel B: Observation of industry distribution

Industry code	Industry names	Number of observations
A	Agriculture, forestry, animal husbandry and fishery	202
B	Mining	185
C0	Food and beverage industry	411
C1	Textiles, clothing, fur industry	424
C2	Wood and furniture industry	0
C3	Paper and printing industry	192
C4	Petroleum, chemicals, and plastic industry	929
C5	Electronics industry	401
C6	Metalwork and non-metal minerals product industry	836
C7	Machinery, equipment and instrument industry	1617
C8	Medicines, biological products	595
C9	Other manufacturing industries	134
D	Electric power, gas and water production and supply industry	348
E	Construction industry	209
F	Transportation and warehousing	331
G	Information technology industry	652
H	Wholesale and retail trade industry	578
J	Real estate industry	305
K	Social service industry	293
L	Communication and cultural industries	32
M	Conglomerates	449
Total		9123

The descriptive statistics of the variables are shown in Table 6.2. The means of HHI and CR4 are 0.070 and 0.386, respectively, which means industry concentration on average is lower in China, product market competition is more intense. The mean and the standard deviation of PCM are 0.105 and 0.141 respectively, similar with prior studies. The mean of |DA| is 0.069, ranging from the minimum value is 0.001 to the maximum value of 0.358; while the mean of REM is −0.043, ranging from −1.106 to 0.951, which indicates companies use real activities to manipulate earnings in both directions − some manage up earnings while others manage down earnings. Abnormal operating cash flow (AbCFO), abnormal production costs (AbProd), abnormal discretionary expenses (AbDisx) have a mean of 0.010, −0.025 and 0.008, respectively. LEV has a mean of 0.490, indicating higher level of average debt ratios of listed companies in China; the BIG4 mean value is 0.063, showing that about 6.3% listed companies are audited by Big 4 CPA firms in China; MARGIN has a mean of 0.047, indicating that there are about 4.7% of listed companies are making a marginal amount of profit; SHRCR1 has a mean of 36%, which means that the first big shareholder holds on average 36% of ownership in the emerging markets. MSHARE has a mean of 0.03%, indicating executives hold lower percentage of ownership in Chinese listed company; IDR has a mean of 0.365, showing independent directors takes up one third of a board; CEOCHG is about 0.189, indicating about one-fifth observations have CEO changes incurred during the year.

In the correlation matrix shown in Table 6.3, DA and |DA| are negatively correlated with market concentration variables (HHI and CR4), indicating that firms confronted with higher

Table 6.2 Descriptive statistics for variables used in earnings management model

Variable	N	Mean	Std. Dev	Minimum	Maximum
DA	9123	0.010	0.095	−0.274	0.324
|DA|	9123	0.069	0.069	0.001	0.358
REM	9123	−0.043	0.3 01	−1.106	0.951
AbCFO	9123	0.010	0.102	−0.325	0.333
AbProd	9123	−0.025	0.189	−0.741	0.647
AbDisx	9123	0.008	0.079	−0.260	0.354
HHI	9123	0.070	0.061	0.020	0.362
CR4	9123	0.386	0.160	0.196	0.898
PCM	9123	0.105	0.141	−0.397	0.559
SIZE	9123	21.797	1.219	19.273	25.416
INAR	9123	0.271	0.181	0.004	0.782
LEV	9123	0.490	0.199	0.056	0.888
ROA	9123	0.061	0.076	−2.682	1.175
BIG4	9123	0.063	0.243	0	1
ANALYST	9123	1.440	1.141	0	3.664
M/B	9123	4.496	3.958	0.807	26.376
SMROE	9123	0.047	0.211	0	1
SOE	9123	0.221	0.415	0	1
SHRCR1	9123	35.977	15.421	8.630	75.840
MSHARE	9123	0.030	0.103	0	0.565
IDR	9123	0.365	0.053	0.091	0.714
CEOCHG	9123	0.189	0.391	0	1

Table 6.3 Pearson's correlation matrix

Pearson correlation matrix for variables used in earnings management model

	(1)	(2)	(3)	(4)	(5)	(6)	(7)	(8)	(9)	(10)	(11)
DA	1.0000										
|DA|	0.2016	1.0000									
	<.0001										
REM	0.2785	0.0920	1.0000								
	<.0001	<.0001									
AbCFO	−0.5965	−0.1397	−0.6675	1.0000							
	<.0001	<.0001	<.0001								
AbProd	0.0940	0.0825	0.9080	−0.4358	1.0000						
	<.0001	<.0001	<.0001	<.0001							
AbDisx	−0.0367	0.0179	−0.6055	0.1788	−0.4173	1.0000					
	0.0005	0.0879	<.0001	<.0001	<.0001						
HHI	−0.0126	−0.0134	−0.0459	0.0304	−0.0372	0.0342	1.0000				
	0.2292	0.2023	<.0001	0.0037	0.0004	0.0011					
CR4	−0.0065	−0.0187	−0.0508	0.0346	−0.0408	0.0359	0.9241	1.0000			
	0.5371	0.0735	<.0001	0.0010	<.0001	0.0006	<.0001				
PCM	0.2219	0.0479	−0.2579	0.2768	−0.2184	0.1045	0.1059	0.1335	1.0000		
	<.0001	<.0001	<.0001	<.0001	<.0001	<.0001	<.0001	<.0001			
MKT	−0.0264	−0.0072	0.0326	−0.0171	0.0430	−0.0012	0.1277	0.1579	0.0098	1.0000	
	0.0117	0.4917	0.0018	0.1023	<.0001	0.9093	<.0001	<.0001	0.3515		
SIZE	0.0598	−0.0238	−0.0345	0.0610	0.0347	0.1252	0.1258	0.1216	0.2162	0.4545	1.0000
	<.0001	0.0231	0.0010	<.0001	0.0009	<.0001	<.0001	<.0001	<.0001	<.0001	
INAR	0.2022	0.1910	0.2471	−0.2658	0.2131	−0.0683	−0.0072	0.0001	0.0612	0.0172	0.0049
	<.0001	<.0001	<.0001	<.0001	<.0001	<.0001	0.4902	0.9940	<.0001	0.1004	0.6416
LEV	−0.1097	0.0878	0.1880	−0.1428	0.2052	−0.0405	−0.0035	0.0111	−0.1296	0.1636	0.3845
	<.0001	<.0001	<.0001	<.0001	<.0001	0.0001	0.7413	0.2887	<.0001	<.0001	<.0001
ROA	0.2452	0.0310	−0.3107	0.2646	−0.2894	0.1414	0.0360	0.0135	0.5043	0.0315	0.0948
	<.0001	0.0031	<.0001	<.0001	<.0001	<.0001	0.0006	0.1988	<.0001	0.0026	<.0001
BIG4	−0.0300	−0.0390	−0.0735	0.0806	−0.0410	0.0727	0.0563	0.0467	0.0757	0.3207	0.3761
	0.0042	0.0002	<.0001	<.0001	<.0001	<.0001	<.0001	<.0001	<.0001	<.0001	<.0001
ANALYST	0.1175	−0.0410	−0.2576	0.1850	−0.2051	0.2428	0.0936	0.0671	0.3480	0.2324	0.5080
	<.0001	<.0001	<.0001	<.0001	<.0001	<.0001	<.0001	<.0001	<.0001	<.0001	<.0001
M/B	0.0420	0.1454	−0.0549	0.0052	−0.0805	0.0213	0.0059	−0.0136	0.0007	−0.0676	−0.2350
	<.0001	<.0001	<.0001	0.6223	<.0001	0.0421	0.5734	0.1926	0.9487	<.0001	<.0001
SMROE	−0.0411	−0.0499	0.0669	−0.0400	0.0626	−0.0509	−0.0273	−0.0307	−0.1314	−0.0312	−0.0273
	<.0001	<.0001	<.0001	0.0001	<.0001	<.0001	0.0092	0.0034	<.0001	0.0028	0.0092
SOE	−0.0197	−0.0538	0.0222	−0.0259	0.0323	0.0080	−0.0015	−0.0155	−0.0510	0.0273	0.1283
	0.0594	<.0001	0.0344	0.0134	0.0021	0.4465	0.8831	0.1394	<.0001	0.0091	<.0001
SHRCR1	0.0315	0.0332	0.0150	0.0205	0.0383	0.0122	0.0882	0.0641	0.1606	0.1234	0.2956
	0.0026	0.0015	0.1523	0.0500	0.0003	0.2427	<.0001	<.0001	<.0001	<.0001	<.0001
MSHARE	0.0549	−0.0362	−0.0174	−0.0219	−0.0307	0.0210	0.0066	0.0044	0.0472	−0.0775	−0.1570
	<.0001	0.0005	0.0960	0.0366	0.0033	0.0448	0.5264	0.6732	<.0001	<.0001	<.0001
IDR	0.0111	0.0151	0.0082	−0.0242	0.0058	0.0052	0.0334	0.0394	0.0046	0.0271	0.0435
	0.2903	0.1497	0.4315	0.0210	0.5769	0.6215	0.0014	0.0002	0.6622	0.0098	<.0001
CEOCHG	−0.0396	0.0593	0.0205	−0.0070	0.0268	0.0063	−0.0110	−0.0115	−0.0339	−0.0207	−0.0319
	0.0002	<.0001	0.0506	0.5059	0.0105	0.5456	0.2935	0.2716	0.0012	0.0476	0.0023

(12)	(13)	(14)	(15)	(16)	(17)	(18)	(19)	(20)	(21)	(22)	(23)
1.0000											
0.2577	1.0000										
<.0001											
–0.0474	–0.2270	1.0000									
<.0001	<.0001										
–0.0577	0.0576	0.0537	1.0000								
<.0001	<.0001	<.0001									
–0.0413	–0.0642	0.3427	0.2307	1.0000							
<.0001	<.0001	<.0001	<.0001								
0.0237	0.0681	0.1273	–0.0503	–0.0070	1.0000						
0.0235	<.0001	<.0001	<.0001	0.5058							
–0.0338	–0.0311	–0.1207	–0.0214	–0.1223	–0.0616	1.0000					
0.0012	0.0030	<.0001	0.0413	<.0001	<.0001						
–0.0108	0.0839	–0.0433	0.0822	0.0046	–0.0500	0.0217	1.0000				
0.3045	<.0001	<.0001	<.0001	0.6625	<.0001	0.0382					
0.0322	0.0663	0.0838	0.1301	0.1712	–0.0381	–0.0365	0.1276	1.0000			
0.0021	<.0001	<.0001	<.0001	<.0001	0.0003	0.0005	<.0001				
0.0332	–0.2671	0.0298	–0.0642	0.1105	–0.0257	–0.0320	–0.1454	–0.0753	1.0000		
0.0015	<.0001	0.0044	<.0001	<.0001	0.0142	0.0023	<.0001	<.0001			
0.0317	–0.0170	–0.0131	0.0331	–0.0002	0.0172	0.0065	–0.0431	0.0402	0.0398	1.0000	
0.0025	0.1039	0.2109	0.0016	0.9846	0.1010	0.5382	<.0001	0.0001	0.0001		
0.0027	0.0415	–0.0443	–0.0273	–0.1003	0.0323	0.0149	0.0057	0.0202	–0.0340	0.0098	1.0000
0.7973	<.0001	<.0001	0.0092	<.0001	0.0020	0.1542	0.5834	0.0543	0.0012	0.3508	

market concentration and less competitive markets are more likely to have lower accrual earnings management. DA and |DA| are positively correlated with price cost margin (PCM), indicating firms with stronger pricing power in the industry are associated with higher accrual earnings management. DA and |DA| are negatively correlated with market share (MKT), which indicates firms with higher market share in the industry are associated with lower accrual earnings management.

HHI (CR4) has a significant and negative correlation with REM and AbProd but a significant and positive one with AbCFO and AbDisx, indicating that firms with higher industry market concentration and lower competitive product market tend to have lower real earnings management. Similarly, market share (MKT) has a positive correlation with real earnings management activities (REM) and abnormal production costs (AbProd), while a negative correlation with abnormal operating cash flow (AbCFO) and abnormal discretionary expenses (AbDisx) shows firms with higher market share in the industry tend to have higher real earnings management activities. PCM has a significant and negative correlation with REM and AbProd but a positive one with AbCFO and AbDisx, indicating that firms with higher competitive position in the industry or stronger pricing power tend to have lower real earnings management activities.

DA and |DA| are positively correlated with REM and AbPROD and negatively correlated with AbCFO and AbDisx, which is consistent with prior studies on accrual earnings management and real earnings management activities (e.g., Cohen and Zarowin 2010; Zang 2012). In addition, the correlations between control variables and earnings management variables are consistent with prior results. INAR, ROA, ANALYS, M/B, SHRCR1, and MSHARE have positive correlations with REM and AbProd and negative correlations with AbCFO and AbDisx, indicating firms with higher inventory and accounts receivables, reporting higher profits, more analyst followings, higher market-to-book ratio, and higher stakeholder and management ownership tend to do earnings management through real activities to achieve specific performance goals. In contrast, State-owned firms with more debts, Big 4 auditors, marginal profits and CEO switches are less likely to do real earnings management, as LEV, BIG4, MARGIN, SOE and CEOCHG have negative correlations with REM and AbProd and positive correlations with AbCFO and AbDisx. All the correlation coefficients among the explanatory variables and controlled variables are lower than 0.40, which means that multicollinearity of regression models is not a major problem, except those between PCM and ROA, MKT and SIZE, ANALYS and SIZE.

To address the possible multicollinearity issues in the regression models, we also calculate VIF scores. None of those are exceeding 10, suggesting that our empirical results are not seriously affected by any potential multicollinearity issues.

Product market competition and earnings management

The multiple regression results on the relationship between product market competition and accrual earnings management are shown in Table 6.4. Discretionary accrual variables (DA and |DA|) and market competition variables (HHI, CR4) are significantly and negatively related, indicating that firms in higher market concentration industry and less product competitive market have lower accrual earnings management. As sensitivity tests, we also perform separate analyses for the groups with positive DA and negative DA (results are not tabled). In the positive DA group, HHI and CR4 have significant and negative coefficients while insignificant in the negative DA group. This indicates that industry concentration effect on accrual earnings management is mainly appear in the firms who manage up their earnings via accruals.

Table 6.4 also shows positive and significant coefficients on PCM but negative ones on MKT, indicating that firms with more pricing power and firms with less market shares in the industry

Table 6.4 Product market competition and accrual earnings management

	DA				|DA|			
	(1)	(2)	(3)	(4)	(5)	(6)	(7)	(8)
HHI	−0.056★★★				−0.020★			
	(3.64)				(−1.77)			
CR4		−0.014★★				−0.010★★		
		(2.35)				(−2.17)		
PCM			0.056★★★				0.017★★★	
			(7.05)				(2.90)	
MKT				−0.220★★★				−0.03
				(6.14)				(−1.09)
SIZE	0.014★★★	0.014★★★	0.013★★★	0.016★★★	0.003★★★	0.003★★★	0.002★★★	0.003★★★
	(11.75)	(11.62)	(10.52)	(12.79)	(3.22)	(3.27)	(2.69)	(3.25)
INAR	0.134★★★	0.134★★★	0.129★★★	0.135★★★	0.070★★★	0.071★★★	0.069★★★	0.071★★★
	(24.87)	(24.85)	(23.82)	(25.1)	(17.39)	(17.40)	(16.88)	(17.41)
LEV	−0.095★★★	−0.094★★★	−0.089★★★	−0.095★★★	0.001	0.001	0.002	0.001
	(15.51)	(15.41)	(−14.51)	(15.58)	(0.10)	(0.10)	(0.51)	(0.16)
ROA	0.247★★★	0.247★★★	0.204★★★	0.244★★★	0.022★★	0.021★★	0.008	0.021★★
	(18.05)	(18.04)	(13.67)	(17.86)	(2.09)	(2.08)	(0.74)	(2.07)
BIG4	−0.027★★★	−0.027★★★	−0.027★★★	−0.023★★★	−0.009★★★	−0.009★★★	−0.008★★★	−0.008★★
	(6.63)	(6.63)	(6.43)	(5.47)	(2.73)	(−2.74)	(−2.64)	(−2.50)
ANALYST	−0.002★★	−0.002★★	−0.003★★★	−0.002★★	−0.003★★★	−0.003★★★	−0.003★★★	−0.003★★★
	(2.04)	(2.10)	(2.75)	(2.09)	(3.62)	(3.67)	(−3.90)	(3.64)
M/B	0.001★★★	0.001★★★	0.001★★★	0.001★★★	0.003★★★	0.003★★★	0.003★★★	0.003★★★
	(4.81)	(4.71)	(4.76)	(5.01)	(13.43)	(13.41)	(13.40)	(13.40)
SMROE	−0.005	−0.005	−0.002	−0.005	−0.011★★★	−0.011★★★	−0.010★★★	−0.011★★★
	(−1.09)	(−1.08)	(−0.51)	(−1.13)	(−3.22)	(−3.25)	(2.98)	(3.21)
SOE	0.001	0.001	0.002	0.001	−0.007★★★	−0.007★★★	−0.007★★★	−0.007★★★
	(0.46)	(0.44)	(0.87)	(0.32)	(4.07)	(4.10)	(−3.90)	(4.08)
SHRCR1	−0.001	−0.001	−0.001★★	−0.001	0.001★★★	0.001★★★	0.001★★★	0.001★★★
	(1.31)	(1.42)	(−2.06)	(1.62)	(3.14)	(3.12)	(2.81)	(3.04)
MSHARE	0.023★★	0.022★★	0.021★★	0.023★★	−0.006	−0.006	−0.007	−0.007
	(2.27)	(2.22)	(2.07)	(2.27)	(−0.85)	(−0.85)	(−0.94)	(−0.88)
IDR	−0.002	−0.002	−0.003	−0.003	0.012	0.012	0.011	0.011
	(−0.10)	(−0.12)	(−0.15)	(−0.15)	(0.89)	(0.91)	(0.86)	(0.85)
CEOCHG	−0.006★★	−0.006★★	−0.006★★	−0.006★★	0.008★★★	0.008★★★	0.008★★★	0.008★★★
	(−2.50)	(−2.50)	(2.51)	(2.54)	(4.42)	(4.41)	(4.42)	(4.42)
Intercept	−0.296★★★	−0.291★★★	−0.270★★★	−0.339★★★	−0.02	−0.018	−0.011	−0.024
	(12.04)	(11.86)	(10.95)	(13.15)	(1.05)	(0.98)	(−0.59)	(−1.22)
Year Dummies	YES	YES	YES	YES	YES	YES	YES	YES
Adj. R^2	0.136	0.135	0.139	0.138	0.076	0.076	0.077	0.076
N	9123	9123	9123	9123	9123	9123	9123	9123

have higher accrual earnings management,. As sensitivity tests, we also perform separate analyses for the groups with positive DA and negative DA (results are not tabled). In the positive DA group, the coefficient of PCM is not significant while it is significant in negative DA group, indicating the firms with stronger pricing power in the industry are more likely to do accrual earnings management to reduce earnings.

The regression coefficient on MKT is significant and negative when DA is the dependent variable, while it is not significant when |DA| is the dependent variable. As sensitivity tests, we also perform separate analyses for the groups with positive DA and negative DA (results are not tabled). The significant regression coefficient of MKT is significantly negative in positive DA samples, but not significant in negative DA samples. Thus, it suggests that firms with higher market shares in the industry are less likely to do accrual earnings management, and such an effect mainly appears in firms who manage their earnings via accruals.

Table 6.5 presents the multiple regression results on the relationship between product market competition and real earnings management. In Panel A, the product market

Table 6.5 Product market competition and real activity earnings management

Panel A: Product market competition and real activity earnings management index (REM)

	Pre.	(1)	(2)	(3)	(4)
HHI	–	−0.125★★★			
		(−2.64)			
CR4			−0.084★★★		
			(4.66)		
PCM	–			−0.309★★★	
				(12.70)	
MKT					0.757★★★
					(6.86)
SIZE	?	0.015★★★	0.016★★★	0.020★★★	0.001
		(4.13)	(4.34)	(5.42)	(0.35)
INAR	+	0.348★★★	0.348★★★	0.374★★★	0.346★★★
		(21.03)	(21.07)	(22.62)	(21.01)
LEV	+	0.087★★★	0.085★★★	0.064★★★	0.103★★★
		(4.61)	(4.56)	(3.41)	(5.54)
ROA	–	−0.858★★★	−0.861★★★	−0.620★★★	−0.827★★★
		(20.40)	(20.47)	(13.57)	(19.65)
BIG4	–	−0.041★★★	−0.041★★★	−0.045★★★	−0.055★★★
		(3.19)	(3.21)	(3.57)	(4.28)
ANALYST	–	−0.056★★★	−0.056★★★	−0.052★★★	−0.052★★★
		(16.51)	(16.61)	(15.33)	(15.11)
M/B	–	−0.003★★★	−0.003★★★	−0.003★★★	−0.011★★★
		(−3.25)	(−3.25)	(3.55)	(5.84)
WEILI	+	0.036★★★	0.035★★	0.024★	0.037★★★
		(2.63)	(2.55)	(1.79)	(2.69)
SOE	+	0.002	0.002	0.002	0.005
		(0.34)	(0.25)	(0.30)	(0.67)

	Pre.	(1)	(2)	(3)	(4)
SHRCR1	+	0.001***	0.001***	0.001***	0.001***
		(4.88)	(4.90)	(5.83)	(4.94)
MSHARE	+	0.081***	0.082***	0.085***	0.074**
		(2.64)	(2.66)	(2.79)	(2.40)
IDR	−	−0.038	−0.034	−0.045	−0.040
		(−0.70)	(−0.63)	(−0.84)	(−0.73)
CEOCHG	−	−0.007	−0.007	−0.007	−0.006
		(−0.99)	(1.01)	(−0.92)	(−0.82)
Intercept	?	−0.407***	−0.400***	−0.501***	−0.114
		(5.37)	(5.31)	(−6.65)	(−1.38)
YearDummies		YES	YES	YES	YES
Adj.R²		0.1901	0.1915	0.2036	0.195
N		9123	9123	9123	9123

Panel B: Product market competition and abnormal production costs (AbProd)

	Pre.	(1)	(2)	(3)	(4)
HHI	−	−0.083***			
		(−2.74)			
CR4	−		−0.050***		
			(4.35)		
	−			−0.158***	
				(−10.11)	
	−				0.281***
					(3.97)
SIZE	?	0.017***	0.018***	0.020***	0.011***
		(7.26)	(7.43)	(8.22)	(4.24)
INAR	+	0.183***	0.184***	0.197***	0.184***
		(17.34)	(17.37)	(18.54)	(17.41)
LEV	+	0.064***	0.063***	0.052***	0.072***
		(5.31)	(5.27)	(4.38)	(6.00)
ROA	−	−0.514***	−0.515***	−0.392***	−0.499***
		(19.10)	(19.16)	(13.38)	(18.51)
BIG4	−	−0.022***	−0.022***	−0.025***	−0.028***
		(2.73)	(2.75)	(3.02)	(3.36)
ANALYST	−	−0.030***	−0.030***	−0.028***	−0.028***
		(13.99)	(14.09)	(13.02)	(12.68)
M/B	−	−0.002***	−0.002***	−0.002***	−0.007***
		(4.08)	(4.09)	(4.02)	(6.04)
WEILI	+	0.023***	0.022**	0.017*	0.023***
		(2.61)	(2.54)	(1.95)	(2.63)

(*Continued*)

Table 6.5 (Continued)

	Pre.	(1)	(2)	(3)	(4)
SOE	+	0.001	0.001	0.001	0.002
		(0.19)	(0.11)	(0.32)	(0.43)
SHRCR1	+	0.001★★★	0.001★★★	0.001★★★	0.001★★★
		(5.01)	(5.01)	(5.72)	(4.97)
MSHARE	+	0.047★★	0.047★★	0.049★★	0.043★★
		(2.38)	(2.40)	(2.48)	(2.20)
IDR	−	−0.028	−0.026	−0.032	−0.029
		(−0.80)	(−0.74)	(−0.93)	(−0.84)
CEOCHG	−	0.001	0.001	0.001	0.001
		(0.11)	(0.09)	(0.18)	(0.24)
Intercept	?	−0.415★★★	−0.410★★★	−0.461★★★	−0.280★★★
		(8.57)	(−8.50)	(−9.54)	(5.26)
YearDummies		YES	YES	YES	YES
Adj.R^2		0.1616	0.1626	0.1702	0.164
N		9123	9123	9123	9123

Panel C: Product market competition and abnormal operating cash flow (AbCFO)

	Pre.	(1)	(2)	(3)	(4)
HHI	+	0.020			
		(1.23)			
CR4			0.017★★★		
			(2.71)		
PCM	+			0.156★★★	
				(18.69)	
MKT					−0.217★★★
					(−5.66)
SIZE	?	−0.002	−0.002	−0.004★★★	0.002
		(1.21)	(−1.36)	(3.37)	(1.16)
INAR	−	−0.135★★★	−0.135★★★	−0.148★★★	−0.133★★★
		(23.44)	(23.46)	(26.03)	(23.26)
LEV	−	−0.016★★	−0.015★★	−0.003	−0.019★★★
		(−2.39)	(2.34)	(−0.48)	(−2.99)
ROA	+	0.281★★★	0.282★★★	0.162★★★	0.275★★★
		(19.29)	(19.32)	(10.30)	(18.81)
BIG4	+	0.017★★★	0.017★★★	0.019★★★	0.021★★★
		(3.74)	(3.76)	(4.34)	(4.61)
ANALYST	+	0.010★★★	0.010★★★	0.008★★★	0.009★★★
		(8.27)	(8.32)	(6.54)	(7.79)
M/B	+	−0.001	−0.001	−0.001	0.001
		(−0.59)	(−0.60)	(0.31)	(0.91)

	Pre.	(1)	(2)	(3)	(4)
WEILI	–	−0.006	−0.006	−0.001	−0.006
		(−1.23)	(1.18)	(−0.06)	(1.31)
SOE	–	−0.007★★	−0.007★★	−0.005★	−0.008★★★
		(2.87)	(2.82)	(−1.94)	(3.06)
SHRCR1	–	−0.001	−0.001	−0.001★★	−0.000
		(−0.75)	(−0.77)	(−2.23)	(−0.84)
MSHARE	–	−0.047★★★	−0.047★★★	−0.049★★★	−0.045★★★
		(4.35)	(4.38)	(4.69)	(4.20)
IDR	+	−0.026	−0.027	−0.024	−0.026
		(−1.39)	(1.44)	(−1.29)	(−1.37)
CEOCHG	+	0.004	0.004	0.004	0.004
		(1.54)	(1.56)	(1.47)	(1.43)
Intercept	?	0.070★★★	0.070★★★	0.123★★★	0.006
		(2.67)	(2.66)	(4.75)	(0.20)
YearDummies		YES	YES	YES	YES
Adj.R²		0.1482	0.1487	0.1795	0.151
N		9123	9123	9123	9123

Panel D: Product market competition and abnormal discretionary expenses (AbDisx)

Abdisx	Pre.				
HHI	+	0.007			
		(0.53)			
CR4	+		0.009★		
			(1.88)		
PCM	+			0.001	
				(0.16)	
MKT	+				−0.251★★★
					(8.12)
SIZE	?	0.003★★★	0.003★★★	0.003★★★	0.008★★★
		(3.08)	(2.94)	(3.15)	(6.79)
INAR	–	−0.021★★★	−0.021★★★	−0.021★★★	−0.021★★★
		(4.53)	(4.55)	(4.48)	(4.44)
LEV	–	−0.010★	−0.010★	−0.010★	−0.015★★★
		(−1.91)	(−1.86)	(−1.95)	(−2.89)
ROA	+	0.053★★★	0.053★★★	0.054★★★	0.042★★★
		(4.47)	(4.50)	(4.14)	(3.59)
BIG4	+	0.002	0.002	0.002	0.007★
		(0.59)	(0.60)	(0.58)	(1.91)
ANALYST	+	0.016★★★	0.016★★★	0.016★★★	0.014★★★
		(16.46)	(16.49)	(16.40)	(14.88)

(*Continued*)

Table 6.5 (Continued)

Abdisx	Pre.				
M/B	+	0.001★★★	0.001★★★	0.001★★★	0.003★★★
		(3.69)	(3.67)	(3.72)	(6.85)
WEILI	−	−0.007★★	−0.006★	−0.007★	−0.007★
		(−1.72)	(−1.68)	(−1.74)	(−1.74)
SOE	−	0.002	0.002	0.002	0.001
		(0.96)	(1.00)	(0.94)	(0.60)
SHRCR1	−	−0.001★★★	−0.001★★★	−0.001★★★	−0.000★★★
		(4.10)	(4.13)	(4.06)	(4.30)
MSHARE	−	0.008	0.008	0.009	0.010
		(0.97)	(0.95)	(0.99)	(1.20)
IDR	+	0.020	0.019	0.020	0.019
		(1.29)	(1.25)	(1.30)	(1.26)
CEOCHG	+	0.006★★★	0.006★★★	0.006★★★	0.006★★★
		(2.90)	(2.91)	(2.89)	(2.72)
Intercept	?	−0.069★★★	−0.069★★★	−0.070★★★	−0.163★★★
		(−3.23)	(−3.23)	(3.27)	(7.01)
YearDummies		YES	YES	YES	YES
Adj.R^2		0.0805	0.0808	0.0804	0.090
N		9123	9123	9123	9123

competition variables (HHI and CR4) are negatively and significantly related to real earnings management measure (REM), indicating that firms with lower market concentration and more competitive product market tend to have higher real earnings management activities. In Panels B, C and D, product market competition variable (CR4) is negatively and significantly related to abnormal production costs (AbProd), positively and significantly related to abnormal operating cash flow (AbCFO) and negatively and significantly related to abnormal discretionary expenditures (AbDisx), which further confirms the results on the relationship between CR4 and REM in Panel A of Table 6.5. The other product market competition variable (HHI) shows similar signs, however, its coefficients in Panels C and D are not significant.

Panel A of Table 6.5 also shows that firm's price cost margin variable (PCM) is negatively and significantly while market share variable (MKT) is positively related to real earnings management measure (REM), indicating that firms with more pricing power in the industry tend to have higher real earnings management activities while firms with more market share in the industry tend to have lower real earnings management. In Panels B, C and D, price cost margin variable (PCM) is negatively and significantly related to abnormal production costs (AbProd), positively and significantly related to abnormal operating cash flow (AbCFO) – which further confirms the results on the relationship between PCM and REM in Panel A – but insignificantly related to abnormal discretionary expenditures (AbDisx). Further, in Panels B, C and D, market share variable (MKT) is positively related to abnormal production costs (AbProd), negatively and significantly related to abnormal operating cash flow (AbCFO) and positively and significantly related to abnormal discretionary expenditures (AbDisx), which further confirms the results on the relationship between MKT and REM in Panel A of Table 6.5.

In addition, in Panel A, the regression coefficients on SIZE, LEV, INAR, MARGIN, SOE, SHRCR1, and MSHARE are significant and positive, indicating firms with larger size, higher levels of inventory and accounts receivable, higher debt ratio, marginal income, higher stakeholder ownership and higher management ownership are more likely have more real earnings management of activities. In contrast, the regression coefficients on ROA, BIG4, ANALYS, IDR, CEOCHG and M/B are significant and negative, indicating firms with more reported profitability, BIG 4 auditors, more analyst followings, more independent directors, CEO changes and market to book ratios are more likely to have more real earnings management of activities. Panels B through D further confirm these findings.

Robustness testing

We perform the following robustness tests:

First, we divide industries into ten groups based on the value of HHI (CR4) and then assign a score of 0–9 to each group accordingly. Using such a market concentration degree ranking for industries (HHI_R and CR4_R), instead of the continuous variables (HHI and CR4), we repeat the regressions and the results are qualitatively the same as those reported. Similarly, we divide firms in the same industry into ten groups based on the value of MKT (PCM) and then assign a score of 0–9 to each group accordingly. Using such competitive positions ranking variables (PCM_R and MKT_R) instead of the continuous variables (PCM and MKT), we find similar results as reported.

Second, in our primary tests above, we use sales to calculate the variables on HHI, CR4 and MKT. As an alternative measure, we use total assets as a basis to calculate market competition concentration (HHI and CR4) and firms' competitive position (MKT) and reperform all the analyses. The results are qualitatively the same as reported.

Third, we use the number of listed companies in the industry as an alternative measure of market competition, and the results are qualitatively the same as those reported. In addition, based on HHI and the number of listed companies in the industry, we build general Herfindal-Hirschman Index (N_HHI, Normalized Herfindahl-Hirshman Index), which is calculated as (HHI-1)/(N-1), as an alternative measure of product market competition. The same approach is also used in Balakrishnan and Cohen (2011). The empirical results with this new measure are essentially the same as reported above.

Fourth, we use the reciprocal of the number of listed companies in the industry to measure the degree of competition in the product market. The results are also qualitatively the same as reported earlier.

Fifth, we include both industry concentration variable (HHI or CR4) and competitive position variable (PCM or MKT) to the same regression model to test whether the impacts of market competition and firm's competitive position on earnings management are still significant if we control one another. The results are qualitatively the same as reported.

Finally, as an alternative measure of firm's competitive position, we use abnormal value of PCM scores (APCM), which is calculated as the difference between a firm's PCM value minus the industry average (PCMi − PCMmean). A higher APCM value represents a higher competitive position in the industry. The regression results with this alternative measure are essentially the same as those reported earlier.

5. Conclusions

Using a sample of observations from the Chinese public companies for the period of 2007–2012, we find that firms confronted with more product market competition are associated with more earnings management. In addition, when a firm is ranked at a higher competitive position in the industry with stronger pricing power, it is less likely to commit accrual earnings management and more likely to manage earnings via real activities.

Our study is not free of limitations. Since our sample includes only selected listed companies, it may not be a good representative of its whole industry. As used in the essay, product market competition measures are based on the observations of listed company data. To the degree that the competition among listed companies in the same industry may not represent the competition in the whole industry, our conclusion may be biased in reflecting the real competition situation in the industry, in particular the competition with or among private companies.

Appendix
VARIABLE DEFINITION

Variable	Definition
Measures of Earnings management	
DA	Discretionary accruals
|DA|	Absolute value of discretionary accruals
AbCFO	Abnormal operating cash flows
AbDisx	Abnormal discretionary expenses
AbProd	Abnormal production costs
REM	An integrated measure of real earnings management. Following Zang (2012), it is calculated as AbProd − AbCFO − AbDisx
Measures of Product market competition	
HHI	Herfindahl–Hirschman index, calculated as the sum of squared market share (Si/S), Si is firm i's revenue, S represents the total revenues in the industry. A small Herfindahl–Hirschman index indicates high competition intensity in the industry.
CR4	The operating income of the top four companies ranked among the industry divided by the total revenue in the industry, Si is firm i's revenues, S represents the total operating revenues. A small CR4 value indicates high industry concentration, and low competition within the industry.
PCM	Price cost margin, calculated as (operating revenue − cost of business − selling expenses − administrative expenses)/operating revenues. It is an approximation of the Lerner index. A higher PCM value represents a higher market power and higher competitive advantage of a company.
MKT	A company's market share based on its revenue divided by total revenues of the industry in the year
Control Variables	
SIZE	Firm size, measures as the natural log of total assets
ROA	Total return on assets, calculated as (net income + interest expenses)/total assets

(Continued)

(Continued)

Variable	Definition
LEV	Leverage ratio, calculated as total liabilities to total assets at the end of the year
DUAL	A dummy variable for CEO's duality, coded as 1 if CEO is the Chairman of the board of directors, and zero otherwise
MSHARE	Managers' percentage of stock share
INAR	Inventory and receivables divided by total assets
SOE	If the ultimate controller is the country, SOE=1, or zero
IDR	Percentage of independent directors in the Board of Directors
SHRCR1	Percentage of company's largest shareholder
BIG4	Dummy variable for auditors, coded as one if a firm is audited by Big 4 international CPA firms, and zero otherwise.
ANALYS	Analysts following, measured as logarithm of (1+M), whereas M is the number of financial analysts who have issued at least one earnings forecast in the specific year
M/B	Market to book ratio
SMROE	Dummy variable for firms with small net income, coded as one if a firm has a ROE (return on equity) of 0–1%, and zero otherwise.
CEOCHG	Dummy variable for CEO change, coded as one if a firm has changed their CEO in year t and zero otherwise.

References

Bagnoli, M., and S. G. Watts. 2010. Oligopoly, Disclosure, and Earnings Management. *The Accounting Review* 85(4), 1191–1214.

Balakrishnan, K., and D. Cohen. 2011. *Product market competition and financial accounting misreporting.* Working paper, University of Pennsylvania and University of Texas, Dallas, TX. Available from: https://scholar.google.com/scholar?hl=en&q=+Balakrishnan%2C+K.+and+Cohen%2C+D.+%282011%29%2C+%E2%80%9CProduct+market+competition+and+financial+accounting+misreporting%E2%80%9D%2C+Working+paper%2C+University+of+Pennsylvania+and+University+of+Texas%2C+Dallas%2C+TX.

Bartov, E., F. A. Gul and J. S. L. Tsui. 2000. Discretionary-Accruals Models and Audit Qualifications. *Journal of Accounting and Economics* 30(3), 421–452.

Beiner, S., M. Schmid, and C. Wanzenried. 2011. Product Market Competition, Managerial Incentives and Firm Valuation. *European Financial Management* 17(2), 331–366.

Bergstresser, D., and T. Philippon. 2006. CEO Incentives and Earnings Management. *Journal of Financial Economics* 80(3), 511–529.

Burgstahler, D., and I. Dichev. 1997. Earnings Management to Avoid Earnings Decreases and Losses. *Journal of Accounting and Economics* 24(1), 99–126.

Burgstahler, D., and M. Eames. 2006. Management of Earnings and Analysts' Forecasts to Achieve Zero and Small Positive Earnings Surprises. *Journal of Business Finance & Accounting* 33(5–6), 633–652.

Christie, A. A., M. P. Joye, and R. L. Watts. 2003. Decentralization of the Firm: Theory and Evidence. *Journal of Corporate Finance* 9(1), 3–36.

Cohen, D., A. Dey, and T. Z. Lys. 2007. *Real and Accrual-based Earnings Management in the Pre- and Post-Sarbanes Oxley Periods. The Accounting Review* 83(3), 757–787

Cohen, D., and P. Zarowin. 2010. Accrual-based and Real Earnings Management Activities Around Seasoned Equity Offerings. *Journal of Accounting and Economics* 50(1), 2–19.

Cunat, V., and M. Guadalupe. 2005. How Does Product Market Competition Shape Incentive Contracts? *Journal of the European Economic Association* 3, 1058–1082.

Cunat, V., and M. Guadalupe. 2009a. Executive Compensation and Competition in the Banking and Financial Sectors. *Journal of Banking & Finance* 33(3), 495–504.

Cunat, V., and M. Guadalupe. 2009b. *Globalization and the Provision of Incentives Inside the Firm: The Effect of Foreign Competition.* Journal of Labor Economics, 27(2), 179–212.

Datta, S., M. Iskandar-Datta, and V. Singh. 2013. Product Market Power, Industry Structure, and Corporate Earnings Management. *Journal of Banking & Finance* 37(8), 3273–3285.

Dechow, P., W. Ge, and C. Schrand. 2010. Understanding Earnings Quality: A Review of the Proxies, Their Determinants and Their Consequences. *Journal of Accounting and Economics* 50, 344–401.

Dechow, P., and D. Skinner. 2000. Earnings Management: Reconciling the Views of Accounting Academics, Practitioners, and Regulators. *Accounting Horizons* 14(2), 235–250.

DeFond, M. L., and J. Jiambalvo. 1994. Debt Covenant Violation and Manipulation of Accruals. *Journal of Accounting and Economics* 17, 145–176.

DeFond, M. L., and C. Park. 1999. The Effect of Competition on CEO Turnover. *Journal of Accounting and Economics* 27, 35–56.

DeGeorge, F., J. Patel, and R. Zeckhauser, 1999. Earnings Management to Exceed Thresholds. *Journal of Business* 72(1), 1–33.

Fama, E. F. 1980. Agency Problems and the Theory of the Firm. *Journal of Political Economy* 88(2).

Fresard, L., and P. Valta. 2013. *Competitive Pressure and Corporate Investment: Evidence from Trade Liberalization.* Working paper. Available from: www.4nations.org/papers/fresardvalta13.pdf.

Fudenberg, D., and J. Tirole. 1995. A Theory of Income and Dividend Smoothing Based on Incumbency Rents. *Journal of Political Economy* 103, 75–93.

Gaspar, J., and M. Massa. 2006. Idiosyncratic Volatility and Product Market Competition. *Journal of Business* 79, 3125–3152.

Graham, J. R., C. R. Harvey, and S. Rajgopal. 2005. The Economic Implications of Corporate Financial Reporting. *Journal of Accounting and Economics* 40, 3–73.

Gunny, K. 2005. *What Are the Consequences of Real Earnings Management?* Working Paper, University of Colorado.

Healy, P. M., and J. M. Wahlen. 1999. A Review of the Earnings Management Literature and Its Implications for Standard Setting. *Accounting Horizons* 13, 365–383.

Hermalin, B., and M. Weisbach. 2012. Information Disclosure and Corporate Governance. *The Journal of Finance*, 67(1), 195–233.

Hou, K., and D. Robinson. 2006. Industry Concentration and Average Stock Returns. *Journal of Finance* 4, 1927–1956.

Karuna, C., K. R. Subramanyam, and F. Tian. 2012. *Industry Product Market Competition and Earnings Management.* Working paper.

Linck, J., J. Netter, and T. Shu. 2010. Can Earnings Management Ease Financial Constraints? Evidence From Earnings Management Prior to Investment. *The Accounting Review*, 88(6), 2117–2143.

Nagar, V. 1999. The Role of the Manager's Human Capital in Discretionary Disclosure. *Journal of Accounting Research* 37(Supplement), 167–181.

Narayanan, N. P. 1985. Managerial Incentives for Short-Term Results. *Journal of Finance* 40, 1469–1484.

Parrino, R. 1997. CEO Turnover and Outside Succession : a Cross-sectional Analysis. *Journal of Financial Economics* 46, 165–197.

Peress, J. 2010. Product Market Competition, Insider Trading, and Stock Market Efficiency. *Journal of Finance* 65(1), 1–43.

Raith, M. 2003. Competition, Risk, and Managerial Incentives. *American Economic Review* 93(4), 1425–1436.

Roychowdhury, S. 2006. Earnings Management Through Real Activities Manipulation. *Journal of Accounting and Economics* 42, 335–370.

Schmidt, K. M. 1997. Managerial Incentives and Product Market Competition. *The Review of Economic Studies* 64(2), 191–213.

Shleifer, A. 2004. Does Competition Destroy Ethical Behavior? *American Economic Review* 94, 414–418.

Tian, Z. Product Market Competition, Management Incentives, and Earnings Management. Dissertation, Xiamen University.

Tinaikar, S., and S. Xue. 2009. *Product Market Competition and Earnings Management: Some International Evidence.* Working paper, University of Florida.

Yang, L., A. Rahman, and M. Bradbury. 2010. *The Trade-off Between Real Earnings Management and Accruals Management by R&D Intensive Firms.* Working paper. Available from: www.researchgate.net/publication/228976807_THE_TRADE-OFF_BETWEEN_REAL_EARNINGS_MANAGEMENT_AND_ACCRUALS_MANAGEMENT.

Zang, A. Y. 2012. Evidence on the Trade-Off between Real Activities Manipulation and Accrual-Based Earnings Management. *The Accounting Review* 87(2), 675–703.

PART III

Managerial accounting

7

BUSINESS STRATEGY, MANAGERIAL EXPECTATION AND COST STICKINESS

Evidence from China

Tingyong Zhong, Jiangna Li

1. Introduction

In traditional cost models, it assumes the costs change symmetrically and proportionally with increases or decreases in activity (Noreen 1991). However, recent empirical researches, on the one hand, demonstrate asymmetry in cost behavior in which costs increase more rapidly with activities than they decrease, which is viewed as cost stickiness (Anderson et al. 2003). On the other hand, costs are "anti-sticky" if they rise less in response to sales increases than they fall when sales decrease equally (Weiss 2010). Therefore, it is important to investigate the determinants of the asymmetry cost behavior.

In this paper, following the strategy theory, we argue that the deliberate managers will match the firm's cost structure to the business strategy by adjusting commit resources initiatively depending on their expectation on the sales, in which the selection of business strategy will affect firm's asymmetric cost behavior. Anderson et al. (2003) argue that it will give rise to adjust costs when the manager selects business strategy, for they have to increase or decrease the necessary or slack resources. Balakrishnan and Gruca (2008) find that reliable cost stickiness only occurs in costs associated with direct patient care, a hospital's core service. Moreover, the cost stickiness for this core service reliably exceeds that for ancillary and support services, which means when a hospital implements the differentiation strategy, the function represents the organization's core competency influences the stickiness of associated costs. Hospital managers will be reluctant to trim costs in core activities related to direct patient care both because of the critical nature of these services to the hospital's mission and because of the (larger) adjustment costs associated with altering this capacity. In contrast, it is much easier and less expensive to adjust capacity levels in outlying support services.

Porter's (1980, 1985) generic business-level strategies, overall cost leadership, differentiation and focus have become a dominant paradigm in the business policy literature. Each of these represents "a fundamentally different approach to creating and sustaining a competitive advantage. Usually a firm must make a choice between them or it will become stuck in the middle" (Porter 1985, p. 17). Moreover, Porter stressed that "achieving cost leadership and differentiation are usually inconsistent, because differentiation is usually costly" (1985, p. 18). The two main business strategies require firms to establish matched cost structures. To achieve a successful differentiation strategy position, it requires a firm to pursue a technology leadership or create a high degree of brand loyalty, which makes the differentiators invest a lot of resources to establish the specialized ability. Consequently, when the market is slumped, the differentiators are reluctant to reduce these slacks, which are useless for other firms but highly expensive to construct. On the contrary, the cost leadership is primarily to gain an advantage over competitors by reducing operation costs below that of others in the same industry, resulting in a lean cost structure and low adjustment costs. Consequently, the choice of business strategy may affect the cost structure and then the cost stickiness.

In addition, managerial expectation may either mitigate or intensify asymmetric cost behavior. All the decisions of strategy and then resource commitment depend on the managerial attitude toward the prediction of the sales' tendency. Dierynck et al. (2012) document that managers increase labor costs to a smaller extent for sales increases but decrease labor costs to a larger extent for sales decreases so that their firms can meet or beat the zero earnings benchmark. Similarly, Kama and Weiss (2013) document that in the presence of incentives to meet earnings targets, managers expedite the trimming of slack resources in response to sales decreases, which results in a lower degree of cost stickiness than under normal circumstances. In contrast, Chen et al. (2012) document that managers' empire-building behaviors leads to cost stickiness, and strong corporate governance mitigates such an asymmetry.

Using the data from China listed companies from 2002 to 2015, we find that: first, different competitive strategies will exhibit different cost behavior. The cost stickiness of differentiation strategy is higher than those choosing a low-cost strategy. Second, different management expectation will affect cost stickiness. Optimistic expectations can increase cost stickiness while pessimistic expectations will reduce cost stickiness. Third, management expectation can adjust the relationship between corporate strategy and cost stickiness. If management expectations tend to be optimistic, the cost stickiness is higher with differentiation strategy than those with low-cost strategy. If management expectations tend to be pessimistic, then cost stickiness is higher with low-cost strategy than those with differentiation strategy. Our study has implications for companies on cost management.

The remainder of the Chapter is as followings. Section 2 discusses previous literature and hypotheses development. Section 3 presents research methodology and data. Section 4 discusses empirical results. Section 5 provides robustness tests, and Section 6 concludes the chapter.

2. Hypotheses development

The different forms of corporate differentiation strategy mainly include customizing differentiated products according to consumer demand differences, maintaining product-specific technology and performance characteristics, etc. (Porter 1996). Companies carried out specialized investment due to the implementation of differentiated strategy, which gradually formed the enterprise's intangible assets or specific assets in accounting. On the one hand, these specific assets enhanced the core competitiveness of companies. However, on the other hand, companies are not free to sell or transfer all of their dedicated resources, such as knowledge of the researchers, workers with specialized production capacity, employees who are proficient in product marketing, managers who are familiar with corporate culture and practices as well as construction of specialized production of machinery and equipment (Williamson 1979; Teece et al. 1997). Therefore, during sales downturn, companies with differentiation strategy will face a higher adjustment costs. Because companies cannot cut costs, they will have to bring these remaining resources into the next period of production until the adjustment costs surpass the costs of the balance bringing about by cutting resources. In addition, because the formation of specialized assets requires a long time to invest and construct, and it is difficult to purchase in the factor market one-time, the specialized assets formed by enterprise investment in the supply side is lack of flexibility, which is actually the threshold of differentiation strategy. No matter it is product D&P innovation or service differentiation strategy, it requires a large range of business costs adjustment. Once the business shrinks and pre-R&D investment cannot be timely digested, it will exert a huge impact on enterprise cost control. When corporate sales decline, companies that choose differentiated strategies are faced with higher upward adjustment costs rather than cutting their investment, which means that companies using a differentiation strategy may show higher cost stickiness than others.

Low-cost strategy is to reduce operating costs through the implementation of effective scale, which makes the cost lower than the competitors. Low-cost strategy companies will do more to control costs in order to provide their products and services at low price. Porter (1980) argues that companies must build efficient, large-scale production facilities, go all out to reduce costs, tightly control costs, manage expenses and R&D, service, marketing, advertising and other costs. Therefore, when the current sales decline, a low-cost strategist tends to cut costs in time in order to maintain or increase its market share. Therefore, low-cost strategy companies have a lower adjustment cost and a more flexible cost structure.

In summary, when corporate sales decline, companies implementing differentiation strategy will maintain the remaining production capacity, while those with low-cost strategy will quickly cut investments or reduce costs. Therefore, we test the following hypothesis:

> *H1: Ceteris Paribus, the cost stickiness of the firms with differentiated strategies will be higher than that of firms with low-cost strategy.*

Managerial expectation is generally divided into optimism and pessimism. In the case of optimism, there may be two conditions: First, if the future sales maintain growth with optimistic expectation, the management tends to expand the scale of production and increase the commitment to resources; Second, if the future sales volume decline, managers will consider it as a temporary adjustment, rather than reduce a variety of the commitment resources, because the reduction of these commitment resources will lead to higher adjustment costs (Banker et al. 2011). As a result, cost stickiness is much higher when sales decline than when sales are meeting with expectations. But if the sales continue to decline, managers will become pessimistic. Under such conditions, managers will significantly reduce investment and production capacity, which will lead to cost anti-stickiness. Thus, here is the second hypothesis:

> *H2: Ceteris Paribus, the optimism of managers will result in cost stickiness, while pessimism will result in cost anti-stickiness.*

Since management expectations may affect cost stickiness, it is possible to adjust the relationship between corporate strategy and cost stickiness. Based on the two-period sales situation, we analyze manager's investment decision-making behavior in firms with different types of strategy. First, assuming that sales in year t−1 is increased, while that in year t is down, managers may still remain optimism. For a firm with differentiated strategy, due to the characteristics of asset exclusivity and higher adjustment costs, managers will not reduce the scale of production, but forward the excess production capacity to the next period. Therefore, compared with other companies, companies with differentiated strategy show higher cost stickiness than others. The firms with low-cost strategy need to keep low adjustment cost and flexible cost structure. Under optimistic expectations circumstances, cost stickiness will be much smaller than companies with differentiation strategy when current sales decline.

However, with two successive period sales decline, managers may become pessimistic and may reduce the resources commitment. Compared to optimistic scenarios, companies that choose a differentiation strategy will cut the excess capacity on a large scale. It is difficult to sell the existing production capacity in a timely manner because asset exclusivity is too strong, and valuable resources for companies that implement differentiation strategies may be less valuable for other businesses. Therefore, it may show a phenomenon of lower cost anti-stickiness. For companies that choose low-cost strategies, because of their lower adjustment cost and cost structure, they will significantly reduce their resource investment and then reduce costs. Therefore, when manager exhibits pessimistic expectation, low-cost strategy companies will show a phenomenon of stronger cost anti-stickiness. Thus, we test the following hypothesis:

> *H3: Ceteris Paribus, if the management is optimistic, the firms that choose the differentiation strategy have higher cost stickiness than those who choose low-cost strategies (H3a); Ceteris Paribus, if the management is pessimistic, the firms that choose the low-cost strategy have higher cost anti-stickiness than those who choose differentiation strategies (H3b).*

3. Research methodology and data

3.1 Econometrics specification

Most of the studies in the literature adopt the cost stickiness model developed by Anderson et al. (2003), which is based on a piecewise-linear relation between logarithm changes in costs and concurrent logarithm changes in sales.

$$\ln(\frac{cost_t}{cost_{t-1}}) = \beta_0 + \beta_1\ln(\frac{Rev_t}{Rev_{t-1}}) + \beta_2\text{Dec}\cdot\ln(\frac{Rev_t}{Rev_{t-1}}) + \varepsilon_t \tag{1}$$

Where, the $\ln(\frac{cost_t}{cost_{t-1}})$ is the logarithm change in costs of firm i in year t, $\ln(\frac{Rev_t}{Rev_{t-1}})$ is the logarithm change in sales revenue, the cost is the sum of selling, general and administrative (SG&A) costs and operating cost. Rev is the revenues of firm i in year t. Dec is a dummy variable taking the value with 1 if the revenues decrease relative to it in the last year and zero otherwise and ε is an error term.

The slope coefficient β1 approximates the percentage change in costs for a 1% sales increase, characterizing the relative importance of variable costs. The coefficient β2 captures the degree of asymmetry in cost response to sales decreases versus increases. Therefore, (β1 + β2) represents the extent of the change in costs with a one unit decrease in sales. If a firm exhibits cost stickiness, the β2 is expected to be negative for the reason that the managers with optimistic managers may not curtail the slack resources as they believe the sale decrease will not last for a longer time and the adjust cost may exceed the earnings due to the reduction of these slack resources, which makes the β2 be negative. However, some companies with pessimistic managers may appear anti-stickiness. When the managers realize the first sale decline and are pessimistic about the following sales, they will significantly cut back on costs at the sales decrease in current period, which makes the β2 be positive.

To check our hypothesis H1, we modify model (1) by adding strategy variable and other control variables. Anderson et al. (2003) argue that the macroeconomic environment, denoted by economic growth, firm-specific characteristics, such as asset intensity (ratio of total assets to sales revenue) and employee intensity (ratio of number of employees to sales revenue), will implement impact on the degree of cost stickiness.

$$
\ln(\frac{cost_t}{cost_{t-1}}) = \beta_0 + \beta_1 \ln(\frac{Rev_t}{Rev_{t-1}}) + \beta_2 Dec_t \cdot \ln(\frac{Rev_t}{Rev_{t-1}}) + \beta_3 Strategy_t \cdot \ln(\frac{Rev_t}{Rev_{t-1}})
$$
$$
+ \beta_4 Dec_t \cdot \ln(\frac{Asset_t}{Rev_t}) \cdot \ln(\frac{Rev_t}{Rev_{t-1}}) + \beta_5 Dec_t \cdot \ln(\frac{Rev_t}{Rev_{t-1}}) \cdot \ln(\frac{Emp_t}{Rev_t}) \quad (2)
$$
$$
+ \beta_6 Dec_t \cdot Suc\_Dec_t \cdot \ln(\frac{Rev_t}{Rev_{t-1}}) + \beta_7 Dec_t \cdot GDP_t \cdot \ln(\frac{Rev_t}{Rev_{t-1}}) + \varepsilon_t
$$

The $Strategy_t$ is the strategy position. $Asset_t$, EMP_t, GDP_t represents the total asset, the number of employees and the growth rate of GDP in year t respectively. Suc_Dec_t is the successive revenue decrease for two years.

We also incorporate the Strategy solely to investigate its indirect impact on the cost change for robustness as follow:

$$
\ln(\frac{cost_t}{cost_{t-1}}) = \beta_0 + \beta_1 \ln(\frac{Rev_t}{Rev_{t-1}}) + \beta_2 \cdot Strategy_t + \beta_3 Dec_t \cdot \ln(\frac{Rev_t}{Rev_{t-1}})
$$
$$
+ \beta_4 Dec_t \cdot Strategy_t \cdot \ln(\frac{Rev_t}{Rev_{t-1}}) + \beta_5 Dec_t \cdot \ln(\frac{Asset_t}{Rev_t}) \cdot \ln(\frac{Rev_t}{Rev_{t-1}})
$$
$$
+ \beta_6 Dec_t \cdot \ln(\frac{Rev_t}{Rev_{t-1}}) \cdot \ln(\frac{Emp_t}{Rev_t}) + \beta_7 Dec_t \cdot Suc\_Dec_t \cdot \ln(\frac{Rev_t}{Rev_{t-1}}) \quad (3)
$$
$$
+ \beta_8 Dec_t \cdot GDP_t \cdot \ln(\frac{Rev_t}{Rev_{t-1}}) + \varepsilon_t
$$

Where the Dec_t is a dummy variable and equals 1 if the revenue decreases in year t compared to it in t−1, otherwise 0. Therefore, the β1 in formula (2) and β2 in (3) measures the change of cost relative to the revenue increase 1%, in other words, when the sales increase 1%, the costs will rise β1% in (1) or β2% in (2). Then the (β1 + β2) represents the percentage of decrease in costs when sales decline 1 unit, that is to say, when the sales fall 1%, the costs shall go down (β1 + β2) %. When the costs exhibit stickiness, we can acquire the β2 > β1 + β2 and then β1 < 0 while they are anti- stickiness, β2 < β1+β2, then β1 > 0. Based on the H1, the β3 in model (2) or β4 in (3) captures the impact of the strategy on the cost stickiness. When these coefficients get greater, the impact of differentiation strategy becomes more. In that case, we expect these parameters to be negative.

To test the H2, H3a and H3b, following the Banker et al. (2013), hereafter, BBCM (2013), we construct a model to investigate the impact of strategy position under different managerial expectations on the cost stickiness.

$$
\ln(\frac{cost_t}{cost_{t-1}}) = \beta_0 + \beta_1^{PInc} \cdot I_{t-1} \cdot \ln(\frac{Rev_t}{Rev_{t-1}}) + \beta_2^{PInc} \cdot Dec_t \cdot I_{t-1} \cdot \ln(\frac{Rev_t}{Rev_{t-1}})
$$
$$
+ \beta_3^{PInc} \cdot Dec_t \cdot I_{t-1} \cdot Strategy_t \cdot \ln(\frac{Rev_t}{Rev_{t-1}}) + \beta_1^{PDec} \cdot D_{t-1} \cdot \ln(\frac{Rev_t}{Rev_{t-1}}) \quad (4)
$$
$$
+ \beta_2^{PDec} \cdot Dec_t \cdot I_{t-1} \cdot \ln(\frac{Rev_t}{Rev_{t-1}}) + \beta_3^{PDec} \cdot Dec_t \cdot Dec_{t-1} \cdot Strategy_t \cdot \ln(\frac{Rev_t}{Rev_{t-1}}) + \varepsilon_t
$$

Where the I_{t-1}, Dec_{t-1} are dummy variables. I_{t-1} equals 1 when sales increase in year t−1 otherwise 0. Dec_{t-1} takes the value 1 if sales decrease in year t−1 otherwise 0. In model (4), β_1^{PInc} captures the percentage of costs increase when sales grow up 1%under the optimistic scenario. (β_1^{PInc} + β_2^{PInc}) represents the percentage of costs decrease if sales decline 1 unit given that the managers are optimistic about future. β_1^{PDnc} measures the percentage of costs increase when sales increase 1%under the pessimistic scenario. (β_1^{PDec} +β_2^{PDec}) represents the percentage of costs decrease if sales decline 1 unit given that the managers are pessimistic about future. H2 expects that a firm will exhibit cost stickiness if the managers are optimistic about future. Therefore, $\beta_1^{\text{PInc}} > (\beta_1^{\text{PInc}} + \beta_2^{\text{PInc}})$, then $\beta_2^{\text{PInc}}<0$; In other words, β_2^{PInc} expected to be significantly negative while costs will appear anti-stickiness under pessimistic scenario in which $\beta_1^{\text{PDec}} < (\beta_1^{\text{PDec}} + \beta_2^{\text{PDec}})$ and then $\beta_2^{\text{PDnc}} > 0$ and β_2^{PDec} is expected to be significantly positive. If β_1^{PInc} and β_1^{PDec} are significantly positive, we anticipate $\beta_1^{\text{PInc}} > \beta_1^{\text{PDec}}$, which implies that the managers with different expectation about future have different preference on investment. Under the H3a and H3b, we expect β_3^{PInc} and β_3^{PDec} are significantly negative.

3.2   Variables and data

The independent variable is cost stickiness. Prior literatures have documented many measurements of cost stickiness, most of which use the percentage of cost change. Considering cost change might vary with many other factors such as managerial decision, cost management, we intend to use the percentage of the sale and administration cost change along with the percentage of operating cost change to measure cost stickiness.

The dependent variable is corporate strategy. The main methods identifying the corporate strategies in existing articles are classified as two types. On one hand, the questionnaire way is used to survey corporate strategy. For example, Dess and Davis (1984) explored a questionnaire to identify a firm's strategy. On the other hand, some articles use existed data to construct an index to recognize the strategy position. In this paper, following Bentley et al. (2015), we use the R&D intensity, growth opportunity, market share, employee intensity and asset intensity to define the strategy.

We also incorporate some other control variables such as (1) China annual real growth rate (GDP) captured by the effect of macroeconomic growth, (2) employee intensity (Emp) represented by the ratio of the number of employees to revenues, (3) asset intensity (Cap) captured by the ratio of asset to revenues, (4) industrial effect (Indy) and year effect (Year). These control variables are commonly used in many studies which indicated they have effects on costs stickiness. All the variables are defined in Table 7.1.

All the financial statement data are collected from Wind database and CSMAR database. The China annual real gross domestic product data come from the National Bureau of Statistics of China. All observations are filtered using the following processes: (1) remove data from ST companies due to extreme and incomplete financial data; (2) remove financial firms as their financial statements are different from others; (3) remove observations with missing number of employees; (4) remove outliers if a firm's assets are less than liabilities and sales, or if its administrative and sale costs are less than zero. As a result, we have a sample with 10148 observations from 2002 to 2015. To handle outlier effect, we have all variables winsorized at the first percentile and 99th percentile.

Table 7.2 reports the descriptive statistics of main variables. The average SG&A cost is 17.54% of sales with a standard deviation of 18.29% and a median of 12.68%. The average operating cost is 92.35% of revenue with a standard deviation of 19.92% and a median of 92%. Average Dec is 0.265, which implies that 26.5% of firms experience sales decrease while most firms gain an

Table 7.1 Variable definitions

Variable		Variable definition
independent variable	$\log(\dfrac{SGA_{i,t}}{SGA_{i,t-1}})$	The logarithm of change in selling, general and administrative (SG&A) costs
	$\ln(Opex_t/Opex_{t-1})$	The logarithm of change in operating costs
Dependent variables	Strategy	Following the Bentley et al.'s (2013) strategy measures
	$\ln(\dfrac{Rev_t}{Rev_{t-1}})$	Logarithm of change in sales revenue
	Dec_t	Dummy variable, equals 1 when the sales of a firm in year t decrease compared to the sales in the prior year t−1, otherwise 0
	Suc_Dec_t	Dummy variable, equals 1 for firm-year observations when revenue declined in the preceding period; otherwise 0.
Control variables	Emp	Defined as the ratio of the number of employees to sales revenue
	Cap	Defined as the ratio of the total assets to sales revenue.
	GDP	Defined as annual the growth rate of China real gross domestic product
	IND	Industrial dummy variable for 18 two-digit SIC industries

Table 7.2 Summary statistics

Variable	mean	p50	sd	min	max
Sales revenue	64.80	11.50	585.00	0.00	28400.00
Selling, general and administrative costs	5.36	1.40	34.40	0.01	1480.00
Operating costs	58.00	10.20	504.00	0.02	25600.00
SG&A costs as a percentage of revenue	17.54	12.68	18.29	1.664	131.2
Operating costs as a percentage of revenue	92.35	92	19.92	47.22	212.5
$\ln(\dfrac{Rev_t}{Rev_{t-1}})$	0.128	0.122	0.346	−1.121	1.55
$\log(\dfrac{SGA_{i,t}}{SGA_{i,t-1}})$	0.145	0.135	0.317	−0.997	1.343
$\ln(Opex_t/Opex_{t-1})$	0.139	0.128	0.32	−0.978	1.398
Strategy	18	18	4.596	6	30
Dec	0.265	0	0.441	0	1

Note: Sales and SG&A costs are in millions of RMB.

increase in sales between Year 2002–2015. The average strategy score is 18 (the maximum is 30 and the minimum equals 6), representing most companies choose differentiation strategy.

4. Empirical results

We first investigate the effect of strategy position on cost stickiness. We regress our model using two alternative dependent variables: SA&G and Cost respectively. In Table 7.3, we estimate three different models using GLS method. The results are listed in Column I through Column III. The estimated result in Column I is based on the model of Anderson et al. (2003), which shows a β1 of 0.427 and a β2 of −0.211. The results are similar to Anderson et al. (2003), Zheng and Hao (2004) and Lei et al. (2012). Its economic meaning is that SA&G costs will increase by 43.7% when sales are up 1% while they decrease only by 21.6% (equals 43.7% minus 21.1%) with sales

Table 7.3 The relationship between strategy position and cost stickiness: using logarithm of change in SG&A as dependent variable

D.V	GLS			Fixed Effect	
	I	*II*	*III*	*IV*	*V*
$Ln(Rev_t/Rev_{t-1})$	0.427***	0.413***	0.409***	0.423***	0.418***
	(26.66)	(47.00)	(45.93)	(42.69)	(41.20)
$Dec*Ln(Rev_t/Rev_{t-1})$	−0.211***	−0.377*	−0.434**	−0.359*	−0.430*
	(−7.66)	(−1.79)	(−2.06)	(−1.75)	(−1.85)
$Dec*Strategy*Ln(Rev_t/Rev_{t-1})$		−0.015***	−0.012***	−0.017***	−0.015***
		(−4.25)	(−3.32)	(−4.52)	(−3.76)
$Dec*Asset*Ln(Rev_t/Rev_{t-1})$		−0.036**	−0.037***	−0.042***	−0.043***
		(−2.57)	(−2.66)	(−2.67)	(−2.72)
$Dec*Emp*Ln(Rev_t/Rev_{t-1})$		−0.037***	−0.038***	−0.035***	−0.038***
		(−3.04)	(−3.11)	(−2.62)	(−2.80)
$Dec*Suc\_Dec*Ln(Rev_t/Rev_{t-1})$		0.112***	0.112***	0.125***	0.127***
		(4.89)	(4.91)	(5.09)	(5.16)
$Dec*Gdp$		−0.001*	−0.001*	−0.001*	−0.001*
		(−1.71)	(−1.77)	(−1.79)	(−1.76)
Strategy			0.001***		0.002**
			(3.07)		(2.45)
_cons	0.077***	0.084***	0.059***	0.074***	0.036**
	(24.80)	(25.78)	(6.71)	(20.30)	(2.29)
N	20947	20945	20945	20945	20945
r2_a	0.154	0.160	0.160	0.036	0.036
Industries effect	No	No	No	Yes	Yes
Year effect	No	No	No	Yes	Yes

Note: t-statistics in parentheses. *, **, *** indicate significance at 10%, 5% and 1% levels, respectively, in two-tailed tests. The sample is collected from CSMAR database from 2000 to 2015 after discarding invalid observations and outliers. The dependent variable is the logarithm of change in SG&A. Three different models are estimated using GLS regression method and the results are listed in Column I through III. To handle fixed effect, we further regress model II and III using GLS fixed effect regression with the results in Column IV and V.

down 1%. The results in Column II and III are for Models (2) and (3). The strategy coefficient β3 is −0. 015 and −0. 012, both significant at 5% and 10% respectively. This supports our first hypothesis that cost stickiness increases with the level of differentiation strategy. We further regress Models (2) and (3) using fixed effects in Column IV and V. The results are similar to GLS estimates but the coefficients are slightly smaller. The cost stickiness coefficient β2 is −0.359 and −0.430, both significant at 5% and 10% respectively. The strategy coefficient β3 is −0.017 and −0.015, both significant at 1%. Once again, these results support H1.

Considering SA&G costs belong to periodic charges which are sensitive to the business activities volume, we then reexamine the association between strategy position and cost stickiness of Model (2) and Model (3) using the logarithm of change in operating costs as the dependent variable. We use both GLS and fixed effect regressions and the results are reported in Table 7.4. The coefficient of strategy is −0.008 and −0.01, both significant at 5% under GLS regression. The

Table 7.4 The relationship between strategy position and cost stickiness: using logarithm of change in operating costs as dependent variable

D.V	GLS			Fixed Effect	
	I	*II*	*III*	*IV*	*V*
Ln(Rev$_t$/Rev$_{t-1}$)	0.872★★★	0.858★★★	0.860★★★	0.859★★★	0.861★★★
	(104.22)	(93.06)	(95.65)	(91.01)	(92.25)
Dec★Ln(Rev$_t$/ Rev$_{t-1}$)	−0.117★★★	−0.646★★★	−0.621★★★	−0.731★★★	−0.702★★★
	(−6.75)	(−3.02)	(−2.91)	(−3.23)	(−3.10)
Dec★Stategy ★ Ln(Rev$_t$/Rev$_{t-1}$)		−0.008★★	−0.010★★	−0.012★★★	−0.013★★★
		(−2.19)	(−2.45)	(−2.90)	(−3.09)
Dec★Asset★ Ln(Rev$_t$/Rev$_{t-1}$)		−0.035★★	−0.034★★	−0.030	−0.029
		(−2.01)	(−1.98)	(−1.60)	(−1.58)
Dec★Emp★ Ln(Rev$_t$/Rev$_{t-1}$)		−0.061★★★	−0.061★★★	−0.071★★★	−0.070★★★
		(−4.68)	(−4.66)	(−5.08)	(−5.02)
Dec★Suc_Dec★ Ln(Rev$_t$/Rev$_{t-1}$)		−0.045★	−0.045★	−0.027	−0.028
		(−1.89)	(−1.90)	(−1.15)	(−1.18)
Dec★Gdp		−0.000★★★	−0.000★★★	−0.000	−0.000
		(−3.05)	(−3.01)	(−1.08)	(−1.06)
Strategy			−0.001★★★		−0.001★
			(−2.69)		(−1.81)
_cons	0.019★★★	0.027★★★	0.038★★★	0.024★★★	0.039★★★
	(12.39)	(13.82)	(7.94)	(10.62)	(4.42)
N	20947	20945	20945	20945	20945
r2_a	0.806	0.813	0.813	0.805	0.805
Industries effect	No	No	No	Yes	Yes
Year effect	No	No	No	Yes	Yes

Note: t-statistics in parentheses. ★, ★★, ★★★ indicate significance at 10%, 5% and 1% levels, respectively, in two-tailed tests. The sample is collected from CSMAR database from 2000 to 2015 after discarding invalid observations and outliers. The dependent variable is the logarithm of change in operating costs. Three different models are estimated using GLS regression method and the results are presented in Column I through III. To handle fixed effects, we further regress model II and III using GLS fixed regression with results reported in Column IV and V.

coefficient becomes slightly smaller with −0.012 and −0.013, respectively. Both are significant at 1%. It implies that the differentiation strategy in the first quartile is 7.2% (0.012 ★ 6 = 0.072) in Column IV, or 7.8% (0.013 ★ 6 = 0.078) in Column V, greater than in the third quartile. The difference in cost stickiness between the first quartile and the third quartile is up to 0.288 (= 0. 012★ 24) in column IV, or 0. 312 (0. 013★ 24) in column V, which further supports our first hypothesis. The signs of other variables are consistent with that in Table 7.3.

We further conduct an empirical analysis on the relationship between managerial expectation and cost stickiness. To examine the second hypothesis, we regress Model (5) with the logarithm change in SA&G costs as dependent variable, using GLS and fixed effect regressions respectively. The results are reported in Column I through III in Table 7.5. The two types of managerial expectation coefficients are measured by the coefficient of β_1^{PInc} (0. 471, significant at 1%) and β_1^{PDec} (0.365, significant at 1%) respectively. The costs will increase 0.471% with sales rising 1% under the optimistic scenario, while the costs could increase 0.365% with sales rising 1% under pessimistic scenario, which implies marginal change in costs due to optimistic managers is 0. 006% (0.471%–0.365%). Meanwhile, β_2^{PInc} is −0.27, significant at 5% and β_2^{PDec} is 0.237, significant at

Table 7.5 The relationship between strategy position, managerial expectation and cost stickiness

D.V	Ln(SGAt/SGAt−1)			Ln(OPECt/OPECt−1)	
	I	II	III	IV	V
	OLS	OLS	FE	OLS	FE
I_{t-1}*ln(Rev$_t$/Rev$_{t-1}$)	0.496★★★	0.488★★★	0.471★★★	0.905★★★	0.899★★★
	(30.9)	(30.21)	(26.27)	(133.05)	(117.92)
D_{t-1}*ln(Rev$_t$/Rev$_{t-1}$)	0.357★★★	0.352★★★	0.365★★★	0.824★★★	0.828★★★
	(15.89)	(15.54)	(15.71)	(63.8)	(62.61)
I_{t-1}*D$_t$*ln(Rev$_t$/Rev$_{t-1}$)	−0.313★★★	−0.258★★	−0.270★★	−0.288★★★	−0.374★★★
	(−9.12)	(−2.49)	(−2.26)	(−5.72)	(−6.99)
D_{t-1}*D$_t$*ln(Rev$_t$/Rev$_{t-1}$)	0.126★★★	0.348★★★	0.237★★★	0.460★★★	0.482★★★
	(3.41)	(2.61)	(3.6)	(5.52)	(5.36)
I_{t-1}*D$_t$*Strategy*ln(Rev$_t$/Rev$_{t-1}$)		−0.029★★★	−0.032★★★	−0.019★★★	−0.025★★★
		(−5.58)	(−5.43)	(−6.73)	(−8.39)
D_{t-1}*D$_t$*Strategy*ln(Rev$_t$/Rev$_{t-1}$)		−0.022★★★	−0.020★★★	−0.028★★★	−0.030★★★
		(−3.51)	(−2.88)	(−6.43)	(−6.35)
_cons	0.073★★★	0.076★★★	0.073★★★	0.020★★★	0.020★★★
	(24.12)	(24.63)	(19.55)	(14.31)	(10.97)
N	20947	20947	20947	20947	20947
r2_a	0.159	0.164	0.143	0.813	0.805
Industries effect	No	No	No	Yes	Yes
Year effect	No	No	No	Yes	Yes

Note: t-statistics in parentheses. ★, ★★, ★★★ indicate significance at 10%, 5% and 1% levels, respectively, in two-tailed tests. We regress Model (5) with the logarithm change in SA&G costs as dependent variable using GLS and fixed effect regressions.

1%. Then $(\beta_1^{\mathrm{PInc}} + \beta_2^{\mathrm{PInc}}) = 0.2$, which is $(0.471-0.270)$, and $(\beta_1^{\mathrm{PDec}} + \beta_2^{\mathrm{PDec}}) = 0.602$, which is $(0.365 + 0.237)$. The former one means costs decrease 0.2% if sales decline 1% under the optimistic scenario while the later one indicates the costs decline 0.602% if the sales decrease 1% under the pessimistic scenario. Because $(\beta_1^{\mathrm{PInc}} + \beta_2^{\mathrm{PInc}}) < (\beta_1^{\mathrm{PDec}} + \beta_2^{\mathrm{PDec}})$ and then $\beta_2^{\mathrm{PInc}} < 0, \beta_2^{\mathrm{PDec}} > 0$, the optimistic managerial expectation will result in cost stickiness, while the pessimistic managerial expectation will result in cost anti-stickiness. We reexamine the results with the logarithm of the change in operating costs as the dependent variables using GLS and fixed effect regressions. Especially, β_2^{PInc} equals -0.288 and -0.374 respectively and both are significant at 1% while β_2^{PDec} is 0.460 and 0.482 both significant at 1%, which further our hypothesis two.

Finally, we provide empirical analysis on the association between strategy position, cost stickiness and managerial expectations. Since managerial expectation affect cost stickiness, it may moderate the relationship between strategy position and cost stickiness. To test this hypothesis, we re-estimate the models and report the results in Table 7.5. The coefficient of $I_{t-1} \star D_t \star$strategy$\star$Ln $(\mathrm{Rev}_t / \mathrm{Rev}_{t-1})$, β_3^{PInc}, is -0.029 and -0.032 in Column II and III, respectively; while the coefficient of $I_{t-1} \star D_t \star$Ln$(\mathrm{Rev}_t / \mathrm{Rev}_{t-1})$, β_2^{PInc}, is -0.258 and -0.270, respectively. Therefore, the absolute value of $(\beta_3^{\mathrm{PInc}} + \beta_2^{\mathrm{PInc}})$ is greater than absolute value of β_2^{PInc}. It implies that the optimistic managerial expectation will strengthen cost stickiness with more differentiation, which supports H3a. When cost stickiness of a firm choosing differentiation strategy is greater than that with cost leadership strategy, the managers with optimistic scenarios will view sales decreases as temporary adjustments, and thus they will be reluctant to cut back costs. Therefore, optimistic managerial expectation will increase cost stickiness.

In addition, the coefficient of $D_{t-1} \star D_t \star$ Strategy$\star$ Ln$(\mathrm{Rev}_t/\mathrm{Rev}_{t-1})$, β_3^{PDec}, is -0.022 and -0.02 (significant at 1%), respectively. β_2^{PDec} is 0.348 and 0.237 in Column II and III, and $(\beta_2^{\mathrm{PDec}} + \beta_3^{\mathrm{PDec}})$ is 0.326 and 0.217, respectively. It indicates that pessimistic managerial expectation will decrease cost stickiness which supports hypothesis H3b. Similarly, we test the results using the logarithm of the change in operating costs and the estimators in Column IV and V, respectively. The results are consistent with the former one. For example, β_3^{PInc} is -0.019 and -0.025 (both significant at 1%) while β_3^{PDec} is -0.028 and -0.030 (both significant at 1%). The results provide further robust evidence on H3b.

5. Robustness test

The unbalanced panel data are used for empirical analysis in the previous analysis. As a robustness test, we use balanced panel data and run GLS and the fixed effect regressions (untabulated). We find that the results are similar to the previous empirical results. Although the significance level may be decreased using the balanced panel data, the signs of the coefficients are consistent as the significance level, which further illustrates that our results are robust.

6. Conclusion and implications

6.1 Conclusions

Seeking a competitive strategy for business development is the key to the success of the business. Based on the data of China A-share listed companies in Shanghai and Shenzhen in 2002–2015, we investigate the relationship between firm's competitive strategy and cost stickiness, and find the following results.

First, the results show that the cost stickiness of firms that choose differentiation strategies is higher than those choosing low-cost strategies. This is because the differentiation strategy maintains or increases its high profit margin by providing quality products or services to customers through a centralized competition (Porter 1996), which requires companies to invest in key areas such as product development, brand building and advertising. However, cost strategy will put more efforts to control costs in order to achieve to provide their products or services with the lowest price, which means that they focus on improving the yield and capacity utilization and minimize the indirect costs and other expenses, based on the actual cost of competitors.

Second, when managers make decisions about whether and how to adjust their resource capacity, they will make the appropriate investment decisions based on current and future sales. Therefore, manager's expectations for the future will affect firm investment decisions and costs. To be specific, management optimistic expectation will strengthen cost stickiness, while pessimistic expectation will ease cost anti-stickiness. If management is optimistic, cost stickiness of companies choosing differentiation strategy will be higher than those choosing low-cost strategy. On the contrary, if the management is pessimistic, cost anti-stickiness of companies with low-cost strategy will be higher than those choosing a differentiation strategy.

6.2   *Implications*

Both the competitive strategy and manager's expectation are core factors influencing cost stickiness. The strategic positioning of firms will influence managers' decision on resource commitment and further reflect the control of cost management. Therefore, this internal mechanism can provide some microcosmic action reference for companies to implement cost management and improve corporate governance mechanisms.

On the other hand, at the level of policy operation, the study provides a new way of cognition for the effectiveness and rationality of the strategic positioning and the management expectation. In addition, it provides innovative ideas for further strategic selection, investment decision and cost control. The empirical results show that different competitive strategies and managers' expectations will produce different cost behaviors. Therefore, to enhance the strategic positioning of companies and management expectations of the effectiveness and rationality, and to constantly improve the internal governance mechanism, managers also need to correctly comprehend the changes in the external environment, and thus achieve effective controls of costs. At the same time, firms should actively guide and standardize the business process, actively play their roles in the market and further optimize and improve the internal and external environment, thus sustaining a harmonious and healthy development.

References

Anderson, M. C., Banker, R. D., and Janakiraman, S. N. (2003). Are selling, general, and administrative costs "sticky"? *Journal of Accounting Research*, 41(1), 47–63.

Balakrishnan, R., and Gruca, T. S. (2008). Cost stickiness and core competency: A note. *Contemporary Accounting Research*, 25(4), 993–1006.

Banker, R. D., Byzalov, D., Ciftci, M., and Mashruwala, M. (2013). The moderating effect of prior revenues changes on asymmetric cost behavior. *Journal of Management Accounting Research*, 26(2), 221–242.

Banker, R. D., Ciftci, M., and Mashruwala, R. (2011). *The Effect on Prior-period Sales Changes on Sticky Cost Behavior*. Working Paper. Temple University.

Bentley, K. A., Omer, T. C., and Sharp, N. Y. (2013). Business strategy, financial reporting irregularities, and audit effort. *Contemporary Accounting Research*, 30(2), 780–817.

Chen, C. X., Lu, H., and Sougiannis, T. (2012). The agency problem, corporate governance, and the asymmetrical behavior of selling, general, and administrative costs. *Contemporary Accounting Research*, 29(1), 252–282.

Dess, G. G., and Davis, P. S. (1984). Porter's (1980) generic strategies as determinants of strategic group membership and organizational performance. *Academy of Management Journal*, 27(3), 467–488.

Dierynck, B., Landsman, W. R., and Renders, A. (2012). Do managerial incentives drive cost behavior? Evidence about the role of the zero earnings benchmark for labor cost behavior in private Belgian firms. *The Accounting Review*, 87(4), 1219–1246.

Kama, I., and Weiss, D. (2013). Do earnings targets and managerial incentives affect sticky costs? *Journal of Accounting Research*, 51(1), 201–224.

Lei, C., Le, S., and Dan, S. (2012). An empirical study on the upward estimation bias in cost stickiness: Evidence from Chinese listed companies. *China Accounting Review*, 1, 3–16.

Noreen, E. (1991). Conditions under which activity-based cost systems provide relevant costs. *Journal of Management Accounting Research*, 3(4), 159–168.

Porter, M. E. (1980). *Competitive strategy: Techniques for analyzing industries and competition*. New York: Free Press.

Porter, M. E. (1985). Technology and competitive advantage. *Journal of Business Strategy*, 5(3), 60–78.

Porter, M. E. (1996). What is strategy. *Harvard Business Review* 74(6), 61–78.

Teece, D. J., Pisano, G., and Shuen, A. (1997). Dynamic capabilities and strategic management. *Strategic Management Journal*, 509–533.

Weiss, D. (2010). Cost behavior and analysts' earnings forecasts. *The Accounting Review*, 85(4), 1441–1471.

Williamson, O. E. (1979). Transaction-cost economics: The governance of contractual relations. *The Journal of Law and Economics*, 22(2), 233–261.

Zheng, S., and Hao, L. (2004). The expense "stickiness" behavior of Chinese listed companies [J]. *Economic Research Journal*, 12, 26–34.

8

EXECUTIVE COMPENSATION IN CHINA

Na Gong

1. Introduction

It is believed that successful entrepreneurs can drive business growth and sustainable development and hence be a driving force for long-term economic growth. The economy of China has made great progress in the last 30 years. Chinese entrepreneurs are the most important subjects in China's reform, and their knowledge, skills and abilities have far-reaching influence on the growth of China's economy.

Managers' compensation contract design is considered to be one of the important factors affecting the behavior of managers. The problem of incentives for top executives has been the focus of interest since the reform and opening up of China. Before 2000, the annual compensations of top executives of listed firms in China were rather low. Moreover, there are obvious differences in compensation levels across industries. In addition, the phenomenon of "Zero Pay" to top executives is grave (Wei, 2000). But executive compensation of listed firms in China has been dramatically increased in the past ten years. The influencing factors of the executive compensation are the focus of the academy.

The compensation format of top executives is monotonic before (Wei, 2000). In December 2005, China issued the *Notice on Promulgating the Measures for the Administration of Equity Incentive Plans of Listed Companies* (For Trial Implementation). It is thought that the executive equity incentive plan can improve the governance structure of listed companies and promote the standard operation and sustained development of listed companies. Since then, more and more companies have implemented stock option plan. The influencing factors of stock option incentive, the economic consequences of stock option incentive and the relationship between corporate decisions and stock option became hot topics.

With the growth of executive compensation, the level and structure of executive compensation in financial institutions have received a great deal of scrutiny after the 2008 financial crisis (Kini and Williams, 2012). In the face of significant declining firm performance, as well as the sticky wage of the grass-roots group employees, sky-high compensation of some executives caused widespread public discontent. Since 2009, China promulgated a number of policies to reduce the gap between executive pay and employee compensation in State-owned enterprises, especially central government-owned enterprises. The compensation dispersion of top management teams and compensation differences between top executives and emloyees are the important issues demanding more attentions from researchers.

To provide insights into Chinese enterprise executive compensation research, this essay covers three main fields regarding enterprise executive compensation in China: institutional background, practice and research. For this reason, the rest of sections in this chapter are arranged as follows: the second section discusses corporate executive cash compensation in China, including the background, practice and research; the third section introduces the corporate stock options in China; the fourth section is the background, practice and research of corporate executive compensation gap in China; the fifth section explores the challenges in executive compensation research in China.

2. Corporate executive cash compensation in China: background, practice and research

2.1 Institutional background and practice of executive compensation of the listed companies in China

Executive compensation of listed firms in China has been dramatically increased in recent years. Executive compensation incentive has been a research focus. The influencing factors of the executive compensation are the problems to which the academic researchers paid most attention in the past decades.

In 1994, an experimental policy was carried out in Shenzhen to examine how the system of annual remuneration could be more effectively applied to the chairperson of the board of directors and/or the general manager (Yu, 2005). The annual remuneration system for general managers in SOEs became standardized in Shenzhen in 1996 (Yu, 2005). In 2004, the State-owned Assets Supervision and Administration Commission published *Interim Measures for Assessment of the Operational Performance of Persons in Charge of Central Enterprises*. According to these rules, the annual remuneration of persons in charge of central enterprises shall consist of basic annual remuneration, performance annual remuneration and long-term incentives. It clearly stipulates a link between executive compensation and firm performance. The salary system reform has achieved substantial breakthrough. Since 2006, the salary of general managers in SOEs has grown rapidly. The average salary of general managers in central SOEs and local SOEs is more than the average salary of general managers in private enterprises. Figure 8.1 demonstrates the average salary trend between 2006 and 2015, based on the data of listed companies of China from the *China Stock Market & Accounting Research Database* (CSMAR).

2.2 Influencing factors of executive compensation

The literature have analyzed how the levels of economic development, capital structure, corporate governance and social networking influence the executive compensation contract of a listed company in China.

2.2.1 Level of economic development

Chen et al. (2010) use the National Economic Research Institute (NERI) index of the marketization of the provinces in China as a proxy to test how marketization affects incentive contract costs and choices. The results show that in years and areas with a higher NERI index, the perks and cash compensations are higher, but perks contracts will be substituted by the cash compensation contracts, and this relation is weakened in protected industries.

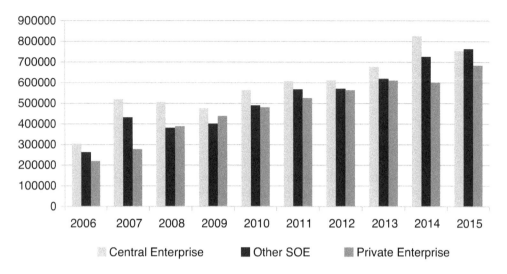

Figure 8.1 The average salary of CEOs in central enterprises, other SOEs and private enterprises in China from 2006 to 2015

Source: CAMAR.

2.2.2 Capital structure

The credit constraints, arising from the imperfect judicial protection on the interests of creditors, have had various degrees of impact on the decisions of listed companies in China. Based on this specific background, there are papers testing the effects of capital structure and the debt maturity constraint on the managerial incentives. The results show that the relationship between capital structure as well as the debt maturity constraint and CEO pay-performance sensitivity are both significantly negative (Wang et al., 2011; Chen and Xu, 2012).

2.2.3 Corporate governance

There is no uniform conclusion about the relationship between the managerial power and the CEOs' compensation. Lu and Zhao (2008) and Quan et al. (2010) investigate the compensation of top managers of SOEs and its effect on firm value. They find that more managerial power of top managers in SOEs leads to higher private benefits. In contrast, Wang and He (2012) argue that since CEO compensation is decided by the State-owned Assets Supervision and Administration Commission (SASAC), CEOs may not be able to influence their compensation even though they are powerful. This means that CEO compensation may not be consistent with managerial power hypotheses in SOEs. Their results show that firm size, monopoly and performance are the most important factors in the contract of CEO compensation, while management power is less significantly related with CEO compensation.

Besides, the effect of characteristics of the board on the compensation is also studied. For example, Zheng et al. (2012) empirically explores excess executive compensation from the perspective of cronyism board culture in China's listed firms. Deng et al. (2015) estimate the influence of overlapping compensation and audit committees on pay for luck in CEO compensation, and the results indicate that overlapping memberships alleviate the sensitivity of CEOs' compensation to luck.

The effect of the controlling shareholder on the compensation is a concern of the academia. Using a dummy on whether ultimate controllers serve on the compensation committee to measure the strength of ultimate controllers' monitoring on executive compensation, Lin et al. (2013) show that executives' pay-for-performance sensitivity (PPS) is higher in companies with ultimate controllers serving on the compensation committee. Zhao and Lu (2015) examine whether the family relationship between CEO and ultimate controller reduces the demand for compensation contract. Their results show that the ultimate controller serving as CEO demands the least for compensation contract.

2.2.4   Social network

Several scholars pay attention to the relationship between social network such as political connections, financial connection and executive compensation. Both Liu et al. (2010) and Tang and Sun (2014) find that, after other economic factors that impact on a CEO's salary and the factors of corporate government are controlled, no matter in SOEs or non-SOEs, all CEOs of politically connected firms obtained significantly high salaries. However, in the SOEs, a CEO's excess compensation resulting from the political connection is negatively related to company's future firm performance. In non-SOEs, the excessive salary resulting from the political link is positively related to a company's future operation performances.

2.3   Economic consequences of executive pay

Most studies find negative economic consequences of executive pay based on the evidence from listed firms in China. These studies suggest that there are managerial entrenchments in determining executive compensation packages, and such managerial entrenchments reduce compensation's incentive effects (Wu and Wu, 2010). The negative effect is more serious in State-owned enterprises. For example, Wang et al. (2014) find that powerful CEOs will pay workers less in State-owned companies. Lu et al. (2014) find that CEOs with administrative experience weaken the role of incentives in implementing effective internal control and the existing practice of politically appointed CEOs in listed State-owned enterprises twists market-oriented incentive mechanism, which jeopardizes the effectiveness of internal controls.

3.   Corporate stock options in China: background, practice and research

3.1   The use of stock options in listed companies in China over the past decade (2006–2016)

The stock option system showed significant effects in the global scope and became the world trend. It is accepted and widely used by Chinese companies during the past decade. On December 2005, China issued the *Notice on Promulgating the Measures for the Administration of Equity Incentive Plans of Listed Companies* (Trial Implementation). The rules stipulate general principles and general provisions on restricted stocks, stock options, implementation procedures and information disclosure, supervision and punishment. Later in 2006, the State-Owned Assets Supervision and Administration Commission of the State Council and the Ministry of Finance formulated the *Trial Measures for Implementing Equity Incentive Plans by State Holding Listed Companies* (Domestic). It is used to standardize the implementation of equity incentive system, establish mid- and long-term incentive mechanism, perfect the corporate governance structure and mobilize the initiative and creativeness of the senior managers and personnel of the listed companies. The Trial Measures stipulate general provisions, an equity incentive plan and its assessment and management.

In order to regulate the recognition, measurement and disclosure of equity-based payment and related information, the MOF formulated the *Accounting Standard for Business Enterprises No.11 – Share-based Payment* in 2006. It included the rules on general provisions, equity-settled share-based payment, cash-settled share-based payment and disclosure.

After the implementation of the rules of the equity incentive plans, there are some incentive plans released by the listed companies. For example, Yili Industrial Group. announced a large amount incentive plans for only three top managers in 2007. Expensive equities incentives led to Yili Industrial Group's huge losses in 2008. The market also has the negative reaction to the expensive equity incentive and firm performance. Soon the China Securities Regulatory Commission formulated *Memorandum No. 1, No. 2 and No. 3 on Issues concerning Equity Incentives*. These Memorandums have more detail rules about the incentive plans.

Recently, in August 2016, China issued the *Notice on Promulgating the Measures for the Administration of Equity Incentive Plans of Listed Companies*. The new rules of equity incentive plans have more details on incentive object, performance assessment index, restricted stocks, stock options and disclosure. Since the release of these rules, the option incentive system in China has been significantly developed. To attract and retain talents, the stock ownership incentive system has become an important measure for many enterprises to solve problems of internal personnel incentive. Many scholars pay increased attention to the influencing factors and economic consequences of stock option incentive and the relationship between the corporate decisions and stock option. The main characteristics of the equity incentive system in China are summarized in Table 8.1.

Table 8.1 Rules and contents of current equity incentive system in China

Year	Rules	Details
2005	The Measures for the Administration of Equity Incentive Plans of Listed Companies (For Trial Implementation).	General Principles; General Provisions; Restricted Stocks; Stock Options; Implementation procedures and information disclosure; Supervision and punishment
2006	The Trial Measures for Implementing Equity Incentive Plans by State Holding Listed Companies (Domestic)	General Provisions; Draft of Equity Incentive Plan; Declaration of equity incentive plan; Assessment and management of equity incentive plan
2006	The Accounting Standard for Business Enterprises No.11 – Share-based Payment	General Provisions; Equity-settled share-based payment; Cash-settled share-based payment; Disclosure
2008	Memorandum No. 1 on Issues concerning Equity Incentives	The extraction problem of incentive fund; Incentive object; The price discount of Restricted stock grant; Installment awarded; Index set of exercise
2008	Memorandum No. 2 on Issues concerning Equity Incentives	The incentive object; Major events in the equity incentive and interval; Shares source
2008	Memorandum No. 3 on Issues concerning Equity Incentives	The equity incentive plan change and cancelation; Equity incentive accounting treatment, Exercise or unlock condition problem, Line arrangement and incentive object scope,

Year	Rules	Details
2016	Measures for the Administration of Equity Incentive Plans of Listed Companies	Incentive object; Performance assessment index; Restricted Stocks; Stock Options; Disclosure

3.2   Influence factors of stock option incentive

Firms take regulations and their own incentive needs into account in making decisions on stock option. Some researchers examine the reason why some listed firms choose stock option. Lu et al. (2011) find that in order to attract and retain talents, firms will have incentives to choose stock option. However, they also show that deficiency in corporate governance and severe agency problems will induce managers to choose stock option for their own welfare. Meanwhile, firms in highly marketed areas and less regulated fields are also inclined to choose stock option. Shen et al. (2011) indicate that stake-raising may be mainly out of political motivation rather than financial.

Some have studied the characteristics and stimulation effect of stock option and purchase plans for stimulation. Lu et al. (2009) analyze the overall characteristics of stock option and purchase plans, and for the first time systematically sum up advisory opinions on distinguishing incentive-driven firms from welfare-driven firms. Wang et al. (2012) find that initial exercise price in the equity incentive plan decreases with managerial power. Shao et al. (2014) indicate that due to the lack of supervision for managers, incentives plans tilt too much for managers' welfare. In contrast, plans of private phases appear more reasonable and function better.

3.3   Economic consequences of stock option incentive

The empirical results of the equity incentive economic consequences are not the same. Zong et al. (2013) investigate how equity compensation affects executive turnover in a competitive manager market and find that equity compensation is inversely related to executive turnover. Lu and Gong (2009) investigate the accounting treatment of equities incentive and its economic consequences under Accounting Standard for Business Enterprises No.11 – Share-based Payment. Using a case study of Yili Industrial Group, they find that expensing equities incentives can affect the company performance. The intensity of amortization can also influence that effect. The market has a negative reaction to the expensing equities incentive and the change on the company performance. The extent of the reaction is directly related to the expensing effect on the performance. Xin and Lu (2012) argue that as the nature of stock-option-incentive plan in SOEs is mixed with incentive, welfare and reward, it inevitably will be in a dilemma in the context of compensation regulation in SOEs.

The operation and management of listed companies in China are more easily manipulated and controlled by executives. Some papers analyze the corporate governance effect of CEO stock incentives from the perspective of earnings management. Xiao et al. (2009) find that listed companies have lower discretionary accruals prior to the announcement of incentive plans compared with control samples, and there is a reversal in discretionary accruals after the announcement. Su and Lin (2010) find that earnings management is positively related to the probability of stock options exercises by the CEOs. Moreover, industry-adjusted ROA significantly declines after CEOs exercises stock options. Xiao et al. (2013) find that not only were the standards of performance evaluation that were set in equity incentive programs significantly lower, but also the performances in the base period were significantly lower than the levels of historical performances.

3.4   The relationship between corporate decisions and stock option

There are several articles about relationship between corporate financing behavior, investment behavior, R&D decision, dividend behavior and stock option incentive of listed companies in China.

3.4.1   Corporate financing behavior and stock option incentive

Hu and Gai (2014) empirically examine the impact of executive stock incentives on bank credit decisions in China's non-SOE firms. They show that bank borrowings firms can obtain increase with the intensity of executive stock incentives. Moreover, based on panel data of Chinese listed corporations from 2003 to 2013, Sheng et al. (2016) find that the relationship between the managerial equity incentive and the adjustment speed of capital structure is significantly positive.

3.4.2   Corporate investment behavior and stock option incentive

There exist both over-investment and under-investment in China's listed companies. Some articles study the effect of China's plan of stimulation in stock ownership on companies' investment. They find that manager shareholding can influence risk – taking (Li and Zhang, 2014). The mechanism of stimulation in stock ownership helps to mitigate companies' inefficient investment behavior. Compared with companies without stimulation in stock ownership, companies with the plan of stimulation in stock ownership have restrained the over-investment behaviors and alleviated under-investment behaviors (Lu and Zhang, 2011; Xu, 2014).

3.4.3   Corporate R&D decision and stock option incentive

Tang et al. (2009, 2011) construct a theoretical framework of stock right incentive, R&D investment and sustainable development of enterprises, and they conduct an empirical analysis on Chinese listed companies. Both the studies indicate that implementing the equity incentive of management has a positive influence on R&D investment.

3.4.4   Corporate dividend behavior and stock option incentive

Xiao and Yu (2012) find that both the cash dividend and the stock dividend and transfer of stock reserve to common shares are significantly higher in the companies announcing equity incentive plans than other companies. The announcement of equity incentives has a positive impact on the levels of stock dividends, cash dividends and transfer of reserve to common shares. The level of stock dividend and transfer of reserve to common shares increases when firms have inadequate capacity of distributing stock dividends and transfer of reserve to common shares. This indicates that firms treat stock dividend and transfer of reserve to common shares as an ideal gold digging tool. However, Lu and Zhang (2012) find the opposite results and show that stock option plans have a negative effect on corporate dividend distribution policy.

Although there are so many articles published about stock option, most of them focus on whether companies have an equity incentive plan. Very few empirical papers have further studied the equity incentive contract of executives, such as the choice of the incentive objects, equity incentive modes and incentive periods. Besides, several scholars have investigated the effect of the equity incentive plan on the corporate financing behavior, investment behavior, R&D decision and dividend behavior. However, future studies need to test the effect of stock options on firm value and the specific path of the effect.

4. Corporate executive compensation gap in China: background, practice and research

4.1 *Executive compensation gap of listed companies in China over the past decade (2008–2016)*

4.1.1 *The first stage (2008–2012)*

The fairness of executive pay has always been the focus of the society. But in the past companies focused more on executive pay level. After the global economic crisis of 2008, in the face of significantly decline of firm performance, the changeless wage of the grass-roots staff, sky-high compensation of some executives caused widespread public discontent. China promulgated a number of policies to reduce the gap between executive pay and employee compensation at SOEs, especially in SOEs owned by central government. In February 2009, the MOF proposed the *Measures for the Management of Financial Compensation, Head of State-Owned and State Holding Enterprises (Draft)*. It covers chairman (vice chairman, executive director), general manager (president, governor), supervisor, deputy general manager (Vice President) and other heads of financial enterprises under the supervision and regulation of the central and state councils. The draft makes clear that the highest basic salary of the head of a financial enterprise shall be no more than five times the fixed salary of on-the-job worker. In September 2009, the Ministry of Human Resources and Social Security, the Ministry of Supervision, MOF, the General Audit Office and the State-Owned Assets Supervision and Administration Commission jointly issued the *Guidelines on Head of the Central Enterprise Salary Management* (hereinafter referred to as the Guidelines). The Guidelines give attention to motivate the head of the central enterprises and worker wage income gap. It links executive annual basic salary with last year's central enterprise on-the-job worker average wage. The performance salary is according to annual business performance assessment results. This is the first time the Chinese government limited pay for executives in a central enterprise for all the industries.

4.1.2 *The second stage (2013–2016)*

After 2013, there was a new round of reform of state compensation. In February 2013, the National Development and Reform Commission, MOF, the Ministry of Human Resources and Social Security issued *Several Opinions on Deepening the Reform of the Income Distribution System* to strengthen the regulation of SOEs' executive compensation. Specially, the regulation caps the salary of the State-owned enterprise executives appointed by the administrative and emphasizes to narrow the salary gap in SOE, and executive pay increases should be lower than regular employee wage growth. In August 2014, the salary system reform plan for central SOEs was approved. It covers the enterprise chairman and secretary of the party committee (party secretary), general manager (CEO, President, etc.), supervisor (chairman of the supervisory board) and other deputy directors. The first batch of reforms involved 72 central enterprises, such as Petrochina, Sinopec and China Mobile. In the past the principal of state compensation consisted of base salary and performance salary. In this reform, the executive pay consists of base salary and performance salary, and term incentive income. Base salary is an average employee wage for a central SOE in the previous year. Performance salary depends on annual evaluation results. Term incentive income is associated with the different term assessment scores. Generally, basic salary will be two times that of an on-the-job worker's average wage. According to the assessment results, performance salary should be no more than twice the basic salary. Term incentive should not exceed 30% of the total annual salary.

The compensation gaps and the multiple of compensation gaps in central SOEs, other SOEs and private enterprises during 2006–2015 of listed companies in China are shown in Figure 8.2 and Figure 8.3, based on the data of listed companies of China from CSMAR.

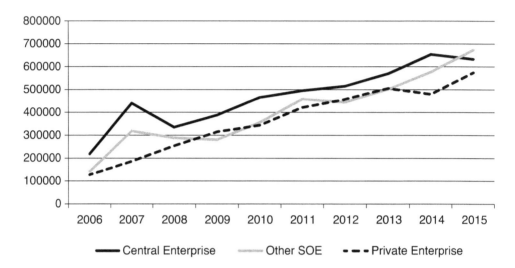

Figure 8.2 The compensation gaps in central enterprises, other SOEs and private enterprises during 2006–2015 in China

Note: Compensation Gaps = Average Salary of General Managers – Average Salary of Employees.

Source: CAMAR.

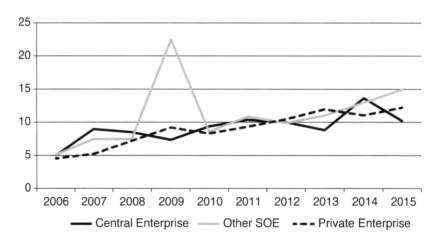

Figure 8.3 The multiple of compensation gaps in central enterprises, other SOEs and private enterprises during 2006–2015 in China

Note: Multiple of Compensation Gaps = Average Salary of General Managers/Average Salary of Employees.

Source: CAMAR.

In the past decade, there are several articles analyzing two types of compensation gaps, that is, the compensation dispersion of top management team and the compensation difference between the top executives and the employees in the Chinese companies.

4.2   *Compensation dispersion of top management team*

Based on tournament theory, Zhang (2007, 2008) propose several hypotheses on the relationship between the compensation dispersion of top management team and firm performance. Both papers find that the relationship between compensation dispersion and firm performance was negative. However, Zhou and Zhu (2010) study the performance of SOE executives from the perspective of tournament incentives. Their theoretical model suggests that a larger degree of payoff dispersion leads to more managerial efforts, and thus better performances.

4.3   *Compensation difference between the top executives and the employee*

Salary difference between the top executives and employees in SOEs has become an upward trend in recent years. Liu and Sun (2010) study the effect of the salary difference in SOEs on firm performance and find that a significant and positive relation between salary difference and firm performance, which supports the tournament theory. Using the sample of SOEs in the manufacturing industry, Li and Hu (2012) provide further evidence that pay dispersion is more likely to motivate employees in SOEs with low pay dispersion, but the relation does not exist in SOEs with high pay dispersion.

Yang and Wang (2014) investigate the impact of firm's internal pay dispersion's impact on earnings management. Empirical evidence suggests a positive effect of internal pay dispersion on earnings management. Further studies show that the above relationship is the joint effect of the shareholders' and executives' motivation, and the existing managerial power intensifies it. Even in the situation where executives are paid more than their peers in the same industry, it doesn't eliminate the effect of internal pay dispersion on earnings management behavior.

5.   The challenges in Chinese enterprise executive compensation research

There are many regulations of executive compensation and the compensation gap in China. However, we know little about this field because some policies of pay reforms in enterprises, especially in SOEs, display ambiguous or even opposite directions. For example, on the one hand, the government encourages the firm to apply an equity incentive plan, which leads to enlargement of the salary difference between the top executive and the employees. On the other hand, they try to decrease the effect of salary difference by restricting the maximum wage of top executives.

The number of articles on the compensation gap is relatively less than those on executive compensation and equity incentive plans. Most papers on the compensation gap focus on the influencing factors and economic consequences of the salary difference and few paper is on the relationship between corporate decisions and compensation dispersion. What is more, fewer scholars paid attention to the joint effect of the stock incentive plan and the compensation gap in China.

References

Chen, Donghua, Liang Shangkun, and Jiang Dequan. How Marketization Affects Incentive Contract Costs and Choices: Perks or Monetary Compensations? *Accounting Research (In Chinese)*, 2010(11): 56–64.

Chen, Ju and Xu Yude. Are the Incentives of CEO Compensation Care for the Interest of Creditor? Empirical Evidence From the view of Debt Maturity Constraint in China, *Accounting Research (In Chinese)*, 2012(9): 73–81.

Deng, Jianping and Chen Aihua. Does Financial Connection Affect Private Enterprise's Pay Contracts? *Accounting Research (In Chinese)*, 2015(9): 52–58.

Deng, Xiaolan, Chen Dong, and Chen Yunsen. Overlapping Membership on Special Committees and Pay for Luck in CEO Compensation: Evidence From Chinese SOEs, *Accounting Research (In Chinese)*, 2015(7): 49–55.

Hu, Guoqiang and Gai Di. Executive Stock Incentives and Bank Credit Decisions_ Empirical Evidence From Private Public Firms in China, *Accounting Research (In Chinese)*, 2014(4): 58–65.

Kini, Omesh and Ryan Williams. Tournament Incentives, Firm Risk, and Corporate Policies, *Journal of Financial Economics*, 2012, 103(2): 350–376.

Li, Wenjing and Hu Yuming. Who Is Encouraged by Pay Dispersion in State-owned Enterprises? *Economic Research Journal (In Chinese)*, 2012(12): 125–136.

Li, Xiaorong and Zhang Ruijun. Equity Incentives Influence Risk-taking: Agency Cost or Risk Averse? *Accounting Research (In Chinese)*, 2014(1): 57–63.

Lin, Le, Xie Deren, and Chen Yunsen. Ultimate Controllers' Monitoring, Industrial Competition and Executive Incentives: Evidence From Privately-owned Listed Companies, *Accounting Research (In Chinese)*, 2013(9): 36–43.

Liu, Chun and Sun Liang. A Study on Relation of Salary Difference and Firm Performance: Evidence From State-owned Enterprises, *NanKai Business Review (In Chinese)*, 2010(2): 30–39.

Liu, Huilong, Zhang Min, Wang Yaping, and Wu Liansheng. Political Connections, Compensation Incentive, and Employee Allocation Efficiency, *Economic Research Journal (In Chinese)*, 2010(9): 109–136.

Lu, Changjiang and Zhang Haiping. The Effect of Stock Option Plans on Corporate Investment Behaviors, *Management World (In Chinese)*, 2011(11): 118–127.

Lu, Changjiang and Zhang Haiping. The Effect of Stock Option Plans on Corporate Dividend Distribution Policy, *Management World (In Chinese)*, 2012(11): 133–143.

Lu, Changjiang, Zhen Huilian, Yan Mingzhu, and Xu Jingjing. The Design for Listed Companies' System of Stimulation by Stock Option and Purchase: Is It an Incentive or Welfare? *Management World (In Chinese)*, 2009(9): 133–147.

Lu, Changjiang, Yan Mingzhu, Zhen Huilian, and Xu Jingjing. Why Corporates Choose Stock Option? Evidence From China, *Accounting Research (In Chinese)*, 2011(1): 68–75.

Lu, Changjiang and Gong Na. Accounting Treatment of Equities Incentive and Its Economic Consequences – A Case Study Based on Yili Industrial Group, *Accounting Research (In Chinese)*, 2009(5): 53–61.

Lu, Changjiang and Zhao Yuheng. A Study on the Effect of the Incentive Given to Managers of State-owned Enterprises, *Management World (In Chinese)*, 2008(11): 99–109.

Lu, Dong, Wang Yunchen, and Fu Peng. Do CEO Incentives Improve the Effectiveness of Internal Control? Empirical Evidence From Listed State-Owned Enterprises, *Accounting Research (In Chinese)*, 2014(6): 66–72.

Quan, Xiaofeng, Wu Shinong, and Wen Fang[J]. Managerial Power, Private Income and Compensation Rigging, *Economic Research Journal (In Chinese)*, 2010(11): 73–87.

Shao, Shuai, Zhou Tao, and Lu Changjiang. Stock Incentive Design Between SOEs and Private Firms: Case Study on Shanghai Jahwa, *Accounting Research (In Chinese)*, 2014(10): 43–50.

Shen, Yifeng, Cu Weihua, and Li Peigong. Stake-raising: Financial Motivation VS. Political Motivation, *Accounting Research (In Chinese)*, 2011(1): 52–60.

Sheng, Mingquan, Zhang Chunqiang, and Wang Ye. Managerial Equity Incentive and Capital Structure Dynamic Adjustment, *Accounting Research (In Chinese)*, 2016(2): 44–50.

Su, Dongwei and Lin Dapang. CEO Stock Incentives, Earnings Management and Corporate Governance, *Economic Research Journal (In Chinese)*, 2010(11): 88–100.

Tang, Qing-quan, Xu Xin, and Cao Yuan. Stock Right Incentive, Research Investment and Sustainable Development of Enterprises: Evidence From Chinese Listed Companies, *Journal of ShanXi Finance and Economics University (In Chinese)*, 2009(8): 77–84.

Tang, Qing-quan, Xia Yun, and Xu Xin. The Equity Incentive of Management and R&D Investment: An Endogenous Perspective, *China Accounting Review (In Chinese)*, 2011(3): 21–41.

Tang, Song and Sun Zheng. The Political Connections, the CEO's Salary, and Firm's Future Management Performances, *Management World (In Chinese)*, 2014(5): 93–105.

Wang, Xiongyuan and He Jie. Monopoly, Firm Size and CEOs' Power Compensation, *Accounting Research (In Chinese)*, 2012(11): 33–38.

Wang, Xiongyuan, He Jie, Peng Xuan, and Wang Peng. Government Intervention, CEO Power in State-owned Companies and Workers' Pay, *Accounting Research (In Chinese)*, 2014(1): 49–56.

Wang, Ye, Ye Ling, and Sheng Mingquan. Managerial Power, Opportunism Motivation and Equity Incentive Plan Design, *Accounting Research (In Chinese)*, 2012(10): 35–41.

Wang, Zhiqiang, Zhang Weiting, and Gu Jiner. Capital Structure, Managerial Entrenchment and Managerial Compensation Level in Chinese Listed Firms, *Accounting Research (In Chinese)*, 2011(2): 72–78.

Wei, Gang. Incentives for Top-Management and Performance of Listed Companies, *Economic Research Journal (In Chinese)*, 2000(3): 32–39.

Wu, Yuhui and Wu Shinong. Executive Compensation: Incentives or Self-Interests? Evidence From Listed Firms in China, *Accounting Research (In Chinese)*, 2010(11): 40–49.

Xiao, Shufang, Zhang Chenyu, Zhang Chao, and Xuan Ran. Earnings Management Prior to the Public Disclosure of an Equity Incentive Plan: Empirical Evidence From Listed Companies in China, *NanKai Business Review (In Chinese)*, 2009(12): 113–127.

Xiao, Shufang and Yu Mengying. Equity Incentive and Dividend Payout Policy: An Empirical Study Based on Listed Firms in China, *Accounting Research (In Chinese)*, 2012(8): 49–57.

Xiao, Shufang, Liu Ying, and Liu Yang. Executives' Earnings Management Behaviors in the Implementation of Equity Incentive: From Perspective of Performance Evaluation for Option Exercise, *Accounting Research (In Chinese)*, 2013(12): 40–46.

Xin, Yu and Lu Changjiang. Incentive, Welfare, or Reward: The Dilemma of Stock-Option: Incentive Plan in State-Owned Enterprises, *Accounting Research (In Chinese)*, 2012(6): 67–75.

Xu, Qian. Uncertainty, Equity Incentive and the Investment Efficiency, *Accounting Research (In Chinese)*, 2014(3): 41–48.

Yang, Zhiqiang and Wang Hua. Internal Pay Dispersion, Ownership Concentration and Earnings Management: Basing on the Salaries Comparative Analysis, *Accounting Research (In Chinese)*, 2014(6): 57–65.

Yu, Guanghua. *The Regulation of Executive Compensation in China*, Working paper, 2005, http://ssrn.com/abstract=1535660

Zhang, Zhengtang. Top Management Team Coordination Needs, Compensation Dispersion and Firm Performance: A Perspective of Tournament Theory, *NanKai Business Review (In Chinese)*, 2007(2): 4–11.

Zhang, Zhengtang. Empirical Research on the Effects of Intra-firm Compensation Dispersion on Organization's Future Performance, *Accounting Research (In Chinese)*, 2008(9): 81–87.

Zhao, Yiyi and Lu Changjiang. Family or Money? The Impact of Family Relationship on Compensation Contract in Family Firms, *Accounting Research (In Chinese)*, 2015(8): 32–40.

Zheng, Zhigang, Sun Juanjuan, and Rui Oliver. Cronyism of Board Culture and Excess Executive Compensation, *Economic Research Journal (In Chinese)*, 2012(12): 111–124.

Zhou, Quanxiong and Zhu Weiping. On the Incentive Effects of SOE Tournament, *China Economic Quarterly (In Chinese)*, 2010(1): 571–596.

Zong, Wenlong, Wang Yutao, and Wei Zi. Do Equity Compensation Reduce Executive Turnover? Empirical Evidence From China's Security Market, *Accounting Research (In Chinese)*, 2013(9): 58–63.

9

EQUITY-BASED COMPENSATION IN CHINA

Liping Xu, Xiankun Jin, Yu Xin[*]

1. Introduction

The history of equity-based compensation in China can be traced back to the Qing dynasty.[1] In the late 19th century, equity incentive plans were applied in early Chinese banks (called "*Piao-hao*", or "*Qianzhuang*" in Chinese) to enhance firm cohesion and performance. "Human-Share System" ("*Shen-Gu-Zhi*" in Chinese), applied by Shan Xi Bank, was one of the most representative ones (Li, 2002). In Shan Xi Bank, the shares were divided into two types. One type was "Silver Shares" owned by initial shareholders who invested the bank with silver. The other type was "Human Shares", which were shares granted to senior employees who met the working period and performance requirements listed in Human-Share System. "Human-Share" enabled employees to share the same right to participate in profit distribution as initial shareholders did, but did not enjoy inheritance, transfer, or voting rights. In the Qing dynasty, in which stability and integrity were valued, Human-Share System performed well and contributed a lot to the success of the Banks. Despite a long history, the launch of equity-based compensation in present-day China is fairly late.[2] Pilot equity incentives were introduced in a small group of State-owned enterprises (SOEs hereafter) around 2000. But for listed firms, equity incentives were not viable until the issuance of the *Regulation on Equity Incentives in Listed Companies (Trial)* (REI-T hereafter) on December 31, 2005. Since then, equity-based compensation appeared and grew in number in China's listed firms. During 2006–2016, there were 1247 announcements of drafts of equity incentive plan (DEIPs hereafter) made by A-share listed firms, among which 1071 were implemented. There has been a large battery of literature documents the design, the motivations, and the economic consequences of equity-based compensation in developed economies especially in the United States, due to its relatively long history. However, the equity-based compensation in Chinese listed firms has not been well documented. The main purpose of this study is to give a general picture on equity-based compensation in China's listed firms, by focusing on the institutional background, the evolution, the contract designs, and the economic consequences.

Executive compensation evolves in response to economic, institutional, and political factors (Murphy, 2013). So is equity-based compensation in China, which emerged from the newly established fledging stock market. In socialist China, equality is greatly valued. Therefore, the regulation on equity incentives is strict, and is even stricter for state-controlled listed companies (SCCs hereafter), due to the concerns of equality from the public. The strong regulation makes weak the motivation for SCCs to implement equity incentives. During 2006–2016, only about 12% of equity incentive plan drafts were announced by SCCs. As for the implemented equity incentive plans, only 8.5% were by SCCs. Compared with equity incentive plans in non-state-controlled listed companies (Non-SCCs hereafter), those in SCCs exhibit smaller grant size, higher ratio of equity instruments granted to executive employees, lower grant-date fair value per executive, longer valid period, and more performance hurdles. Due to restrict regulation, option backdating is not possible because the whole process of granting equity incentives is under close investigation and listed firms shall disclose to the public within two working days upon the approval of drafts of equity incentive plans by the board of directors. China's accounting standards have converged to IFRSs since 2006, the beginning year of equity incentives emerged. Accounting for share-based payments follows the rule of grant-date fair value expensing. This partially discourages the use of equity incentives in top management compensation. By the end of 2016, about 30% of listed firms announced equity incentive plans, and 27% of listed firms carried out the plan.

We carefully survey the contract design of equity incentive plans by looking at the terms in the DEIPs announced during 2006–2016. Here are the main features: (1) the grant size, as the percentage of the number of shares granted to total shares outstanding, declines over time. The average grant size is 2.85% of total shares. (2) The relative percentage of equity instruments granted to executive managers also declines over years. On average, 24.19% of equity instruments granted are to executive managers, and the rest to the core employees. The average fair value of equity instruments granted is RMB 48.91 million. For each executive recipient, the average fair value of equity instruments granted is RMB 1.95 million. (3) Over the years, restricted stocks have gradually replaced stock options, becoming the dominant form of equity-based compensation. (4) The typical valid period of equity instruments used under compensation plan is four or five years, both for restricted stocks and stock options. (5) The vesting pattern is graded vesting. Typically, for each tranche of vested instruments, only one-year exercise period is allowed. (6) The vesting conditions are mainly accounting performance-based. Various forms of profitability measures are referred as performance hurdles. (7) The grant price of restricted stocks is half of the exercise price of stock options. This possibly explains the increasing popularity of restricted stocks. Overall, the scale of equity-based compensation in China is small and the valid period is short. The equity-based compensation in China is more like middle-term compensation, rather than long-term.

Except political and institutional influence, academics use efficient contracting vs. managerial power arguments to explain managerial compensation. We conduct simple regressions to test which argument applies in China by regressing contract terms of equity incentives on corporate governance and firm characteristic variables. The regression results reveal that larger shareholders associate with smaller grant size and longer valid period. Bigger board size and higher ratio of independent board are related with more grants of restricted stocks and more performance hurdles. Overall, these results suggest rent extractions view of equity-based compensation in China. The opportunistic view of equity-based compensation is further supported by earnings management strategies around granting vesting and exercising period of equity incentives. In China, the exercise price of equity incentives cannot be adjusted, except in case of distributing cash dividends or stock dividends. The dividend distribution typically results in strong stock price. Therefore, in China firms with equity-based compensation plans distribute more dividends (Xiao and Yu, 2012). Managers' equity incentives also increase manager's propensity to commit corporate fraud (Hass et al., 2016). Even so, the stock market reaction to the announcement of equity incentive plans is positive (Fang et al., 2015). Equity-based compensation also relates to better firm performance (Fang et al., 2015), more accurate analyst forecasts, and more favorable investment recommendations (Liu, 2017). In fact, the efficient contracting view and rent extraction view of equity incentive are not mutually exclusive (Murphy, 2013). Managerial power affects the design of equity incentives. Managers also have incentives to manage earnings and dividend payout to exploit benefits from equity incentives. At the same time, equity incentives can motivate managers to improve firm performance.

The remainder of this study is organized as follows: Section 2 introduces the institutional background. Section 3 presents a descriptive survey on the equity-based compensation during 2006–2016 in China. Simple regressions are carried out in Section 4, aiming to reveal the factors influencing contract design of equity incentive plans. Section 5 discusses the consequences of equity incentives. Section 6 concludes the study.

2. The institutional background

China's stock market started in the early 1990s with the establishment of Shanghai Stock Exchange in 1990 and Shenzhen Stock Exchange in 1991. Though young, both stock exchanges now are among the top 10 stock exchanges in the world in terms of market capitalization.[3] As a market started from scratch, the market infrastructures have been developed on a try and see process. In 1990s, many former SOEs were transformed to jointed stock companies and subsequently got listed in the stock exchanges. During this process, the employees of joint-stock companies were allowed to subscribe stocks and stock certificates, called them internal employee shares. But these employee shares had a lock-up period of three years and could not be traded outside the company. Directors and managers could also subscribe these shares and share certificates. However, due to the malpractices, such as issuing shares to illegal subscribers, the China Securities Regulatory Commission (CSRC hereafter) shut down the issuance of internal employee shares in 1998. Note that these employee shares were not granted to the top management as part of the compensation package, but as one of the fund-raising channels for SOEs. Therefore, employee shares are not equity-based compensations discussed in this study.

During China's transformation from the communist planned economy to the socialist market economy, how to manage the huge state assets was a major concern. To reform the low efficient, dying SOEs, the equity incentive was introduced as an experiment. In 1999, eight Beijing Government Agencies issued the *Guiding Opinions on Pilot Implementation of Future Stock Incentives for Executives in SOEs*. According to the opinion, SOEs can grant future stocks to its chairman of the board and the general manager, up to 5%–20% of the company's total shares. The chairman or manager needs to purchase these shares and the shares have a two-year lock-up period. In the same year, the 15th Central Committee of the Communist Party of China (CCCPC hereafter) issued the *Decisions of the CCCPC on Several Major Issues Concerning the Reform and Development of SOEs*. The decision recommended the implementation of annual salary systems and shareholding plans in a small number of SOEs. In 2002, such pilot equity incentive practices were extended to the R&D personnel and managers in State-owned high-tech enterprises. However, according to the relevant regulation, the number of pilot enterprises shall not exceed five for each province.

Before 2005 in China, the IPO firms' shares were categorized into tradable shares and untradable shares. The founder's shares (including the State-owned shares in partially privatized companies) were not tradable in the stock exchanges, and only could be transferred on the negotiation basis at a great discount outside the exchanges. In addition, share repurchase was strictly banned. The sources of shares and the tradability of shares were controversial if equity incentive plans were applied to listed firms. Therefore, the above-mentioned pilot equity incentive practices were applied to the non-listed SOEs only. Although some listed companies had tried to adopt equity incentives during this period, most of them ended up in failure because of the hurdles that came from both capital markets and laws. However, during this period (1990–2005), the Red Chip firms that are incorporated outside mainland China and listed on the Hong Kong stock exchange can issue stock compensation plans in catering the demand of foreign investors. Chen et al. (2013) document that by the end of 2005, 91% of 76 state-controlled Red Chip firms have granted stock options, so have the 65% of 103 non-state-controlled Red Chip firms. Chen et al. (2013) further point out that state-controlled Red Chip firms forced the directors to forfeit a significant percentage of their vested in-the-money stock options due to a conflict between the high-powered stock option compensation and state-controlled firm's unique managerial labor market.

In 2005, the CSRC launched the share-spit reform. The reform continued to 2006, made the un-tradable shares tradable. After the share-split reform, all the common shares of listed companies become tradable and identical in every aspect. To motivate listed firms to embrace the share-split reform, the CSRC and other four central government agencies issued the *Guiding Opinions on the Share-Split Reform of Listed Companies* in 2005. According to the opinion, listed companies that have completed the share-split reform shall be given priority in raising funds from the secondary market, and they may implement equity incentives to their management team. Subsequently, the Standing Committee of the National People's Congress (SCNPC) revised the *Company Law* and the *Security Law*. Accounting to the revised *Company Law*, listed companies can repurchase its own shares and award the shares to employees, up to 5% of outstanding shares. These regulations cleared the barriers of equity incentives. The share-split reform enables the controlling shareholders to trade their shares in the capital market, and thus make their personal wealth sensitive to stock price. The revised *Company Law* permits shareholders grant shares to managers.

The starting point of equity incentives in listed companies was the issuance of the REI-T by the CSRC at the end of 2005. The REI-T (2005) specifies the general rules for companies to grant employees equity-based compensation. According to the REI-T (2005) the general procedure for implementing equity incentives can be divided into several steps as shown in Figure 9.1. First, the DEIPs shall be proposed by the compensation committee and approved by the board of directors. Subsequently, lawyers are hired to provide professional advice and issue legal opinions on DEIPs. After that, relevant materials, such as the detailed written plans, board resolutions, and legal opinions, are required to be filed to the CSRC and the copies of those documents be sent to the stock exchanges and the local securities regulatory agencies at the same time. If there is no objection raised by the CSRC within 20 working

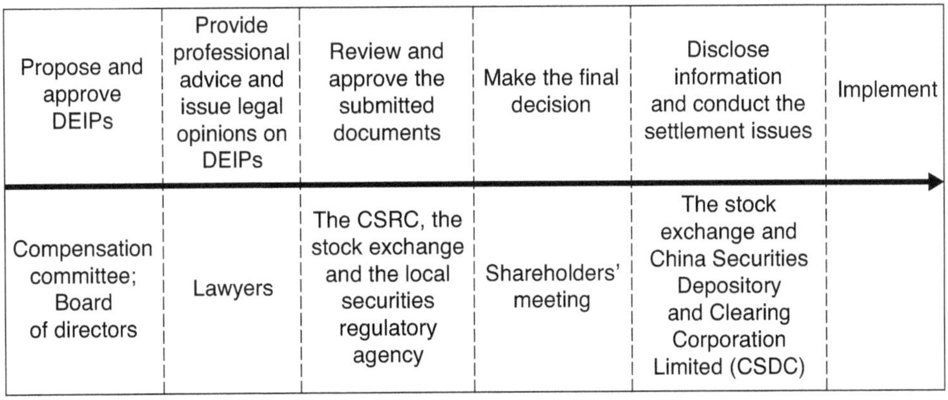

Propose and approve DEIPs	Provide professional advice and issue legal opinions on DEIPs	Review and approve the submitted documents	Make the final decision	Disclose information and conduct the settlement issues	Implement
Compensation committee; Board of directors	Lawyers	The CSRC, the stock exchange and the local securities regulatory agency	Shareholders' meeting	The stock exchange and China Securities Depository and Clearing Corporation Limited (CSDC)	

Figure 9.1 The procedures of equity incentive plans in China

days from the date of receipt of documents, the general shareholders' meeting can be held to make the final decision. After the approval of equity incentive plans (EIPs hereafter) by shareholders' meeting, the related documents are required to be disclosed to the public at the information disclosure platform in the stock exchanges and the settlement issues should be done via the China Securities Depository and Clearing Corporation (CSDC). Only when all of these have been done, can a firm start to implement the EIPs.

In 2006, the China State-Owned Assets Supervision and Administration Commission (SASAC hereafter) and the Ministry of Finance (MOF hereafter) issued two additional regulations on equity incentives, which are applied to SCCs only.[4] These regulations raise more conditions and restrictions for SCCs to initiate EIPs in terms of corporate governance, the upper limit of the value of equity-based compensation, and the procedure of implementing EIPs. As the regulations specify, EIPs to be implemented shall be audited by the agency or the department that is responsible for the management of State-owned assets before the general shareholder meetings. Moreover, the prospective gains of a senior manager from equity incentive plans shall not exceed 40% of his/her total compensation for offshore SCCs and 30% for domestic SCCs.

To provide more specific rules, the CSRC issued *Memorandums on Relevant Issues of Equity Incentives 1–3* (MREI (1-3) hereafter) in 2008. In the same year, another regulation, which provided supplementary guidance on implementation issues of EIPs in SCCs, was issued by the SASAC and the MOF.[5] According to the new regulation, the ratio of the equity incentive compensation obtained by an incentive object to his/her total compensation shall not exceed 40% for state-controlled domestic or H-share listed firms and 50% for state-controlled Red Chip firms. After that, tax issues related to equity incentives were specified in a series of regulations issued by the MOF and the State Administration of Taxation (SAT hereafter) in 2009. According to these tax regulations, the gains generated from equity incentives shall be taxed at the same rate as salary income on the exercise day.

China's accounting standards (CAS) converge with IFRSs when the MOF issued the new accounting standards in 2006. The new accounting standards became effective for annual period beginning 2007. CAS 11, consistent with IFRS 2, requires grant-date fair value of share-based payments to be expensed over the vesting period. Equity incentive plans appeared in 2006, in responsive to the issuance of the REI-T (2005). Firms launched equity incentive plans in 2006 did not recognize stock compensation expenses but postponed them to 2007 and adjusted to beginning return earnings of 2007 fiscal year. The stock compensation expense can be huge because it was determined by the grant-date fair value. For example, Inner Mongolia Yili Industrial Group recognized RMB 0.46 billion stock option expenses in 2007, in addition to RMB 5.06 million adjusted to beginning return earnings. The RMB 0.46 billion stock option expense in 2007 directly led to the negative net income for its 2007 fiscal year.

In 2014, to catering the diversified ownership reform, the CSRC issued the *Guiding Opinions on Pilot Implementation of Employee Stock Ownership Plans for Listed Companies*. Since then, employee stock ownership plans (ESOPs hereafter) flourished in China's listed firms. By the end of 2016, there were about 600 cases of ESOPs announced by the listed firms. However, the purpose of ESOP is to tie the capital providers and labor providers together and make them an interest community. By law, the grant of ESOP does not require performance conditions. The equity-based compensation in this study does not include ESOPs.

To improve the administrative process of equity incentive plans and to unify the regulations in the REI-T (2005) and the MREI (1–3) (2008), the CSRC issued formal *Regulation on Equity Incentives in Listed Companies* (REI hereafter) in 2016. At the same time, the REI-T (2005) and MREI (1–3) (2008) phased out. The REI (2016) also tries to resolve the problems arising from implementing equity incentive plans during the past 10 years. The general principal of the REI (2016) is to relax regulation, but improve monitoring. The REI (2016) makes it clear that the objects of equity incentive plans do not include independent directors, supervisors, and the shareholder with 5% or more ownership and his spouse, parents or children. However, employees with foreign nationality can be the subject. The REI (2016) also establishes a claw-back mechanism to require the top management to pay back the granted instruments and the returns from exercising them in case of false financing reporting and misleading information disclosure. The REI (2016) relaxes the lower bond of performance conditions and the ratio of reserved equities (from 10% to 20%). The REI (2016) raises standards on information disclosure of implementing equity incentives. We expect more firms will initiate EIPs following the issuance of the REI (2016).

3.   A descriptive survey on equity-based compensation in China

3.1   *An overview of equity incentive plans during 2006–2016*

After the issuance of the REI-T at the end of 2005, equity incentives emerged in 2006, therefore, our investigation started from 2006. Table 9.1 presents the distribution of the equity incentive plans in China's A-share listed firms during 2006–2016. Panel A reports distributions according to years. During this 11-year period, 1247 DEIPs were announced and 1071 of

Table 9.1 Distributions of announcements of DEIPs and EIPs made by A-share listed companies during 2006–2016

Panel A: Announcements of DEIPs and EIPs according to years

Year	*Announcements of DEIPs*		*Announcements of EIPs*	
	Number	*Percentage*	*Number*	*Percentage*
2006	37	2.97%	20	1.87%
2007	13	1.04%	5	0.47%
2008	67	5.37%	21	1.96%
2009	21	1.68%	11	1.03%
2010	78	6.26%	43	4.01%
2011	130	10.43%	98	9.15%
2012	123	9.86%	127	11.86%
2013	156	12.51%	136	12.70%
2014	165	13.23%	166	15.50%
2015	208	16.68%	220	20.54%
2016	249	19.97%	224	20.92%
Total	1247	100.00%	1071	100.00%

Panel B: Announcements of DEIPs and EIPs according to the type of controlling shareholder

Controlling shareholder	*Announcements of DEIPs*		*Announcements of EIPs*	
	Number	*Percentage*	*Number*	*Percentage*
State	149	11.95%	91	8.50%
Non-State	1098	88.05%	980	91.50%
Total	1247	100%	1071	100%

Panel C: Industry distributions of DEIPs and EIPs

Industry	No. of DEIPS	% to Total DEIPs	No. of firm with DEIPs by 2016	No. of firms by 2016	% of firms with DEIPs by 2016	No. of EIPs	% to Total EIPs	No. of firm with EIPs by 2016	% of firms with EIPs by 2016
A. Agriculture, forestry, animal husbandry, and fishery	15	1.20%	14	45	31.11%	12	1.12%	11	24.44%
B. Ming	10	0.80%	9	78	11.54%	8	0.75%	7	8.97%
C0. Food and beverage	42	3.37%	31	117	26.50%	36	3.36%	28	23.93%
C1. Textile, fur, and apparel	36	2.89%	23	78	29.49%	29	2.71%	19	24.36%
C2. Wood and furniture	10	0.80%	9	22	40.91%	7	0.65%	7	31.82%
C3. Paper and print	18	1.44%	17	47	36.17%	15	1.40%	14	29.79%
C4. Oil, chemicals, and plastics	105	8.42%	80	298	26.85%	95	8.87%	72	24.16%
C5. Electronics	99	7.94%	69	177	38.98%	83	7.75%	61	34.46%
C6. Metals and nonmetals	70	5.61%	56	223	25.11%	58	5.42%	50	22.42%
C7. Machine, equipment, and instrument	284	22.77%	213	652	32.67%	244	22.78%	193	29.60%
C8. Medicine and biological products	83	6.66%	67	174	38.51%	71	6.63%	59	33.91%
C9. Other Manufacturing	5	0.40%	5	18	27.78%	5	0.47%	5	27.78%
D. Electricity, gas, and water	12	0.96%	10	96	10.42%	8	0.75%	7	7.29%
E. Construction	36	2.89%	24	89	26.97%	30	2.80%	23	25.84%
F. Transportation	9	0.72%	8	86	9.30%	8	0.75%	7	8.14%
G. Information technology	228	18.28%	145	287	50.52%	204	19.05%	138	48.08%
H. Wholesale and resale trade	44	3.53%	31	156	19.87%	38	3.55%	29	18.59%
I. Financials	1	0.08%	1	68	1.47%	0	0.00%	0	0.00%
J. Real estate	55	4.41%	39	126	30.95%	41	3.83%	34	26.98%
K. Social services	57	4.57%	39	122	31.97%	53	4.95%	35	28.69%
L. Communication and culture	23	1.84%	13	54	24.07%	22	2.05%	12	22.22%
M. Comprehensive	5	0.40%	5	23	21.74%	4	0.37%	4	17.39%
Total	1247	100.00%	908	3036	29.91%	1071	100.00%	815	26.84%

them have been implemented (may subject to revision) by the end of 2016. Generally, there is a growing trend both in the number of announcements of DEIPs and that of EIPs. Panel B compares the announcements of drafts and implementation of EIPs in SCCs and Non-SCCs. The majority of DEIPs and EIPs were announced by Non-SCCs and those announced by SCCs only occupy 12% of DEIPs and 8.5% of EIPs. Note that during this period, 43.29% of listed firms are ultimately state-controlled. There are several explanations why disproportionately fewer SCCs launched equity incentives. First, the rules related to EIPs in SCCs are stricter. One possible reason for the strict regulations imposed to SCCs is the information disadvantage of state assets management agencies. State-owned assets management agencies have informational disadvantages and difficulties in observing the operating performance of SCCs at a low cost. Therefore, designing an effective equity-based compensation contract is almost impossible. Implementing strict rules to regulate executive compensation seems to be the only solution. Moreover, in response to public's pursuit of social equality, the government has intention to lower executives' compensation in SCCs and narrow the wealth gap between executives and employees. Besides, the majority of executives of SCCs are appointed by the government instead of being selected from the managers' market (Xin and Lv, 2012). Executives of SCCs are not only managers but also potential officials. With stronger expectation of political promotion, senior executives are willing to accept less compensation and therefore a smaller compensation gap (Bu et al., 2016). Since there are so many restrictions on setting cash or equity incentive compensation in SCCs, self-interested executives may conduct opportunistic behaviors such as perk consumption. Chen et al. (2016) find that perks are provided when the relative pay between top executives and average employees is low. The equity-based compensation in Non-SCCs is more flexible and more market-oriented.

Panel C reports the industry distributions.[6] Of the 1247 announcements of DEIPs and 1071 announcements of EIPs, roughly 40% were made by firms in information technology industry and machine, equipment and instrument industry. These firms rely more on human capital and so equity incentives are more important for them. The rest of Panel C reports the frequency of DEIPs and EIPs on firm level. By the end of 2016, there were altogether 908, about 30% of listed firms, announced DEIPs. Of these, 815, or 26.84%, implemented EIPs. Human capital-intensive industries show the greatest enthusiasm to award employees equity instruments to retain talents and motivate them to work hard. Among them are information technology, electronics, medicine and biological products industries. The similar pattern can be seen in the industry distributions of EIPs.

Due to strict regulations, only one financial listed company announced DEIPs but failed to implement.[7] Public outrage over excessive pay of executives in financial industry might also be the reasons. High level of executives' compensation in financial sector, which is considered excessive, conflicts with people's pursuit of social equality. In addition, risk-taking incentives, which are endogenous in EIPs and regarded as one of the expected effects of EIPs, are exactly what financial listed companies try to circumvent, especially after the subprime financial crisis. Bhagat and Bolton (2014) provide the evidence that incentives generated from executive compensation programs are correlated with excessive risk-taking by banks. Moreover, it is argued that risk-taking incentives induced by stock options will increase not only banks' total risk and insolvency risk (Minhat and Abdullah, 2016), but also their contributions to systematic distress risk and systematic crash risk (Kim et al., 2016). To maintain the stability of financial system and prevent the recurrence of financial crisis, equity incentives are not encouraged to be implemented in financial industry or even banned in state-controlled financial listed firms since the issuance of the *Notice on the Compensation Regulation on the Responsible Persons of State-owned Financial Enterprises* in 2009 by the MOF.

3.2   *Incentive objects and the grant size*

Executives and core employees, who play an important role in company's operation and development, are the main incentive objects of EIPs in China. According to the REI-T (2005), grant size of EIPs shall not exceed 10% of total outstanding shares and for each recipient, equities granted from EIPs is not permitted to exceed 1% of total shares outstanding. For SCCs, the ratio of the equity compensation received by a recipient shall not exceed 40% of his/her total compensation for firms incorporated in mainland China and 50% for firms incorporated overseas. Such strict regulations on grant size in SCCs, in return, lead to deficiency of equity incentives and increase managers' propensity to influence the design of other elements of EIPs, which have not been specifically regulated, toward welfare-orientation.

Compared with EIPs that have been approved by shareholders, DEIPs are the better choice for motivation analysis (Lv et al., 2009). We collected the data of DEIPs proposed by A-share listed companies in China from 2006 to 2016.[8] Table 9.2 reports the grant size and incentive objects of DEIPs. Panel A shows that the grant size, the percentage of shares covered by DEIPs to total shares outstanding, has a mean and median value of 2.85% and 2.47% respectively. This level is much lower than the maximum 10% grant size specified in the REI-T (2005). Table 9.2 also shows that the grant size has a continuing downward trend and the mean (median) value of size declines dramatically from 6.06% (6.03%) to 2.17% (1.83%) during 2006–2016.[9] As for SCCs, due to compensation regulation and prevention of losses of state assets, the grant size is quite small. The median value of grant size in SCCs is less than half of that in Non-SCCs (1% vs. 2.58%).[10]

Table 9.2 also shows that on average 10.84% of recipients are executive managers and 24.19% of shares are granted to executive managers. There have been sharp declines both in proportion of executive recipients to total recipients and that of executive equity grants to total equity grants. These declining trends show that the importance of core employees is gradually recognized, and they appear to become the main objects of EIPs. In addition, both the mean and median value of the proportion of executive recipients to total recipients in SCCs are significantly higher than those in Non-SCCs. Therefore, Non-SCCs stress more the contributions made by core employees, and thus offer more equity grants to them.[11]

Table 9.2 further presents the fair value of equity incentives as disclosed in DEIPs. On average, the fair value of equity instruments granted amounts to RMB 48.91 million. Since 2008, the fair value of equity instruments granted declines. The average fair value of equity incentives granted per executive is RMB 1.95 million. Typically, the equity instruments granted vest in three tranches and expires one year after the instruments become vested. The RMB 1.95 million fair value is expected to be realized in successive three years with RMB 0.65 million per year. Although the fair value of total equity grants is bigger in SCCs, the fair value of equity grants per executive in SCCs is only about 60% of that in Non-SCCs. This is mainly due to the regulation on the upper bond of equity-based compensation per executive in SCCs.

3.3   *The incentive forms*

Table 9.3 summarizes the forms of equity incentive plans. Panel A of table 9.3 shows that stock options and restricted stocks are the two main forms of EIPs in China. Restricted stocks are the most popular (accounts for 60.86%, which is 51.80% + 8.66% + 0.40%), followed by stock options (accounts for 47.23%, which is 37.77% + 8.66% + 0.8%). Share appreciation rights were rarely used. Approximately 10% of DEIPs contain combinations of stock options, restrict stocks, and share appreciation rights. SCCs use more stock options (account for 58.48%, which is 57.72% + 0.76%). But Non-SCCs use more restricted stocks (account for 63.48%, which is

Table 9.2 Proposed grant size, incentive objects, and fair value of equity grants in DEIPs

Year	Grant Size (1)			Proportion of executive recipients to total recipients (2)			Proportion of executive grants to total grants (3)			Fair value of total grants (in RMB Million) (4)			The fair value of grants per executive recipient (in RMB Million) (5)		
	N	Mean	Median	N	Mean	Median	N	Mean	Median	N	Mean	Median	N	Mean	Median
2006	34	6.06%	6.03%	23	39.88%	31.82%	32	50.66%	46.72%	0	NA	NA	0	NA	NA
2007	12	3.15%	3.02%	10	23.63%	9.21%	11	35.44%	34.53%	1	11.88	11.88	1	0.68	0.68
2008	61	4.10%	3.62%	52	25.64%	10.49%	64	39.66%	33.10%	7	110.96	13.84	7	4.44	0.64
2009	20	3.46%	3.39%	21	6.11%	4.55%	21	23.61%	21.92%	14	74.66	34.05	14	2.97	1.63
2010	78	3.07%	2.72%	78	14.03%	5.63%	80	27.84%	18.91%	71	88.33	46.98	66	3.07	2.03
2011	126	3.07%	2.86%	135	8.07%	5.41%	134	22.18%	18.08%	126	49.55	33.86	119	2.02	1.40
2012	123	3.27%	2.94%	142	9.73%	4.33%	142	21.92%	18.00%	140	38.61	22.73	128	1.43	0.98
2013	155	2.93%	2.58%	187	11.69%	4.35%	187	25.40%	19.69%	182	37.82	20.13	159	1.34	0.91
2014	165	2.49%	2.41%	188	8.68%	4.14%	188	22.56%	16.01%	187	44.67	28.16	169	1.50	1.05
2015	208	2.45%	2.04%	221	10.16%	3.49%	221	24.20%	18.01%	215	49.52	29.22	191	2.74	1.17
2016	249	2.17%	1.83%	265	7.85%	2.53%	266	18.27%	11.52%	261	50.77	29.14	216	1.84	0.93
Total	**1231**	**2.85%**	**2.47%**	**1322**	**10.84%**	**4.15%**	**1346**	**24.19%**	**18.01%**	**1204**	**48.91**	**28.03**	**1070**	**1.95**	**1.06**
Non-SCCs	1090	2.97%	2.58%	1190	10.43%	4.00%	1208	23.85%	17.80%	1103	46.78	27.59	976	2.02	1.10
SCCs	141	1.95%	1.00%	132	14.50%	6.63%	138	27.17%	20.48%	101	72.12	38.19	94	1.20	0.74
T-test	5.8891***			-2.2213**			-1.6197			-3.4998***			2.2085**		
Wilcoxon-Z	7.889***			-3.668***			-1.951*			-3.000***			3.306***		

Notes: This table reports the grant size, incentive objects, and fair value of equity incentives in DEIPs announced during 2006–2016. Grant size referred to the number of equity instruments granted to the total number of shares outstanding. There are 16 cases in which grant size is related to company's performance and hence not clearly specified in the DEIPs. We treat simultaneous grants of stock options, restricted stocks or SARs as separate grants in columns (2)–(5). Some firms do not disclose details of fair values, therefore the sample size in columns (4) and (5) are smaller. ****, **, and * indicate the differences in means/medians are statistically significant at 1%, 5%, and 10% levels respectively.

Table 9.3 Distributions of incentive forms

Pane A: Equity incentive forms

Forms	Full sample		Non-SCC sample		SCC sample	
	Obs.	%	Obs.	%	Obs.	%
RS	646	51.80%	585	53.28%	61	40.94%
SO	471	37.77%	385	35.06%	86	57.72%
SAR	7	0.56%	7	0.64%	0	0.00%
RS+SO	108	8.66%	108	9.84%	0	0.00%
RS+SAR	5	0.40%	4	0.36%	1	0.67%
SO+SAR	10	0.80%	9	0.82%	1	0.67%
Total	1247	100%	1098	100.00%	149	100.00%

Panel B: Distributions of equity incentive forms according to years

Year	Restricted Stocks		Stock options		Stock appreciation rights		Number of DEIPs
	Number	Percentage	Number	Percentage	Number	Percentage	
2006	11	29.73%	27	72.97%	1	2.70%	37
2007	2	15.38%	11	84.62%	0	0.00%	13
2008	14	20.90%	53	79.10%	2	2.99%	67
2009	5	23.81%	17	80.95%	0	0.00%	21
2010	20	25.64%	58	74.36%	2	2.56%	78
2011	43	33.08%	91	70.00%	4	3.08%	130
2012	71	57.72%	68	55.28%	3	2.44%	123
2013	105	67.31%	84	53.85%	0	0.00%	156
2014	121	73.33%	63	38.18%	4	2.42%	165
2015	166	79.81%	52	25.00%	3	1.44%	208
2016	201	80.72%	65	26.10%	3	1.20%	249
Total	759	60.87%	589	47.23%	22	1.76%	1247

Notes: This table reports the distributions of incentive forms in DEIPs announced during 2006–2016. "RS" refers to restricted stocks; "SO" refers to stock options; "SAR" refers to stock appreciation rights. The percentages in panel B is the percentage of the number of certain forms to the number of total DEIPs in that specific year. Since there are DEIPs that contain two equity incentive forms, the total percentage of these three forms is beyond 100%.

53.28% + 9.84% + 0.36%). Panel B reports the time-series evolution of the incentive forms. The general trend is that restricted stocks become more and more popular. In 2016, more than 80% of DEIPs used restricted stocks, compared with about 30% in 2006. On the contrary, in 2006, about 73% of DEIPs adopted stock options, but in 2016, the percentage dropped to 26%.

Compared with stock options, restricted stocks are more punitive and bonding. The holders of stock options, who have reached the vesting conditions, have the right to exercise the options or choose to give up when the gains generated from exercising are below their expectations without any cost being paid in terms of money. But when granted restricted stock, the holders have to pay to purchase stocks before the decision on holding or selling. Even if the same amount of money can be returned to the holders when they choose not to continue EIPs due to low stock prices or not meeting vesting conditions, the time cost of money has already occurred. Therefore, restricted stocks are more bonding and can motivate managers to improve performance.

However, restricted stocks are more favorable to managers in terms of exercise price. According to the REI-T (2005), the exercise prices of stock options shall not be lower than either the stock price on the trading day before the announcement date of DEIPs or the average stock price of 30 trading days before the announcement date of DEIPs. The minimum grant price of restricted stocks, specified in the MREI (1–3) (2008), can be as half of the average stock price of 20 trading days before the pricing date. Xiao et al. (2016) find that the tendency of choosing restricted stocks instead of stock options is stronger when the proportion of senior executives in the incentive objects is higher during 2009–2014 and such tendency seems more obvious in the companies with more managerial power. Moreover, the bear market and low stock market performance during or after the financial crisis in 2008 may also contribute to the preference for restricted stocks because managers are pessimistic about future stock prices and believe that stock options are very likely to be out of money during the valid period.

3.4 The valid period

Valid period, which refers to the period from grant date to expiration date, generally includes two parts: vesting period, and exercise period for stock options or unlock period for restricted stocks. In China, the dominant vesting pattern is "graded vesting", e.g. 25% of the options vest each year for four years, rather than "cliff vesting" (all vested at once). The exercise period and unlock period are rather short in China, typically 1 year. Figure 9.2 illustrates the vesting process of a stock option plan with a four-year valid period. As shown in Figure 9.2, 30%, 40%, 30% of the options vest each year for the three years following the grant date. The exercise period is one year following the vesting date for each tranche of stock options vested. Therefore, the valid period is 4 years.

According to the REI-T (2005), vesting period shall be no shorter than one year, and valid period shall be no longer than ten years. As for equity incentives in SCCs, the vesting period shall be two years and the exercise period or unlock period shall be no shorter than three years. Table 9.4 reports the valid period of equity instruments in DEIPs. Among the 1247 DEIPs, 1238 explicitly disclosed information on valid period.[12] As presented in Panel A, the mean value of

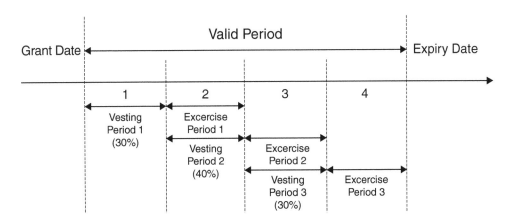

Figure 9.2 The schedule of a stock option plan with 4–year valid period

Table 9.4 Valid period and vesting period of equity incentives in DEIPs

Panel A: Valid period and vesting period (in years)

Sample	Valid period			Vesting Period		
	Obs.	Mean	Median	Obs.	Mean	Median
Full Sample	1238	4.63	4	1224	3.14	3
Non-SCCs	1092	4.49	4	1087	3.15	3
SCCs	146	5.66	5	137	3.07	3
T-test	−12.3876★★★			1.4781		
Wilcoxon-Z	−10.731★★★			1.442		

Panel B: Time length distributions of valid period

Year	Full sample		Non-SCC sample		SCC sample	
	Obs.	%	Obs.	%	Obs.	%
1	2	0.16%	2	0.18%	0	0.00%
2	4	0.32%	3	0.27%	1	0.68%
3	37	2.99%	34	3.11%	3	2.05%
3.5	2	0.16%	2	0.18%	0	0.00%
4	628	50.73%	613	56.14%	15	10.27%
4.5	16	1.29%	16	1.47%	0	0.00%
5	415	33.52%	323	29.58%	92	63.01%
5.5	10	0.81%	10	0.92%	0	0.00%
6	71	5.74%	64	5.86%	7	4.79%
7	15	1.21%	9	0.82%	6	4.11%
8	10	0.81%	6	0.55%	4	2.74%
10	28	2.26%	10	0.92%	18	12.33%
Total	1238	100.00%	1092	100.00%	146	100.00%

Panel C: Time Length Distributions of vesting period

Year	Full sample		Non-SCC sample		SCC sample	
	Obs.	%	Obs.	%	Obs.	%
1	4	0.33%	3	0.28%	1	0.73%
2	66	5.39%	65	5.98%	1	0.73%
3	938	76.63%	815	74.98%	123	89.78%
4	192	15.69%	181	16.65%	11	8.03%
5	22	1.80%	21	1.93%	1	0.73%
6	2	0.16%	2	0.18%	0	0.00%
Total	1224	100.00%	1087	100.00%	137	100.00%

Notes: This table reports descriptive statistics of valid period and vesting period. There are 9 (23) cases in which valid period (vesting period) is not clearly specified. When there is a difference in valid period between two incentive forms included in one DEIP, we choose the longer one. ★★★★indicates the difference between SCCs and Non-SCCs are statistically significant in means by T-test and in medians by Wilcoxon-Z test at 1% level.

valid period is 4.63 years and the median is four years. The graded vesting typically lasts three years in three tranches and for each tranche the exercise or unlock period is only one year after vested. But in the United States, the valid period for restricted stocks is typically five years, and that for stock options is ten years (Aggarwal, 2008). Therefore, in China, the equity-based compensations are medium-term compensation. Panel B reports the distribution of valid periods and vesting period. For full sample, about half (50.73%) of DEIPs design the valid period of four years, and 33.52% five years. Only 2% have the maximum ten-year period. Typically, the vesting period is three years, accounts for more than 3 fourths (76.63%) of all samples. In the United States, stock options may become vested in three years and may have another seven years to maturity. In China, once the restricted stocks or options are vested, they are supposed to be unlocked or exercised during the next one or two years. The limited period of unlocking or exercising in China is likely to result in managers' opportunistic behaviors. Table 9.4 also reports the valid period for equity instruments in DEIPs of SCCs and Non-SCCs, respectively. It shows that for SCCs, the valid period is longer with 5.66 years in mean and five years in median. Panel B show that almost two thirds (63.01%) of SCCs propose five-year valid period equity incentive plans, compared with less than one third (29.58%) in Non-SCCs.

The short valid period might indicate the managerial power hypothesis of CEO compensation. Lv et al. (2009) provide the evidence that CEO duality increases the tendency of choosing short valid period. They also find that when the chairman of the board does not get compensation from the listed companies, the probability of choosing longer valid period is higher. Similarly, Cadman et al. (2013) suggest that firms with more powerful CEOs and weaker governance grant options with shorter vesting periods. Qu et al. (2016) find that more independent boards, a well-structured remuneration committee and the separation of CEO and board chair appear to encourage the use of longer vesting period. The results from these studies support managerial power hypothesis. These findings also suggest good corporate governance has a positive role in restraining managers from rent extraction in compensation contracting.

3.5 Vesting conditions

The rules on vesting conditions were initially specified in the REI-T (2005). But the specific guidance in how to set performance-based vesting conditions had not been provided until the issuance of the MREI (1-3) (2008). According to the MREI (1-3) (2008), performance-based vesting conditions, such as growth rate of net income and ROE, are supposed to be no lower than the historical levels. And the net profit after extraordinary gains and losses during vesting period shall not be either negative or lower than the average level of the last three fiscal years prior to the grant date. Except financial performance measures, market value and relative performance in the industry are also encouraged to be set as the benchmarks. The finalized REI issued in 2016 relaxes the vesting conditions. The requirement that vesting conditions shall not be lower than the historical levels and shall not be negative was removed.

Table 9.5 shows the vesting conditions specified in DEIPs. Panel A reports the number of vesting conditions. There are only six DEIPs that do not set any performance hurdles. Most DEIPs set one or two vesting conditions (84.12% = 32.64% + 51.48%), and the number of vesting conditions can be up to five. Panel B reports the types of vesting conditions. Growth rate of net income is most widely used (81.48%), followed by ROE (46.99%), then by the absolute level or the growth rate of operating income and revenue (26.14%). Most vesting conditions are profitability related accounting measures. Stock price and market value are seldom used (only 1.52%). Compared with Non-SCCs, SCCs set more vesting conditions (2.40 vs. 1.76 in means).

Table 9.5 Vesting conditions specified in DEIPs

Panel A: Number of vesting conditions specified in DEIPs

No. of vesting conditions	Full sample		Non-SCC sample		SCC sample	
	Obs.	*%*	*Obs.*	*%*	*Obs.*	*%*
0	6	0.48%	4	0.36%	2	1.34%
1	407	32.64%	390	35.52%	17	11.41%
2	642	51.48%	582	53.01%	60	40.27%
3	167	13.39%	108	9.84%	59	39.60%
4	23	1.84%	12	1.09%	11	7.38%
5	2	0.16%	2	0.18%	0	0.00%
Total	1247	100%	1098	100.00%	149	100.00%
Mean	1.8396		1.7632		2.4027★★★	
Median	2		2		2★★★	

Panel B: Types of vesting conditions

Types of vesting conditions	Full sample		Non-SCC sample		SCC sample	
	Obs.	*%*	*Obs.*	*%*	*Obs.*	*%*
ROE	586	46.99%	471	42.90%	115	77.18%
Growth rate of net income	1016	81.48%	907	82.60%	109	73.15%
Net income	241	19.33%	230	20.95%	11	7.38%
EPS	23	1.84%	15	1.37%	8	5.37%
Operating income and revenue	326	26.14%	260	23.68%	66	44.30%
Other profitability indexes	43	3.45%	12	1.09%	31	20.81%
Stock price and market value	19	1.52%	15	1.37%	4	2.68%
Cash flow	8	0.64%	6	0.55%	2	1.34%
Others	32	2.57%	20	1.82%	12	8.05%
Total	2294		1936		358	

Notes: This table reports descriptive statistics of the number of vesting conditions and types of vesting conditions in DEIPs announced during 2006–2016. ★★★★indicates the difference between SCCs and Non-SCCs are statistically significant in means by T-test and in medians by Wilcoxon-Z test at 1% level.

The design of vesting conditions, which determines how much effort managers should pay for getting equity interests, is directly related to what role EIPs play. Setting more performance hurdles which are not easy to be overcome is preferred by shareholders in the hope of gaining more profits from managers' efforts. But for managers, the less and lower performance hurdles make more benefits. Wu and Wu (2010) argue that vesting conditions of EIPs in China are so loose that managers can easily reach them with little effort being paid, which obviously reflect managers' selfish behaviors in the design of EIPs. Similarly, Qu et al. (2016) and Abernethy et al. (2015) find that more powerful CEOs appear to influence the granting of equity incentives with less restrictive vesting conditions and less challenging targets, negating some of the beneficial effects. In addition, to circumvent performance hurdles and prevent failure of vesting, powerful managers tend to lower the performance-based vesting conditions by earnings management to lower the financial performance in the benchmark year (Xiao et al., 2013).

3.6 *Grant (exercise) prices*

In China, information disclosure and pricing of equity incentive plans are strictly regulated. The floor of grant prices or exercise prices is settled at the announcement date of DEIPs. Option backdating, which is often used as a proxy for misconduct in corporate governance literature, is not applicable in China. The REI-T (2005) and the MREI (1-3) (2008) set the lower bonds of exercise price of stock options and the grant price of restricted stocks. And these prices are to be disclosed in DEIPs. Typically, the firm chooses the lowest price available. Table 9.6 reports the suggested prices in DEIPs. In Panel A of Table 9.6, the mean grant price of restricted stocks is RMB 12.25, and the mean exercise price of stock options is RMB 22.49. Some may argue that the two means are not directly comparable because they are from different firms. Fortunately, we have 104 DEIPs which simultaneously grant restricted stocks and stock options. Based on these pair grants, we still observe the big difference between the grant price of restricted stocks and exercise price of stock options (RMB 11.64 vs. 23.62 in means). These differences, of cause, are statistically significant. Such differences exist both in SCCs and Non-SCCs. The exercise price of restricted stocks is about half of that of stock options. The direct reason for the difference lies in the regulations that specified in the REI-T (2005) and the MREI (1-3) (2008). Finally, the grant/exercise prices of equity incentives in SCCs are lower than those in Non-SCCs.

Table 9.6 Incentive forms and exercise (grant) prices

Panel A: Grant prices for restricted stocks and exercise prices for stock options

Price	Restricted Stocks			Stock Options			T-test	Wilcoxon-Z
	N	Mean	Median	N	Mean	Median		
All	719	12.25	8.87	584	22.49	16.84	−11.7186★★★	−14.786★★★
Pair	104	11.64	7.31	104	23.62	14.60	−4.0102★★★	−6.882★★★

Panel B: The price difference between Non-SCCs and SCCs

Price	Non-SCCs			SCCs			T-test	Wilcoxon-Z
	N	Mean	Median	N	Mean	Median		
Restricted Stocks	669	12.46	8.94	50	9.45	7.26	1.8360★	2.313★★
Stock Options	500	23.63	17.80	84	15.69	12.47	3.4234★★★	4.452★★★

Notes: This table reports grant prices and exercises prices and T-test and Wilcoxon-Z test of the difference in them. There are 104 DEIPs that contain both restricted stocks and stock options and their corresponding prices are reported as "Pair" sample. ★★★, ★★, and ★ indicate the differences in means/medians are statistically significant at 1%, 5%, and 10% levels respectively.

3.7 Implementation vs. termination

The DEIPs that have been approved by the board of directors may not be implemented when either the CSRC or the shareholders raise objections. Once objections are raised, DEIPs are subject to revisions. If the revised DEIP fails to meet the CSRC's or shareholders' concerns, it ends up with termination. Sometimes, the issuance of new regulations may also impede the approval of DEIPs due to changes in new requirements. Many DEIPs that had been announced but had not been passed around the issuance of the MREI (1–3) (2008), for example, may fail to meet the new regulation which imposes more restrictions on the design of EIPs, and therefore be terminated. Table 9.7 summarizes the progress of DEIPs during 2006–2016. Among 1247 DEIPs that have been put forward, 9.30% (116/1247) of them were terminated before being approved by shareholders, 87.49% (1091/1247) of them reached the stage of implementation.[13]

Even if approved by shareholders, EIPs may still be terminated during the process of implementation. In the United States or other countries, repricing is permitted when changes in capital market environment or other relevant factors occur, which make the initial version of EIPs ineffective or unviable. But in China, key elements of EIPs such as incentive forms, grant or exercise prices are prohibited from being arbitrarily adjusted according to the MREI (1–3) (2008), unless these adjustments are made due to ex-right, ex-dividend or other relevant events. Still, EIPs can be terminated due to changes in environment, poor operating performance, or other reasons. Among 1091 EIPs approved by shareholders, 9.53% (104/1091) of them were terminated in the stage of implementation.

Table 9.7 Progress of EIPs and reasons for termination

Panel A: Progress of EIPs

Progress	Number of DEIPs	Number of EIPs	Total
Termination	116	104	220
Non-termination	40	987	1027
Total	156	1091	1247

Panel B: Reasons for termination

Type	DEIPs		EIPs		Total	
	Number	%	Number	%	Number	%
Change in environment	63	54.31%	37	35.58%	100	45.45%
Poor operating performance	–	–	53	50.96%	53	24.09%
Change in incentive objects	9	7.76%	5	4.81%	14	6.36%
Change in stock prices	2	1.72%	3	2.88%	5	2.27%
Disapproval on DEIPs	8	6.90%	–	–	8	3.64%
Issuance of new regulations	29	25.00%	2	1.92%	31	14.09%
Occurrence of other events	2	1.72%	4	3.85%	6	2.73%
Unspecified reasons	3	2.59%	–	–	3	1.36%
Total	116	100.00%	104	100.00%	220	100.00%

Notes: This table reports the progress of EIPs and reasons for termination. Here, "DEIPs" refer to those DEIPs announced during 2006–2016 have not been approved by shareholders by the end of March 2017, while "EIPs" refer to those that have already been passed and implemented. So, the number of EIPs here (1091) is larger than that of announcements of EIPs (1071) accounted for the period of 2006–2016.

To explore why DEIPS and EIPs were terminated, we collected the reasons for termination from termination announcements and divided them into eight categories: (1) change in environment (including business environment, policy environment, and capital market environment); (2) poor operating performance; (3) change in incentive objects;[14] (4) change in stock prices; (5) disapproval of shareholders, the CSRC, or other regulators of DEIPs; (6) issuance of new regulations such as the MREI (1-3) (2008); (7) occurrence of other events;[15] and (8) unspecified reasons. As shown in Table 9.7, change in environment and issuance of new regulations are the main reasons for termination of DEIPs. Poor operating performance contributes to the failure of EIPs most, followed by change in environment. Overall, change in environment is the most widely used reason for termination. However, the information contained in this reason is little and not specific. Firms may use change in environment as an excuse for their unwillingness to disclose the real reasons behind termination. More research needs to be done to detect the real reasons behind the vague expressions used by firms.

This section surveys the equity-based compensation in China's listed firms during 2006–2016 in terms of the frequency, the incentive objects, the grant size, the incentive forms, the valid period, the vesting schedule, the vesting conditions, the grant/exercise price, the progress status, and the reasons for termination. To summarize, by the end of 2016, about 30% of listed firms in China have proposed DEIPs, and 27% of listed firms implemented EIPs. But around 90% of firms implementing EIPs are Non-SCCs. The grant size has been declining and on average is 2.85%, well below the 10% maximum as specified by regulations. The proportion of equity grants to executives has also been declining and average fair value per executive grants is 1.95 million RMB. Like in the United States since 2006 (Murphy, 2013), restricted stocks have gradually dominated stock options and become the main form of equity-based compensation in China since 2012. The vesting pattern is typically graded vesting in three years. The average valid period is 4.63 years. Therefore, the stock-based compensation in China is at most mid-term compensation. Performance hurdles are set for the stock compensation to be vested and various accounting-based profitability measures are used as hurdles. The exercise price of restricted stocks is only half of that of stock options. This might explain the popularity of restricted stock. Most of DEIPs successfully progress to the implementation stage. But there do have DEIPs and EIPs been terminated. Changing environments and poor performance are the main reasons claimed for the termination. Finally, due to strict regulation, the equity-based compensations in SCCs are much fewer in frequency, smaller in grant size, longer in valid period, and having more performance hurdles, compared with those in Non-SCCs.

4. A simple test on the contract design of equity incentive plans

The design of EIPs fundamentally determines what kind of effects EIPs can bring about. According to efficient contracting argument, equity incentive plans are used to align interests of executives or core employees with those of shareholders. The design of plan will reflect a competitive equilibrium in the market for managerial talent and incentives are structured to optimize firm value (Core and Guay, 1999). On the contrary, managerial power hypothesis argues that high level of equity-based compensation is the result of managers' ability to set their own pay. To further distinguish which motivation dominates in equity incentive plans in China, we use corporate governance variables and proxies of managerial power to predict contract design characteristics. If better corporate governance and weak managerial power lead to more incentive-oriented contract design, managerial power hypothesis will be supported; otherwise, efficient contracting hypothesis will be supported.

4.1 Factors influence contract design

According to the managerial power hypothesis, as self-interested individuals, managers take an active part in the design of compensation packages instead of being the one who accepts the "optimal" contracts set by shareholders or other groups passively. Managers will ex ante influence the design to maximize the gains for their own welfare, especially in presence of deficiency in corporate governance and severe agency problems. For example, Davila and Penalva (2006) find that firms with stronger managerial power put more weight on accounting-based measures of performance, compared with stock-based performance measures. Abernethy et al. (2015) and Qu et al. (2016) provide the evidence that firms with powerful CEOs attach less challenging targets or less restrictive vesting conditions in stock option plans. Cadman et al. (2013) find that firms with more powerful CEOs and weaker governance grant options with shorter vesting periods.

Studies on China's listed firms also find that higher managerial power is related with lower exercise price (Wang et al., 2012) and higher likelihood of granting restricted stocks (Xiao et al., 2016). Managers are documented to set target performance measures which are too easy to be met (Wu and Wu, 2010). The equity incentive plans that set very low target performance measures are called welfare-oriented equity incentives (Lv et al., 2009; Xin and Lv, 2012). Thus, EIPs are more likely to be welfare-oriented when there are powerful managers. The power of managers inflates when the CEO chairs the board and when managerial ownership gets bigger. Therefore, based on the managerial power hypothesis, we predict that CEO duality and managerial ownership are positively related with the probability of setting welfare-oriented incentive contracts.

Good corporate governance can counterbalance the opportunistic behavior of managers. Since the board of directors is the one who makes the first move toward the approval of DEIPs, we predict that board characteristics are important determinants of the design of EIPs. A more independent board is assumed to have lower probability of being controlled by managers and hence to set incentive-oriented EIPs (Lv et al., 2009; Fang et al., 2015). Although large boards can result in less effective coordination, communication and decision-making (Jensen, 1993), but can also pose counterbalance for managerial power. Laux and Laux (2009) find that board monitoring can relieve earnings management induced by CEO equity incentives. Therefore, we argue that independent board and large board can lower the probability of managers' serving their own interests through effective control over the company by setting welfare-oriented EIPs.

Shareholder activism can also relieve managerial powers. Large shareholders and institutional shareholders, taking active part in corporate governance, can supervise the behaviors and performance of the management (Shleifer and Vishny, 1986; Agrawal and Mandelker, 1990; Gillan and Starks, 2000). Large stakes of these two types shareholders not only have the passion and energy to monitor managers, but also enjoy information advantage which is lack of for smaller, passive investors. The probability of designing incentive-oriented EIPs, therefore, increases with both the proportion of large shareholders and that of institutional shareholders. Therefore, we predict that companies with higher proportion of large shareholders and institutional shareholders are more inclined to design incentive-oriented EIPs.

Finally, we control for ownership type. Executive compensation in SCCs is under strong regulations, partly due to the praise of social equality in socialist China, and partly due to the negative impact of managerial power when managers enjoy de facto control rights. The design of EIPs in SCCs is confronted with stricter rules. The SASAC and the MOF set upper bounds for executive compensation from incentive plans in SCCs. Equity incentives in State-owned financial companies were suspend since 2009. The waiting period for SCCs is required to be at least two years, but for Non-SCCs 1 year is the minimum. Thus, compared with Non-SCCs, the valid periods are longer and vesting conditions are stricter in SCCs.

4.2 Research design

DEIPs, as discussed before, are the better choice for motivation analysis. Therefore, our initial sample comprises the 1247 DEIPs announced during 2006–2016. We exclude 77 DEIPs that were announced in the same year as initial public offerings. In addition, we remove 8 DEIPs that were announced either by financial company or companies in financial trouble (labeled as special treatment (ST) by the stock exchange). Finally, we obtain 1100, 1110, 1106, and 1113 observations for grant size test, incentive form test, valid period test, and vesting condition test, respectively, after deleting missing data. Our data come from the Wind database and the CSMAR database, and we checked the filings of stock-based compensation for detailed contract terms. To mitigate the influence of outliers, all continuous variables are winsorized at the 1st and 99th percentiles.

Grant size, incentive form, valid period, and vesting conditions are key elements of EIPs. These contract design characteristics are regressed on firm characteristics using the following model:

$$EIPs_{i,t} = \alpha_0 + \alpha_1 SC_{i,t} + \alpha_2 Big10_{i,t-1} + \alpha_3 Institutional_{i,t-1} + \alpha_4 BoardSize_{i,t-1}$$
$$+ \alpha_5 Independent_{i,t-1} + \alpha_6 CEODuality_{i,t-1} + \alpha_7 Managerial_{i,t-1}$$
$$+ \sum_{j=1}^{n} \beta_j Controls_{i,t-1} + \varepsilon$$

The dependent variable *EIPs* includes four variables of contract characteristics of DEIPs, which are used interchangeably. The four variables are: *Grant Size*, measured as the proportion of shares will be granted to the total shares outstanding; *Valid Period*, measured as the length of time from grant date to expiry date; *Incentive Form*, measured as the proportion of equity grants in form of restricted stocks to total equity grants; and *Vesting Conditions*, measured as the number of vesting conditions.

As for the predictors, *SC* is a dummy variable for state control, equals 1 when the listed firm is controlled by state owners and 0 otherwise. *Big10* is a measure of ownership concentration, calculated as the proportion of shares owned by top ten shareholders. *Institutional* is a variable measuring the proportion of shares held by institutional shareholders. *BoardSize* refers to the size of board of directors. *Independent* is a variable for the ratio of independent directors to the number of directors on the board. *CEODuality* is an indicator variable, coded 1 for firms with CEO serves the chair of the board, and 0 otherwise. *Managerial* is the proportion of shares held by managers. These variables will capture the effect of managerial power (*CEODuality, Managerial*), shareholder counterbalance (*Big10, Institutional*), board monitoring (*BoardSize, Independent*), and government regulation (*SC*). We also control other firm characteristics, include firm size (*SIZE*), growth opportunity (*Q*), leverage (*LEV*), cash holding (*CASH*), profitability (*ROE*), cash dividend (*DIV*), agency cost (*AC*). In addition, marketization index (*MI*) is controlled to account for governance environmental factors. Finally, industry and year fixed effects are controlled. Table 9.8 gives the variable definitions.

4.3 Empirical results

Table 9.9 presents descriptive statistics for variables used in empirical tests. Grant size has a mean and median value of 2.85% and 2.47%. Among all the equity grants, restricted stocks take up 55.8% on average. The mean value of valid period is 4.64 years. The median of number of vesting conditions is 2. These contract terms are very close to the descriptions in Section 3. Table 9.9 also reports firm characteristics of firm-years with DEIPs announcements, against all firm-years

Table 9.8 Definition of variables

Variable name	Definition of variables
Grant Size	The proportion of shares covered by DEIPs to total outstanding shares.
Incentive Form	The proportion of equities granted in the form of restricted stocks to total equity grants.
Valid Period	The time length of valid period and if there is difference between two incentive forms in one DEIPs, the longer one is chosen.
Vesting Conditions	The number of vesting conditions.
SC	An indicator variable with a value of "1" if the company is controlled by the state and "zero" otherwise.
Big10	The proportion of shares hold by top 10 big shareholders to total outstanding shares.
Institutional	The proportion of shares hold by institutional shareholders to total outstanding shares.
BoardSize	The number of directors in the board.
Independent	The proportion of independent directors to all directors in the board.
CEODuality	An indicator variable with a value of "1" if the CEO also work as board chair and "zero" otherwise.
Managerial	The proportion of shares hold by managers to total shares outstanding.[1]
Size	Natural logarithm of book value of total assets.
Q	Tobin's Q, the ratio of market value of equity plus book value of debt to book value of total assets.
LEV	The ratio of debts to total assets.
CASH	Cash assets scaled by total assets.
ROE	Return on book value of equity.
DIV	Cash dividend per share.
AC	The ratio of general and administrative expenses to revenue.
MI	The marketization index announced by Wang et al. (2017) minus the average value of the index in each year.[2]

[1] Here, the range of managers is followed the statements of the CSRC including directors, supervisors and senior managers.

[2] The marketization index is a comprehensive province-level index that measures the progress of marketization reform and the degree of marketization from five aspects: ① the relationship between the government and market; ② the development of non-State-owned economy; ③ the development of product market; ④ the development of production elements market; ⑤ the development of market intermediary organizations and legal system environment. There are two versions of marketization index. The version announced in 2011 includes observations from 1997 to 2010, while the version announced in 2016 includes observations from 2008 to 2014. We use the 2011 version of marketization index for observation before 2008 and the 2016 version of marketization index for observation in 2008 and beyond. Since the calculation has changed slightly in 2016 version, we use the value of marketization index minus the average value in the year instead of absolute value to reduce the impact of the difference of calculation between these two versions. Besides, for observations in 2015, we use interpolation methods to infer the marketization index approximately.

over the same period. There are only 12.85% of DEIPs in our sample were announced by SCCs. However, during the same period, 43.29% of the firms were controlled by state institutions. For firms with DEIPs, on average, 62.43% of shares are owned by the top ten largest shareholders, and 32.28% by institutional shareholders. The median board size is 9, and one third of them

Table 9.9 Descriptive statistics

Variables	Firm-Years with DEIP announcements						All Firm-Years				
	No. of Obs.	Mean	Median	Std. Dev	Min	Max	No. of Obs.	Mean	Median	T-test	Wilcoxon-Z
Grant Size	1100	0.0285	0.0247	0.0197	0.0014	0.0978	—	—	—	—	—
Incentive Form	1110	0.5580	1.0000	0.4789	0.0000	1.0000	—	—	—	—	—
Valid Period	1106	4.6415	4.0000	1.1085	3.0000	10.0000	—	—	—	—	—
Vesting Conditions	1113	1.8625	2.0000	0.7234	1.0000	4.0000	—	—	—	—	—
SC	1113	0.1285	0.0000	0.3348	0.0000	1.0000	20113	0.4329	0.0000	-20.2426***	-20.050***
Big10	1113	0.6243	0.6415	0.1400	0.2491	0.8998	20113	0.5813	0.5925	8.8839***	9.163***
Institutional	1113	0.3228	0.2861	0.2379	0.0000	0.8694	20113	0.3345	0.3144	-1.5571	-1.202
BoardSize	1113	8.5948	9.0000	1.6360	5.0000	14.0000	20113	9.0391	9.0000	-7.6759***	-6.759***
Independent	1113	0.3765	0.3333	0.0604	0.3333	0.6000	20113	0.3670	0.3333	5.9662***	22.687***
CEODuality	1113	0.3333	0.0000	0.4716	0.0000	1.0000	20113	0.2084	0.0000	9.9016***	9.879***
Managerial	1113	0.2186	0.1232	0.2329	0.0000	0.7230	20113	0.0973	0.0001	20.7323***	20.996***
Size	1113	21.6078	21.3896	1.1160	19.8050	25.2974	20113	21.8797	21.6634	-6.6212***	-6.471***
Q	1113	3.4569	2.7705	2.4206	0.9548	13.7987	20113	2.5539	1.9522	15.6767***	16.234***
LEV	1113	0.3552	0.3315	0.2011	0.0349	0.8219	20113	0.4525	0.4568	-14.7860***	-14.602***
CASH	1113	0.2810	0.2307	0.1861	0.0290	0.7948	20113	0.2010	0.1543	16.4008***	15.557***
ROE	1113	0.1106	0.1038	0.0724	-0.0689	0.3397	20113	0.0753	0.0783	10.0355***	11.269***
DIV	1113	0.1556	0.1000	0.1743	0.0000	1.0000	20113	0.1077	0.0500	10.3513***	13.191***
AC	1113	0.1105	0.0906	0.0815	0.0138	0.4242	20113	0.0943	0.0752	6.4534***	8.343***
MI	1113	1.9978	2.4242	1.3414	-2.0148	3.9690	20113	1.4870	1.8110	10.1343***	9.467***

Notes: This table reports descriptive statistics of all variables used in empirical tests. Since there are cases in which grant size is related to performance and valid period is not clearly specified, the observations for grant size, incentive form and valid period is less than those of other variables. The definitions of all variables are shown in table 9.8. **** indicates that the differences in means/medians are statistically significant at 1% level.

are independent directors. About one third of firms have their CEOs serve as the chairman of the board. The average managerial ownership is 21.86%, but the range of managerial ownership is 0%–72.3%. This shows a great variation in managerial power among firms. Compared with the whole listed firms sample over 2006–2016, firms announced DEIPs have more concentrated ownership, smaller boards, higher independent boards ratio, more likely to have CEO serve as the chairman, and higher managerial ownership. DEIP firms are also smaller, with higher valuation, lower leverage, higher cash holding, more profitable, distribute more dividends, have higher administration costs, and locate in more developed areas. Therefore, DEIP firms have big shareholders, strong boards, strong managerial power, as well as strong financial performance.

Table 9.10 reports the regression results. In the first column of Table 9.10, grant size is the dependent variable. Consistent with compensation regulation in SCCs, the coefficient on *SC* is significantly negative. Therefore, equity-based compensation in state-controlled companies displays relatively low incentive intensity. The negative and significant coefficient on *Big10* suggests that companies with higher proportion of big shareholders are likely to limit the grant size. It seems that big shareholders can be a counterbalance to prevent managers overpaying themselves by issuing more equity-based compensation. It is reasonable to find that grant size in big companies is smaller, because in general, big firms have more total shares outstanding. The coefficient on growth opportunity is negative and significant, which is opposite to the hypotheses proposed by Smith and Watts (1992) and the findings of Core and Guay (1999). Besides, high leveraged companies are more likely to grant more equities, which may be a substitute for cash compensation due to debt pressure. The intensity of equity incentives is at a relatively high level in companies with higher agency cost. In general, these results support managerial opportunistic hypothesis of equity incentive.

In the second column of Table 9.10, the dependent variable is the ratio of restricted stocks. Due to the lower grant price, it is argued that restricted stocks are more favorable to managers. However, when restricted stocks are granted, and the vesting conditions are met, managers need to use their own money to first purchase the stocks, of cause at much lower price. On the contrary, the stock options are granted to managers for free, only condition on performance hurdles and working period. As such, it is argued that restricted stocks are more binding. Since there are no extra rules specifying which form of equity incentives SCCs should take, there is no significant difference in incentive form between SCCs and Non-SCCs. Most of the coefficients on corporate governance structure and managerial power variables are insignificant except board size, independent board and CEO duality, whose coefficients are marginally significant. Companies with larger boards and higher percentage of independent boards are more likely to grant restricted stocks rather than stock options. Firms with CEO serves simultaneously as chair of the board are more likely to grant stock options rather than restricted stocks. It seems that powerful board prefer restricted stocks, but powerful managers prefer stock options, supporting the bonding hypothesis of restricted stocks.

The results of regression on valid period are reported in the third column of Table 9.10. Due to stricter rules on valid period, the valid periods of DEIPs announced by SCCs are relatively longer. Moreover, we do find the positive role of big shareholders in guiding the design of EIPs toward incentive orientation. Finally, firm size and growth opportunities are positively related with valid period. But leverage is negatively related with valid period.

Generally, more vesting conditions make vesting more difficult. For shareholders, more vesting conditions in some degree ensure that incentives are not granted for free but require some efforts to be made, reflecting the primary goal of equity-based compensation. The empirical results of the regression on the number of vesting conditions are presented in the last column of Table 9.10. SCCs set more vesting conditions to convey the signal to the public that equity incentives are

Table 9.10 Empirical results

Variables	(1) Grant size	(2) Incentive form	(3) Valid period	(4) Vesting conditions
SCt	−0.0148★★★	−0.0518	0.9277★★★	0.6500★★★
	(0.002)	(0.049)	(0.146)	(0.076)
Big10t−1	−0.0075★	−0.0810	0.4961★	0.2378
	(0.005)	(0.110)	(0.299)	(0.155)
Institutional t−1	−0.0030	−0.0147	−0.1959	0.0993
	(0.003)	(0.066)	(0.165)	(0.087)
BoardSize t−1	0.0002	0.0189★	−0.0050	0.0305★★
	(0.000)	(0.011)	(0.028)	(0.015)
Independent t−1	−0.0143	0.4863★	1.0711	0.7553★
	(0.009)	(0.250)	(0.751)	(0.389)
CEODuality t−1	0.0009	−0.0520★	−0.0299	−0.0403
	(0.001)	(0.028)	(0.063)	(0.037)
Managerial t−1	−0.0036	−0.1010	−0.1126	−0.0491
	(0.003)	(0.067)	(0.146)	(0.086)
Size t−1	−0.0046★★★	−0.0705★★★	0.1995★★★	−0.0269
	(0.001)	(0.019)	(0.056)	(0.028)
Q t−1	−0.0021★★★	−0.0124	0.0369★	−0.0285★★★
	(0.000)	(0.008)	(0.021)	(0.009)
LEV t−1	0.0157★★★	−0.0314	−0.4746★	−0.0688
	(0.004)	(0.105)	(0.243)	(0.142)
CASH t−1	−0.0024	−0.0351	0.0205	0.4266★★★
	(0.004)	(0.098)	(0.215)	(0.134)
ROE t−1	0.0120	−0.1816	0.7542	0.4914
	(0.010)	(0.235)	(0.629)	(0.332)
DIV t−1	0.0041	0.1771★	−0.2116	−0.3341★★★
	(0.003)	(0.092)	(0.195)	(0.117)
AC t−1	0.0177★★	0.1842	−0.6550	−0.2549
	(0.008)	(0.221)	(0.428)	(0.295)
MI t−1	0.0004	0.0129	−0.0187	−0.0091
	(0.000)	(0.010)	(0.028)	(0.016)
Constant	0.1608★★★	1.3431★★★	−0.2489	1.4992★★
	(0.017)	(0.449)	(1.275)	(0.688)
Year FE	YES	YES	YES	YES
Industry FE	YES	YES	YES	YES
Observations	1,100	1,110	1,106	1,113
R-squared	0.292	0.268	0.228	0.394

Notes: This table reports the empirical results from OLS regressions. All variables are defined in table 9.8. Robust standard errors are shown in parentheses. ★★★, ★★, and ★ represent the coefficient is statistically significant at 1%, 5%, and 10 % levels respectively.

serving as the tool for motivating managers to work hard rather than increasing managers' private welfare. In addition, the number of vesting conditions is positively related with board size and independency. Therefore, big and independent board help to set the equity incentive plan toward an efficient contracting. The number of vesting conditions is negatively related with growth opportunities and cash dividend payment, but positively related with the level of cash holding.

To summarize, equity incentive plans in SCCs have smaller grant size, longer valid period, and more performance hurdles. However, the seemingly more incentive-oriented contracting is actually the results of government regulation. The by-product of the stricter regulation is that it makes equity incentives less attractive. In addition, stronger corporate governance results in more incentive-oriented contracting, which can be seen from the following observations: the presence of big shareholder results in smaller grant size and longer valid period. The bigger and the more independent the board, the more likely that restricted stocks are used, and the more performance hurdles are set. The above evidence points toward a managerial power story of equity-based compensation in China.

5. The consequences of implementing equity-based compensations

5.1 *Manage earnings to meet vesting conditions*

The primary goal of introducing performance hurdles in equity incentive plans is to motivate managers to work hard. However, since accounting-based performance hurdles are subject to managers' discretions and market-based performance hurdles can be influenced by manager's financial reporting strategy, managing earnings is another way to meet vesting conditions. Benmelech et al. (2010) show that in a dynamic rational expectations model with asymmetric information, stock-based compensation not only induces managers to exert costly effort, but also induces them to conceal bad news about future growth options, and choose sub-optimal investment policies to support the pretense. Findings in empirical research supports the earnings management prediction. For example, Cheng and Warfield (2005) document that managers with high equity incentives are more likely to report earnings that meet or just beat analysts' forecasts. They are also less likely to report large positive earnings surprise to reserve earnings for the future. Bergstresser and Phlilippon (2006) find that CEO equity incentives are associated with accrual management. Efendi et al. (2007) conclude that the larger the value of a CEO's stock option holdings, the greater his/her incentive to misstate the financial statements to support the stock price. There are other arguments, however. Laux and Laux (2009) predict that directors will adjust their oversight effort in response to a change in CEO incentives and an increase in CEO equity incentives, therefore, does not necessarily increase earnings management. Consistent with this conjecture, Erickson et al. (2006) and Armstrong et al. (2010) find no consistent evidence that managers' equity incentives are positively associated with accounting fraud or irregularities.

Equity incentive induced earnings management was documented in China. Xiao et al. (2013) find that firms manage earnings downwards before the announcement of DEIPs to lower exercising price and performance hurdles and the extent of earnings management is positively related to the managerial power. Studies also find that the earnings management pattern perfectly corresponds to the equity incentive schedules. Earnings are managed upwards during vesting and exercising period and downwards after the exercising period (Su and Lin, 2010; Liu et al., 2016). Liu (2017) provides evidence for Chinese listed firms that analysts forecast accuracy is noticeably higher for listed firms with higher levels of management compensation. Liu (2017) thus suggests the alignment view of managerial incentives in China since managerial compensation improves information environments. However, it is also possible that the higher analysts forecast accuracy is the results of managers reporting strategy to meet the analysts' expectations (Cheng and Warfield, 2005).

5.2 More dividends, more gains?

To maximum their gains, managers have strong tendency to not only lower grant (exercise) prices but also increase current stock prices. Due to strict regulations on information disclosure and pricing, there exist no opportunities for managers to alter the grant date to choose a relatively low grant price or exercise price. However, equity incentives are dividend-protective in China. The grant (exercise) prices can be adjusted downwards accordingly whenever there is cash or stock dividend announced. At the same time, investors respond positively to payments of both cash dividends and stock dividends. Therefore, distributing dividend is an effective way to enhance the fair value of equity incentives in China.

Where executive stock options are generally not dividend-protective, dividends are reduced relative to expected dividends in firms with executive stock options (Lambert et al., 1989). Fenn and Liang (2001) find a negative relationship between dividends and stock options, as well as a positive relationship between repurchases and stock options, indicating a shift from dividends to share repurchases for companies awarding equities. Using a sample of European countries (including the UK, Germany, France, Italy, the Netherlands, and Spain), De Cesari and Ozkan (2015) find that executive stock option holdings and stock option deltas are negatively associated with both dividend payments and total payout.

When equity incentives are dividend-protective, equity incentives can increase dividend payouts. Aboody and Kasznik (2008) find that dividend-protective restricted stocks have been used increasingly, and the use of restricted stocks related with increases in firms' payouts. Using a sample of Chinese listed companies, Xiao and Yu (2012) provide the evidence that the announcement of equity incentives has a positive impact on the levels of stock dividends, the transfer of reserve to common shares, and cash dividends. Similarly, Han et al. (2012) find that companies that implement stock incentives are more likely to issue high stock dividends and the probability of issuing high stock dividends increases with the degree of stock incentives.

5.3 The incentive effect of equity-based compensation

One of the objectives of equity incentives is to motivate managers taking reasonable risks. However, managers are documented to taking too much risk because of equity incentives (e.g. Bhagat and Bolton, 2014). What's more, equity portfolios can even provide managers incentives to take risks in a distorted way, e.g. misreporting (Armstrong et al., 2013). Literature also documents risk-taking effect of equity incentives in Chinese firms. For example, Wang and Wu (2016) find that vega is positively related with risk-taking in China. Chen and Zhou (2014) documents that incentive-oriented EIPs are related with higher R&D expenses.

Another objective of equity incentives is to attract talented managers. Zong et al. (2013) and Chen et al. (2017) both find that firms with equity incentives have lower top management turnover. There is also evidence that equity incentives relieve agency costs and improve performance. Studies using Chinese firms as research sample have find that equity incentives can improve the efficiency of internal control systems (Yu and Wu, 2015), reduce cost stickiness (Liang, 2016), reduce auditing fees (Ni et al., 2017), improve investment efficiency (Lv and Zhang, 2011), facilitate debt financing (Hu and Gai, 2014; Sheng et al., 2016), and accelerate leverage adjustment toward target leverage (Yang et al., 2016). There are also studies that directly examine the market performance and operating performance of equity-based compensation and find positive results (Xie and Chen, 2010; Liu and Ma, 2013; Fang et al., 2015).

In this section, we draw from the literature to discuss the agency problems arising from the implementation of equity incentive plans, such as earnings management and opportunistic dividend policy. We also review the empirical findings on the incentive effect of equity incentive plans in China's listed firms. In doing this, we find evidence supporting both managerial power hypothesis and efficient contracting hypothesis. Although the related studies are just starting, and the above evidence is preliminary, we still find that the two hypotheses are not mutually exclusive, but can coexist.

6. Conclusion

Despite a long history, equity incentives in modern China are not viable until the issuance of the REI-T at the end of 2005. Since then, great progress of regulation on equity incentive has been witnessed and the popularity of equity incentives has increased. This study presents a general picture on equity incentives in China's listed firms. Especially, we introduce the regulatory background, the evolution and the status of, the contract design and the consequences of equity incentive plans in listed firms. The regulation on equity incentives is rigid in China, especially for SCCs. Strict regulatory rules were set in terms of qualifications, vesting conditions, grant price, valid period, disclosure, etc. By analyzing the contract design, we concluded that the role of equity incentives is more appropriate to be defined as medium-term incentives rather long-term incentives. We further show that SCCs are more likely to announce DEIPs with smaller grant size, longer valid period, and more vesting conditions, due to stricter regulation. Moreover, the monitor function of big shareholders and independent directors is observed in the design of DEIPs. Finally, we find both evidence of managerial power hypothesis and efficient contracting hypothesis of equity incentives in China's listed firms. The managerial power hypothesis is indicated by the contract design, the earnings management arising from and dividend policies triggered by equity incentives. The efficient contracting argument is supported by the evidence on the consequences of equity incentives in terms of investment efficiency, announcement date return, and operating performance after granting equity incentives.

Appendix 1
A LIST OF ABBREVIATIONS

CCCPC	Central Committee of the Communist Party of China
CSDC	China Securities Depository and Clearing Corporation
CSRC	China Securities Regulatory Commission
DEIP	Draft of Equity Incentive Plan
EIP	Equity Incentive Plan
ESOP	Employee Stock Ownership Plan
MOC	Ministry of Commerce
MOF	Ministry of Finance
MOST	Ministry of Science and Technology
MREI (1–3)	Memorandums on Relevant Issues of Equity Incentives (1–3)
NDRC	National Development and Reform Commission
Non-SCCs	Non-State-Controlled Companies
PAOSC	Production Affairs Office of the State Council
PBC	People's Bank of China
REI-T	Regulation on Equity Incentives in Listed companies (Trial)
REI	Regulation on Equity Incentives in Listed companies
SASAC	China State-Owned Assets Supervision and Administration Commission
SAT	State Administration of Taxation
SCCs	State-Controlled Companies
SCET	State Commission for Economic and Trade
SCNPC	Standing Committee of the National People's Congress
SCRES	State Commission for Restructuring the Economic System
SCSC	Securities Committee of the State Council
SOEs	State-Owned Enterprises

Appendix 2

SUMMARY OF LAWS AND REGULATIONS RELATED TO EQUITY INCENTIVES IN CHINA

Panel A: Laws and regulations on equity incentives

Title of laws and regulations/Issuing authorities/Issuing date/Effective date
• Key Items

[1] *Regulation on Pilot Project of Joint-Stock Enterprises*/SCRES, NDRC, MOF, PBC, and PAOSC / 05–15–1992 / 05–15–1992
• In pilot joint-stock enterprises established though private placements, employees are allowed to hold stocks and stock certificates. But these stocks and stock certificates cannot be traded outside the enterprises.

[2] *Regulatory Opinions on Limited Liability Companies*/SCRES / 05–15–1992 / 05–15–1992
• In limited liability companies established through private placements, stock certificates held by employees can be traded among legal persons and employees within the companies.
• Legal persons shall not transfer State-owned shares, warrants and preferred shares to their employees, or purchase shares using collective welfare fund, reward fund or public welfare fund and grant the shares to employees.
• The shares held by employees shall not be transferred within 3 years after the company's placements.
• Directors and managers shall not transfer their shares within 3 years of their service, and the shares transferred after the locking period and during their tenures shall not exceed half of their total shares. Share transfer by directors and managers shall be approved by the board of directors.

[3] *Opinions on Immediately Suppressing Malpractices in Issuing Internal Employee Shares*/SCRES, SCET, and SCSC / 04–03–1993 / 04–03–1993
• Due to the negative impact arising from the malpractices in issuing shares to employees, such as issuing shares to those who are not allowed to hold shares or illegal trading of stock certificates, the local governments are required to immediately restrict and suspend the approval of new establishment of companies which issue shares to employees.

[4] *Notice on the Shutoff of the Issuance of Internal Employee Shares*/CSRC / 11–25–1998 / 11–25–1998
• The limited shareholding companies shall not issue internal employee shares since the issuance of this notice.

---

[5] *Guiding Opinions on Pilot Implementation of Future Stock Incentives for Executives in State-owned Enterprises* / 8 Beijing Government Agencies / 07–28–1999 / 07–28–1999

- State-owned Enterprise can grant future stocks to its chairman of the board and the general manager. With the approval of shareholders and the board, other senior managers who are willing to hold shares could invest in the company with cash.
- Managerial ownership shall range from 5% to 20% of company's total shares. The shares held by the chairman of the board and the general manager should exceed 10% of managerial ownerships.
- The amount of capital contributed by managers shall not be less than 100,000 Yuan. The number of managerial shares generally ranges from 1 to 4 times of their capital contribution.
- Managerial shares could be transferred after 2 years of serving the office.

[6] *Decisions of the Central Committee of the Communist Party of China on Several Major Issues Concerning the Reform and Development of State-owned Enterprises*/ the 15th CCCPC / 09–22–1999 / 09–22–1999

- The trial implementation of annual salary systems, shareholding systems, and other distribution forms was allowed in State-owned enterprises.

[7] *Guiding Opinions on the Pilot Work of Equity Incentives for State-owned High-tech Enterprises*/MOF and MOST / 08–21–2002 / 08–21–2002

- The scope of pilot enterprises of equity incentives covers the state-owed high-tech enterprises (excluding listed companies) whose R&D expenses (R&D personnel) account for more than 5% (10%) of annual sales (total employees) and cumulative added-value of net assets generated from net profit exceeds 30% of enterprises' net assets over the past three years. The incentive objects include R&D personnel and managers who have made outstanding contributions.
- Incentive forms can be equity shares awarded, equity shares selling at a specific price, and equities shares for patented technology or non-patented technology.
- The value of equity incentives shall not exceed 35% of the added-value generated from net profit after tax over the past three years and the proportion of equities shares awarded shall not exceed 50% of total equities under the incentive plans.

[8] *Notice on Relevant Issues of Implementation of "Guiding Opinions on the Pilot Work of Equity Incentives for State-owned High-tech Enterprises"*/MOF and MOST / 11–18–2002 / 11–18–2002

- The number of pilot enterprises shall not exceed 5 for each province, autonomous region, municipality directly under the Central Government, or municipalities with independent planning status.

[9] *Notice on the Pilot Work of Equity Incentives for Central State-owned High-tech Enterprises*/SASAC and MOST / 04-30-2004 / 04-30-2004

- The scope of pilot equity incentives enterprises covers the central state-owed high-tech enterprises (excluding listed companies) for which the revenues from high-tech production accounts for more than 50% of total revenues and conditions listed in the *Guiding Opinions on the Pilot Work of Equity Incentive for State-owned High-tech Enterprises* are met.

[10] *Company Law of the People's Republic of China* (2005 Revision)/the SCNPC / 10–27–2005 / 01–01–2006

- A company can repurchase its own shares to award its employees with the approval of the meeting of shareholders. The shares repurchased shall not exceed 5% of the total shares already issued by this company. The funds used for the share acquisition shall be paid from the after-tax profits of the company. The shares purchased by the company shall be transferred to the employees within 1 year.
- The directors, supervisors and senior managers of the company shall file to the company the shares held by them and the changes thereof. During the term of office, the shares transferred by any of them each year shall not exceed 25% of the total shares of the company he/she holds. The shares of the company held by the aforesaid persons shall not be transferred within 1 year from the date the company gets listed. The aforesaid persons shall not transfer the shares of the company he/she holds within six months from the date being removed from his post.

(Continued)

[11] *Guiding Opinions on the Share-Split Reform of Listed Companies* /CSRC, SASAC, MOF, PBC, MOC / 08–23–2005 / 08–23–2005

- Listed companies that have completed the share-spit reform shall be given priority in raising funds from the secondary market, and may implement equity incentives to their management team.

[12] *Regulation on Equity Incentives in Listed Companies (Trial)* /CSRC / 12–31–2005 / 01–01–2006

- *Incentive forms:* This regulation shall be applicable to the equity incentive plans implemented by a listed company through the granting of restricted stocks, stock options, and by other ways as permitted by law or administrative regulation.
- *Incentive objects:* The equity incentive objects may include the directors, supervisors, senior executives, and core employees of a listed company, and other employees that the company may deem necessary, but shall not include independent directors.
- *Grant size:* The aggregate stock involved in all the effective equity incentive plans of a listed company shall not exceed 10% of the total equity of the company. Without the approval of the special resolution of the shareholders' meeting, the accumulated stock granted to any incentive object shall not exceed 1% of the total equity of the company.
- *Valid period:* The interval between the grant date and the first vesting date of stock options shall not be less than 1 year and the valid period shall not exceed 10 years. During the valid period, the vesting of stock options shall be vested over several periods and the vested stock options shall be exercised during their respective exercise period, otherwise these stock options will expire.
- *Exercise price:* The exercise price of stock options shall be no less than the following prices, whichever is higher: (1) the stock price of the company at one trading day before the announcement date of the DEIP; and (2) the average stock price of the company within 30 trading days before the announcement date of the DEIP.
- *Adjustments of exercise price or the number of stock options:* In case a listed company needs to adjust the exercise price or the number of stock options due to ex-right or ex-dividend of the target stocks or other reasons, it may make adjustment according to the principles and ways as set forth in the stock option plan.
- *Financing to objects prohibited:* A listed company shall not provide loans and any other form of finance subsidy to any incentive object according to the equity incentive plan, including provide guarantee for his loans.
- *Procedures and information disclosure:* (See Section 2 of the body text)

[13] *Regulation on Equity Incentives in State-Controlled Companies Listed on Offshore Stock Exchanges (Trial)* /SASAC, MOF / 01–27–2006 / 03–01–2006

- *Grant size:* Within the valid period of EIPs, the prospective gains of a senior manager from equity incentive plans shall not exceed 40% of his/her total compensation.
- *Vesting schedule:* In principle, the vesting period shall not be less than 2 years and the unlock period or exercise period shall not be less than 3 years, during which the rights (here refers to the rights to exercise stock options or to unlock restricted stocks) shall be exercised in uniform speed and by batches.
- *Procedures:* The State-owned shareholders of a listed company shall, before the shareholders' meeting deliberates and approves an EIP, report the EIP to be implemented by the listed company to the organ or department that performs the duties of owner of state assets for review. The final opinions of State-owned shareholders on approving the EIP or not should be in accordance with the review result.

[14] *Regulation on Equity Incentives in State-Controlled Companies Listed on Domestic Stock Exchanges (Trial)* /SASAC and MOF / 09–30–2006 / 09–30–2006

- *Incentive objects:* The objects of equity incentive plans shall be, in principle, limited to the directors, senior managers of a listed company, and core technical personnel and managerial backbones that have direct influence on the overall performance and sustainable development of the listed company. The objects of the equity incentive plans shall not include supervisors, independent directors and the outside directors assumed by the personnel other than the holding company of a listed company.
- *Grant size:* Within the valid period of an EIP, the prospective returns of individual equity incentive of a senior manager shall not exceed 30% of his/her total compensation.
- *Vesting schedule:* Essentially the same as in the *Regulation on Equity Incentive in State-owned Companies Listed on Offshore Stock Exchanges (Trial)*.

[15] *Memorandum on Relevant Issues of Equity Incentives No.1/CSRC/03–17–2008 /03–17–2008*
- ***Incentive objects:*** In general, a shareholder holding 5% or more of the company's shares or the actual controller of the company shall not participate in an EIP, unless the shareholders' meeting approves its participation provided that all affiliated shareholders excuse themselves when vote at the shareholders' meeting. The spouse or a blood relative of a major shareholder holding 5% or more of the company's shares or the actual controller of the company may be a plan participant if the spouse or blood relative meets the conditions for participants. Attention shall be paid to whether the equity instruments granted to him or her corresponds with his or her position in the company, provided that all affiliated shareholders excuse themselves when vote at the shareholders' meeting.
- ***Grant price:*** The price discount for the granted restricted stocks shall obey the following rules: (1) If the underlying stock comes from share repurchase, the relevant provisions on stock repurchase in the *Company Law* shall apply; (2) If the underlying stock comes from private placement, the grant price shall not be lower than 50% of the company's average stock price for the 20 trading days prior to the base date for pricing.
- ***Vesting conditions:*** Vesting conditions shall refer to the performance of the company. In general, the performance-based vesting conditions (for example, earnings per share, weighted average return on equity, and net profit growth rate) shall not be lower than its historical levels. Moreover, market value and relative performance in the industry are encouraged, but the benchmark shall be no lower than the market index or the industry average performance.

[16] *Memorandum on Relevant Issues of Equity Incentives No.2/CSRC/05–06–2008 /05–06–2008*
- ***Incentive objects:*** To ensure the independence of the supervisors of listed companies and maximize their supervisory role, the supervisors of listed companies shall not be participants in any EIPs.
- ***Vesting conditions:*** A listed company may set vesting conditions suitable for the company according to its actual circumstances. The vesting conditions shall consist of financial indicators and non-financial indicators. If a performance indicator involves accounting profit, the company shall adopt the net profit after deduction of non-recurring profits and losses under the new accounting standards. Costs of stock options shall be listed under recurring profits and losses.

[17] *Memorandum on Relevant Issues of Equity Incentives* No.3/ CSRC/ 09–16–2008/ 09–16–2008
- ***Termination of EIPs:*** A listed company is prohibited from modifying the grant price or form of incentive plans without good reasons. If a listed company intends to modify the grant price or the form of incentive plan, its board of directors shall deliberate a resolution on cancelation of the original EIP and announce it to the public. At the same time, the listed company shall file an application with the CSRC to terminate the original equity incentive plan.
- ***Vesting conditions:*** An EIP of a listed company shall state that during the vesting period, the net profit attributed to the shareholders of the listed company and the net profit attributed to the shareholders of the listed company after deduction of non-recurring profits and losses shall be no lower than the average for the three accounting years prior to the grant date and shall not be negative.

[18] *Notice on Issues Concerning the Implementation of the Equity Incentive System in State-Controlled Listed Companies/SASAC and MOF/ 10–21–2008 / 10–21–2008*
- ***Vesting conditions:*** The target performance for granting equity instruments shall not be lower than the average performance of the company in the last three years, or the industry average performance, or the 50-percentile performance of benchmarking firms.
- ***Exercise conditions:*** The exercise condition shall be higher than vesting condition. The target performance for exercising equity incentive instruments shall be no lower than the performance at the vested year, no lower than the industry average performance (or 75-percentile performance of benchmarking firms).
- ***Vesting conditions for restricted stocks:*** The target performance for granting restricted stocks shall be no lower than the higher of average performance of in the last three years, the actual performance in the previous year, and the industry average performance (or 50-percentail performance of benchmarking firms).

(Continued)

- *Grant size:* During the valid period, the ratio of the equity incentive compensation obtained by an incentive object to his/her total compensation (including equity incentive returns, same below) shall not exceed 40% for a domestic listed company or an overseas H-share company, or 50% for an overseas red chip company. If the actual equity incentive compensation exceeds the above-mentioned ratio, the stock option (or stock appreciation right) that has not been exercised yet shall not be exercised any more, or the returns from exercising shall be turned in to the company.

[19] *Notice on the Compensation Regulation on the Responsible Persons of State-owned Financial Enterprises*/MOF / 01–13–2009 / 01–13–2009
- All State-owned financial enterprises shall suspend the implementation of EIPs and employee stock ownership plans.

[20] *Guiding Opinions on Pilot Implementation of Employee Stock Ownership Plans for Listed Companies*/CSRC / 06–20–2014 / 06–20–2014
- The implementation of ESOP is the independent decision of the company. Employees participate in ESOP on voluntary basis. List companies shall not force employees to participate in the company's ESOP in the way of apportionment or forced distribution.
- The holding term for each ESOP shall be no less than 12 months and, if the underlying stocks are issued via private placements, shall be no less than 36 months.
- The total number of shares covered by the ESOP of the listed company shall not exceed 10% of the total outstanding shares of the company. The total number of shares of the individual employees shall not exceed 1% of the total shares of the company.

[21] *Regulation on Equity Incentives in Listed Companies*/CSRC/ 07–13–2016 / 08–13–2016
- *Incentive objects:* Incentive objects may include the directors, senior executives, and core employees of a listed company, and other employees having direct impacts on the company's performance and development, but shall not include independent directors and supervisors. An employee of foreign nationality who serves as a director, senior executive, core technician or core business specialist of a listed company in China may be the incentive objects. A shareholder or an actual controller that solely or aggregately holds 5% or more shares of a listed company and his or her spouse, parents and children shall not be incentive objects.
- *Internal accountability mechanism and improper benefit taking-back mechanism:* A listed company shall enter into an agreement with the incentive objects, confirm the content of the EIP, and agree on both parties' other rights and obligations in accordance with this regulation. The listed company shall promise that the information disclosure documents relating to the equity incentive plan do not have any false records, misleading statements or material omissions. All incentive grantees shall promise that if the listed company fails to comply with the arrangements on the grant or exercise of equities because of any false record, misleading statement or material omission in the information disclosure documents, the incentive objects shall, after the false record, misleading statement or material omission in the relevant information disclosure documents are confirmed, return all the proceeds obtained from the EIP to the company.
- *Vesting conditions:* Vesting conditions shall include the company's performance indicators and personal performance indicators for incentive objects. The relevant indicators shall be objective, open, clear and transparent, shall comply with the company's actual circumstances, and be conducive to the enhancement of the company's competitiveness.
- *Grant price:* A listed company shall, when granting restricted stocks to incentive objects, determine the grant price or methods for determining the grant price. The grant price shall not be lower than the face value of stocks, and in principle, shall not be lower than the following price, whichever is higher: (1) 50% of the average trading price of the company's stocks of the trading day before the issuance of the draft equity incentive plan; (2) 50% of average trading price of the company's stocks 20 trading days, 60 trading days or 120 trading days before the issuance of the DEIP.

- **Exercise price:** A listed company shall, when granting stock options to incentive grantees, determine the exercise price or the methods for the determination of exercise price. The exercise price shall not be lower than the face value of the stocks, and shall in principle, not be lower than the following price, whichever is higher: (1) average trading price of the company's stocks of the trading day before the issuance of the draft equity incentive plan; (2) any of average trading price of the company's stocks 20 trading days, 60 trading days or 120 trading days before the issuance of the DEIP.
- **Vesting schedule:** The interval between the date of grant of stock options or restricted stocks and the first vesting date shall not be less than 12 months. Within the valid period, a listed company shall provide vesting by several periods, and each period shall not be less than 12 months. The proportion of equities (restricted stock or stock options) vested during each period shall not exceed 50% of the total amount of the equities covered in the EIP. Where the vesting conditions for the current period are not met, restricted stocks (stock options) shall not be unlocked (exercised) or deferred to the next period.
- **Procedures and information disclosure:** More rigorous.

Panel B: Laws and regulations relevant to the accounting treatment of equity incentives

Title of laws and regulations/Issuing authorities/Issuing date/Effective date
- Key Items

[22] *Accounting Standards for Enterprises No. 11 – Share-based Payments*/MOF/ 02–15–2006 / 01–01–2007
- The share-based payments shall consist of equity-settled share-based payments and cash-settled share-based payments.
- For an equity-settled share-based payment in return for services of employees, if the right may be exercised immediately after the grant, the fair value of the equity instruments shall, on the grant day, be recorded in the relevant cost or expense and the capital surplus shall be increased correspondingly. For an equity-settled share-based payment in return for employee services, if the right cannot be exercised until the vesting period ends or until the prescribed performance conditions are met, then on each balance sheet date within the vesting period, the services acquired in the current period shall, on the basis of the best estimate of the number of vested equity instruments, be recorded in the relevant costs or expenses and the capital surplus at the fair value of the equities instruments on the grant date.
- For a cash-settled share-based payment instruments, if the right may be exercised immediately after the grant, the fair value of the liability incurred by the enterprise shall, on the grant day, be recorded in the relevant costs or expenses, and the liabilities shall be increased correspondingly. For a cash-settled share-based payment, if the right may not be exercised until the vesting period ends or until the specified performance conditions are met, on each balance sheet date within the vesting period, the services acquired in the current period shall, based on the best estimate of the information about the exercisable right, be recorded in the relevant costs or expenses and the corresponding liabilities at the fair value of the liability incurred by the enterprise.

[23] *Notice on Relevant Issues of Accounting Treatments after the Implementation of the Company Law*/MOF/ 03–15–2006 / 04–01–2006
- In respect to the stocks repurchased due to the implementation of EIPs, the stocks to be repurchased shall not be more than 5% of the total amount of outstanding stocks, and the capital used to repurchase shall be within the amount of profits that can be distributed to the investors in the current term.

Panel C: Laws and regulations relevant to the tax issues of equity incentives

Title of laws and regulations/Issuing authorities/Issuing date/Effective date
- Key Items

[24] *Notice on the Issue of Levying Individual Income Taxes on Incomes from Individual Stock Options* (No.35 [2005])/MOF and SAT/ 03–31–2005/ 07–01–2005
- When an employee exercises stock options, if the actual purchase price (exercise price) at which an employee gets stocks from the enterprise is lower than the stock price on the purchase day, the difference is

(Continued)

the incomes relating to his/her service and employment due to his/her performance and accomplishments in this enterprise, therefore, the individual income taxes on such kind of incomes shall be levied pursuant to the provisions on "incomes from wages and salaries".

- If an employee transfers the stocks obtained by exercising the stock options and the transfer price is higher than the stock price on the exercise day, the individual income taxes on such price difference shall be levied pursuant to the tax collection and exemption provisions on "incomes from transfer of property".
- The individual income taxes on the incomes of an employee from the distribution of enterprise after-tax profits due to its holding stocks shall be levied pursuant to the provisions on "incomes from interests, dividends and bonuses".

[25] *Supplementary Circular on the Relevant Issues Regarding the Individual Incomes Taxes Levied on Incomes Generated from Stock Options* (No. 902 [2006] of the SAT)/ SAT/ 09–30–2006 / 09–30–2006
- The term "net incomes generated from the transfer of stock options" as described in item (2), Article 2 of Document No. 35 [2005] of the MOF generally refers to the incomes generated from the transfer of stock options. Where any employee purchases any stock options at a discount, the balance reached after deduction of the actual payment of the discounted stock options from the incomes generated from the transfer of stock options shall be deemed as the net income generated from the transfer of stock options.
- The term "granting price per share as paid by an employee to obtain the stock options" as prescribed in item (2), Article 2 of Document No. 35 [2005] of the MOF generally refers to the price per share as actually paid by the employee by exercising his stock options. If any employee obtains his stock options at a discount, the aforesaid granting price may include the price as actually paid by the employee when he purchased the stock options at a discount.

[26] *Notice on the Issues Concerning the Imposition of Individual Income Tax on Incomes from Stock Appreciation Right and Restricted Stock/* MOF and SAT/01–07–2009/ 01–07–2009
- The calculation and levy of the individual income tax on the incomes which individuals obtain from their stock appreciation rights and restricted stocks in listed companies shall be governed, by analogy, by the relevant provisions of the No.35 [2005] of the MOF and the Letter No. 902 [2006] of the SAT.

[27] *Notice on Relevant Issues Concerning Individual Income Taxes Levied on Income Generated from Stock Options of Senior Managers of Listed Companies /*SAT/05–04–2009 / 05–04–2009
- When exercising the stock option rights obtained by senior managers of listed companies, if it is indeed difficult for them to pay the tax upon approval of the tax authorities, the individual income taxes may be paid in installments within six months from the date of the exercise of the stock option.

[28] *Notice of the Issues Concerning the Individual Income Tax on Equity Incentives (Letter No. 461 [2009] of the SAT)/* SAT/ 08–24–2009/ 08–24–2009
- A listed company shall multiply the average price of the stock price of the date on which the restricted stocks under the incentive plan are registered with CSDC (or overseas securities depository and custody institution) and the stock price of the unlock date by the number of this batch of stocks, and then subtract the actual amount of money paid for obtaining the restricted stocks corresponding to the number of this batch of stocks which the restrictions are lifted, and difference is the taxable income.

Notes: The laws and regulations were collected from the websites of the promulgating institutions and the Perking University Law database (www.pkulaw.cn/) were referred to compile the English versions of these laws and regulations.

Notes

* The authors acknowledge the financial support from the China National Social Science Foundation Key Research Project (Project No. 17ZDA086): Research on Reforms and Innovations of Monitoring System in State-Owned Enterprises.
1 The Qing dynasty (from A.D. 1636 to A.D. 1912) was the last feudal dynasty in China's history.
2 Started in the 1990s, shareholding companies could issue employee shares. These shares were not part of the compensation package but more like the fund-raising from employees. Initially employee shares could not be traded in the stock exchange, but later they became tradable. Employee shares were prohibited since 1998.
3 According to Bloomberg, the market capitalization of China's listed sector is now second in the world, after the United States.
4 *"Regulation on Equity Incentives in State-Controlled Companies Listed on Offshore Stock Exchanges (Trial)"* and *"Regulation on Equity Incentives in State-Controlled Companies Listed on Domestic Stock Exchanges (Trial)"*.
5 *"Notice on Issues Concerning the Implementation of Equity Incentive System in State-Controlled Listed Companies"*.
6 In our study, we follow the industry category issued by the CSRC in 2001 and use two-digit codes for manufacturing industry and one-digit codes for the others.
7 Some financial companies listed in Hong Kong such as Bank of Communications and China Life have announced DEIPs or EIPs. But most of them ended up in suspension or termination due to regulatory ban on equity incentives in financial SCCs in the beginning of 2009.
8 We extract equity incentive plan data from Wind database and checked relevant information from the Shanghai Stock Exchange or the Shenzhen Stock Exchange when necessary.
9 According to Murphy (2013), the average annual option grant measured as % of common shares for S&P 500 firms during 1992–2005 runs between 1.1% and 2.6%.
10 Note that the grant size would be mechanically small due to the relative large assets base in SCCs. However, even controlling the size effect, the grant size is still smaller in SCCs as shown in Table 9.10.
11 For the sake of convenience, we use the word "managers" to stand for incentive objects including both executives and core employees in the remainder of this essay.
12 If two types of instruments were used, such as restricted and stock options, and their valid periods differ, we report the longer one. There are only six cases with different valid periods. In five cases, they differ in one year, and in one case they differ in two years.
13 The other DEIPs are still being revised and reviewed. They do not belong to either termination group or implementation group.
14 Termination is likely to occur when there is a turnover of initial objects or the need to expand the range of incentive objects.
15 According to the REI-T (2005), equity incentives are not permitted for the companies that are investigated and penalized by the CSRC due to fraud. So, termination is mandatory when fraud is detected and penalized. Other than that, material assets reorganization may also impede the implementation of EIPs.

References

Abernethy, M. A., Y. F. Kuang, and B. Qin. 2015. The influence of CEO power on compensation contract design. *The Accounting Review* 90(4): 1265–1306.
Aboody, D., and R. Kasznik. 2008. Executive stock-based compensation and firms' cash payout: The role of shareholders' tax-related payout preferences. *Review of Accounting Studies* 13: 316–251.
Aggarwal, R. K. 2008. Executive compensation and incentives. In *Handbook of Empirical Corporate Finance*, edited by B. E. Eckbo, 498–534. London: North Holland.
Agrawal, A., and G. N. Mandelker. 1990. Large shareholders and the monitoring of managers: The case of antitakeover charter amendments. *The Journal of Financial and Quantitative Analysis* 25(2):143–161.
Armstrong, C. S., A. D. Jagolinzer, and D. F. Larcker. 2010. Chief executive officer equity incentives and accounting irregularities. *Journal of Accounting Research* 48(2): 225–271.
Armstrong, S. S., D. F. Larcker, G. Ormazabal, and D. J. Taylor. 2013. The relation between equity incentives and misreporting: The role of risk-taking incentives. *Journal of Financial Economics* 109: 327–350.
Benmelech, E., E. Kandel, and P. Veronesi. 2010. Stock-based compensation and CEO (Dis) incentives. *Quarterly Journal of Economics* 125(4): 1769–1820.

Bergstresser, D., and T. Phlilippon. 2006. CEO incentives and earnings management. *Journal of Financial Economics* 80(3): 511–529.

Bhagat, S., and B. Bolton. 2014. Financial crisis and bank executive incentive compensation. *Journal of Corporate Finance* 25: 313–341.

Bu, D., C. Zhang, and T. Lin. 2016. Will political promotion expectation decrease the pay gap in state-owned enterprises in China? *China Journal of Accounting Studies* 4(1): 53–78.

Cadman, B. D., T. O. Rusticus, and J. Sunder. 2013. Stock option grant vesting terms: Economic and financial reporting determinants. *Review of Accounting Studies* 18(4): 1159–1190.

Chen, D., O. Z. Li, and S. Liang. 2016. Perk consumption as a suboptimal outcome under pay regulations. *Asia-Pacific Journal of Accounting & Economics* 23(4): 373–399.

Chen, J., Y. Liu, and Q. Qiu. 2017. Equity compensation and executive turnover: Empirical data from listed companies. *Modern Finance and Economics – Journal of Tianjing University of Finance and Economics (in Chinese)* 3: 23–34.

Chen, X., and J. Zhou. 2014. Top management stock compensation plan and R&D expenditure: Empirical evidence from Chinese A-share market. *Securities Market Herald (in Chinese)* 2: 33–41.

Chen, Z., Y. Guan, and B. Ke. 2013. Are stock option grants to directors of state-controlled Chinese firms listed in Hong Kong genuine compensation? *The Accounting Review* 88(5): 1547–1574.

Cheng, Q., and T. D. Warfield. 2005. Equity incentives and earnings management. *The Accounting Review* 80(2): 441–476.

Core, J., and W. Guay. 1999. The use of equity grants to manage optimal equity incentive levels. *Journal of Accounting and Economics* 28(2): 151–184.

De Cesari, A., and N. Ozkan. 2015. Executive incentives and payout policy: Empirical evidence from Europe. *Journal of Banking & Finance* 55: 70–91.

Davila, A., and F. Penalva. 2006. Governance structure and the weighting of performance measures in CEO compensation. *Review of Accounting Studies* 11(4): 463–493.

Efendi, J., A. Srivastava, and E. Swanson. 2007. Why do corporate managers misstate financial statements? The role of option compensation and other factors. *Journal of Financial Economics* 85(3): 667–708.

Erickson, M., M. Hanlon, and E. L. Maydew. 2006. Is there a link between executive equity incentives and accounting fraud? *Journal of Accounting Research* 44(1): 113–143.

Fang, H., J. R. Nofsinger, and J. Quan. 2015. The effects of employee stock option plans on operating performance in Chinese firms. *Journal of Banking & Finance* 54: 141–159.

Fenn, G. W., and N. Liang. 2001. Corporate payout policy and managerial stock incentives. *Journal of Financial Economics* 60(1): 45–72.

Gillan, S. L., and L. T. Starks. 2000. Corporate governance proposals and shareholder activism: The role of institutional investors. *Journal of Financial Economics* 57(2): 275–305.

Han, H., C. Lv, and R. Li. 2012. Inefficient pricing, managerial stock incentives and stock dividends. *Journal of Finance and Economics (in Chinese)* 38(10): 47–56.

Hass, L. H., M. Tarsalewska, and F. Zhan. 2016. Equity incentives and corporate fraud in China. *Journal of Business Ethics* 138(4): 723–742.

Hu, G., and D. Gai. 2014. Executive stock incentives and bank credit decisions: Empirical evidence from private public firms in China. *Accounting Research (in Chinese)* 4: 58–65.

Jensen, M. 1993. The modern industrial revolution, exit and the failure of internal control systems. *The Journal of Finance* 48(3): 831–880.

Kim, J., L. Li, M. L. Z. Ma, and F. M. Song. 2016. CEO option compensation and systemic risk in the banking industry. *Asia-Pacific Journal of Accounting & Economics* 23(2): 131–160.

Lambert, R. A., W. N. Lanen, and D. F. Larcker. 1989. Executive stock option plans and corporate dividend policy. *The Journal of Financial and Quantitative Analysis* 24(4): 409–425.

Laux, C., and V. Laux. 2009. Board committees, CEO compensation, and earnings management. *The Accounting Review* 84(3): 869–891.

Li, Y. 2002. The interpretation of incentive systems in Shan Si Bank. *Accounting Research (in Chinese)* 3: 31–35.

Liang, S. 2016. Will the incentive intensity of equity compensation affect enterprise's cost stickiness? *The Journal of World Economy (in Chinese)* 6: 168–192.

Liu, B., H. Luo, and W. Zhou. 2016. Exercising limitations of equity incentives and the pecking-order of earnings management. *Management World (in Chinese)* 11: 141–155.

Liu, G., and Y. Ma. 2013. Does the equity incentive implemented in Chinese listed companies really work? An empirical study based on the annual reports of Chinese listed companies from 2005 to 2012. *China Soft Science (in Chinese)* 7: 110–121.

Liu, S. 2017. The impact of equity incentive plans on analysts' earnings forecasts and stock recommendations for Chinese listed firms: An empirical study. *Journal of International Accounting, Auditing and Taxation* 29: 1–13.

Lv, C., and H. Zhang. 2011. The effect of the stock option plans on corporate investment behaviors. *Management World (in Chinese)* 11: 118–126.

Lv, C., H. Zheng, M. Yan, and J. Xu. 2009. The design for listed companies' system of stimulation by stock option and purchase: Is it an incentive or welfare? *Management World (in Chinese)* 9: 133–147.

Minhat, M., and M. Abdullah. 2016. Bankers' stock options, risk-taking and the financial crisis. *Journal of Financial Stability* 22: 121–128.

Murphy, K. J. 2013. Executive compensation: Where we are, and how we got there. In *Handbook of the Economics of Finance*, edited by George Constantinides, Milton Harris, and Rene Stulz, 211–356. North Holland: Elsevier Science North Holland.

Ni, X., D. Dai, and D. Zhang. 2017. Equity incentives and audit fees: Empirical evidence from China. *Auditing Research (in Chinese)* 1: 69–77.

Qu, X., M. Percy, J. Stewart, and F. Hu. 2016. Executive stock option vesting conditions, corporate governance and CEO attributes: Evidence from Australia. *Accounting and Finance*, forthcoming. Online version 2016, 1–31. Available from: https://onlinelibrary.wiley.com/doi/epdf/10.1111/acfi.12223

Sheng, M., C. Zhang, and Y. Wang. 2016. Managerial equity incentive and capital structure dynamic adjustment. *Accounting Research (in Chinese)* 2: 44–50.

Shleifer, A., and R. W. Vishny. 1986. Large shareholders and corporate control. *Journal of Political Economy* 94(3): 461–488.

Smith, C. W., and R. L. Watts. 1992. The investment opportunity set and corporate financing, dividend, and compensation policies. *Journal of Financial Economics* 32(3): 263–292.

Su, D., and D. Lin. 2010. CEO stock incentives, earnings management and corporate governance. *Economic Research Journal (in Chinese)* 11: 88–100.

Wang, D., and D. Wu. 2016. Equity incentive and risk taking: Evidence from China's listed companies. *Nankai Business Review (in Chinese)* 19(3): 157–167.

Wang, X., G. Fan, and J. Yu. 2017. *Marketization index of China's provinces: Neri report 2016*. 1st ed. Beijing: Social Sciences Academic Press (China).

Wang, Y., L. Ye, and M. Sheng. 2012. Managerial power, opportunism motivation and equity incentive plan design. *Accounting Research (in Chinese)* 10: 35–41.

Wu, Y., and S. Wu. 2010. A study on the selfish behavior of the high-raking managers and on its influencing elements. *Management World (in Chinese)* 5: 141–149.

Xiao, S., Y. Liu, and Y. Liu. 2013. Executives' earnings management behaviors in the implementation of equity incentive: From perspective of performance evaluation for option exercise. *Accounting Research (in Chinese)* 12: 40–46.

Xiao, S., Q. Shi, T. Wang, and S. Yi. 2016. The preferences of equity incentive mode of listed companies: From the prospect of incentive objects. *Accounting Research (in Chinese)* 6: 55–62.

Xiao, S., and M. Yu. 2012. Equity incentive and dividend payout policy: An empirical study based on listed firms in China. *Accounting Research (in Chinese)* 8: 49–57.

Xie, D., and Y. Chen. 2010. Performance-based equity incentive plans, performance hurdles, and shareholder wealth. *Journal of Financial Research (in Chinese)* 12: 99–114.

Xin, Y., and C. Lv. 2012. Incentive, welfare, or reward: The dilemma of stock option incentive plan in state-owned enterprises. *Accounting Research (in Chinese)* 6: 67–75.

Yang, Z., S. Shi, B. Shi, and X. Cao. 2016. Mixed ownership structure, equity incentives and managerial entrenchment in financial decision-making: Evidence based on dynamic trade-off theory. *Journal of Finance and Economics (in Chinese)* 42(8): 108–120.

Yu, H., and Y. Wu. 2015. Equity incentives and effectiveness of internal controls. *Auditing Research (in Chinese)* 5: 57–67.

Zong, W., Y. Wang, and Z. Wei. 2013. Does equity compensation reduce executive turnover? Empirical evidence from China's securities market. *Accounting Research (in Chinese)* 9: 58–63.

10

DIGITAL TRANSFORMATION OF FINANCE FUNCTION AND SHIFT STRATEGY

Xiaomei Guo, Liqun Yuan, Wei Gao[1]

1. Introduction

Digitalization, the process of transforming any kind of activity or information into digital formats that can be electronically collected, stored, retrieved and analyzed (CFO Research and SAP, 2015), is gathering pace all over the world. Digitalization changes the nature of products and the process of value chains, and it has significant implications on how firms attain and sustain competitive advantage. Digitalization has forced many firms to revisit their strategy and business model to sustain in a complex business environment. Built on the digital revolution, the fourth industrial revolution, characterized by a fusion of technologies that is blurring the lines between the physical, digital and biological spheres, is occurring. It is evolving at an exponential pace, disrupting almost every industry, heralding the transformation of the entire business system. The finance function, the center of the required data and analytical techniques, is ideally placed to push the transformation. The financial team is looked upon to help the board "understand what the digital developments and wider megatrends mean for their businesses and develop the strategies needed to respond"(PWC, 2015, p. 6). What can the finance team do to meet the current demand for business transformation?

There are many streams of strategic models of competitive advantage, such as the industry structure view, the resource-based view, the dynamic capabilities approach and recently the network-centric view, which can be used to find the superior performance of a company in a competitive environment.

The traditional industrial organization model raised in the 1970s assesses competition within an industry (Porter, 1981). IO theory places a premium on the environment and is explicitly concerned with the opportunities and threats stemming from the environment. According to the IO theory, industry forces in which a firm operates are very important for the firm to maintain profitability. Porter's Five Forces framework (Porter, 1979) focuses on evaluating suppliers, customers and the threat of new entrants and/or substitute products. Yet it's not up to date to disclose the value capture in most of the new industries.

The resource-based view (RBV) of the firm emerged in the 1980s and the 1990s (Barney, 1991). Unlike the IO view that advocates on the importance of anticipating the external forces, the RBV approach contends the importance of having control over the internal forces. VRIO analysis as suggested by Barney, stands for four questions that ask if a resource is: valuable? rare? costly to imitate? And is a firm organized to capture the value of the resources?

The dynamic capabilities framework (Teece et al., 1994, 1997; Teece, 2007) analyzes competitive advantage based on firms operating in environments of rapid technological change. Dynamic capability is "the firm's ability to integrate, build and reconfigure internal and external competences to address rapidly changing environments" (Teece et al., 1994, p. 537). The competitive advantage of firms rests on distinctive processes (ways of coordinating and combining), shaped by the firm's (specific) asset positions (such as the firm's portfolio of difficult-to-trade knowledge assets and complementary assets), and the evolution path(s) it has adopted or inherited. It is increasingly providing the intellectual infrastructure for both theoretical and applied analyses of strategic management.

However, the above approaches are challenged by the emergence of digital technology, along with a new network-centric view which explains the competitive environment of firms being confronted with digital technology and its affordances. Based on the network-centric view, the firms may achieve competitive advantage by actively shaping the digital environment (i.e. applying a logic of effectuation) and by value co-creating the interconnected firms in the digital environment (Iansiti and Lakhani, 2014; Teece, 2012). Today companies are embedded in multiple complex relationships that make them interdependent on each other for success. It makes sense to "suggest that a company be viewed not as a member of a single industry but as part of a business ecosystem that crosses a variety of industries" (Moore, 1993, p. 76). A business ecosystem is "an economic community supported by a foundation of interacting organizations and individuals-the organisms of the business world"(Moore, 1996, p. 26). The ecosystem is structured around core firms, an organization serving as a richly-connected hub wielding significant influence in a business network (Iansiti and Levien, 2004a). Various entities including suppliers, producers, retailers and customers work in tandem to create value (Moore, 1996).

The development of a business ecosystem enhances procurement processes, an optimized product mix, operational efficiency and enhanced information sharing (Iansiti and Levien, 2004b), thus facilitating the co-creation of effective and timely innovations (Adner, 2006). Under these premises, creating value has become more complex. Value creation processes in an emerging digital environment are based on the contribution of multiple stakeholders who integrate and apply resources for themselves and for others. Value is thus always co-created (Koch and Windsperger, 2017). Basics of the four streams of strategy are listed in Table 10.1.

In the 1980s, management accounting was criticized for not adequately serving the needs of senior managers in the formulation of strategy and sustaining a competitive advantage. To answer the criticism a body of literature emerged around the development of strategic management accounting, and some practices were advocated, such as competitor analysis (Simmonds, 1981; Ward, 1992), competitive advantage (Porter, 1980, 1985), strategic cost management (Shank and Govindarajan, 1989, 1993) and value chain analysis (Shank and Govindarajan, 1992). Accountants are viewed as business partners when they support the strategic management process.

In the digitalized world, it is recognized that the traditional way of thinking about strategy is limited in the amorphous, unbounded and fluid business network (Iansiti and Levien, 2004a; Teece, 2007). How should strategy be redesigned, and in particular, how can the accountants help to support the strategy? To answer this question, the authors present a case based on Midea, one of the leading top five white electrical appliance manufacturers of the world, which has shifted its strategy since 2011 and has built a new business model, incorporating the philosophy of internet and digitalization. During that process, its finance function was redesigned. Many innovated practice were introduced, including efficiency management, finance platform, to name but a few. In this paper, the authors discuss some of the financial practices, construct a process model of the shift of the strategy, explore the links between the financial practice and

Table 10.1 Four streams of strategy management

Representative Research Streams	Industry Structure View	Resource-Based View	Dynamic Capabilities Approach	Network-Centric View
Unit for analysis	Industry: Positioning	Firm: Resources VRIO resources,	Firm: Dynamic Capabilities intangible assets soft assets	Inter-organizational network structure, Business ecosystem
Environment	Stable, predictable	Relatively stable industries, internal organization	turbulent	Complex turbulent
Value creation	Sequential value chain	Firm-owned resources	Dynamic capabilities(intangibles)	Value Network of firms Value co-creation
Analysis Tool	PE five forces	BCG, value chain analysis	Sensing, seizing transforming,	value analysis Network Ecosystem mapping

Source: Koch, T. and Windsperger, J. (2017). Seeing through the network: Competitive advantage in the digital economy. *Journal of Organization Design*, 6(6). Modified.

the strategy. The insights from the case may shed some light on the management accounting practice that functions in the digital economy and provides some actionable practice for the practitioners.

The case study method, "an empirical inquiry that investigates a contemporary phenomenon in depth and within its real-world context" (Yin, 1984, p. 23), is used in the study. Semi-structured interviews were carried out with the managers of the company, supplemented with direct observation, documents and artifacts, and internal documentation as well. Cross verification of the record was done to ensure coherency. The process of shift strategy and financial strategy was reconstructed, and the underlying value creation system was discussed.

The following section comes with a discussion of the company's shift strategy, then follows an analysis of the company's major practice of the finance function to help build and implement the new strategy and finally some insights are drawn and the conclusions are made.

2. Midea's shift strategy in the digital world

2.1 Company profile

Midea Group is a leading global manufacturer of electrical home appliance, headquartered in Beijiao, Guangdong, China. Founded in 1968, it went into the industry in the 1980s. Now, Midea offers a uniquely broad product range, including consumer appliances (kitchen appliances, refrigerators, laundry appliances and various small home appliances), HVAC (residential air-conditioning, commercial air-conditioning, heating & ventilation) and robotics and industrial automation (Kuka Group and Yaskawa joint venture). The electrical appliance division of the company went listed in 1993, delisted in 2013, and later the whole group was relisted as Midea Group on the Shenzhen Stock Exchange. As of 2013, the firm employed approximately 100,000 people in China and overseas across 21 manufacturing plants and 260 logistics centers across 200 countries.

It has been listed on the Fortune Global 500 since July 2016. After nearly 50 years of continued growth, Midea now generates annual global revenue of more than USD 22 billion. Midea is the world's largest producer of major appliances and the world's No. 1 brand of air-treatment products, air-coolers, kettles and rice cookers. On November 18, 2015, Moody's, Standard & Poor's and Fitch Ratings respectively assigned A3 / A-/A- ratings to Midea Group, with outlooks all being stable. The ratings are in a leading position among home appliance manufacturers worldwide, as well as among Chinese non State-owned enterprises.

After ten years of rapid growth, when turnovers grew tenfold from RMB 10 Billion in 1990, to 100 Billion in 2010, Midea became the top five white electrical appliance manufacturer of the world. The success was mainly due to the low-cost advantages achieved through scale of economics, which was the common practice in the industry. However since 2011, most companies in the industry suffered a loss. There was a great downturn of performance in the main products of Midea.

Recognizing that the traditional business model of low cost and scale of economy had become ineffective, Midea revisited its strategy and began the transformation since 2011.

Instead of focusing on scale, the company focused on profitability and later, on value creation. A new strategy was set, including: product leadership, efficiency-driven and globalization.

(1) Product leadership: the company increased its spending on R&D and product innovation, upgrading its product lines, abandoning the low-end ones and focusing on the high end ones (including the smart appliances).
(2) Efficiency-driven: the company relied on efficiency management controls rather than the traditional cost cutting tools.
(3) Globalization: the company sought globalization by setting up overseas manufacture bases, shifting from OEM/ODM to OBM, and enhancing its own brands.

Some steps were taken, including the redesign of the organization structure, merging with the companies in the robotic and internet industry, and designing a new business model.

2.1.1 Redesigning the organizational structure

The organization structure of Midea used to be a divisionalized one, similar to that of GE's, which was established in 1997. However, in 2011, the organization structure was redesigned into a flattening one, which turned the divisions into SBUs that focused on customers. Seven platforms were formed to better serve the SBUs, and the administrative functions were kept at the headquarters (see Figure 10.1).

The new structure is made of nine divisions, eight functions and seven platforms. The nine divisions were originally different divisions in charge of different product lines. As customers orientated and self-contained SBUs, the divisions became the operating centers of the whole value chain. Redesign of the value chain followed, linking them closely with the customers and suppliers. The managers were transformed into business partners with highly delegation of power. The SBUs are highly motivated and specialized in their own fields and expand quickly and healthily.

The eight functions, such as finance, IT and administration are centralized in the headquarters and provide share service to the group company and its subsidiaries, the nine SBUs and other platforms. In this way, share of professional resources becomes possible, efficiency is increased and value is added.

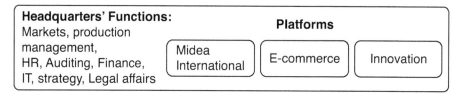

> **9 Divisions (SBUs) :**
> Home appliance, kitchen appliance, A/C, Refrigeration, laundry, water appliances, components ect
> Full responsibility, self contained, orientated to customers, profit center with high delegation of power

> **Platforms :**
> Logistics, customers service, Cash MGT, Purchase
> Customers focused, relying on digital technology, share value on centralized share service and information

> **Headquarters' Functions:**
> Markets, production management, HR, Auditing, Finance, IT, strategy, Legal affairs
>
> **Platforms**
> Midea International | E-commerce | Innovation

Figure 10.1 New organization structure

The seven newly built platforms, including R&D, logistic, E-commerce, cash management and customer service, are structured into two types. The first type, i.e. logistics, customer service, cash management and purchase platforms are self-contained and more independent, providing service to the whole group. Digital technology including E-commerce are used to help the platforms serve the company. With uniform product system, inventory system and other back up data system enhancing the service capability, visualized inventory management was provided on the logistic platform to SBUs. Resources synergy is realized, customers experience is enhanced and the efficiency is increased. Data on customer behavior is collected on the customer service platform, when post-sale services are provided, giving feedback to SBUs to help the latter better understand the needs of the consumers and come out with new products. The second type of platform, consisting of Innovation, E-commerce, and Globalization platforms, are placed under the group head office. All these platforms are data driven, that is problems are discovered, analyzed and solved through data. It intensifies the sharing of resources and information and strengthens the operation of its own functions as well. It not only promotes the intelligent management of enterprises, but it also lays a structural foundation for the efficiency management of the value chain and provides the basic premise for enterprises to enhance the overall value.

2.1.2 *Embracing the developments of technology-smart strategies*

The widespread use of the internet, and the advances in IT technology, have greatly changed consumer behavior (increasingly built upon access to mobile networks and data), forcing companies to change the way they design, market and deliver products and services. Integrating big data, the internet of things and cloud computing into the operation process, Midea began to promote its new business model, which is intelligent and of high efficiency, compared to the traditional one that depends on the advantages of low cost, scale economy to achieve growth. Since 2012, Midea has proposed two Smart Strategies, i.e. smart manufacture and smart home appliance. Relying on its complete industry chain, Midea actively promoted the automation of production and operation through the large-scale use of robots and other automation devices. Through capital investment or mergers, Midea stepped into the new robot industry, building up strategic alliances with several overseas robot manufacturing companies, including Kuka, a German robotics company (the acquisition of the company was highly publicized). The IT system was redesigned, helping Midea to connect the whole value chain from R&D to post-sale service and push it beyond the boundary of Midea with the introduction of a smart phone application. Automation helped Midea to reduce its reliance on labor and increase its efficiency. At the same time, the internet thinking, intelligent technology and modern management concepts were combined into the operation process, realizing the intelligent management and optimizing the business process and organizational structure.

The integration of different industries is the trend of the digital economy, which helps to make better use of complementary resources in the industry chain to achieve mutual benefits and a win-win success in the whole industry chain ecosystem. In 2014, cooperating with Xiaomi, Jingdong, Alibaba and other internet companies, Midea's home appliance system was built on the platform of Suning, Ali and Jingdong, the three major electricity suppliers. Based on the advanced hardware, software and the cloud system, Midea finally launched the "M-Smart" smart home appliance system, transforming itself from a single product manufacturer to a product maker and integrated system solution provider.

2.1.3   Setting up new business model

In 2015, Midea actively redesigned its differentiated value chain and built a value orientated new business model as shown in Figure 10.2. The business model is made up of three modules, namely, products, platforms and customers. The products module is the fundamental activity of value creation, which consists of R&D, manufacture and marketing of the internal value chain. The platforms module is cross functional and includes innovation, finance, customer service, E commerce and logistic. These platforms, dealing with information, logistics and funds management, are viewed as supportive activities of the value chain. The customer module goes beyond the firm boundary and is an assessment of the result of value creation of the firm. The philosophy of the model is that value is created through efficiency and links. On one hand, the company makes efforts to increase the efficiency of each of the value chain activities centered on products and customers, and business units. On the other hand, it relies on its unique range of product lines and various layers of cooperation with many partners, to make full use of the complementary capabilities of each party, creating new value from the links along the value chain.

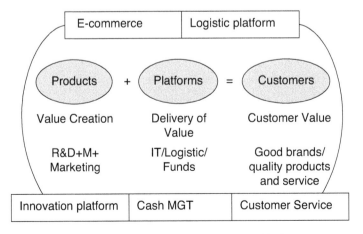

Figure 10.2   New business model (value created through efficiency and links)

2.2 Performance after shift strategy

Significant improvements were realized from the shift strategy. Investment in fixed assets were cut down by 30%, and head counts by 46.4%, the increase in revenue was slowed down, and the idle capacity was got rid of. Investment in R&D was increased, with R&D talents accounting for 47% of administrative personnel and ratio of R&D/Sales reaching to the highest in the industry. 32 000 patents were obtained in five years after the shift strategy, Midea succeeded in upgrading the product lines by abandoning the low-end products and focusing on the high end ones (an increase from 20% to 50% after the shift).

Turnovers dropped in 2012 due to the transition, but have increased since then. By 2016 turnover hit 159.044 Billion Yuan. The average increase rate of turnover was 9%, as compared to 15%–20% before the transition. Net profit margin on sales increased from 4.95% in 2011 to 9.97% in 2016, with net profit changed from 6.6 Billion Yuan to 15.8 Billion in 2016. Accumulated profit for five years from 2012 to 2016 amounted to 55.5 Billion, signaling the successful transition of the company from the goal of revenue increase to profit increase. At the same time, net cash flows from operation increased greatly. The ratio of operating cash flows to profit increased from 0.6183 in 2011 to 1.683 in 2016. Cash cycle was shortened to 4.2 days in 2015 and one day in 2016, as compare to 26.7 days in 2011. The efficiency of cash management was greatly improved. By the time the annual report of 2016 was published, the total market value of Midea was over RMB200 Billion.

3. Financial practices boosting the transition of business strategy

3.1 Restructuring finance function into three platforms

As the business strategy shifted, the finance function changed too. Its goal was changed from cost control to value management. The financial professionals identify problems from the perspective of managers and analyze and solve problems, which are digitalized. The financial system was adopted, integrating the financial process with the operational process and providing management controls with high transparency. The structure of the financial function was redesigned into a large platform, which consisted of three interlinked ones: financial share service, operational finance and cash management platform.

(1) Financial share service platform: as technology advanced, most of the transaction record activities were replaced by automation. The processes, procedures and information system of the whole group of the company were standardized and centralized on the share service platform, providing information and reports to its users for the group company in a timely, standardized and comparable way, with deep insights and meticulous support for the business.

(2) Business and finance integration platform. with deep understanding of the needs of business, the finance team was actively involved in the redesign of the business model by participating in the whole process of operation and, providing fine management in all aspects of the value chain that have impacts on value creation. As a result, the value chain was redesigned, the boundary was expanded and the industrial ecosystem was formed. A cross functional efficiency management model over the whole value chain was applied.

(3) The cash management platform is a globalized one that consists of four parts: cash pool, financing platform, product platform and foreign exchange management platform. The cash pool is mainly responsible for the collection of cash and notes of companies within

the group, be it domestic or overseas, providing cash service, settlement and integration of global financial resources. The financing platform is mainly responsible for domestic and foreign financing at home and abroad; the product platform relies on the financial company that was incorporated and licensed in 2010 to provide internal and external financing and guarantee to the group members of the Midea. The foreign exchange management platform is responsible for hedging exchange rate risk, which is based on the actual needs of the group and operation globally.

As strategy shifted, the finance department has changed into a global platform that integrates with the business and provides various services to the whole group, making use of the advanced technology. Centralized management of global capital and intensive control of resources helped Midea to better control the financial risk, to increase the efficiency of fund management and to create value for parties of the ecosystem.

3.2 Cooperation with the business units to launch whole value chain management

As the strategy shifted, the finance team helped to design the new business model, which is customer orientated and meets the customers' demands through innovative products and platforms that have the effect of synergy. The finance function focused on the value chain to upgrade and optimize the industry structure and to increase the operational efficiency, leading to a new cost management model which includes whole value chain cost management and whole value chain efficiency management.

3.2.1 Whole value chain cost management

An end to end approach was used to implement analysis encompassing activities from the development of strategy and the operational activities starting from R&D to post-sale customer services. As the strategy shifted, the finance professionals helped the SBUs to upgrade its product structure. With refined and detailed profitability analysis, SBUs deleted unprofitable products and focused on high margin products, which accounted for more than 66% of all products by the end of 2014, as compared to 20% before the restructure. At the same time, life cycle management was implemented, the number of product models was cut down and the parts and components were standardized. Cost management is treated as a feed forward rather than a feedback tool, which covers the whole value chain and is cross functional. Closely cooperating with the operational department, the accountants of Midea systematically analyze core activities such as investment, research, manufacturing, marketing, after-sale etc., to seek cost drivers, while at the same time focus on efficiency of resources invested in R&D, marketing and brand building. Attention is also paid to the synergy of resources, synergy between upstream and downstream parties in the industry ecosystem and collaboration between HR, financial and business sectors. The analysis showed that most of the costs were locked in the R&D phase and logistic, warehouse and post-sale service cost together accounted for 20% of total cost. So it was realized that cost cutting should be focused on both ends of the value chain. As a result, the finance function was actively involved in the operation of the value chain, and closed loop management control was exerted over the whole value chain. A cross functional team of R&D, marketing and finance was formed at the early stage of R&D, and success rate and other management measures were used to identify potential problems, with variance analyzed based on benchmarks and data. In this way, causes were found and corrective measures for the troubles were taken. Goal achieving rate was used to assess the performance of responsible managers, providing data to improve performance. In addition to that detailed cost, reports were made to help SBUs make better decisions.

3.2.2   *Whole value chain efficiency management*

In the internet economy, with the buyer dominating the market, the consumers are extremely sensitive to the rate to market. Excess inventories lower the efficiency of marketing channels and prevent the launch of new products, which have adverse impacts on value creation. Abandoning the traditional "push" system and focusing on the customer value proposition under the internet economy, Midea implemented a "T+3" value chain management model, which put the orders of the end users as the starting point to pull the overall operational process, based on the internet technology. The model starts from the customer order delivery cycle (T cycle), through the production material organization cycle (T + 1 cycle), the finished product cycle (T + 2 cycle), and the logistics delivery cycle (T + 3 cycle), to achieve customer order satisfaction. Production is made based on sales prospects, forcing the supply chain including R&D, manufacturing and quality management, to respond quickly. As a result, efficiency is increased and rate to market is improved, which increases the value of the whole chain. Benefits are obvious, inventory and related number of moves are reduced, the logistics channels are streamlined and the market response speed is accelerated, delivery cycle is shortened, requirements on warehouse and inventory are reduced and inventory turnover and capital turnover are greatly accelerated

Midea enjoyed a broad range of product lines and is at the hub of the industry value chain, which helps it to establish a strategic alliance with the suppliers and the dealers. It cooperated with the suppliers in new technology applications and new material research, while providing various support to its suppliers. Through logistics platforms, the integrated service capability of delivery and installation are enhanced. Both online and offline channels are launched to enhance user experience. The upstream and downstream of the industry chain have been closely connected, which promotes the lean process and digitalization of the supply chain. Midea has built a sharing platform for supply chain partners, implementing electronic settlement, setting the transparent trading rules, sharing information with the partners and providing convenient industrial chain financial services to the partners, thereby creating a new business ecosystem. In this way, efficiency of the whole value chain was increased and value was co-created and shared by the partners.

3.3   *Integration of industrial-finance capital*

To enhance the competitiveness of the industrial chain and the business ecosystem, and to further promote the transformation and upgrading of the business, Midea started integration of Industrial-finance capital, by means of various financial instrument through its financing platform.

As the core firm in the business ecosystem, with various suppliers, distributors, agents and consumers from the upstream and downstream of the value chain, and a large number of employees at different level of the subsidiary and affiliated companies in the group, Midea enjoys a large customer base of the global cash platform mentioned before. The financial platform provides financial service, such as Internal settlement, internal financing, internal loans, trade financing for various parties within the business ecosystem, which is convenient and lower the transaction cost. As the efficiency of the value chain increased, larger amount of cash inflows are generated, which become the low-cost source of financing for the ecosystem. Innovated financial products are developed and delivered, and a new form of financial industry is established. Loans are provided to suppliers using the accounts receivable as a pledges, with the limit of credit adjusted based on the balance of Accounts Receivables. As to the dealers, inventory pledged loans are provided. With new technology of mobile payment, various types of instruments, such as Midea pocket, Midea smart loan, E loan, U loan, easy loan and loans to employees based on the internet, tailored asset management and innovated application carriers are designed and sold in a fast and low-cost way. As data is shared among the members of the ecosystem, credit investigation is quick and reliable, so risk is under control. As the targeted users are within the ecosystem, various forms of outlets, platforms and channel resources are available for the promotion of the financial products, which lowers the operating cost of financial management.

The supplier finance helps the partners to cope with the financial difficulties, ensures the overall operation of Midea's value chain, frees up its cash flows and increases returns on cash management. It also helps the company to maintain the supplier-buyer relationship at a low cost, leading to the overall health of the value chain and an increase of the value. The customer finance and tailored loan provides fund to the end consumers at a favorable rate, stimulating consumption of potential customers while collecting data of customers' value. This service enhances customer satisfaction and stimulates consumption, leading to the increase in turnover for SBUs and the resulting increase in cash flows from operation, adding the source of capital for the finance platform in return. In this way, Midea makes full use of the complementary capabilities of the two industries, and the integration of the industry and finance capital is realized.

4. Discussions

According to Porter (1980), there are two competitive strategies: low-cost leadership and differentiation. The changing demand of the consumers under the digital internet economy, and the continuing price rise in energy, raw materials and labors, have made low-end products out of place and unprofitable. An upgrade of the products is inevitable. Envisioning the trend in 2011, Midea started to shift its strategy toward differentiation. As greater ability to outsource almost anything and everything has made the traditional competitive sources of differentiation based on economies of scale and scope outdated, Midea revisited its strategy to find new sources of differentiation and competitive advantages. Product leadership, efficiency-driven and globalization are the cores of Midea's strategy.

Product leadership was the initial attempt to be differentiated. As value will not be created unless the product is delivered to the customers, Midea put customer value on top of its priority list. To meet customer demand, investment on R&D was greatly increased. The redesign of the value chain led to the restructure of the organization structure and the emergence of various platform, which increased the efficiency of the whole group company, i.e. the value chain redesigned was driven by efficiency. During these transformations, the value chain was first extended beyond the boundary of the group and later integrated with other industries. The merger with the automation and robotic industry, and the strategic alliance with the internet industry, are all examples of cross industry integration. As the company makes its products and services smarter, smarter management was launched too. It came with upgrading products, redesigning the industry value chain, cross industry integration and finally arriving at the new business model, where the strategic goal is value creation. E-commerce and globalization are two factors compelling the business to change. The increased use of the internet, mobile phones and other IT has make it easier to communicate around the world. As value is derived from various parties, i.e. outsourcers, marketers, manufacturers, even raw material suppliers, who became global, globalization became the choice of Midea. "Globalization is a process of worldwide integration of strategy formulation, implementation and evaluation activities" (David, 2007, p. 101). With globalization,

Midea is able to build globalized platforms that increase the efficiency further and replicate its business model beyond the country boundary.

As mentioned before, approaches for explanation of competitive advantage and strategy evolve over time. As the environment has changed greatly by globalization and advances in technology, companies innovate their business models to compete differently. Business models explain how firms work, including how they make money and how they deliver value to customers at an appropriate cost (Magretta, 2002). As business models can be conceived as a set of relations and feedback loops between variables and their consequences, strategic management should aim at developing these to create virtuous cycles, leading to an evolution of the business model (Casadesus-Masanell and Ricart, 2010). A business model is more generic than a business strategy. Coupling strategy and business model analysis is needed to protect competitive advantage resulting from new business model design (Teece, 2010). Competitive advantage (or differentiation) could be realized by offering a better business model or the same business model in a different market. (Magretta, 2002)

Based on the relationship of strategy and business model, further analysis of the new business model as proposed by Midea is necessary. From 2011, Midea shifted its strategy in two phases, first from scale of economy to profitability, and then from profitability to value creation. As can be seen from Fig X.2, customer value, represented in brands and quality products and services, is created through products and platforms. Products are designed, manufactured and marketed through the operational value chain. T + 3 management was applied to make the value chain slim and flexible, shortening the time from design to market. The value chain was extended to link suppliers and customers. Platforms, including internal platforms and external platforms and later, cross industry platforms, are used to deliver value to the customers.

As value creation is at the heart of business models, management accounting, which is "the sourcing, analysis, communication and use of decision-relevant financial and non-financial information to generate and preserve value for organizations" (CGMA, 2014, p. 8), can help to design and implement the business model and strategy. Management accountants work across the business, not just in finance. They advise managers on the financial implications of big decisions and help the formulation of business strategy. As strategy goals changed, the goal of financial strategy and its determinants changed too. It started with cost control to profit maximization and finally to value management (See Table 10.2). A change in unit for analysis can be observed, when the finance changes its focus from the manufacture process to the cross-industry, platform based business ecosystem. Various accounting practices were applied to help value creation.

In the first stage, the traditional tool of contribution analysis was applied, which helped the company to delete unprofitable products. It was soon recognized that focus should be placed on R&D, so value chain analysis and target costing were applied, under the name of whole value chain cost management. With T + 3 management, cycle time of operation was greatly reduced, and value was created. The decrease of the cycle time is deemed as operational efficiency management in Midea. As to the cash management, globalized cash platform was formed which centralized and synergized

In the second stage, as digital developments to sharpen efficiency has freed up finance to provide more decision support and value for the enterprise, more emphasis was placed on co-creation of value (structural efficiency as used by Midea). Whole value chain efficiency management and integration of industry and finance capital was applied. End to end approach was applied in T + 3 management, which involves various suppliers, channels and customers. The three platforms, the R&D logistic platform and the post service helped to link different parties together in the process of the co-creation of value, with the sharing of data and information along the value chain. Strategic alliance with E-business platforms increased the efficiency further, and

Table 10.2 Change of financial strategy as the strategy shifted

Time frame	Before 2011	2011–2015	2016-
Strategy Goal	Economic of Scale	Profit maximization	Value Creation
Financial strategy (goal) and determinants	Cost control factors of production	Profit maximization Profit = Sales margin*turnovers (efficiency)	Value Management Value = efficiency*link (integration)
Unit of analysis as value creating systems	Manufacture – a process in the internal value chain	Internal Value chain – Industry value chain – value chain extension Focus on two ends: R&D and Post-Sale service	Extension – value chain integration – Business Ecosystem Focus on Platforms and integration
Accounting practice	Traditional management accounting tools, Variance analysis, etc.	Contribution analysis, Value chain analysis, Target costing -whole value chain cost management, T + 3 management	Whole value chain efficiency management, Cross industry ecosystem-integration of industry and finance capital
Role of accountants	Information provider	Business partner	Value integrator

the business ecosystem began to take shape. Based on the network-centric approach, firms' resources and capabilities should extend beyond firm boundaries and be embedded in sets of relationships between firms to create value. Instead of being rigidly grouped around a specific business of manufacturing, Midea began to draw together mutually supportive companies from multiple industries to create differentiated products and services and to co-create value. Ample cash reserves as a result of efficient management of the whole value chain becomes the low-cost source of funding for the development of finance platforms. With IT technology, the platform integrates different parties of the ecosystem, solves the problem of shortage of cash of various parties and increases the efficiency of fund use. In this sense, a collaborative, intertwined networking mindset has been created and the accountants are on the way to change from business partners to value integrators.

5. Conclusions

In the digital economy, value is created through integration and cooperation. Instead of the sequential value chain, the platform based ecosystem has become the value creation system. As a result, the strategy and the business model should be redesigned. The finance function needs to transform accordingly. The transformation of the finance function of Midea in the support of shift strategies shows how the accountants can help push the shape of the platform based business ecosystem and the creation of value. The practice of whole value chain management by Midea evolves over time to become a cross industry management tool applicable to the business ecosystem. It focuses on increasing efficiency of both the operation and the link of partners of the ecosystem. Value is created when the value chain is redesigned and extended to both ends and finally integrated with the partners of the business ecosystem. Through co-determination and co-creation in the whole value chain and the business ecosystem, finance together with management help reshape the strategy in the digital world.

Note

1 The authors would like to acknowledge the support of the Canada China Scholarship Exchange Program (CCSEP), a scholarship undertaken with the assistance of the Government of Canada, and co-administrated with the Chinese Scholarship Council (CSC).

References

Adner, R. (2006) Match Your Innovation Strategy to Your Innovation Ecosystem. *Harvard Business Review*, 84(4), 98–107.

Barney, J. B. (1991) Firm Resources and Sustained Competitive Advantage. *Journal of Management*, 17(1), 99–120.

Casadesus-Masanell, R. and Ricart, J. (2010) From Strategy to Business Models and onto Tactics. *Long Range Planning*, 43(2–3), 195–215.

CFO Research and SAP. (2015) *Thriving in The Digital Economy: The Innovative Finance Function*. Boston, MA, USA, CFO Publishing.

CGMA. (2014) *Global Management Accounting Principles*. London, UK, CGMA.

David, F. (2007) *Strategic Management*. Prentice Hall, New Jersey, USA.

Iansiti, M. and Lakhani, K. (2014) Digital Ubiquity: How Connections, Sensors, and Data Are Revolutionizing Business. *Harvard Business Review*, 92(11), 91–99.

Iansiti, M. and Levien, R. (2004a) *The Keystone Advantage: What the New Dynamics of Business Ecosystems Mean for Strategy, Innovation, and Sustainability*. Boston, Harvard Business School Press.

Iansiti, M. and Levien, R. (2004b) Strategy as Ecology. *Harvard Business Review*, 82(3), 68–78.

Koch, T. and Windsperger, J. (2017) Seeing Through the Network: Competitive Advantage in the Digital Economy. *Journal of Organization Design.* [online] 6 (6). Available from: https://doi.org/10.1186/s41469-017-0016-z [Accessed: 30th November 2017].

Magretta, J. (2002) Why Business Models Matter. *Harvard Business Review*, 80(5), 86.

Moore, J. (1993) Predators and Prey: A New Ecology of Competition. *Harvard Business Review*, 71(3), 75–84.

Moore, J. (1996) *The Death of Competition: Leadership and Strategy in the Age of Business Ecosystems*. New York, HarperBusiness.

Porter, M. E. (1979) How Competitive Forces Shape Strategy. *Harvard Business Review*, 57(2), 137–145.

Porter, M. E. (1980) *Competitive Strategy: Techniques for Analysing Industries and Competitors*. New York, The Free Press.

Porter, M. E. (1981) The Contributions of Industrial Organization to Strategic Management. *The Academy of Management Review*, 6(4), 609–620.

Porter, M. E. (1985) *Competitive Advantage: Creating and Sustaining Superior Performance*. New York, The Free Press.

PWC. (2015) *Leading From the Front: Redesigning Finance for the Digital Age: Making Sense of the Changing Role of Finance in the Digital Economy*. New York, US, PWC.

Shank, J. K. and Govindarajan, V. (1989) *Strategic Cost Analysis: The Evolution From Managerial to Strategic Accounting*. Hinsdale, Illinois, Richard D Irwin.

Shank, J. K. and Govindarajan, V. (1992) Strategic Cost Management: The Value Chain Perspective. *Journal of Management Accounting Research*, 4, 179–197.

Shank, J. K. and Govindarajan, V. (1993) What "Drives" Cost? A Strategic Cost Management Perspective. *Advances in Management Accounting*, 2, 27–46.

Simmonds, K. (1981) Strategic Management Accounting. *Management Accounting*, 59, 26–29.

Teece, D. (2007) Explicating Dynamic Capabilities: The Nature and Micro Foundations of (Sustainable) Enterprise Performance. *Strategic Management Journal*, 28(13), 1319–1350.

Teece, D. (2010) Business Models, Business Strategy and Innovation. *Long Range Planning*, 43(2–3), 172–194.

Teece, D. (2012) Next-generation Competition: New Concepts for Understanding How Innovation Shapes Competition and Policy in the Digital Economy. *Journal of Law, Economics, and Policy*, 9(1), 97–118.

Teece, D. and Pisano, G. (1994) The Dynamic Capabilities of Firms: An Introduction. *Industrial and Corporate Change*, 3(3), 537–556.

Teece, D., Pisano, G. and Shuen, A. (1997) Dynamic Capabilities and Strategic Management. *Strategic Management Journal*, 18(7), 509–533.

Teece, D. and Pisano, G. (1994) The Dynamic Capabilities of Firms: An Introduction. *Industrial and Corporate Change*, 3(3), 537–556.

Ward, K. (1992) *Strategic Management Accounting*. Oxford, Butterworth-Heinemann.

Yin, R. (1984) *Case Study Research: Design and Methods*. Thousand Oaks, California, US, Sage Publications.

PART IV

Auditing

11

AUDIT QUALITY
AND AUDIT FEES IN CHINA

Feng Liu, Fan Ye, Xiaoxiao Yu[1]

1. Introduction

In this essay, we present an overview of China's audit market and mainly discuss the most important and distinctive features that may affect audit quality and fees. China resumed its professional accounting service in the early 1980s when it opened its door to foreign investments. Before this, all enterprises were State-owned, meaning that they were not supposed to assume financial risk, such as losses and cash deficits. China even had no income tax and sales tax until 1978. However, starting in the early 1980s, China opened its doors to the world, introduced market mechanisms and encouraged private investment. The first so-called joint venture company was founded in April 1980,[2] necessitating a true and fair accounting system and an independent auditing system. It was under these circumstances that the Ministry of Finance (MOF) issued the *Provisional Regulations for Establishing the Accounting Advisory Office*[3] in 1980 and the *Accounting System for Joint Ventures* in 1983.

When China founded the Shanghai Stock Exchange in 1990 and the Shenzhen Stock Exchange in 1991, certified public accountants (CPAs) began to provide independent audit services to listed companies. By the end of 2016, the market capitalizations of the exchanges were USD$4.0988 trillion and USD$3.2127 trillion respectively, the fourth- and sixth-largest market capitalizations worldwide at the time.[4] And with the expansion of the exchanges came a simultaneous expansion of China's audit market. Our work thus responds to international investors' and academics' demand for current knowledge of China's audit market. There are a variety of research opportunities and challenges both at home and abroad, partly occasioned by a series of auditing reforms over a brief period. For example, DeFond et al. (1999) discuss government regulation and the demand for independent auditors in China, and Gul et al. (2013) use Chinese data to investigate the effects of individual auditors.

Some special features differentiate China's audit market from developed ones. First, China's audit firms have expanded via mergers and acquisitions of other audit firms or CPA teams in response to compulsory regulatory intervention. However, the Chinese audit market is still less concentrated compared with developed markets, especially the US audit market. The international Big 4 accounting firms differ from Chinese domestic firms not only in size but also in the natures of their respective clienteles and management strategies.

Second, data on individual auditors is available in China because audit reports must not only name the audit firm but also be signed by two or three CPAs. In addition, Chinese clients form relationships with their individual auditors rather than audit firms, which challenges the theory of firm size and audit quality that DeAngelo (1981) proposes and provides some new perspectives for auditing research.

Third, audit risk in China mainly arises from administrative penalty. China has had a policy of mandatory rotation of signing auditors since 2005, but its implications for audit quality still need to be assessed. In particular, individual auditors may try in various ways to circumvent the policy and maintain continuous, individual relationships with their clients.

In sum, the distinctive features of China's audit market that differentiate it from the US market imply that it may not be well described or explained by current auditing theory, which mainly focuses on the US market. Researchers should be aware of such distinctive features when they analyze audit quality and audit fees in China.

By discussing the institutional background of China's audit market, we expect to help both academics and practitioners better understand that market's distinctive issues. Differences between the US and Chinese audit markets raise an interesting question about the validity of current U.S.-oriented auditing theories for the Chinese case. In addition, China's audit market can provide fresh and distinctive research settings in which one can investigate auditing topics relevant to institutional development generally.

The structure of this chapter is as follows: the next section describes audit reports, audit fees and the regulatory environment. Section 3 discusses distinctive features of China's audit market. Section 4 concludes the chapter.

2.   Overview of China's audit market

2.1   *The product: audit reports and opinions*

The output of audit services is an audit report. Publicly listed companies in China must disclose audit reports in a standard format. The most recently revised standards for audit reports were issued in 2016 (in accordance with revisions to international auditing standards). Table 11.1

Table 11.1 Contents of audit reports

Previous reporting standard	Revised reporting standard
(1) Title (Auditor's Report);	(1) Title (Auditor's Report);
(2) Addressee;	(2) Addressee;
(3) Introductory paragraph;	**(3) Auditor's opinion (including introductory paragraph);**
(4) Management's responsibilities for financial statements;	**(4) Basis for opinion;**
(5) Auditor's responsibilities for audit of the financial statements;	(5) Management's responsibilities for financial statements;
(6) Auditor's opinion;	(6) Auditor's responsibilities for audit of the financial statements;
(7) Name and signature of CPAs;	**(7) Other reporting responsibilities;**
(8) Name, address and signature of audit firm;	(8) Name and signature of CPAs;
(9) Date of auditor's report.	(9) Name, address and signature of audit firm;
	(10) Date of auditor's report.

presents the contents of audit reports under the previous standard and the current, revised standard.[5] The most important change is that the opinion section must now be presented earlier in the report to better attract users' attention.

The report must also present supplementary information, such as (1) emphasis of matter paragraphs: these cover matters that the financial statements appropriately present or disclose but that, in the auditor's judgment, deserve special emphasis because they are fundamental to users' broader understanding of the statements; and (2) other matter paragraphs: these cover matters that the financial statements do not present or disclose and that, in the auditor's judgment, are relevant to users' understanding of the audit, auditor's responsibilities or audit reports.

The revised standards, which are generally consistent with the new auditing standards adopted by AICPA and IAASB, require new information to be disclosed. These include (1) key audit matters: these are the matters that, in the auditor's professional judgment, are of most significance to the audit of the financial statements of the current period. They are selected from matters communicated with those charged with governance; (2) going concerns: information falling under this heading is now presented in a separate section titled "Material Uncertainty Related to Going Concerns"; and (3) a separate section, titled "Other Information", is required and replaces the "Other Matters" section. The information in question is financial or non-financial information other than financial statements and the audit report thereon that is included in an entity's annual report.

The revised standards will be in effect for most listed companies from 2018, but they had already been adopted by 93 companies as of 2016's annual reports. Among these, 63 companies were audited by Big 4 accounting firms.[6] 19 companies disclosed one key audit matter, 23 companies disclosed two matters, 38 companies disclosed three matters, 11 companies disclosed four matters and only two companies disclosed five matters. We find that about 49% of the matters pertained to impairment provision, 12% to revenue recognition and another 12% to consolidation.

China follows international auditing standards in audit opinions. There are five types of opinions. (1) Clean (or unqualified) opinion: the financial statements are prepared, in all material respects, in accordance with the applicable financial reporting framework, and realize the fair presentation; (2) unqualified with explanatory notes; and (3) Modified. Table 11.2 presents three types of modified opinions: the qualified opinion, the adverse opinion and the disclaimer of opinion.

When academics use audit opinions as a proxy for audit quality, they always code the variable as 0 only if the opinion is clean and 1 otherwise. They regard the unqualified opinion with explanatory notes as a quasi-qualification opinion (Chen et al. 2000; Chen et al. 2001a). They also use restatement, financial reporting quality, accrual quality, below-the-line items and small profits as audit quality measures (Gul et al. 2013).[7] Table 11.3 reports the distributions of audit opinions received by publicly listed firms in the period 2001 to 2016. Clean opinions

Table 11.2 Types of audit opinions

The matters	*The effects or possible effects on the financial statements*	
	Material but not pervasive	*Both material and pervasive*
Misstatements	Qualified	Adverse
Unable to obtain sufficient appropriate audit evidence	Qualified	Disclaimer

Table 11.3 Distribution by year and type of audit opinions

Year	Clean	Unqualified with explanatory notes	Qualified	Disclaimer	Total
2001	1,007	93	43	20	1,163
2002	1,063	102	43	20	1,228
2003	1,183	59	27	21	1,290
2004	1,228	69	52	30	1,379
2005	1,203	78	60	33	1,374
2006	1,307	81	39	30	1,457
2007	1,447	92	15	17	1,571
2008	1,512	77	18	18	1,625
2009	1,656	86	13	19	1,774
2010	2,011	87	23	7	2,128
2011	2,248	92	19	4	2,363
2012	2,402	72	15	3	2,492
2013	2,446	61	22	7	2,536
2014	2,554	71	18	9	2,652
2015	2,742	80	14	6	2,842
2016	3,030	75	21	10	3,136
Total	29,039	1,275	442	254	31,010

account for 93.64% of the total, and that proportion keeps increasing during the period. The listed companies have received no adverse opinions since 2001. The audit opinions on the 2016 annual reports under the revised standards were all clean opinions, except one unqualified with explanatory notes.

2.2   The price: audit fees

Although China began to introduce market mechanisms in the early 1980s, its economy still largely operates under central planning and strong governmental regulation. For instance, there is a governmental agency called the Bureau of Commodity Prices that has the authority to set prices for all kinds of commodities and services, including audit services. Thus, from its inception, audit pricing in China was based not primarily on competitiveness and quality but on central regulation.

In 1989, the MOF mandated that audit services should be priced in accordance with government guidance but with some latitude. Under that scheme, auditors can negotiate with their clients to determine their fees within a price range set by the government. The pricing criteria are specified by provincial governments, based on client business characteristics, auditor's workload, demand for expertise and so on. The purpose of such regulation is to mitigate low balling of the competition. The revised regulations released in 2010 distinguish audit, capital verification and accounting consultation services. Under those regulations, audit and capital verification services charge a government-advised price, whereas accounting consultation service use market-adjusted pricing (that is, auditors negotiate with clients autonomously). At the same time, the 2010 regulations prescribe piece-charging and timing-charging. This practice was discontinued in 2014, when the National Development and Reform Commission, the parent unit of the Bureau of Commodity Prices, ended the regulation of audit fees and began to let markets determine the final price.

Under government-advised pricing, provincial governments set out the specific pricing criteria in a tiered pricing model based on clients' total assets or revenue. However, some provinces have not enacted the relevant regulations, and there are large disparities between provinces (Huang et al. 2015). For example, the regulations in Guangdong Province set prices according to whichever of the client's assets or revenue is higher, whereas Jiangsu Province's regulations, although also pricing according to asset or revenue, select which one according to the nature of the asset. In addition, audit fees at the same tier of service vary by region. For assets ranging from RMB10 million to 50 million, the standard fee in Guangdong Province is 0.5‰, but that in Jiangsu Province is 0.4‰, and in Shanxi Province it is an absolute value. Furthermore, the fluctuation of audit fees also varies by province. Lastly, the rigor with which authorities implement fee rules also varies across regions. For instance, in Fujian Province, listed companies can choose to follow the fee rules or negotiate with auditors.

How does pricing regulation affect audit fees? Are all audit firms affected to the same degree? Does price regulation improve or hurt audit quality? These questions need to be answered. However, studies of audit fees and related topics neglect them and presuppose theories appropriate to the US market, wherein audit fees are mainly fixed by market competition. Such theories may also pertain to the Chinese market, but to settle that, we need to explore the effect of China's unique institutional setting on the audit pricing process.

Listed companies have been required to disclose audit fees since 2001.[8] From 2001 to 2016,[9] the average audit fee rose from RMB 0.44701 million (about USD $54,010) to RMB 1.08232 million (about USD $156,020), and increased year by year (Table 11.4). The average audit fees divided by total assets decreased slightly, which is partially due to the trend of audit fees and the number of listed companies.

Table 11.4 Description of audit fees (in 000)

Year	n	RMB		USD		The average of audit fees/ total assets
		Mean	Median	Mean	Median	
2001	1,068	447.01	380.00	54.01	45.91	0.041%
2002	1,129	451.38	400.00	54.53	48.32	0.040%
2003	1,178	467.37	400.00	56.47	48.33	0.037%
2004	1,209	480.23	400.00	58.02	48.33	0.037%
2005	1,154	483.51	400.00	59.91	49.57	0.036%
2006	1,139	546.89	450.00	70.04	57.63	0.038%
2007	1,191	637.21	450.00	87.23	61.61	0.040%
2008	1,372	667.56	500.00	97.67	73.16	0.040%
2009	1,536	684.73	500.00	100.28	73.23	0.042%
2010	1,747	711.10	520.00	107.37	78.52	0.038%
2011	2,041	814.22	580.00	129.22	92.05	0.035%
2012	2,437	840.93	600.00	133.79	95.46	0.034%
2013	2,485	885.27	630.00	145.20	103.33	0.032%
2014	2,610	925.08	690.00	151.18	112.76	0.031%
2015	2,810	1,035.60	700.00	159.48	107.80	0.030%
2016	3,101	1,082.32	800.00	156.02	115.32	0.030%

2.3 The regulatory environment

The main regulators in China's audit market include the following. (1) The MOF: according to the *Law of Certified Public Accountants* and *Accounting Law*, the MOF has the authority to discipline the accounting profession, including to formulate and enforce standards and regulations, and to issue policy recommendations, such as the "bigger and stronger" policy. (2) The Chinese Institute of Certified Public Accountants (CICPA): by name, CICPA is equivalent to AICPA in the US. However, by nature, CICPA is quite, if not totally, different from its American peer. The entire management team of CICPA has to be nominated and approved by the MOF. Thus, empowered by the MOF, CICPA has complete regulatory authority for the Chinese accounting profession. Its responsibilities include drafting auditing standards (approved by the MOF), organizing CPA examinations, registration, peer review and so on. After the PCAOB was founded in 2002, removing regulatory authority of audit firms from AICPA, the MOF followed suit and removed authority for registration and administration of audit firms from CICPA in 2005. (3) The China Securities Regulatory Commission (CSRC), Shanghai Stock Exchange and Shenzhen Stock Exchange: insofar as all listed companies must have their annual reports audited, CSRC and its two subordinate exchanges have regulatory authority over the CPA profession. For example, no audit firms can audit annual reports for listed companies without CSRC's approval, and CSRC can also punish auditors who violate regulations. CSRC regulates annual report disclosure, which may affect auditors' performance. (4) The State-owned Assets Supervision and Administration Commission of the State Council (SASAC): there are many State-owned enterprises in SASAC's charge in China that are major clients of the large audit firms. If audit firms intend to have such entities as their clients, they must meet the criteria set by SASAC. Thus, the behavior of audit firms may be affected by SASAC.

The *Law on Certified Public Accountants* and *Accounting Law* are the top-level laws that regulate the accounting profession.[10] The first regulates CPAs and CPA firms' registration and business scope, and CICPA's duties. The second prescribes basic institutions of accounting, supervision and personnel. In 1995, China began to establish auditing standards systematically. CICPA drafted and the MOF approved the first set of *Independent Auditing Standards for Certified Public Accountants* in that year. In 2006, China formally formulated auditing standards following the international auditing standards, namely the *Auditing Standards for Certified Public Accountants*. Later in 2010, the MOF amended 38 auditing standards to achieve continuous comprehensive convergence with the international auditing standards following amendments to the latter. Furthermore, China formulated regulations on professional ethics in 1992 and amended them in 1996, 2002 and 2009.

Distinctive of the Chinese audit market is that many regulations that influence the behavior of auditors and firms, in addition to the laws and standards mentioned above, come from multiple regulators. For instance, there are a variety of qualifications for auditing different kinds of clients, thresholds to enter into the securities market and guiding policies for firms' development. In the third section, we introduce some of these regulations.

3. Features of China's audit market

3.1 Changes of audit firms

In the past two decades, CPA firms have expanded their size quickly because of the development of China's economy and securities markets and of regulatory intervention. Figure 11.1 presents the annual revenue of the top 10 CPA firms by year. The revenue of the top firm has increased

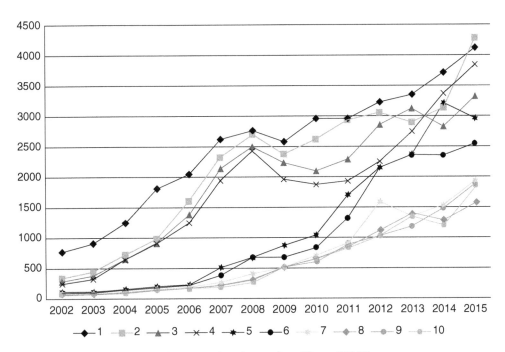

Figure 11.1 Annual revenue of the top ten firms by year (in millions of RMB)

from less than RMB 1 billion (about USD $154 million) in 2002 to more than RMB 4 billion (about USD $616 million) in 2015.[11]

As we mention above, although China has allowed some market mechanisms for almost 40 years, there are still many regulations from different governmental agencies. For audit services, different governmental agencies might set up varied benchmark requirements and a licensing system for admission to the audit market. CSRC and the MOF jointly issue licenses for audit firms that qualify to perform annual report auditing for listed companies, while SASAC selects a short list of audit firms to audit State-owned enterprises controlled by central government. Different governmental agencies and different licensing schemes require different benchmark requirements, such as requirements on the number of CPAs, annual revenue and ranking among all CPA firms.[12] Minimum firm size is a common requirement but not the only one. For example, as of 1993, CPA firms with at least 8 CPAs who had passed the national securities auditor examinations[13] were eligible to audit listed companies in mainland China, and that threshold number rose to 200 CPAs in 2012.

Moreover, regulators have directly encouraged CPA firms to expand their size by issuing so-called "bigger and stronger" policies many times since 2006. Such policies mandate "establishing 10 firms that are international and big" and "encouraging mergers between strong firms".[14] The most efficient and widely used way to expand is to merge with or acquire other CPA firms, and thereby to acquire their clients. Figure 11.2 presents the number of CPA firms that were able to audit listed companies in mainland China between 1993 and 2015.[15] Although the securities market (and thus the number of companies and amount of audit fees) grew rapidly during that period, the number of licensed audit firms qualified to sign up listed companies continually decreased from 2000 to 2015. That implies that firm size has expanded enormously. There are only 40 firms in the market now, and almost all of them have been involved in at least one merger.

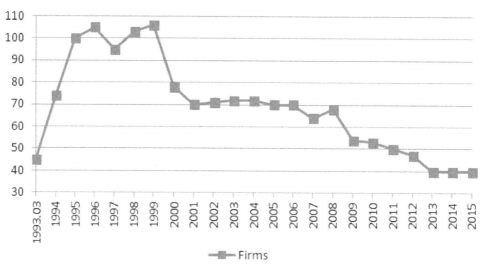

Figure 11.2 Number of firms

The potential benefits and shortcomings of so-called regulation-driven mergers of audit firms merits further study. The main question is whether the new and bigger accounting firm is really integrated or not. Studies of firm mergers and audit quality yield mixed results. Wu (2006) and Li (2011) find little evidence that mergers improve audit quality. They even find that audit quality of some merged firms may diminish. Chan and Wu (2011) show that more than half of mergers do not improve audit quality and that only multi-license mergers result in greater auditor independence and audit quality improvement. Yet Zeng and Zhang (2010) find that discretionary accruals of clients decrease and audit quality improves after mergers. Studies also find that audit fees increase after mergers (Cai et al. 2011; Li et al. 2012).

In China's audit market, the international Big 4 firms have a special status. The Big 4 began to provide services in China in 1992 (when they were the Big 6), and they had to form cooperative firms (a type of joint venture) with local audit firms because regulations did not permit foreign accounting firms to do business independently in China. For example, they set up the cooperative firms Andersen Huaqiang, Deloitte-Huayong, Ernst & Young Huaming and KPMG-Huazhen. All of these names include "Hua", which indicates China and the MOF.

Due to changes in CPA law in 2012, they have begun to change their organizational forms to limited liability partnerships, the same form used by domestic firms. Yet their governance systems and internal management structures remain different from those of domestic firms, and they are much less frequently involved in mergers.[16] In their studies, academics typically try to control for the effect of Big 4 firms or simply regard them as higher-quality firms. The audit fees of Big 4 firms are always higher than those of domestic firms (Qi et al. 2004; Tian and Liu 2013). Nevertheless, the differences between the Big 4 and large domestic firms and between Big 4 operations in China and those in other countries remain to be studied in detail. Chan et al. (2012) treat the Big 4 as a benchmark to predict the opinions of non-Big 4 clients. Liu et al. (2002) find that Big 4 firms may also acquire clients by hiring auditors away from other firms. Ke et al. (2015) compare clients listed only in mainland China with clients cross-listed in Hong Kong and conclude that the weak institutional environment in China induces Big 4 firms to provide lower quality services to the former.

Table 11.5 Number of clients and quantity of audit fees in 2015 (in 000)

Type of firm	Number of clients	RMB		USD	
		Mean	Median	Mean	Median
Big 4	155	3,313.21	2,250.00	510.23	346.50
Big 6	1,555	956.71	742.00	147.33	114.27
Non-Big 10	1,100	826.17	675.00	127.23	103.95
In total	2,810	1,035.60	700.00	159.48	107.80

Apart from the Big 4, 21 audit firms (36 firms in total) have joined international accounting networks or alliances, such as RSM International, BDO International and so on. Among them, Pan-China CPA, Reanda International and ShineWing CPA originate in China.[17] Studies find that the audit quality of these firms tends to be higher than that of others (Wang and Wang 2012; Zeng and Zhang 2014).

Overall, the concentration of China's audit market is still low after two decades of development. Academics usually divide audit firms into two groups by size, namely Big 4 and non-Big 4 (or Big 10 and non-Big 10). In China, the international Big 4 firms are among the largest. PwC ranked as the largest firm in 2015, and the ranks of Deloitte, Ernst & Young and KPMG were third, fifth and sixth respectively.[18] So we can divide audit firms into three types: the international Big 4, the Big 6 (that is, the Big 10 less the international Big 4) and the non-Big 10. Table 11.5 exhibits the number of clients and quantity of audit fees by type of CPA firm in 2015. The Big 4 had much fewer clients than other firms, but their client size was bigger. The market share of Big 6 firms by number of clients was 55.34%. However, there was no significant difference between their clients and non-Big 10 firms' clients with respect to size or fees charged. Thus, we may infer at least that the clients of Big 4 firms are quite distinctive. This requires consideration when we analyze the audit quality of the Big 4 firms.

Studies show that office features affect audit quality, but the effect is not as strong in the US market (Gul et al. 2013). Office size is also related to audit fee size. For example, Wang and Xin (2010) find that audit quality and audit fees of office are lower, and they are positively related to the size of office. Chen et al. (2010b) suggest that the relationship between client importance, measured at the office level, and audit opinions is sensitive to model specification and sample composition.

3.2   *Individual auditors*

In China, not only audit firms but also individual auditors need to sign audit reports. Therefore, we have a set of unique data that is not available for US and other markets. Furthermore, we are able to collect more information about individual auditors through disclosures on the CICPA website, such as age, date of qualification, educational background and so on. In addition, two or three CPAs must cosign an audit report at the same time. One of them supervises the fieldwork, and the other is responsible for the review work. This requirement was implemented in 1993, but it was written into auditing standards for the first time in 2016 when the revised standards were released. The revised standards further require auditors to mark the engagement partner.[19] In practice, two or three CPAs sign audit reports. A series of studies published in international journals use Chinese data to investigate audit quality and audit fees at the individual level (Chen et al. 2010b; Gul et al. 2013; Huang et al. 2015; Guan et al. 2016; Chen et al. 2016).

Tracing the co-movement of individual auditors and their clients from one firm to another suggests that there is a strong bond between individual auditors and clients in China's audit market. In the wake of the disaffiliation reform, many local audit firms obtain clients via auditors' close relationships with local governments (Chan et al. 2006). Audit firms also encourage individual auditors to obtain clients, and auditors audit the clients they recruit (Chen et al. 2001b; Chen 2013). Because of a lack of incentives to demand high-quality auditors, it is more efficient for relationships with clients to belong to individual auditors (Tan 2006).

In addition, we find that when individual auditors join another CPA firm because of mergers or because of auditing failures at their former firms, their clients usually choose to follow them to the new firm at the same time. In the two years after Da Hua firms merged with Ernst & Young in 2002, many auditors and their clients moved to other firms together (Chen et al. 2010a). In 2001, authorities terminated or suspended the licenses of eight audit firms, forcing their auditors and clients to leave. About half of the clients followed their auditors to their new firms. Specifically, about 27.1% of clients were signed by their former auditors in the first year, and the proportion in the second and third years rose to 49.3% and 55.9%, respectively (Chen et al. 2009). More generally, half of clients will follow their auditors (Wang et al. 2010).[20] Xue et al. (2013) find that clients also tend to change firms when their auditors leave. Even in cases where auditors do not leave a firm, we find evidence of a close relationship between clients and their auditors because the latter consistently sign the audit reports for the same clients over a long period of time at the individual auditor level (Li and Wu 2006). Firth et al. (2012b) also find that although Chinese regulators mandate auditor rotation, 46.4% of clients' auditors will rotate back after the cooling-off period. Thus, in effect, clients may be signed to individual auditors rather than the CPA firms to which the auditors belong.

Future studies are needed to explore the economic consequences of this kind of relation between clients and individual auditors. A few studies begin to investigate relevant issues, but their findings are mixed.[21] Future studies ought to expand from the audit firm level to the individual auditor level (auditors' characteristic or competencies) and to examine the experience and behavior of individual auditors.

3.3   Engagement risk

In 1998, regulators introduced the disaffiliation program. Prior to that time, most audit firms were government-affiliated. Others were university-affiliated or were joint ventures with an international accounting firm (DeFond et al. 1999). In fact, the Chinese partners in those joint ventures were mainly the MOF or the local bureau of finance on behalf of the local government.[22] After the disaffiliation reform, Chinese audit firms could adopt the organizational forms of limited liability or of partnership. Most firms chose limited liability. Thereafter, audit firms became independent legal entities. Both firms and individual auditors became exposed to litigation risk (Yang et al. 2001; Gul et al. 2009). In 2010, audit firms were required to take the form of limited liability partnerships (LLP), although whether individual auditors have unlimited liability depends on the degree and cause of audit failure.[23] Thus, litigation risk rose after the disaffiliation reform. Although the litigation risk in China may be lower than that in the developed market because of China's weak institutional environment, such risk is not negligible (Firth et al. 2012a). Studies conclude that the changes of organizational form improve audit quality at the audit firm and individual auditor level (Yang et al. 2001; Gul et al. 2009; Firth et al. 2012a; Liu and Wang 2014; Liu et al. 2015). However, there is no evidence that the changes are related to audit fees (Li et al. 2013b).

Risk in China mainly comes from the punishments of CSRC, not from lawsuits. There were 21 cases of punishment after 2010. In nine of them, the punishments for CPA firms or auditors were monetary fines, suspension or termination of practice (Table 11.6). We find that the

Table 11.6 Punishments for audit firms and individual auditors (in millions of RMB)[1]

Disclosure time	Firms		Signing auditors	
	Name	Punishments	Name	Punishments
10/2013	Zhong Lei	Fines: 2.94 million (revenue of 0.98 million) Termination of practice	Wang Yue, Huang Guohua	Fines: 0.1 million; 0.1 million Termination of practice
05/2013	Shenzhen Peng Cheng	Fines: 1.20 million (0.6 million) Termination of practice	Yao Guoyong, Liao Fushu	Fines: 0.1 million; 0.1 million Termination of practice
09/2013	Da Xin	Fines: 1.8 million (0.6 million)	Hu Xiaohei, Wu Guomin	Fines: 0.1 million; 0.05 million Termination of practice
02/2014	Reanda	Fines: 1.80 million (0.6 million)	Huang Cheng, Wen Jinghui	Fines: 0.1 million; 0.1 million Suspension of practice for 10 years
10/2013	Da Hua	Fines: 1.8 million (0.9 million)	Wang Haibin, Liu Chunkui	Fines: 0.1 million; 0.05 million Suspension of practice for seven years
08/2016	Shenzhen Peng Cheng	NA	Li Hong, Liu Tao	Fines: 0.1 million Suspension of practice for five years
11/2015	Reanda	Fines: 1.9 million (0.95 million)	Wen Jinghui, Wang Wei	Fines: 0.1 million Suspension of practice for five years
07/2016	Beijing Xing Hua	Fines: 12.8976 million (3.2244 million)	Wang Quanzhou, Yang Yihui, Wang Quansheng	Fines: 0.1 million Suspension of practice for five years, five years and three years
03/2016	Reanda	Suspension of undertaking new business until September 30, 2016	NA	

[1] The data come from the CSMAR database and the disclosures of CSRC and the Shanghai and Shenzhen Stock Exchanges. There are other kinds of punishment, such as a warning. In the fraud case of the company Sheng Jing Shan He, CSRC gave the audit firm Zhong Shen Guo Ji and its auditors a warning and would not receive their documents for 36 months. CICPA can summon auditors for risky engagements.

This table exhibits cases of punishment by monetary fine and suspension or termination of practice from January 2010 to December 2016. There are another 12 cases in which the only punishment is monetary fines. There are nine cases in which the Shanghai and Shenzhen Stock Exchanges execute the punishment.

monetary fines for the CPA firms were no more than four times the revenue of the project. The highest fine was RMB 12.8976 million (about USD $1.8592 million).[24] Only two firms were punished with termination of practice, but even in those cases, auditors other than the signing ones simply joined other firms along with their clients (Fang 2014). The highest fine for the signing auditors was no more than RMB 10,000 (about USD $14,415), and 16 auditors were punished with suspension or termination of practice. All signing auditors bear the same responsibility and will be punished at the same time, even when they do not actually participate in the auditing work.[25] So cosigning is an assumption of collective responsibility. Overall, compared with the fines for CPA firms and auditors, suspension or termination of practice is a more severe punishment, especially for the signing auditors. Auditors will thus pay more attention to their personal risk and to the audit quality of their clients than to risk to the CPA firm and the other auditors.

Studies also examine the effect of the punishments on audit quality and audit fees, but their conclusions are inconsistent. Using the sample of clients and firms punished by the CSRC, Wang et al. (2011) find that the punishments did not significantly improve audit quality of firms' or auditors' clients. However, Liu (2013) suggests that the punishments would make auditors work harder to improve audit quality and regain their reputation, leading to increases in audit cost and audit fees.

Reputation risk is another factor that drives auditors to elevate audit quality. In China's audit market, it is uncertain whether the reputation mechanism is valid. Liu et al. (2010) find that audit firms did not lose their clients after their reputations had been damaged, although their clients' share prices declined. Moreover, Chinese CPA firms change their names frequently, partially due to mergers.

3.4 *Mandatory rotation*

The policy of mandatory signing auditor rotation was issued in 2003 and took effect in 2004. Signing auditors are not allowed to provide audit services for the same clients for more than five consecutive years, and they should not provide audit services for clients within two years of being rotated off.[26] However, the effect of mandatory rotation on audit quality is uncertain because individual auditors may try to circumvent the policy. For example, studies find that individual auditors may choose interim successors via their personal relationships after they are rotated off, so that it will be easier for them to rotate back. They can even control their clients after they are rotated off (Li and Wu 2006; Zhang et al. 2011; Firth et al. 2012b; Li et al. 2013a; Lennox et al. 2014). Furthermore, CPA firms are not allowed to provide audit services for the same central State-owned enterprises for fewer than two years and more than five years, although if those firms can audit companies listed in Hong Kong or rank among the top 15, they can extend their tenure.[27]

4. Conclusions and discussion

This essay presents an overview of audit reports and audit fees in China's audit market and mainly discusses the distinctive features of audit firms, individual auditors and their clients in that market. Figure 11.3 shows the framework of extant studies. Institutional factors affect the supply of audit services. They also affect audit quality via auditors' incentives and competencies (DeFond and Zhang 2014) and affect audit fees via audit risk and auditors' effort (Simunic 1980). So the first step is to understand the institutional background when one participates in China's market or performs China-related auditing research. Notably, China's market is different from those on

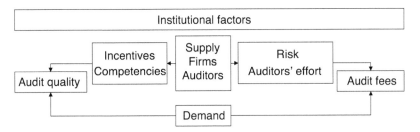

Figure 11.3 Research framework: Institutional factors and the audit market

which prevailing theories are based, namely those in the developed markets, such as the US market. For example, regulatory intervention has accelerated audit firm mergers, and the mandatory changes of organizational form may improve litigation risk.

Thus, it is valuable to discuss the fundamental features of the Chinese audit market and their distinctive effects, and doing so fills a gap in the research. We offer some directions for future research. The regulations in the Chinese market set some thresholds for audit firms. Yet this raises the question of whether auditors have an incentive to supply high audit quality or just to meet the requirements. There are different kinds of CPA firm in China, such as Big 4 firms, firms belonging to international accounting networks or alliances, domestic non-Big 10 firms and so on. Can we explain differences in their service quality just by their size or quasi-rents? In addition, concentration in the Chinese audit market is low. Audit fees should be decided by supply and demand in the market and not just by auditors' risk and effort. The auditing work is executed by individual auditors or audit teams. Data on individual auditors is available in China, so we can investigate the individual auditing process. Moreover, because the bond with clients may belong to individual auditors, it will not be appropriate to restrict research to the firm level. Finally, we can take informal institution analysis (e.g., of culture or social capital) into the auditing research fields.

Factors influencing demand for audit services include corporate governance and internal controls. For example, Wang et al. (2008) investigate the demand of central State-owned enterprises for audit services. Audit quality and audit fees should be decided by supply and demand in the audit market. Yet there is a question of whether clients demand high-quality audits in China.

In addition, beyond the availability of useful data, such as those on the identities of individual auditors, there are many distinctive institutional features of China, such as dual auditing, political connections and financing constraints. There are a variety of opportunities to study institutional factors and audit quality, and the possible results have implications for policy makers, regulators, investors and practitioners in China and similar emerging markets.

Notes

1 We thank Professor Haiyan Zhou for helpful comments. All errors are our own. Liu Feng acknowledged financial support from National Science Foundation of China (71672159) and National Distinguished Accounting Professor Development Project, Accounting Society of China.

2 In April 11, 1980, Beijing Air Catering Co., Ltd., was approved by the State Administration for Industry and Commerce under the registration "Joint Venture 001".

3 The MOF issued the *Provisional Regulations for Establishing the Accounting Advisory Office* on December 23, 1980. It marked the resumption of the certified public accounting profession. According to most literature and textbooks, the first audit firm was established in Shanghai on January 1, 1981, but in fact, an audit firm in Gansu Province had been established on September 1, 1980 (Liu and Lin 2000). Because certified public accountants were regarded as capitalist and thus discriminated against in China up to the 1970s, the MOF used the Accounting Advisory Office to avoid the sensitive term "certified public

accountant". Nevertheless, the Accounting Advisory Office provided what were, in effect, certified public accountant services.

4 See the *WFE (World Federation of Exchanges) Annual Statistics Guide 2016.*

5 In the *Regulations for Auditing, Verifying and Reporting for CPAs 1988* (the previous set of standards in China), audit reports must include scope paragraphs, explanation paragraphs and opinion paragraphs. The revised standards require more to be disclosed.

6 The revised standards should come into effect in 2017 for those companies cross-listed in mainland China and Hong Kong. The regulator encourages companies to adopt the revised standards in advance. Auditors of companies cross-listed in mainland China and Hong Kong are mostly Big 4 firms.

7 The validity of the measures remains to be evaluated. Before 2003, the names of five types of opinion were different in Chinese. Some studies use going concern as the audit quality measure, but it requires manual collection. The revised standards require disclosure of going concern information.

8 The *Q&As related to the Information Disclosure of Listed Companies No. 6 2001.*

9 Our data in this study come from the CSMAR database. We delete the observations with missing information and winsorize the variables at 1% and 99%. We show the result in RMB. We use the exchange rate at the end of the year.

10 The *Law on Certified Public Accountants* and *Accounting Law* were both enacted in 1986. They were later amended.

11 The ranking of audit firms comes from the annual report of the top 100 Chinese audit firms released by CICPA.

12 Many regulations come from the MOF and CSRC and have been revised many times.

13 The MOF and CSRC jointly created a license for CPAs to qualify to perform annual report auditing for listed companies. The exam was held for the first time in 1997. In 2007, the licensing regime was revised so that only firms and not individual CPAs had to be licensed.

14 See the related regulations of 2000, 2006, 2007, 2009, 2011 and 2012.

15 The data come from the reports and yearbooks of CSRC and CICPA.

16 See the regulations of 2012. Mergers involving Big 4 firms include those (1) between the Ernst & Young and Shanghai Da Hua firms, (2) between the Deloitte, Beijing Tian Jian and Shenzhen Tian Jian Xin De firms, (3) between the PwC and Guangzhou Yang Cheng firms, and (4) between the PwC and Andersen firms.

17 See the disclosures on the websites of CICPA and audit firms.

18 The ranking of audit firms comes from the annual report of the top 100 Chinese audit firms released by CICPA. All of the Big 6 firms (that is, the Big 10 less the Big 4) have joined or established international accounting networks.

19 The earlier regulation is the *Provisional Regulations on Issuance and Trading of Securities 1993.* The revised standards of 2016 require that audit reports be signed by both the engagement partner and the CPA who is responsible for the project.

20 After clients' auditors left their firms, 55 clients did not change their auditors but did change firms. 66 clients changed their auditors but not their firms.

21 See Chen et al. (2010a), Chen et al. (2009), Wang et al. (2010) and Firth et al. (2012b). For example, Chen et al. (2009) find that clients with greater earnings management activities are more likely to follow their auditors between firms, and this kind of client will become more aggressive in the two post-switch years.

22 The Chinese partner of Anderson, Ernst & Young and KPMG was the MOF. The Chinese partner of Deloitte was the Shanghai bureau of finance. The Chinese partner of Cooper & Lybrand was a central State-owned enterprise. Only the Chinese partner of Price Waterhouse was not a government entity (Liu and Zhou 2007).

23 (1) In cases of auditing failure due to willful misconduct or gross negligence, those partners are liable without limit who engage in such misconduct or negligence, whereas others face only limited liabilities. (2) In cases of failure not through willful misconduct or gross negligence, all of the partners need to take unlimited liabilities. Big 4 firms also began to take the limited liability partnership form in 2012.

24 Beijing Xing Hua received the highest fines. According to CICPA, in 2016, its total revenue was RMB 760.5524 million (about USD $109.6371 million), per capita revenue was RMB 0.3404 million (about USD $49,070) and per CPA revenue was RMB 1.1755 million (about USD $169,454). In some cases, only the individual auditors were punished (Wu 2007; Wu 2008).

25 See the fraud cases of Zhong Tian Qin (Yin Guang Xia companies) and Shen Zhen Hua Peng (Mai Ke Te companies).

26 Regardless of whether the auditors work in the same firm during the period, the maximum is five years. If both of the signing auditors have provided services for five years at the same time, one of them is allowed to extend to a maximum of one more year.

27 See the regulations of 2004, 2006 and 2011.

References

In English

Chan, K. H., Lin, K. Z., Mo, P. L.-L. A political-economic analysis of auditor reporting and auditor switches[J]. *Review of Accounting Studies*, 2006, 11(1): 21–48.

Chan, K. H., Lin, K. Z., Wang, R. R. Government ownership, accounting-based regulations, and the pursuit of favorable audit opinions: Evidence from China[J]. *Auditing: A Journal of Practice & Theory*, 2012, 31(4): 47–64.

Chan, K. H., Wu, D. Aggregate quasi rents and auditor independence: Evidence from audit firm mergers in China[J]. *Contemporary Accounting Research*, 2011, 28(1): 175–213.

Chen, C. J. P., Chen, S., Su, X. Profitability regulation, earnings management, and modified audit opinions: Evidence from China[J]. *Auditing: A Journal of Practice & Theory*, 2001a, 20(2): 9–30.

Chen, C. J. P., Shome, A., Su, X. How is audit quality perceived by big 5 and local auditors in China? A preliminary investigation[J]. *International Journal of Auditing*, 2001b, 5: 157–175.

Chen, C. J. P., Su, X., Wu, X. Auditor changes following a big 4 merger with a local Chinese firm: A case study[J]. *Auditing: A Journal of Practice & Theory*, 2010a, 29(1): 41–72.

Chen, C. J. P., Su, X., Wu, X. Forced audit firm change, continued partner-client relationship, and financial reporting quality[J]. *Auditing: A Journal of Practice & Theory*, 2009, 28(2): 227–246.

Chen, C. J. P., Su, X., Zhao, R. An emerging market's reaction to initial modified audit opinions: Evidence from the Shanghai Stock Exchange[J]. *Contemporary Accounting Research*, 2000, 17(3): 429–455.

Chen, F., Peng, S., Xue, S., Yang, Z., Ye, F. Do audit clients successfully engage in opinion shopping? Partner-level evidence[J]. *Journal of Accounting Research*, 2016, 54(1): 79–112.

Chen, S., Sun, S. Y. J., Wu, D. Client importance, institutional improvements, and audit quality in china: An office and individual auditor level analysis[J]. *The Accounting Review*, 2010b, 85(1): 127–158.

DeAngelo, L. E. Auditor size and audit quality[J]. *Journal of Accounting and Economics*, 1981, 3(3): 183–199.

DeFond, M., Wong, T. J., Li, S. The impact of improved auditor independence on audit market concentration in China[J]. *Journal of Accounting and Economics*, 1999, 28(3): 269–305.

DeFond, M., Zhang, J. A review of archival auditing research[J]. *Journal of Accounting and Economics*, 2014, 58(2–3): 275–326.

Firth, M. A., Mo, P. L. L., Wong, R. M. K. Auditors' organizational form, legal liability, and reporting conservatism: Evidence from China[J]. *Contemporary Accounting Research*, 2012a, 29(1): 57–93.

Firth, M. A., Rui, O. M., Wu, X. Rotate back or not after mandatory audit partner rotation?[J]. *Journal of Accounting and Public Policy*, 2012b, 31(4): 356–373.

Guan, Y., Su, L., Wu, D, et al. Do school ties between auditors and client executives influence audit outcomes?[J]. *Journal of Accounting and Economics*, 2016, 61(2–3): 506–525.

Gul, F. A., Sami, H., Zhou, H. Auditor disaffiliation program in China and auditor independence[J]. *Auditing: A Journal of Practice & Theory*, 2009, 28(1): 29–51.

Gul, F. A., Wu, D., Yang, Z. Do individual auditors affect audit quality? Evidence from archival data[J]. *The Accounting Review*, 2013, 88(6): 1993–2023.

Huang, H.-W., Raghunandan, K., Huang, T.-C., et al. Fee discounting and audit quality following audit firm and audit partner changes: Chinese evidence[J]. *The Accounting Review*, 2015, 90(4): 1517–1546.

1Ke, B., Lennox, C. S., and Xin, Q. The effect of China's weak institutional environment on the quality of big 4 audits. *The Accounting Review*, 2015, 90(4), 1591–1619

Lennox, C., Wu, X., Zhang, T. Does mandatory rotation of audit partners improve audit quality?[J]. *The Accounting Review*, 2014, 89(5): 1775–1803.

Li, X., Xu, H., Zhang, M. *Mandatory audit partner rotation and audit quality effect of personal relationships between audit partners[J].* Working paper, 2013a. Available from: http://mitsloan.mit.edu/events/2013-asia-conference-in-accounting/pdf/Mandatory_Audit_Partner_Rotation.pdf

Simunic, D. A. The pricing of audit services: Theory and evidence[J]. *Journal of Accounting Research*, 1980, 18(1): 161–190.

Wang, Q., Wong, T. J., Xia, L. State ownership, the institutional environment, and auditor choice: Evidence from China[J]. *Journal of Accounting and Economics*, 2008, 46(1): 112–134.

Yang, L., Tang, Q., Kilgore, A., et al. Auditor-government associations and auditor independence in China[J]. *The British Accounting Review*, 2001, 33(2): 175–189.

In Chinese

Cai, C., Sun, T., Ye, J. Study on the effect of China's local accounting firms mergers – Based on the audit fee premium of "big four"[J]. In Chinese. *Accounting Research*, 2011, 1: 83–89+96.

Chen, B. A study of internal governance and its effect on Chinese audit firms – Evidence from a survey and factor analysis[J]. In Chinese. *The Chinese Certified Public Accountant*, 2013, 7: 64–71.

Fang, H. *If auditor size is gone, where does audit quality attach? – A case study based on auditors change[D].* In Chinese. Xiamen: Xiamen University, 2014.

Li, J., Song, H., Deng, J. The influence of switching auditor organizational forms on audit fee[J]. In Chinese. *Auditing Research*, 2013b, 2: 99–105.

Li, M. Could the merger of accounting firms improve audit quality[J]. In Chinese. *Economic Issues in China*, 2011, 1: 98–107.

Li, M., Zhang, J., Liu, X. The effect of audit firm mergers on audit pricing: Evidence from Chinese stock market[J]. In Chinese. *Accounting Research*, 2012, 5: 86–92+94.

Li, S., Wu, X. Rotation of signing auditors: Natural state and mandatory rule's initial effect in Chinese securities market[J]. In Chinese. *Accounting Research*, 2006, 1: 36–43+93.

Liu, F., Lin, B. The disaffiliation program and the choice of government: An explanation[J]. In Chinese. *Accounting Research*, 2000, 2: 9–15.

Liu, F., Zhang, L., Carroll, R. Auditing market in China and auditor's selection: A case analysis[J]. In Chinese. *Accounting Research*, 2002, 12: 22–27+50.

Liu, F., Zhao, J., Tu, G., et al. The importance of auditor engagement power arrangements – From the perspective of auditors' reputation[J]. In Chinese. *Accounting Research*, 2010, 12: 49–56.

Liu, F., Zhou, F. Does size really matter? – A perspective of conservatism test[J]. In Chinese. *Accounting Research*, 2007, 3: 79–87+94.

Liu, Q., Guo, J., Tang, Y. Audit firms' organizational form, legal liability, and audit quality: An individual auditor level analysis[J]. In Chinese. *Accounting Research*, 2015, 4: 86–94+96.

Liu, X. Auditor sanction and audit pricing – Based on the data of listed clients of auditors disciplined by CSRC[J]. In Chinese. *Auditing Research*, 2013, 2: 90–98.

Liu, X., Wang, K. Did auditors' organizational transformation have an impact on audit quality?[J]. In Chinese. *Accounting Research*, 2014, 4: 88–94+96.

Qi, H., Chen, H., Zhang, Y. The size, brand, audit quality of audit firms – The audit fees and audit quality of international Big 4 firms in China[J]. In Chinese. *Auditing Research*, 2004, 3: 59–65.

Tan, Y. Impact of control rights of the client's list, private benefits of control rights on audit firm's merger[J]. In Chinese. *Accounting Research*, 2006, 6: 41–47+96.

Tian, L., Liu, X. Brand premiums of international big 4 and audit fees of China's listed companies[J]. In Chinese. *China Accounting Review*, 2013, 11: 55–70.

Wang, B., Li, J., Tang, Y. Do administrative penalties improve the audit quality? Evidence from enforcement of China Securities Regulatory Commission[J]. In Chinese. *Accounting Research*, 2011, 12: 86–92.

Wang, B., Xin, Q. Do office practice of audit firms influence audit quality and fees?[J]. In Chinese. *Auditing Research*, 2010, 2: 70–76.

Wang, S., Tang, S., Li, Z., et al. Earnings management, ownership of clients and audit quality – Empirical evidence from Chinese capital market[J]. In Chinese. *Auditing Research*, 2010, 1: 55–64.

Wang, Y., Wang, P. A study on the effect of China's CPA firms becoming a member of international accounting firms[J]. In Chinese. *Management World*, 2012, 3: 61–71.

Wu, X. Accounting firm combination and quality control: The case of zhongtianqin[J]. In Chinese. *Accounting Research*, 2006, 10: 79–85+96.

Wu, X. Consequence of regulatory sanction on an individual auditor without the audit firm: Empirical evidence[J]. In Chinese. *Accounting Research*, 2008, 8: 23–31+94.

Wu, X. Regulatory propensity toward auditor liability in audit failures: An empirical analysis[J]. In Chinese. *Accounting Research*, 2007, 7: 53–61+96.

Xue, S., Ye, F., Hong, Y. Partner-client relationship and auditor switcher[J]. In Chinese. *Accounting Research*, 2013, 9: 78–83+97.

Zeng, Y., Zhang, J. The audit quality of membership of international accounting firms – Based on the preliminary research on the Chinese audit market[J]. In Chinese. *Auditing Research*, 2014, 1: 96–104+112.

Zeng, Y., Zhang, J. The effect of audit firm mergers on audit quality[J]. In Chinese. *Auditing Research*, 2010, 5: 53–60.

Zhang, J., Huang, Z., Li, M. Is mandatory rotation of signing auditors improving the audit quality? – Empirical evidence from the public listed companies in China[J]. In Chinese. *Auditing Research*, 2011, 5: 82–89.

12

INDEPENDENT AUDITING IN CHINA

A historic perspective

Songsheng Chen, Qingqing Liu

1. Introduction

Since the implementation of economic reform and opening-up policies in China in 1978, an increasing number of Chinese firms have chosen to open listings on domestic and overseas exchanges. Meanwhile, an increasing number of foreign companies have established their branches or have joint ventures with local firms in China. As investors need reliable accounting information to make their business decisions, they demand firms to have independent auditors. It is important for investors to understand the role of independent auditing, especially for the international investors.

Besides independent audits above, there are other two types of audits in China: government audit and internal audit. Government audit has a long history in China, which can be traced back to the Zhou Dynasty (1046–771 B.C.). In Tang (618–907 A.D.), Song (960–1279 A.D.), Ming (1368–1644 A.D.) and Qing (1644–1911 A.D.) Dynasties, official government offices were established for government audit. Today's National Audit Office in China (hereafter NAO) was established in 1983. The office is to supervise the financial issues of government agencies and State-Owned Enterprises (hereafter SOEs), similar to General Accountability Office (hereafter GAO) in the US. However, the difference between China's NAO and the GAO in the US is that the GAO is supervised by the Congress, while NAO is supervised by the State Council in China. With respect to internal audit, Chinese firms started to implement their internal audit in 1985 under the requirement of NAO. The development of internal audit is very sluggish in China. Now the internal audit is supervised by the CEO or audit committee. Compared with independent audit, government audit serves the government and internal audit is regarded as the assistant of management. Among the three types of audit, investors and creditors relay more on independent audit. Therefore, we focus on independent audit in this chapter.

1.1 Independent audit prior to reform and opening-up policies (1911–1980)

During the early 20th century, independent audit was introduced by a few famous scholars who studied abroad and learned the practice of accounting firms, such as Lin Xie (who received a bachelor's degree from Japan) and Xulun Pan (who received a Ph.D. from Columbia University in the US). After the foundation of the People's Republic of China (hereafter China) in 1949, the government implemented a planned economy, in which all the economic activities were managed by the government. All the firms were State-owned enterprises. Resources and net income in SOEs were attributed to central government. Firms were not required to disclose financial statements nor have them audited. So, there was no need for an independent audit. In 1979, China's government implemented a series of political and economic reforms, which represented a milestone for independent audit. In this section, we illustrate independent audit before and after the 1979 reform and opening-up policies (See Figure 12.1)

Independent audit during 1911–1949

In 1911, Sun Yat-sen lead the Xinhai Revolution, overthrew the Qing Dynasty and established the Republic of China. During 1913–1915, the *Law of Partnership Enterprise* was enacted. The separation between ownership and management drove the demand for third-party supervision. In 1918, the Beiyang government promulgated the *Temporary Constitution of Accountants*. It was the first act regarding CPAs in China history. Lin Xie, who studied business at Meiji University in Japan, became the first Certified Public Accountant (hereafter CPA), and he helped set up the first group of accounting firms in China. There were ever 2619 CPAs during the peak time. However, CPAs did not play an important role in the private economy. In 1927, most SOEs collapsed due to weak controls of central government, while private companies were undergoing a golden age. But the development of independent audit in China was stopped due to World War II and the civil war in China.

Independent audit during 1949–1979

At the beginning of PRC, China implemented the planned economy policy, under which most business activities were arranged by the government. There was no demand for third-party supervision. China's economy suffered a heavy depression because of the "Great Famine" in 1959–1961 and the Great Cultural Revolution in 1966–1976. Accordingly, independent audit was discontinued for many years.

Independent audit after 1980

The development of China's independent audit can be divided into four periods: (1) restoration and reestablishment; (2) formalization of independent audit system; (3) institutional innovation; and (4) international development (Chen, 2008).

1.2 Restoration and reestablishment of independent audit (1980–1990)

In December of 1978, China's government announced the guideline of *Opening up to the Outside, Invigorating the Inside*. On the one hand, China's vast market prospects attracted a large number of foreign firms to set up branches; on the other hand, all the domestic firms in China were State-owned at that times, lacking technology and competitive advantage. In order to promote the development of domestic enterprises, the Chinese government encouraged foreign enterprises to form Sino-foreign joint ventures. However, the not-for-profit accounting system was then modeled after the former Soviet Union and served a planned economy, to provide reliable

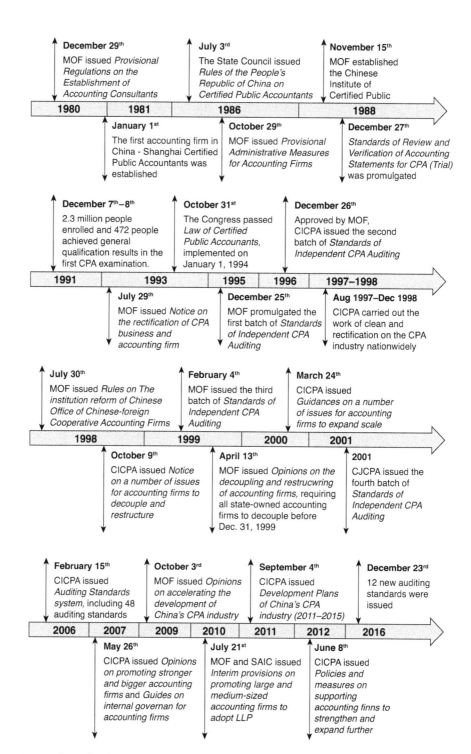

Figure 12.1 Chronicle of events (1980–2016)

information to foreign investors. There was an urgent demand for professionals who could prepare the financial statements serving public interest in capital markets.

The CPA system was restored by the Ministry of Finance (hereafter MOF) with the approval of the State Council in 1980. In the early 1980s, Shanghai became one of the most developed areas in the early stages of economic reform due to its geographical advantage. Accordingly, the CPA industry emerged in Shanghai first. At the beginning of 1981, China's first accounting firm, Shanghai Accounting firm, was set up, which was the subordinate unit of Shanghai Financial Bureau.

In July 1986, the State Council issued *Regulations of the People's Republic of China on Certified Public Accountants*, which was the predecessor of the *Law of People's Republic of China on Certified Public Accountants*. In November 1988, the Chinese Institute of Certified Public Accountants (hereafter CICPA) was founded by MOF based on international conventions, and local areas built provincial CICPA in succession.

Independent audit was not fully restored until 1991. More than 459 accounting firms were set up around the country, and 6722 CPAs were authorized to perform a variety of types of services such as bookkeeping, capital evaluation or tax. These audit firms played an important role in the improvement of investment environment. Four factors – practitioners (CPAs), professional institutions (audit firms), laws (regulations of the People's Republic of China on Certified Public Accountants) and regulators (CICPA) helped develop the independent audit practice.

1.3   Emerging independent audit system (1991–1997)

Shanghai Stock Exchange and Shenzhen Stock Exchange were set up in November 1990 and July 1991 respectively. At the end of 1992, China's government further clarified a new goal of economic reform to establish a market-oriented economy. The formation of China's capital market and the establishment of market-oriented economy greatly promoted the demand for independent audit. In 1992, the Big 6 (now Big 4) entered the market in the format of joint audit firms.

However, a few accounting scandals occurred in the following years due to lack of regulation. In 1993, three serious accounting fraud cases – the Shenzhen Yuanye scandal, the Changcheng Jidian scandal and the Hainan Zhongshui scandal – occurred successively, which resulted in a series of regulations to reorganize audit profession. By the end of 1997, 520 audit firms and 1447 branches were closed; 1181 audit firms were punished; 4871 practitioners were suspended and 2748 practitioners were sanctioned. In 1991, CICPA designed CPA examinations. In 1994, the *Law of People's Republic of China on Certified Public Accountants* was enacted. During 1995 and 1996, auditing standards were developed and the first batch of auditing standards were issued in December 1996. To enhance the independence of auditors, accounting firms were required to be separate from their sponsoring organizations, mostly government agencies and research institutes, before the end of 1998. Since then, China's independent audit has gradually normalized.

1.4   Institutional reform (1998–2004)

In the early stage of accounting firms' development, each accounting firm was supervised by government agencies. These government agencies supervised and regulated accounting firms, such as hiring CPAs, paying CPAs and dismissing CPAs. These government agencies often required their affiliates to hire CPAs whom they supervise, which impaired the independence of the auditing profession. From 1998, accounting firms were separated from government agencies and other non-profit organizations. Thus governments would not intervene in the operation and development of accounting firms, and accounting firms undertook their own business risk. In 2000, CICPA required accounting firms to merge or enlarge their size to obtain their competitive advantages. In this period of time, accounting firms became more independent and competitive in the market. They tried to get more market share through expanding their size and improving their audit quality.

1.5   International development phase (2005–present)

To meet the demand for economic globalization, especially after China's entry into WTO, China's government encouraged firms to implement the strategies of the "going out", and many Chinese enterprises actively adopted international collaborations and extended their markets and resources worldwide. This also encouraged the CPAs in China to expand their international business. In 2005, the CICPA established its own globalization objectives. The strategies include: talent training, converging Chinese auditing standards with international auditing standards, promoting more competitive and larger accounting firms, developing non-audit services and integrating of information technology.

2.   Evolution of independent auditing standards

In August 2001, Guangxia (Yinchuan) Industrial Co., Ltd. (referred to as Yinguangxia), which was known as "China's first blue-chip" for its impressive performance and attractive prospect, was investigated by MOF, China Securities Regulatory Commission (hereafter CSRC) and CICPA. From 1998 to 2001, Yinguangxia inflated its net profit of 771.567 million yuan by forging purchase and sales contracts, export declarations, VAT invoices, tax documents and financial instruments and other means. The Zhongtianqin accounting firm, which audited Yingguangxia, not only failed to give due attention to the authenticity of audit evidence, but also failed to implement any necessary audit procedures before issuing an unqualified opinion. The CPAs lacked professional caution in the course of practice. The MOF revoked the CPA qualification of the two partners-in-charge, suspended the practice qualification of Zhongtianqin CPAs and revoked its business license of securities and futures business. The case is known as "China's Enron scandal".

Another striking fraud case happened in 2013. Hunan Wanfushengke Co., Ltd. fabricated lies in order to meet listing requirements. By inflating the construction in progress and prepaid accounts and forging sales contracts, Wanfushengke made the net profit eight times larger than the actual one. The revenue in its prospectus was inflated by 740 million with a net profit by 160 million yuan from 2008 to the first half of 2011. However, Zhonglei accounting firm, which was responsible for the annual audit of the company, failed to correct its major misstatement. Finally, the Zhonglei accounting firm had confiscated business income of 1.38 million yuan and imposed a twofold fine, revoking its securities license. The relevant partners-in-charge were fined, and they were given a life-long ban on the securities market.

Frequent audit failures in China show that there are still various loopholes that need to be fixed in auditing standards. As a factor to improve audit quality, China's auditing standards have undergone a series of changes to align with international standards.

In order to ensure audit quality, CICPA, based on *Regulations on Certified Public Accountants (1986)*, developed *Standards of Review and Verification of Financial Statements for CPAs* (hereinafter refer to the *Standards*). The *Standards* were approved by the MOF and implemented in December 1988. The *Standards* included general requirements, standards, verification scope, methodology, procedures, regulations on evidence collection, working paper and contents of audit reports. The

Table 12.1 Summary of the evolution of independent auditing standards

Releasing date	Implementation date	Auditing Standards	Content	Legal basis
Dec.27, 1988	Dec. 27, 1988	Standards of Review and Verification of financial Statements for CPA	Standards of reviewing and verifying financial statements of various economic organizations for CPA	Regulations of CPAs (Released on July 3, 1986)
From 1995 to 2003	From 1996 to 2003	Independent Auditing of Standards	6 batches and 48 projects in total	the CPA act (Released on October 31, 1993)
Feb. 15, 2006	July 1, 2007	Practicing Standards of CPA	48 Rules	
Nov. 1, 2010	Jan. 1, 2012	Practicing Standards of CPA (Modified version in 2010)	Modified 38 standards; abolished 35 items in Practicing Standards (2006) and keeping 13 items	
Dec. 23, 2016	Jan. 1, 2017	12 Standards including No. 1504 Standards of CPA Auditing-Recording Crucial Items in Auditing Reports	Formulated new Rules: No. 1504 Rules-Recording crucial items in auditing reports; modified and adjusted a few Standards	

Standards played an active role in promoting the professionalism of the CPA industry in China. In this section we discuss the development of independent auditing standards in different stages, and we summarize these in Table 12.1.

2.1 Development of Independent Auditing Standards (1995–2003)

CICPA promulgated *Independent Auditing Standards* under the *Certified Public Accountants Act* (released on October 31, 1993) and *Accounting Standards for Business Enterprises* (implemented on July 1, 1993). *Independent Auditing Standards* was approved and published by the MOF in six batches between 1995 through 2003, covering 48 items (see the summary in Table 12.2).

Independent Auditing Standards consists of three levels: the first level is general standards; the second level are specific standards and a statement of independent auditing practices; the third level are guidelines on independent auditing practices. The overall structure is as shown in Figure 12.2.

2.2 Revision of CPA Practice Standards (2006)

With economic growth, the accounting firms are able to expand their business from audit to other audit services such as consulting services. To meet the demand of business diversification, the *CPA Practice Standards* were comprehensively modified in 2006 based on the new *Accounting Standards for Business Enterprises* (See Table 12.3). In February 2006, CICPA publicized 48 auditing standards (hereinafter refer to *New Auditing Standards*), which came into effect in January 2007. The *New Auditing Standards* included assurance service standards, other service standards and quality control standards. The structure of the *Standards* is presented in Figure 12.3.

Table 12.2 Contents of *Independent Auditing Standards*

Category	Number of items
Preface	1
General standards	1
Specific standards	28
Statement of independent auditing practices	10
Guidelines on independent auditing practices	5
General standards of ethical conduct	1
General standards of quality control	1
General standards of continuing professional education	1

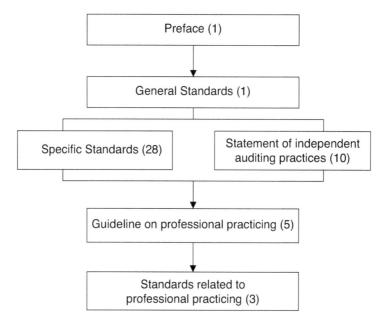

Figure 12.2 Basic framework of independent auditing standards

Table 12.3 Main Contents of *2006 CPA Practice Standards*

Category	Number (48 in total)
General standards of CPA Assurance Service	1
CPA Auditing Standards (No. 1101–1633)	41
CPA Review Standards (No. 2101)	1
Other Assurance Standards (No. 3101 and No. 3111)	2
Other Service Standards (No. 4101 and No. 4111)	2
Quality Control Standards (No. 5101)	1

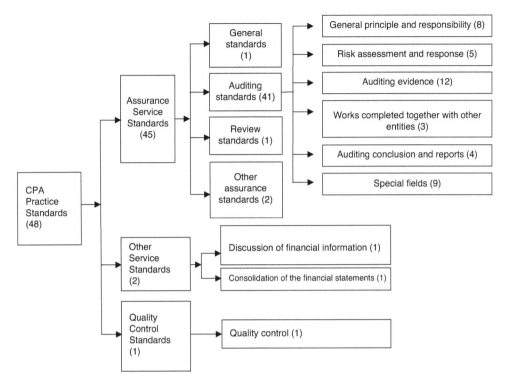

Figure 12.3 Basic Framework of *2006 CPA Practice Standards*

2.3 *Revision of* CPA Practice Standards *(2010)*

The CPA Practicing Standards of China (modified version in 2010) was released in 2010, with large-scale modification of 38 items *Standards (2006)*. The modified *Standards* were implemented in January 2012, in which 35 items in *CPA Practicing Standards (2006)* were abolished and 13 items were maintained.

2.4 *2016 Revision of* CPA Practice Standards

On December 28, 2016, a new standard *Recording Substantial Auditing Items in Audit Reports* was added into the *CPA Auditing Standards of China*, while another 11 items were modified. The releasing and implementation of the new auditing report standards will trigger active changes in the following three aspects: (1) more information contents in audit reports, which have an important role in relevance decisions; (2) an increased level of transparency of auditing practice; and (3) an increased level of responsibility of CPAs.

3. Regulators for independent auditing

Two main groups of professionals practiced independent audit in China before 1995. Certified Public Accountants, who were give their charge by the Chinese Institute of Certified Public Accountants, and Certified Public Auditors, who were regulated by the Chinese Institute of Certified Public Auditors. These two kinds of practitioners provided similar services, and the two regulators competed for power and members, to align with international practice and promote healthy competition. In June 19, 1995, the two groups merged into today's CICPA, ending the chaotic situation of "two practitioners", "two firms" and "two institutes". CPAs in China are supervised by the MOF and the CICPA, along with the CRSC (China Securities Regulatory Commission) and the National Audit Bureau (NAB, mainly responsible for government audit).

3.1 Government supervision – Ministry of Finance and its local agencies

Under the *CPA Act*, Ministry of Finance and local governments, supervise the practice of CPAs. Specific supervision functions of MOF and its local agencies include: (1) business supervision to assure accounting firms comply with laws, regulations and auditing standards, (2) disciplinary actions on CPAs who violate rules, acts, regulations and auditing standards, finding warning, suspension of practice and revoking CPA licenses, and (3) audit fee regulations at province level (in conjunction with the Department of Price at the province level) based on the workload of CPAs.

3.2 CICPA and local boards

CICPA was set up on September 8, 1992, which was a combination of the Chinese Institute of Certified Public Accountants (established in November 15, 1988, guided by the MOF) and the Chinese Institute of Certified Public Auditors (established on June 19, 1995, and guided by the National Audit Bureau). CICPA joined the Confederation of Asian and Pacific Accountants (CAPA) and the International Federation of Accountants (IFAC) in October 1996 and May 1997 respectively, and they established close cooperation with more than 50 foreign organizations of accountants.

Up to June 30, 2016, CICPA had 8411 member firms. Among them, 40 accounting firms could audit firms listed on the Shanghai and Shenzhen Stock Exchanges, and 11 large accounting firms could audit firms listed on the Hong Kong Stock Exchange. The number of individual members was around 220,000 of which the number of CPA was 101,855, and non-practicing members was 119,719. Local institutes of CPAs supervise local accounting firms and CPAs.

Besides the MOF and the CICPA, the CSRC (China Securities Regulatory Commission) and the National Audit Bureau (mainly responsible for government audit) are also regulators on CPAs and accounting firms. Among them, the CSRC is mainly responsible for supervising accounting firms who audit listed firms. The National Audit Bureau, like the MOF, also has sanction power on accounting firms.

4. Accounting firms

The first CPA firm with partnership torment emerged in the mid-1980s. In November 1985, three retired accountants raised 3,000 yuan and created the Daxin accounting firm in Wuhan, Hubei Province. Because there were no other corresponding rules to follow, the business sector had to approve the Daxin accounting firm registered as a partnership firm, in accordance with the provisions of the Finance Committee of the State Council in 1951. It was the first partnership accounting firm in China after the restoration and reconstruction of the CPA system. However, most accounting firms were affiliated with the government for a long period of time.

4.1   The organizational reform of accounting firms

The early accounting firms were affiliated with government agencies or institutions, and thus by nature they were the subsidiary body of the government or institutions. Meanwhile, the assets were owned by the state and the legal liability was also borne by the state (for details, see Gul et al., 2009).

The 1993 *CPA Act* specifies that the organization forms of accounting firms can be partnership or limited liability. In April 1997, in accordance with the unified deployment of the State Council, the Shenzhen municipal government promulgated the *Measures for the Implementation of Shenzhen Accounting Firm System Reform* as the first to implement deregulation reform. In 1998, all accounting firms started to disaffiliate from their superior government agencies, and firms could be independent and take on their own responsibility. By the end of 1999, 4805 accounting firms disaffiliated with their previous organizers and were established under "partnership" or "limited liability". Most of the reformed accounting firms choose "limited liabilities". By October 2009, there were 6659 accounting firms, among which, the number of accounting firms in "limited liability" was 4363 (66%). Moreover, among the top 100 accounting firms in 2009, 97 firms chose limited liability. Some accounting firms adopted the operation model of "combined limited liability and partnership". There are high litigation risks and management problems in this management model, such as confusion with the internal management structure and low management efficiency. Besides, the interests of the partner cannot be effectively protected, and the staff incentive is weakened.

In 2006, the revised *Partnership Enterprise Law* was formally promulgated, which added the relevant provisions of Limited Liability Partnership (hereafter LLP). According to the provisions of the *Partnership Enterprise Law*, LLP is a special form of general partnership but not an independent new law and is suitable to the professional service institutions, which provides compensable service for customers with professional knowledge and expertise. In accounting firms with Limited Liability Partnership, one partner (or several partners), who brought down their indebtedness owing to his (or their) misconduct or gross negligence, should bear unlimited liability or unlimited joint liability, while other partners should assume liability limited by property share in the partnership enterprise. The new organization form of Limited Liability Partnership in *Partnership Enterprise Law* provides legislative authority for the organizational reform of accounting firms.

On July 21, 2010, the MOF also issued the *Interim Provisions on the Promotion of Large and Medium-sized Accounting Firms to adopt the Form of Limited Liability Partnership*, where accounting firms are required to change limited liability partnership. Accounting firms, whose market shares ranked in the top 12 of the market, were transformed to limited liability partnerships between 2011 and 2012. By the end of 2013, 40 Chinese accounting firms, which hold the qualification of auditing listed firms, had changed their limited liability partnership.

The transformation of auditing firms from limited liability to partnership reduced the positive discretionary accruals of their clients, and they are more likely to issue modified opinions; that is, the transformation improved listed firms' audit quality (Wang and Dou, 2015).

4.2   The international Big 6 (or Big 4) in China

In 1992, the Big 6 (or Big 4) international accounting firms were allowed to enter China in the form of joint venture. In January 1981, Chinese government allowed Price Waterhouse to establish an office in Shanghai and founded the first branch of international accounting firms. Since 1992, the Big 6 international accounting firms have been allowed to establish Sino-foreign cooperative accounting firm. Since Price Waterhouse and Coopers & Lybrand merged, and

Andersen went bankrupt after Enron scandal, Big 6 became Big 4 accounting. Currently Chinese accounting firms cooperated with Big 4, under the names of PWC-Zhongtian, EY-Huaming, Deloitte-Huayong and KPMG-Huazhen.

In 2012, the Big 4 accounting firms implemented a localization and transformation project. The essence of the project is that the Sino-foreign cooperative firms, whose cooperation contract was expired according to the cooperation contract in 1992, should be controlled by Chinese partners and transformed to limited liability partnership firms. The transformation process included two phases. In the first stage, after the cooperative contract was expired, new accounting firms adopted limited liability partnership, while the original cooperative accounting firms should be liquidated. In the second stage, the Big 4 must gradually reach their goal of localization in management teams during a transition period of five years (by the end of 2017). The percentage of foreign partners should be reduced to less than 20% of total partners from the previous 40%. So far, the first phase of localization of the Big 4 was finished during the period from July 2012 to December 2012. In particular, local offices of KPMG, Ernst & Young, Deloitte & Touche and Price WaterhouseCoopers were established on July 5, July 27, September 14 and December 24 in 2012, respectively.

4.3 The development of Chinese domestic accounting firms

On January 1, 1981, the first accounting firm – Shanghai CPAs – was established. In March 1986, BDO China Shu Lun Pan CPAs LLP, which was set up in 1927, resumed its operation. Simultaneously, a large number of accounting firms had been founded in the whole country.

On January 22, 1996, the MOF approved that Shaanxi Yuehua, Zhongyu and Shenzhen Beicheng CPAs LLP jointly establish Yuehua (group) CPAs LLP, which marked the breakthrough of a cross-regional group of accounting firms, and China's first national accounting firm was born.

In 1998, following the deregulation and transformation policy, the two largest accounting firms in Beijing – Beijing CPAs and Jingdu CPAs – were merged into Beijing Jingdu CPAs LLP, which marked the prelude of substantial mergers and reorganizations in the CPA industry in China. In March 2000, to meet the demand for an increasing number of large enterprises, the MOF issued the *Guidance on Several Issues on Expanding the Scale of Accounting Firms* to promote business expansion, including mergers, establishment of new branches and recruiting more professional CPAs.

4.3.1 Accounting firms' merger

The First Merger Wave came in 2000. In March 2000, when the MOF issued the *Guidance on Several Issues of Expanding the Scale of Accounting Firms*, it also issued the *Interim Methods for Administrating Accounting Firms' Merger* to standardize merger procedures in accounting firms. Under the encouragement of a series of documents issued by the MOF and the CICPA, the CPA industry produced a huge wave of merger. The number of accounting firms was reduced to 152 after the merger of 411 accounting firms. The main goals of merger reasons is to obtain business qualifications in auditing listed firms, meet the qualification requirements of other statutory audit business and enhance their competitive advantages in the marketplace, such as participating in government project bidding and producing scale economy effects.

The Second Merger Wave came in 2007. On May 26, 2007, the CICPA released the *Opinions on Promoting the Accounting Firm to Become Bigger and Stronger*, and the CPA industry fully launched the third strategy for the development of the industry – accounting firms became bigger and stronger, after the strategy of talent cultivation and the strategy of international convergence in standards. The primary motivations of this merger wave were to enable CPA firms to provide accounting service for Chinese enterprises who plan to do their business abroad, and to enhance the competitiveness of domestic accounting firms. The main characteristics of this merger include: megamerger and higher competitive advantages in these accounting firms after the merger. Examples include the merger of Tianjian Guanghua and Chongqing Tianjian CPAs LLP, the merger of Beijing Jingdu and Tianhua CPAs LLP, RSM China CPAs LLP merged by Zhongruihua Hengxin and Yuehua CPAs LLP.

The Third Merger Wave came in 2009. In October 2009, the MOF issued the notice of *Some Opinions on Speeding up the Development of CPA Industry in China*, and clearly suggested that China's government would spend five years facilitating ten large accounting firms to promote their competencies. In November 2009, the MOF and the Securities Regulatory Commission developed the *Pilot Work Plan of Accounting Firm Engaged in Audits of H-share Enterprise*, which regulated the qualification of auditors in auditing listed firms. The MOF further regulated the minimum requirements for accounting firms, such as minimum revenues, audit fees, the number of listed firms, audit revenues and the number of CPA professionals. Accounting firms, which would meet their requirements via merger, could be qualified to audit firms listed in the Hong Kong Stock Exchange.

In 2009, accounting firms such as WUYIGE, Wanlong Asia, Grant Thornton, Reanda, Zhejiang Pan-China Dongfang, Pan-China Guanghua, ShineWing and China Audit Asia-Pacific LLP had successfully met the requirements specified by the pilot plans after their mergers. According to the CICPA, by December 31, 2009, the number of accounting firms with qualifications to audit public firms was reduced from 100 to 54.

Besides meeting the requirements of audit qualifications of H-shares, the purpose of the merger was to increase CPA firms' rankings, as well as obtain some special or new accounting business, such as internal control audit, management consulting business and overseas accounting business. This merger wave was characterized as megamerger, and a more rational choice of partner. Gong et al. (2016) studied 18 merger cases in Chinese accounting firms between 2005 and 2009, and compared the audit efficiency before and after the merger. They found that audit quality did not decrease, although audit time was reduced. They concluded that mergers improved audit efficiency while did not driving down audit fees because of increased audit efficiency.

4.3.2   Set up branch offices of accounting firms

In March 2000, *Guidance on Several Issues of Expanding the Scale of Accounting Firms* issued by the MOF stated that accounting firms can expand by setting up their branch offices. At the same time, the MOF published the *Interim Measures for the Approval and Management of Accounting Firms' Branch offices*. The provisions stated that accounting firms' branch offices were not a separate legal entity, which can be established by accounting firms outside their location city or county to engage in business activities for their business demand. The provisions also address the requirement and procedures of establishing accounting firms' branch office across different provinces.

On January 15, 2010, the MOF issued the *Interim Measures for the Administration of the Branch Offices of Accounting Firms*, which demanded that accounting firms and their branch offices should be unified substantiality in the aspects of personnel, finance, business, technical standards and information management. By December 2016, there were 7469 accounting firms and 993 branch offices in China.

There are two main management models between headquarters of accounting firms and their branch offices. One model is that headquarters of accounting firms implement their vertical management for their branch offices, and the other mode is that accounting firms are partitioned into management headquarters (head firms) and business segments (branches). Compared with the former, the latter provides more autonomy to branch offices.

4.4 Audit market and accounting firm competition in China

4.4.1 Audit market structure in China

Compared with a stable and mature audit market system in the developed countries, such as the US, the audit market in China is still in an emerging entity, full of high competition and low market concentration (Chen et al., 2010). The average market share of the Big 4 is only 17% based on the number of clients, which is far below the 61% of their counterpart in US (Francis et al., 2013).

The CICPA issued the *Opinions on Promoting Accounting Firms to Become Bigger and Stronger* on May 26, 2007, as did the Chinese government. Since then, the market share of the non-Big 4 accounting firms has increased year by year. In 2012, the annual revenue of RSM China exceeded that of KPMG for the first time, and ranked fourth in the nation. In 2013, the annual revenue of RSM China and BDO exceeded Ernst and KPMG, and separately ranked third and fourth. These non-Big 4 accounting firms have gradually grown and can compete with the international Big 4.

In summary, the market shares of the international Big 4 in China audit market have reduced, while non-Big 4 accounting firms show a rising trend of market concentration. The distribution of client resources becomes more concentrated in non-Big 4 leading accounting firms (e.g., RSM China and BDO).

4.4.2 Low balling

In the Chinese audit market, the international Big 4 do not occupy a majority of the market share, resulting in high competition in the audit market. In order to retain or obtain more clients, low balling in the Chinese audit market is very common. To resolve this issue, the MOF issued *Administration Measures for the Service Charges of Accounting Firms* in 2010, and the *Notice on Further Implementation* was released in 2011. However, the implementation was not effective, and low balling was still widely practiced in the audit market. In July 2012, a special investigation of the Anhui Provincial Institute of CPAs showed that there were three accounting firms which had seriously low balled their clients. Some revenues in audit fees are less than 50% of the fee standard set by the province. Obviously, the audit quality is not assured in its low audit revenues. In the future, the CICPA should strengthen accounting firms' legal responsibility, increase their litigation costs, improve corporate governance and optimize audit market environment competition.

5. Certified public accountants

5.1 The education of CPAs

5.1.1 The undergraduate education of CPAs

In 1994, the CICPA selected 22 universities as China's pilot institutions for CPA undergraduate education. They implemented quality teaching evaluation. In 2006, 2007 and 2011, the CICPA prepared teaching quality assessment respectively. The latest evaluation index system includes 25 specific items of six categories. In 2016, the number of universities approved by the CICPA to launch CPA undergraduate education is 19, of which ten are directly supervised by the Ministry of Education, 11 universities are in its 211 Project[1] and six universities in its 985 Project.[2]

Besides the 19 universities who receive funds from the CICPA, there were a small number of regional business colleges setting up their undergraduate CPA major. The CPA major was also set up in private colleges (including some independent campuses of public universities). 15 of the 19 universities sponsored by the CICPA have Ph.D. programs in accounting along with master's programs and undergraduate programs; regional business colleges usually have master's programs in accounting and undergraduate programs; while private colleges and independent campuses of public universities operate only undergraduate programs.

5.1.2 CPAs continuing education

In January 1997, the CICPA issued the *General Standards for Professional Follow-up Education of Chinese Certified Public Accountants* to standardize CPAs' continuing education and improve CPAs' professional competence level. Following the promulgation of the *Guidance on the Chinese Institute of Certified Public Accountants on Strengthening the Training of Professionals* in 2005, the *Continuing Education and Training System for Chinese Certified Public Accountants* was issued in September 2006. These are to regulate the format and requirements of continuing education, the organization and the assessment.

China's CPA continuing education is partitioned into organized and non-organized forms. Organized forms of continuing education include training courses, seminars, academic reports and other forms organized by the CICPA or its local branches. Non-organized forms of continuing education include the participation of research programs, foreign firm internships and other forms of self-learning. At present, China's CPAs' continuing education takes every two years as an assessment cycle (from January 1 of the starting year to December 31 of the following year). Each assessment cycle of continuing education requires every CPA to be trained in no less than 80 credit hours. Ethics training for each CPA should not be less than four credit hours in each assessment cycle.

5.2 The qualification exam of CPAs

In December 1980, *Interim Provisions on the Establishment of Accounting Consultants* was promulgated. After CPAs practice was interrupted for nearly 30 years, there was an urgent demand for CPA practices. In March 1987, the MOF promulgated the *Interim Measures for the Examination and Assessment of Certified Public Accountants*, which regulated subjects, scope, application criteria and procedures of CPA qualification exams in detail. In December 1991, China held a national uniform exam of CPAs for the first time. Since then, the CPA exam has been held once a year. Those who have a bachelor's degree or higher, or are a medium rank (or above) accountant or related professional, were allowed to sit in on the exam. The *Law of People's Republic of China on Certified Public Accountants*, which came into force on January 1, 1994, further empowered the CICPA with the function of supervising the exam. The law clarified the provisions of exam registration and exemption. By December 31, 2015, a total of 204,600 professionals had obtained CPA certificates, which formed an important supply of professionals of audit profession.

According to the *Outline of the National Examination of Certified Public Accountants* in 2015, there are six subjects, i.e., Accounting, Auditing, Financial Management, Corporate Strategy & Risk Management, Business Law and Tax. The integrated stage mainly tests whether applicants hold an integrated competence of special knowledge and whether they understand professional values and ethics, and if they have an ability to solve some practical problems.

The CPA exam is organized by the CICPA, and the outcome is released with a confirmation from the MOF. Grades are in percentile format, with 60% as a passing mark. The single-pass test grades of the professional stage are valid for five years, while the test grades of the integrated stage do not have valid term requirements. The CPA candidates can apply for score reviews after the exam grades are published in five to ten working days.

5.3   Mandatory rotation of partner-in-charge

In 2002, the Sarbanes-Oxley Act in the US was issued, which required that partners of a CPA firm should not provide auditing and review service for a listed company for more than five consecutive years, and should not provide audit service for the same client during two years after the rotation. In China, there are similar mandatory rotation requirements on CPAs. On October 8, 2003, the CSRC and MOF issued the *Regulation on the Regular Rotation of Signing Certified Public Accountants for Securities and Futures industries*, which prevented CPAs from providing audit service for IPO firms for more than two years; partners-in-charge and the managers are not allowed to serve for the same listed company after five years. Besides, even if individual CPAs changed their CPA firm, they cannot serve the same client within the first two years after the rotation.

In 2004, the MOF stipulated that the State-owned and state holding non-financial enterprises should require accounting firms to change their partners-in-charge after providing audit service for the same client for five consecutive years. The new audit standard issued in 2006 required accounting firms to regularly change the project leader auditing their clients (NO. 5101 *Business quality control*).

The empirical studies also documented the impact of partner rotation on audit quality. Lennox et al. (2014) used audit adjustment as a proxy variable of audit quality and found that audit quality was higher when rotation year was closer, and audit quality was significantly higher in the last year before the rotation and the first year after the rotation. Bandyopadhyay et al. (2014) also found that audit quality improved highly within three years after the rotation based on the data from Chinese listed firms between 2004 and 2009.

In 2005, the State-owned Assets Supervision and Administration Commission (SASAC) issued the *Notice on Strengthen the Audit of the Financial Accounts of Central Enterprises*. The notice requests that accounting firms provide audit service for the same central enterprise should not be shorter than two years, but should not be longer than five years.

In sum, at present, China issued a series of rules and regulations for the rotation of the partners-in-charge. As to the rotation of accounting firms, China only made rotation requirements for the central enterprises.

5.4   Legal liability of certified public accountants

When the following circumstances occur, CPAs and their accounting firms need to take legal responsibilities.

(1) *Default.* One or several parties of the contract fail to meet the requirements of the contract. In this case, accounting firms fail to fulfill their obligation in accordance with the business agreement within the required period.

(2) *Ordinary negligence.* CPAs do not maintain reasonable prudence and do not fully comply with the requirements of audit standards.

(3) *Gross negligence.* CPAs do not maintain the minimum professional prudence, and do not follow the basic requirements of audit standards.

(4) *Fraud.* CPAs do not report any material misstatements when they are aware of them.

There are five criteria to define CPA's liabilities: (1) whether the misstatement is significant; (2) whether the internal control is invalid; (3) whether the control test is in place; (4) whether the substantive procedures are in place; and (5) whether the CPA has the motivation of fraud. The specific way is shown in Figure 12.4.

If CPAs cause losses for their clients or third parties due to default, negligence or fraud, they have administrative liability, civil liability or criminal liability. CPAs may assume a type of liability or combined types of liabilities concurrently. The legal liabilities and penalties which CPAs or accounting firms may bear by the reason of default, negligence or fraud are presented in Table 12.4.

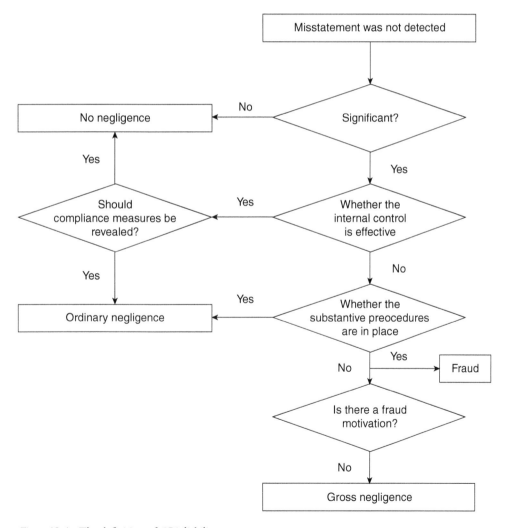

Figure 12.4 The definition of CPA liability

Table 12.4 Penalties of CPAs and accounting firms

Types of liability Subject of legal responsibility	Administrative liability (Due to default or negligence)	Civil liability penalties and related articles (Due to default, negligence or fraud)	Criminal liability (Due to fraud)
Certified Public Accountant	**Warning; suspend the operation; revoke the certificate of certified public accountant** Paragraphs 2, Article 39 of *CPA Law* (modified in 2014) Paragraphs 1 and 2 of Article 207 of *Corporation Law* (modified in 2013) Paragraphs 1 and 2 of Article 45; 201, 223 of the *Securities Law* (modified in 2014)	**Compensate the loss of the victim; pay liquidated damages** Article 42 of the Law on *CPA Law* (modified in 2014) Paragraph 3, Article 207 of the *Corporation Law* (modified in 2013) Article 173 of the *Securities Law* (modified in 2014)	**Fixed-term imprisonment of not more than five years or criminal detention** Article 229, Paragraphs 1 and 2 of the *Criminal Law* (modified in 2009)
Accounting firm	**Warning; suspension of the operation; withdrawal; confiscation of illegal income; fine** Paragraphs 1, Article 39of *CPA Law* (modified in 2014) Paragraphs 1 and 2 of Article 207 of *Corporation Law* (modified in 2013) Paragraphs 1 and 2 of Article 45; 201, 223, and 226 of the *Securities Law* (modified in 2014)	**Compensate the loss of the victim; pay liquidated damages** Article 42 of the Law on *CPA Law* (modified in 2014) Paragraph 3, Article 207 of the *Corporation Law* (modified in 2013) Article 173 of the *Securities Law* (modified in 2014)	**Give criminal sanctions** Paragraphs 3, Article 39 of *CPA Law* (modified in 2014)

6. The development of China's independent audit market

China's CPA industry is in the process of marketization in the audit profession. With the economic transformation from planned to socialist market economy, independent audit was reestablished, the government intervene was reduced and industry practice was more developed and standardized. Also, the accounting firms were more competent, more innovative and internationalized.

The development trend of China's CPAs reflects the development of the economy and that of their clients (China's enterprises). According to the Institution Change Theory, a political and economic system is composed of a set of complex systems with special connections. Therefore, in this complex constitution, the institution development of CPAs in China is closely related to the development of the economy and enterprises in it.

6.1 Emergence and current development of independent audit market

In 1976, Chinese government leaders were replaced, but the economic strategy had not been fundamentally changed until 1978. With per capita GDP of around 200 USD, China was one of the poorest countries in the world, and thus economic transition was urgently needed. By the end of 1978, the policy of reform and opening up was developed. Introducing foreign investment via Chinese-foreign joint venture was one of the important measures. This helped change the landscape of economy, as there were only State-owned enterprises in China, who were government agencies and adopted the government accounting system. Such an accounting model is different from for-profit peers worldwide, and it was difficult to understand by foreign investors. In addition, foreign investors demand the assurance of an independent third party.

Because there was no precedent, Chinese economic reforms had to follow the reform strategy of "fumbling the way across the river" and the pragmatism of "a good cat should be good at catching rats". So, the goal and route of reform were not very clear. Accordingly, the development of the initial independent audit systems was also a pragmatic model of "walk while seeing". Without comprehensive design and mature theoretical guidance, many policies were driven by events or followed the international practice. However, with the maturity of China's audit market, the focus of policy-making now shifts to institutional innovation and design.

Institution Change Theory (North, 1981) defines the change mode of institutions into induced change, gradual change and prompt change. Liu and Wang (2008) argued that the evolution of China's CPAs was a top-down mandatory system change driven by the government, along with increased gradual change. CPA reform was introduced and implemented through the commands and laws of the government. The imposed change has the advantages of the scale economy, and the government's authorities make the implementation of the system more guaranteed and the change time shorter. Meanwhile, China's CPAs experienced gradual changes. For example, the reform of the accounting firms' format was not imposed, and accounting firms were encouraged to finish the reform within a certain period of time. Besides, big, medium and small firms took turns to implement the reforms gradually. The CPA industry reforms were usually changed locally, then nationally. For example, the disaffiliation program was first implemented in some cities as pilots and then was extended to the whole country, this process helped identify and fix some problems in and assured the smoothness of the overall transition.

6.2 The future development of independent audit in China

First, future development modes should switch from factor-driven to efficiency-driven, even to innovation-driven. The World Economic Forum (WEF) divides the world's countries into three specific stages in its Global Competitiveness Report (2006–2007): factor-driven, efficiency-driven and innovation-driven. At present, China's independent audit is still in the stage of factor-driven (such as the forced merger of domestic firms). In the future, the inherent efficiency of the audit profession needs to be improved, and a more innovative system needs to be developed.

Second, future reform should expand from a single aspect of accounting firm to multiple aspects. Not only do accounting firms need to be reformed, but also the corresponding politics, culture and institutional environment should be taken into consideration. The relationship among the three mechanisms, i.e., government, market and society, should be integrated. Moreover, all parties need to be defined by their boundaries for the purpose of reducing transaction costs.

Third, it is important to promote the transformation of government functions and system optimization. On one hand, the government should only provide limited services, and local governments should reduce the interference of accounting firms. On the other hand, related institutional settings should be optimized, such as the reform of the tax system (e.g. tax and fee reduction), the reduction of approval procedures and repeated inspection of the same client and reduction in report burden.

Fourth, future auditors should play a more active role in the international market. Along with the convergence with international audit standards, the Chinese auditors should be encouraged to compete with their peers worldwide.

Notes

1 The 211 Project is a project of National Key Universities and Colleges initiated by the Ministry of Education in 1995, with the intent to raise the research standards of highly ranked universities and cultivate strategies for socio-economic development.
2 The 985 Project is a project that was first announced by Chinese President Jiang Zemin at the 100th anniversary of Peking University on May 4, 1998 to promote the development and reputation of the Chinese higher education system by founding world-class universities in the 21st century. It is named after the date of the announcement, May 1998, or 98/5, according to the Chinese date format.

References

Bandyopadhyay, Sati P., Changling Chen, and Yingmin Yu. Mandatory audit partner rotation, audit market concentration, and audit quality: Evidence from China. *Advances in Accounting*, 2014, 30(1): 18–31.

Chen, Shimin, Sunny Y. J. Sun, and Donghui Wu. Client importance, institutional improvements, and audit quality in China: An office and individual auditor level analysis. *The Accounting Review*, 2010, 85(1): 127–158.

Chen, Yugui. The four stages of the development in Chinese CPA industry. *The Chinese Certified Public Accountant*, 2008, 11: 12–17.

Francis, Jere R., Paul N. Michas, and Scott E. Seavey. Does audit market concentration harm the quality of audited earnings? Evidence from audit markets in 42 countries. *Contemporary Accounting Research*, 2013, 30(1): 325–355.

Gul, Ferdinand A., Heibatollah Sami, and Haiyan Zhou. Auditor disaffiliation program in China and auditor independence. *Auditing: A Journal of Practice & Theory*, 2009, 28(1): 29–51.

Gong, Qihui, Oliver Zhen Li, Yupeng Lin, and Liansheng Wu. On the benefits of audit market consolidation: Evidence from merged audit firms. *The Accounting Review*, 2016, 91(2): 463–488.

Lennox, Clive S., Xi Wu, and Tianyu Zhang. Does mandatory rotation of audit partners improve audit quality? *The Accounting Review*, 2014, 89(5): 1775–1803.

Liu, Minghui, and Wang Taocheng. The evolution of Chinese CPA system in thirty years of reform and opening. *The Accounting Research*, 2008, 12: 15–23.

North, Douglass Cecil. *Structure and change in economic history.* New York: Norton, 1981.

Wang, Chunfei, and Dou Huan. Does the transformation of accounting firms' organizational form improve audit quality? Evidence from China. *China Journal of Accounting Research*, 2015, 8(4): 279–293.

PART V

Taxation

13

TAX ISSUES IN CHINA

Tao Zeng

1. Introduction

Since the establishment of both national stock exchanges on the mainland of China – the Shanghai and Shenzhen Stock Markets – in 1990, China has become the world's fastest-growing economy. It is the world's second largest economy by GDP with its stock markets being the second largest stock market in the world. It has the largest population and has the greatest growth potential. Investors and corporations around the world have paid increasing attention to the investment and business opportunities in this dynamic and energetic country. Meanwhile, the demand for government regulations and policy disclosures have increased, accompanied by a set of domestic tax reforms. To date there are studies that offer a comprehensive guide for academics, management, and practitioners on the current tax issues in China. The existing literature generally examines taxation in OECD countries and rarely examines it in developing countries such as China. As argued by Bahl and Bird (2008), both tax legislation and enforcement in developing countries are much different from those in developed countries. As a result, the structure of taxation, the enforcement of taxation, as well as taxpayers' attitudes and compliance behavior are much different from those in developed countries.

To fill this gap, this essay reviews the tax system and its development in China in recent years. It also surveys and discusses two major areas of research in accounting related to Chinese taxes. They are: corporate governance, ownership structure and tax aggressiveness; and corporate reactions to the 2008 corporate tax reform. In addition, this essay examines inter-temporal income shifting as well as the impact of ownership structures on income shifting during the 2008 corporate tax rate reduction. Using Chinese listed real estate firms during 2007 and 2008, this study shows that firms had a significantly higher total income for the quarter ending March 2008 – the first quarter of tax rate cut, suggesting that firms shifted income to the low-tax periods. Further analysis shows that these results also hold for operating income but not for non-operating income. It also shows that corporate ownership structures, including large shareholders and state ownership, are important factors in connection with both total and operating income shifting. However, institutional shareholding and inside shareholding do not affect firms' income shifting decisions.

The rest of this paper is organized as follows. In Section 2, I review the tax system and its development in China in recent years. In Section 3, I survey and discuss two major areas of literature in accounting that are related to Chinese taxes. In Section 4, I examine inter-temporal income shifting among Chinese real estate firms in the wake of the 2008 corporate tax rate cut. I develop the hypotheses, design empirical models, specify data collection and variable measurement, and present testing results. Finally, a conclusion and summary is provided in Section 5.

2. Overview of taxation in China

Through the continuous reform on the tax system, the simple single tax system used in the central-planning economy before the 1990s was replaced by a tax system with a variety of taxes. The current major taxes enforced in China include value added tax (VAT), business tax, consumption tax,[1] income tax (including enterprise and individual income tax), and tariff. The following table reports the dollar amount of the major taxes and the total amount of tax revenue between 1996 and 2015. Table 13.1 shows that all major taxes have increased dramatically over the past two decades.

Table 13.2 presents the percentage of each tax over the total amount of tax revenue during the past two decades. It reveals that the percentage of VAT over total tax revenue has decreased from over 40% in 1996 to about 25% in 2015. The percentage of enterprise income tax over the total tax revenue has increased from 10% in the 1990s to about 20% in the 2010s. On the other hand, the weights of other major taxes were simply fluctuating over time.

Table 13.1 Dollar amount of major taxes from 1996 to 2015 (in billion RMB)

Year	Total	VAT	Business Tax	Consumption Tax	Enterprise Income Tax	Individual Income Tax	Tariff
2015	12,492	3,111	1,931	1,054	2,713	862	256
2014	11,918	3,086	1,778	891	2,464	738	284
2013	11,053	2,881	1,723	823	2,243	651	263
2012	10,061	2,642	1,575	788	1,965	582	278
2011	8,974	2,427	1,368	694	1,677	605	256
2010	7,321	2,109	1,116	607	1,284	484	203
2009	5,952	1,848	901	476	1,154	395	148
2008	5,422	1,800	763	257	1,118	372	177
2007	4,562	1,547	658	221	878	319	143
2006	3,480	1,278	513	189	704	245	114
2005	2,878	1,079	423	163	534	209	107
2004	2,417	912	358	150	396	174	104
2003	2,002	724	284	118	292	142	92
2002	1,764	618	245	105	308	121	70
2001	1,530	536	206	93	263	100	84
2000	1,258	455	187	86	100	66	75
1999	1,068	388	167	82	81	41	56
1998	926	363	158	81	93	0	31
1997	823	328	132	68	96	0	32
1996	691	296	105	62	97	0	30

Source: National Bureau of Statistics of China.

Table 13.2 Percentage of major taxes over total tax revenue from 1996 to 2015

Year	VAT (%)	Business Tax (%)	Consumption Tax (%)	Enterprise Income Tax (%)	Individual Income Tax (%)	Tariff (%)
2015	24.90	15.46	8.44	21.72	6.90	2.05
2014	25.89	14.92	7.48	20.67	6.19	2.38
2013	26.07	15.59	7.45	20.29	5.89	2.38
2012	26.26	15.65	7.83	19.53	5.78	2.76
2011	27.04	15.24	7.73	18.69	6.74	2.85
2010	28.81	15.24	8.29	17.54	6.61	2.77
2009	31.05	15.14	8.00	19.39	6.64	2.49
2008	33.20	14.07	4.74	20.62	6.86	3.26
2007	33.91	14.42	4.84	19.25	6.99	3.13
2006	36.72	14.74	5.43	20.23	7.04	3.28
2005	37.49	14.70	5.66	18.55	7.26	3.72
2004	37.73	14.81	6.21	16.38	7.20	4.30
2003	36.16	14.19	5.89	14.59	7.09	4.60
2002	35.03	13.89	5.95	17.46	6.86	3.97
2001	35.03	13.46	6.08	17.19	6.54	5.49
2000	36.17	14.86	6.84	7.95	5.25	5.96
1999	36.33	15.64	7.68	7.58	3.84	5.24
1998	39.20	17.06	8.75	10.04	0.00	3.35
1997	39.85	16.04	8.26	11.66	0.00	3.89
1996	42.84	15.20	8.97	14.04	0.00	4.34

Source: National Bureau of Statistics of China.

There are some differences between the Chinese tax structure and those in OECD economies. For example, in China, individual income tax is less than 10% of the total tax revenue, and the sum of individual and enterprise income tax is under 30% of the total tax revenue. On the other hand, individual income tax is over 20% of the total tax revenue, and the sum of individual and corporate income tax is over 30% of the total tax revenue in OECD countries.[2]

The VAT was first implemented in 1979. It is one of the most important taxes imposed in China. It generally applies to the sales of goods, provisions of services such as processing, repairs and replacement, and the importing of goods into China (Hao et al. 2005). Multiple rates are applied to the VAT, depending on the taxpayers' sales, type of goods and services, and type of industrial sectors. For example, the general rate is 17%, while it is only 3% for small-scale taxpayers.

The VAT system has been reformed continuously in recent years. In 2009, China reformed its VAT and shifted it from production-based to consumption-based, which means taxpayers can claim a credit for the VAT paid on purchases against the VAT payable when they sell their goods or provide services. To solve the double tax issues on goods and services (VAT and business tax), in 2011, the State Council Standing Committee decided that starting in 2012, VAT would be expanded to include certain service industries, such as transportation, tele-communication, etc., which were originally subject to business tax. In 2016, all service industries became subject to the VAT instead of the business tax (Jin and Jin 2013).

The business tax was first levied in the 1950s. It is a tax imposed on transferring intangible assets, selling real estate properties and natural resources, as well as provision of certain services, including construction, transportation, postal and tele-communication, banking and insurance, and media and entertainment (Hao et al. 2005). Business tax rates vary from 3% to 20%, with the most common rates being 3% and 5%.

The business tax is levied on gross turnover and sales. It is not a creditable tax to the extent that the input tax cannot be removed (Stoianoff 2011). As indicated above, under the VAT reform, service sectors such as transportation and tele-communication are subject to the VAT and are no longer subject to the business tax. It is expected that replacing the business tax by the VAT for all sectors will be one of the most important tax reforms pursued in the near future.

The consumption tax is mainly levied on prescribed luxury goods and nonessential goods, such as jewelry, luxury watches, yachts, and golf equipment, products harmful to health or the environment, such as alcohol, tobacco, and fireworks, high resource consumption products, such as motor vehicles, and certain petroleum products. The consumption tax is computed based on sales with tax rates that vary from 3% to 45%, depending on the type of goods. The consumption tax generates revenue for local governments. In 2016, consumption tax reform was introduced and was underway with the purposes of increasing tax revenue, increasing equity and fairness, and increasing enforcement.

Personal income tax was introduced in China less than 20 years ago. It is a tax on income earned by individuals. Tax source, tax base, allowable deductions, and tax rates are the main components of the personal income tax. Tax rates differ depending on the source of the income earned. For example, employment income is taxed based on progressive tax rates of 3% to 45%. Income from business is taxed at rates from 5% to 35%. Property income such as interests, dividends, rental income, and royalty income is taxed at a flat rate of 20%. The tax reform on individual income tax focuses on allowable deductions and rates with the purpose of narrowing the income gap.

The enterprise income tax was introduced in the 1950s. It is a tax on profit made by enterprises. In the past, domestic enterprises, including State-owned enterprises, collectively owned enterprises, and private enterprises, followed different sets of tax laws. Since the 1994 tax reform, all domestic enterprises were subject to the same tax system with a tax rate of 33%. However, foreign enterprises followed a different tax law, which allows them to access to various favorable treatments. For instance, rate reductions are available for foreign enterprises located in specific economic zones or cities.

In 2007, a new enterprise income tax law was passed, which replaced the old tax laws and provided a unified income tax system for both domestic and foreign enterprises (Zeng 2010a). Under the new enterprise law, the income tax rate is 25% for all enterprises. A rate reduction of 5% applies to small-scale and low-profit enterprises. A rate reduction of 10% applies to enterprises in the high and new technology sector. The new law was enacted at the beginning of 2008.

Tax research in accounting is dominated by the studies on corporate income tax (see Shackelford and Shevlin 2001 and Hanlon and Heitzman 2010 for reviews). Studies of corporate income tax in China are motivated by the growing importance of China's role in the world economy. They are also motivated by the fact that China provides a very unique setting with a high level of state ownership and a high level of ownership concentration in the capital market. It has become an interesting topic for academics and policy makers to investigate the tax reporting behavior of firms with such a unique ownership structure. In addition, these studies are motivated by the corporate income tax reform in China in recent years, in particular, the introduction of the new enterprise income tax law in 2008.

In the next section, I review and discuss two main areas of literature in accounting that are related to Chinese taxes. They are: corporate governance, ownership structure and tax aggressiveness; and corporate reactions to the 2008 corporate tax reform.

3. Tax research in accounting related to Chinese corporate tax

3.1 *Ownership structure and tax avoidance*

Tax avoidance has become a worldwide issue in recent years, and a greater number of academic tax studies have investigated what is associated with tax avoidance activities (see Hanlon and Heitzman 2010 for a review).

I follow Hanlon and Heitzman (2010) and define tax avoidance broadly as any activity that reduces tax liability, which implies that,

> If tax avoidance represents a continuum of tax planning strategies where something like municipal bond investments are at one end (lower explicit tax, perfectly legal), then terms such as 'noncompliance', 'evasion', 'aggressiveness', and 'sheltering' would be closer to the other end of the continuum. A tax planning activity or a tax strategy could be anywhere along the continuum depending upon how aggressive the activity is in reducing taxes.
>
> *(Hanlon and Heitzman 2010, p. 137)*

There are three basic measures for tax avoidance in accounting and tax literature. They are, the GAAP effective tax rate, the cash effective tax rate, and the book-tax difference

The GAAP effective tax rate is defined as total income tax expenses divided by pre-tax income, where total income tax expenses are the sum of current and deferred income tax expenses. The cash effective tax rate is defined as the cash tax paid to the tax agency in the year divided by pre-tax income. The book-tax difference measures the deviation of taxable income from accounting income given the fact that accounting principles and tax laws are not the same. It is defined as pre-tax earnings less taxable income, where taxable income is calculated as total income tax expenses over the statutory tax rate.

Several studies of tax avoidance in China focus on corporate ownership structure given the fact that listed firms in China have a very unique ownership structure – a high level of state shareholding, e.g., state owner enterprises (SOE), and the existence of large shareholders, i.e., high level of ownership concentration.

Cao and Dou (2007) examine the effect of state ownership on a firm's effective tax rate and find that State-owned firms pay higher taxes compared to non-State-owned firms.

Zeng (2010b) explores how the role of ownership concentration and state ownership affect a firm's tax reporting. Using a sample of publicly traded firms in China between 1998 and 2008, she shows that firms with highly concentrated ownership engage in tax avoidance, and firms whose largest shareholders are government-related engage in less tax avoidance than firms whose largest shareholders are non-government-related. Chan et al. (2013) find similar results using Chinese listed firms for the time period from 2003 to 2009. In addition, they find that corporate governance, such as board shareholdings and the CEO serving as board chairman, is also linked to tax aggressiveness. Bradshaw et al. (2013) also find that State-owned enterprises paid higher effective tax rates than other firms, which implies that the State-owned enterprises make tax decisions in favor of the state (the controlling shareholder) at the expense of other shareholders.

Zeng (2011) posits that corporate inside ownership and macro institutional environments such as marketization are important for firms' tax reporting practices in China. Using a sample of 780 listed firms for eight years from 1998 to 2005, she finds that firms located in regions with more developed institutions and marketization generally have higher effective tax rates compared to those located in less developed institutions and marketization. She also finds that inside ownership mitigates this relationship.

Wu et al. (2012) argue that the relationship between firm size and tax avoidance depends on whether or not the firms are controlled by the state. They find that, for privately controlled firms, lager firms exhibit higher effective tax rates, consistent with the political cost theory (Zimmerman 1983), while for state-controlled firms, larger firms exhibit lower effective tax rates, consistent with political power theory (Adhikari et al. 2005).

Li et al. (2014) examine the relationship between ownership structure and tax avoidance during the share structure splitting reform in 2005. They find that State-owned enterprises have been more tax aggressive after the reform while non-State-owned enterprises have not. They argue that this is because State-owned enterprises, after the reform, put more weight on value creation and tax efficiency.

Finally, Zhang et al. (2016) examine the impact of pyramid ownership structures on firms' tax liability measured as effective tax rates. Using Chinese listed firms from 2004 to 2011, they find that a pyramidal structure in local State-owned corporations significantly reduces the corporate tax burden. They argue that tax is used as a channel for increasing firm value in state-controlled pyramidal business groups.

3.2   Tax planning practices around tax law change

Another area of Chinese tax-related research is the income shifting around a tax rate cut. Existing studies show that firms will engage in inter-temporal income shifting or earnings management across periods when facing an anticipated tax rate reduction (Scholes et al. 1992; Guenther 1994; Roubi and Richardson 1998; Madzharova 2012; Balachandran et al. 2013; Choi and Lee 2013).

The new Enterprise Income Tax Law, which was passed by the Chinese 10th National People's Congress on March 16, 2007, and took effect on January 1, 2008, provides a unified 25% corporate tax rate for all enterprises. Given this is the largest corporate tax rate cut for domestic enterprises since 1994, it is an interesting tax issue to examine firms' tax planning activities around the tax rate cut. Several studies investigate tax planning activities, such as income management during periods when the tax law changes.

Zeng (2014) finds some evidence showing that real estate firms managed income in response to the tax rate cut. In particular, she finds that firms managed earnings, including both accrual-based earnings and real earnings, to decrease income in the fourth quarter of 2007 and to increase income in the first quarter of 2008. This finding implies that firms managed income downward in the high-tax period while managing income upward in the low-tax period.

Lin et al. (2014) examine the response of both public and private firms to the 2008 tax rate cut. They document that private firms used current accounting accruals to decrease more income in 2007 than in 2008 and private firms used current accounting accruals to decrease more income than public firms in 2007. They conclude that private firms, in response to the 2007 tax rate cut, shifted income from 2007 to 2008 to save taxes.

Though the new Enterprise Income Tax Law cut tax rates for domestic enterprises, it removed many preferential tax treatments for foreign investment enterprises. It is expected that the new tax law may affect tax planning activities in foreign investment enterprises. An and Tan (2014) examine the response of foreign investment enterprises to the new tax law. They use the Chinese Industrial Enterprise Data during 2002 to 2008 and find that foreign investment enterprises responded to the new law by shifting income out of China.

4. Ownership structure and income shifting

In this section, I examine income shifting, including total income and operating income shifting in the real estate sector in response to the 2008 tax rate cut. In addition, I examine how corporate ownership structures (i.e., large shareholders, state ownership, inside ownership, and institutional ownership) affect income shifting practices.

4.1 Large shareholding and income shifting

Similar to the firms in many Asian and South American countries, Chinese publicly traded firms generally have large and controlling shareholders, i.e., the firms are controlled by a small number of shareholders. Wang (2014) documents that, during the period 2003–2011, shares of listed firms in China were held in the hands of a few largest shareholders, although the degree of concentration has reduced gradually.

Shleifer and Vishny (1997) argue that, where there is a lack of controlling shareholders, the dispersed investors have little incentive to monitor managers' behavior, including tax-planning activities. Conversely, as ownership becomes more concentrated, holding a large stake in a firm encourages the large shareholders to ensure that the managers behave in ways that will benefit shareholders. Therefore, large shareholding discourages managerial opportunism and mitigates agency problems, and hence tax planning activities are likely to benefit shareholders. As argued by Klassen (1997), firms with less diffuse ownership are more concerned with tax saving and therefore are more likely to adopt tax saving strategies, such as realizing capital losses but deferring capital gains. Desai and Dharmapala (2005) argue that whether or not tax avoidance activities benefit shareholders depends on a firm's corporate governance. They find that, for well-governed firms, tax avoidance increases their market values. Wilson (2009) examines whether firms' tax sheltering activities lead to value increase or to managerial opportunism, and find that for well-governed firms, tax sheltering increases market value. Zeng (2010b) shows that, in China, firms have lower effective tax rates when they have concentrated ownership.

Hence I expect that firms with large shareholders engaged in more inter-temporal income shifting in response to the 2008 tax rate cut.

4.2 State ownership and income shifting

Many publicly traded firms have three types of shares: state shares, legal person shares, and individual shares. In spite of institutional reforms in the financial and economic areas, many are still closely connected to the government. In these firms, shares were held by the central government, local government, or a State-owned enterprise (SOE). Wang (2014) documents that state shares had been the main type of shares in China during 2003 to 2011.

The association between state/non-state ownership and tax reporting practices has not been sufficiently explored, and the few relevant studies available come to divergent conclusions. On the one hand, Adhikari et al. (2005) argue that in non-Western developing countries such as East Asian countries, the economic system is relationship oriented rather than market-oriented, where firms are able to obtain government support and preferential tax treatments by virtue of their political connections. They find that firms with more State-owned shares pay lower taxes since they are more likely to have political connections and hence receive more government support. Wu et al. (2012) have similar findings to the extent that, for Chinese state-controlled firms, larger firms have lower effective tax rates. Kim and Zhang (2016) also find that politically connected firms are more tax aggressive than non-connected firms in the US. Finally, Mindzak and Zeng (2016) find that, in Canada, pyramid ownership structure is linked to more political connections and hence leads to more tax avoidance activities.

On the other hand, it has been argued that firms with state ownership pay higher taxes. This is based on the literature of management career concerns. First, as shown by Groves et al. (1995) and Kato and Long (2006), managers in Chinese SOEs are appointed by the government and act as government officials. Given the objective of pursuing social or political goals beyond the economic goal of minimizing tax payments, the government is more likely to appoint those who are willing to achieve such goals. Furthermore, managers paying more taxes or avoiding paying less tax will increase their political capital and enlarge their chances of promotion (Cao and Dou 2007). Zeng (2010b) find that Chinese listed firms pay a higher tax when they are controlled by the government. Bradshaw et al. (2013) also find that, in China, State-owned firms exhibit higher effective tax rates than non-State-owned firms, and paying more taxes increases the probability for a manager to be promoted to a higher position.

Finally, Salihu et al. (2014) explore the relationship between government ownership and tax avoidance for Malaysian firms and the results are inconclusive. They find that government ownership is associated with only two of the four measures of tax avoidance.

Therefore, it is an empirical question whether or not firms with state ownership shifted more income to the low-tax time periods in response to the 2008 tax rate cut.

4.3   *Inside ownership, institutional ownership, and income shifting*

The association between inside ownership and tax avoidance activities has not been sufficiently explored, either, and the few existing studies on this association have mixed results.

A study by Chen et al. (2010) argues that, for family-owned firms, a dominant owner-manager may have motivations to engage in excess tax saving activities since he can obtain a large part of the benefits from tax savings by virtue of large shareholding in the firm. However, by doing this, the owner-manager has to face a share price discount, since minority or outside shareholders are sensitive to the potential rent extraction from the tax saving activities. Furthermore, penalties by tax agencies for aggressive tax behavior would be more severe for the owner-manager, since his shares are less diversified. Chen et al. (2010) conclude that for a risk-averse owner-manager, the latter explanation dominates, and thus he is less likely to be tax aggressive.

Nevertheless, inside shareholding is used as a corporate governance mechanism to mitigate agency problems and increase alignment between shareholders and managers. Given that tax saving activities are likely to benefit all shareholders, including management shareholders, firms with inside shareholders are likely to embark on tax planning strategies to reduce their tax liabilities. For example, Scholes et al. (1992) find that closely-held firms are more likely to take tax saving opportunities even though these opportunities will reduce accounting income. Klassen (1997) investigates the association between insider-ownership concentration and gains/losses realized from divesting operating units and finds that firms with concentrated inside ownership are more concerned with tax saving rather than accounting reports and therefore are more likely to embark on tax saving strategies, including realizing capital losses, but will defer capital gains.

Hence, it still remains an empirical question whether firms with inside ownership exhibited similar or different tax planning practices than other firms in response to the 2008 tax rate cut.

Finally, I add institutional ownership to the empirical model since prior literature finds that this ownership is associated with firms' tax avoidance. However, the results are mixed (Kholbadalov 2012; Khurana and Moser 2013; Khan et al. 2017). Khurana and Moser (2013) argue that institutional ownership is likely to discourage management's tax avoidance practices since such practices increase potential for management opportunism or reduce information transparency. They find that firms with high levels of long-term institutional ownership are engaging in less tax avoidance practices. On the other hand, Khan et al. (2017) provide evidence showing that institutional ownership and tax avoidance are positively associated with each other. However, Kholbadalov (2012) examines the relationship between tax avoidance and the cost of borrowing and finds that institutional ownership has no significant effect on this relationship.

Hence, it is still an empirical question whether firms with institutional ownership exhibited similar or different income shifting practices compared to other firms in response to the 2008 tax rate cut.

4.4   Regression models and data collection

To examine income shifting around the 2008 tax rate cut and to determine the impact of the corporate ownership structure on income shifting, I designed the following regression model.

$$
PRO_{it} = \gamma_0 + \gamma_1 TAX_t + \gamma_2 OWN_{it} + \gamma_3 STA_{it} + \gamma_4 INST_{it} + \gamma_5 INSD_{it} \\
+ \sum_k \mu_k CONTROL_{it} + \varepsilon_{it}
\tag{1}
$$

where
PRO_{it}: pre-tax income in the first quarter of 2007 and 2008, deflated by book value
TAX_t: difference in statutory tax rate in year t, i.e., 0% for 2007, and −8% (25%–33%) for 2008
OWN_{it}: existence of large shareholders, an indicator variable, equal to 1 if shareholding by the top five shareholders is more than 50%, and 0 otherwise
STA_{it}: state ownership, measured as the percentage of shares held by the state
$INST_{it}$: institutional ownership, measured as the percentage of shares held by institutions
$INSD_{it}$: inside ownership, measured as the percentage of shares held by inside shareholders including senior managers and directors
$CONTROL_{it}$: a set of control variables

I choose three control variables that might influence income shifting decisions (Zimmerman 1983). They are firm size (*SIZE*), measured as log of total assets; leverage (*LEV*), measured as the ratio of long-term debts over total assets; and auditor quality, measure as an indicator variable, equal to 1 if firms are audited by a top ten auditor, and 0 otherwise. Figure 13.1 shows the relation between the dependent variable (*PRO*) and the explanatory variables (*TAX, OWNERSHIP, CONTROL*).

I predict that $\gamma_1 < 0$. That is, firms shifted income to the first quarter of 2008, the low-tax period. I also predict that $\gamma_2 > 0$. That is, firms with large shareholders engaged in more inter-temporal income shifting around the tax rate cut.

Financial data have been collected from the China Stock Market Financial Statement Database (CSMAR). Information about corporate ownership information has been manually collected from the SINA finance database. The SINA finance database covers a lot of financial and accounting data of Chinese listed firms such as annual financial reports, financial analysis, share price, ownership structure changes, top ten shareholders, etc.

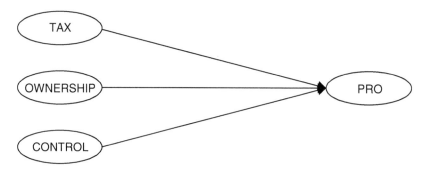

Figure 13.1 The relation between the dependent variable (*PRO*) and the explanatory variables (*TAX, OWNERSHIP, CONTROL*)

CSMAR database covers all corporations listed on the Shanghai Stock Exchange or the Shenzhen Stock Exchange for their financial statements since 1990. The firms selected for this study meet the condition that they are real estate firms with financial statements available from 2005 to 2008. There are 304 firm-year observations. I delete 97 observations whose third quarter pre-tax income is negative. I further delete 13 observations whose book value is negative. As a result, I end up with a sample size of 194 observations.

4.5 Testing results

Table 13.3 reports the results from regression model 1, which tests the effect of the ownership structure on income shifting decisions around the 2008 tax rate reduction. As expected, the coefficient on *TAX* is positive and statistically significant at 0.01 level, which shows that firms responded to the anticipated tax rate cut by moving income to the low-tax time periods. The coefficient is -0.539 for a rate reduction of 8%. Since the average book value is RMB 1,169 million, firms actually shifted about RMB 79 million of income (1,169 ×0.539/8) for each percent of the tax rate reduction.

Table 13.3 also shows that, consistent with my expectation, the coefficient on *OWN* is positive and statistically significant at the 0.05 level, suggesting that firms with large shareholders defer more income to the first quarter of 2008. In addition, the coefficient on *STA* is negative and statistically significant at the 0.05 level, which implies that firms with higher level of state ownership defer less income to the low-tax time periods. This is consistent with the management career concerns (Groves et al. 1995; Kato and Long 2006; Cao and Dou 2007; Zeng 2010b).

However, Table 13.3 shows that the coefficients on *INST* and *INSD* are not significant, suggesting that institutional ownership and inside ownership are not associated with a firm's income shifting activities during the 2008 tax rate cut.

Table 13.3 also documents the results on control variables. It reveals that *LEV* is positively associated with *PRO*, suggesting that firms with high levels of debt shift more income to the first quarter of 2008. Firm size and auditor quality, on the other hand, are not associated with a firm's income shifting activities.

Scholes et al. (1992) indicate that firms can defer income in many ways when a tax rate cut is anticipated. Firms can postpone revenue sales or accelerate tax deductible expenses, such as accelerating depreciation deductions on fixed assets, accelerating R&D expenditures, or accelerating advertisement campaigns. To analyze further which category of income (i.e., operating income *vs.*

Table 13.3 Basic testing results

Parameter	Predicted signs	Est value	t student	Prob(> |t|)
Intercept		− 0.053	− 0.246	0.81
TAX	−	− 0.538	− 2.543★★★	0.01
OWN	+	0.041	2.086★★	0.04
STA	?	− 0.080	−1.973★★	0.05
INST	?	0.010	0.121	0.90
INSD	?	3.218	0.689	0.49
SIZE	?	0.006	0.245	0.81
LEV	?	0.254	2.526★★★	0.01
AUD	?	0.010	0.574	0.57
R2(adj)	0.06			
F	2.64			

★★★ significant at 0.01 level; ★★ significant at 0.05 level; ★ significant at 0.1 level.

Regression model:

$$PRO_{it} = \gamma_0 + \gamma_1 TAX_t + \gamma_2 OWN_{it} + \gamma_3 STA_{it} + \gamma_4 INST_{it} + \gamma_5 INSD_{it}$$
$$+ \sum_k \mu_k CONTROL_{it} + \varepsilon_{it}$$

PRO: pre-tax income in the first quarter of 2007 and 2008, deflated by book value

TAX: difference in statutory tax rate in year t, i.e., 0% for 2007, and − 8% (25% − 33%) for 2008

OWN: existence of large shareholders, an indicator variable, equal to 1 if shareholding by the top five shareholders is more than 50%, and 0 otherwise

STA: state ownership, measured as the percentage of shares held by the state

INST: institutional ownership, measured as the percentage of shares held by institutions

INSD: inside ownership, measured as shares held by the percentage of inside shareholders including senior managers and directors

SIZE: firm size, measured as log of total assets

LEV: leverage, measured as the ratio of long-term debts over total assets

AUD: an indicator variable, equal to 1 if firms are audited by a top ten auditor, and 0 otherwise

non-operating income) is shifted to the low-tax time periods, I decompose the dependent variable *PRO* into operating income and non-operating income. Operating income is generated by the firm's regular businesses and operations while non-operating income includes investment gains or some other atypical gains or losses. Non-operating income is usually not recurring and is therefore excluded from evaluating firm performance. Therefore, I specify the following two models.

$$OPRO_{it} = \alpha_0 + \alpha_1 TAX_t + \alpha_2 OWN_{it} + \alpha_3 STA_{it} + \alpha_4 INST_{it} + \alpha_5 INSD_{it}$$
$$+ \sum_k \varphi_k CONTROL_{it} + \varepsilon_{it} \qquad (2)$$

$$NOPRO_{it} = \alpha_0 + \theta_1 TAX_t + \theta_2 OWN_{it} + \theta_3 STA_{it} + \theta_4 INST_{it} + \theta_5 INSD_{it}$$
$$+ \sum_k \delta_k CONTROL_{it} + \varepsilon_{it} \qquad (3)$$

where

$OPRP_{it}$: pre-tax operating income, deflated by book value

$NOPRO_{it}$: pre-tax non-operating income, deflated by book value

Table 13.4 Testing results with dependent variable of operating profit

Parameter	Est value	t student	Prob(> |t|)
Intercept	−0.054	−0.252	0.80
TAX	−0.522	−2.477★★★	0.01
OWN	0.042	2.140★★	0.03
STA	−0.078	−1.938★★	0.05
INST	0.010	0.120	0.90
INSD	3.167	0.681	0.50
SIZE	0.006	0.240	0.81
LEV	0.261	2.607★★★	0.01
AUD	0.010	0.624	0.53
R2(adj)	0.06		
F	2.66		

★★★ significant at 0.01 level; ★★ significant at 0.05 level; ★ significant at 0.1 level.
Regression model:

$$OPRO_{it} = \alpha_0 + \alpha_1 TAX_t + \alpha_2 OWN_{it} + \alpha_3 STA_{it} + \alpha_4 INST_{it} + \alpha_5 INSD_{it}$$
$$+ \sum_k \varphi_k CONTROL_{it} + \varepsilon_{it} \tag{2}$$

OPRO: pre-tax operating income in the first quarter of 2007 and 2008, deflated by book value
TAX: difference in statutory tax rate in year t, i.e., 0% for 2007, and −8% (25% − 33%) for 2008
OWN: existence of large shareholders, an indicator variable, equal to 1 if shareholding by the top five
   shareholders is more than 50%, and 0 otherwise
STA: state ownership, measured as the percentage of shares held by the state
INST: institutional ownership, measured as the percentage of shares held by institutions
INSD: inside ownership, measured as shares held by the percentage of inside shareholders including
   senior managers and directors
SIZE: firm size, measured as log of total assets
LEV: leverage, measured as the ratio of long-term debts over total assetsAUD: an indicator variable,
   equal to 1 if firms are audited by a top ten auditor, and 0 otherwise.

Table 13.4 presents the results from model 2, which tests the impact of the ownership structure on a firm's decision to shift operating income around the 2008 tax rate reduction. It shows that operating income is negatively associated with tax rates, statistically significant at the 0.05 level. The coefficient on *TAX* is −0.522 for a rate reduction of 8%. That is, firms shifted about RMB 76 million of operating income (1,169 ×0.522/8) for each percent of the tax rate reduction.

Similar to the results in Table 13.3, Table 13.4 shows that *OWN* is positively associated with *OPRO*, suggesting that firms with large shareholders defer more operating income to the low-tax periods. *STA* is negatively associated with *OPRO*, which implies that firms with a high level of state ownership defer less operating income to the low-tax time periods.

Table 13.5 reports the results from model 3, which tests the impact of ownership structure on a firm's decision to shift non-operating income around the 2008 tax rate reduction. It shows that the coefficient on *TAX* is not significant. Overall, the results in Tables 13.4 and 13.5 suggest that firms defer operating income rather than non-operating income to the first quarter of 2008 in response to the tax rate reduction.

Table 13.5 Testing results with dependent variable of non-operating profit

Parameter	Est value	t student	Prob(>|t|)
Intercept	0.001	0.105	0.92
TAX	−0.016	−1.534	0.13
OWN	−0.001	−0.888	0.38
STA	−0.002	−0.869	0.39
INST	0.000	0.028	0.98
INSD	0.051	0.216	0.83
SIZE	0.000	0.118	0.91
LEV	−0.007	−1.387	0.17
AUD	−0.001	−0.942	0.35
R2(adj)	NA(<0)		
F	0.93		

★★★ significant at 0.01 level; ★★ significant at 0.05 level; ★ significant at 0.1 level.

Regression model:

$$NOPRO_{it} = \alpha_0 + \theta_1 TAX_t + \theta_2 OWN_{it} + \theta_3 STA_{it} + \theta_4 INST_{it} + \theta_5 INSD_{it}$$
$$+ \sum_k \delta_k CONTROL_{it} + \varepsilon_{it} \tag{3}$$

NOPRO: pre-tax non-operating income in the first quarter of 2007 and 2008, deflated by book value

TAX: difference in statutory tax rate in year t, i.e., 0% for 2007, and -8% (25% − 33%) for 2008

OWN: existence of large shareholders, an indicator variable, equal to 1 if shareholding by the top five shareholders is more than 50%, and 0 otherwise

STA: state ownership, measured as the percentage of shares held by the state

INST: institutional ownership, measured as the percentage of shares held by institutions

INSD: inside ownership, measured as shares held by the percentage of inside shareholders including senior managers and directors

SIZE: firm size, measured as log of total assets

LEV: leverage, measured as the ratio of long-term debts over total assets

AUD: an indicator variable, equal to 1 if firms are audited by a top ten auditor, and 0 otherwise.

5. Conclusion and discussion

For the past three decades, China has adopted an open-door policy and transformed from a central-planning economy to a market-oriented economy. It has become the world's fastest-growing economy. Today it is the world's second largest economy with enormous growth potential. It attracts investors and corporations around the world looking for investment and business opportunities. Meanwhile, the legal and institutional system is much different from that in developed countries. While prior literature generally examines industrial countries, only a few studies examine developing countries such as China.

This paper contributes to the existing studies on Chinese legal or institutional perspectives by reviewing the tax system and its development in China. It also surveys and discusses two major areas of research in accounting related to Chinese taxes. They are corporate governance, ownership structure, and tax aggressiveness; and corporate reactions to the 2008 corporate tax reform.

In addition, this paper examines inter-temporal shifting of net income and operating income by publicly traded real estate firms in the wake of the 2008 corporate tax rate reduction. Using panel data of two-year time periods from 2007 to 2008, I document that firms have significantly higher pre-tax income in the first quarter of 2008 (the first quarter in which the corporate tax rate is reduced to 25% from 33%). Further analysis shows that these results also hold for operating income but not for non-operating income. I also find that corporate ownership structures, including large shareholders and state ownership, are important factors in connection to both total and operating income shifting. However, institutional ownership and inside ownership are not associated with a firm's income shifting activities. This paper contributes to a better understanding of tax planning practices by examining firms' income shifting activities around corporate tax rate changes. It also examines how ownership structure affects these income shifting activities.

This essay is of interest to policy makers, professionals, and scholars who wish to understand taxation in China and conduct research on the Chinese tax system. It is also of interest to policy makers, corporate management, and academics who wish to examine how economic and institutional factors, as well as corporate ownership structures, are associated with corporate tax planning practices around government tax policy changes.

Notes

1 Value added tax (VAT), business tax, and consumption tax are combined and called turnover tax.
2 Source: Revenue Statistics – Tax Structure – OECD, available at www.oecd.org/tax/taxpolicy/revenue-statistics-tax-structures.htm

References

Adhikari, A., Derashid, C., and Zhang, H. (2005), "Political policy, political connections, and effective tax rates: Longitudinal evidence from Malaysia", *Journal of Accounting and Public Policy*, Vol. 25 No. 4, pp. 574–595.

An, Z. and Tan, C. (2014), "Taxation and income shifting: Empirical evidence from a quasi-experiment in China", *Economic Systems*, Vol. 38 No. 4, pp. 588–596.

Bahl, R. W. and Bird, R. M. (2008), "Tax policy in developing countries: Looking back and forward", *National Tax Journal*, Vol. 61 No. 2, pp. 279–302.

Balachandran, B., Hanlon, D., and Tu, H. (2013), "Tax-induced earnings management within a dividend imputation system", *Australian Tax Forum*, Vol. 28 No. 3, pp. 555–582.

Bradshaw, M. T., Liao, G., and Ma, M. (2013), *Ownership structure and tax avoidance: Evidence from agency costs of state ownership in China*, Available at SSRN: http://ssrn.com/abstract=2239837 or http://dx.doi.org/10.2139/ssrn.2239837

Cao, S. J. and Dou, K. (2007), *Determinants of the variability of corporate effective tax rates: Evidence of listed company in China*, Working Paper, Chong Qing University, Chong Qing.

Chan, K. H., Mo, P. L. L., and Zhou, A. Y. (2013), "Government ownership, corporate governance and tax aggressiveness: Evidence from China", *Accounting and Finance*, Vol. 53 No. 4, pp. 1029–1051.

Chen, S., Chen, X., Cheng, Q., and Shevlin, T. (2010), "Are family firms more tax aggressive than non-family firms?", *Journal of Financial Economics*, Vol. 95 No. 1, pp. 41–61.

Choi, W. and Lee, H. (2013), "Management of accruals components in response to corporate income tax rate changes: Evidence from Korea", *The Journal of Applied Business Research*, Vol. 29 No. 5, pp. 1421–1436.

Desai, M. A. and Dharmapala, D. (2005), *Corporate tax avoidance and firm values*, NBER Working Paper No. 11241.

Groves, T., Hong, Y., McMillan, J., and Naughton, B. (1995), "China's evolving managerial labour market", *Journal of Political Economy*, Vol. 103 No. 4, pp. 873–892.

Guenther, D. (1994), "Earnings management in response to corporate tax rate changes: Evidence from the 1986 Tax Reform Act", *The Accounting Review*, Vol. 69 No. 1, pp. 230–243.

Hanlon, M. and Heitzman, S. (2010), "A Review of Tax Research", *Journal of Accounting and Economics*, Vol. 50 No. 1, pp. 127–178.

Hao, C., Rao, Y., and Hou, Y. (2005), *Chinese Taxation*, Nankai: Nankai University Publisher.

Jin, D. and Jin, W. (2013), "On the development strategy of China's Value-Added Tax (VAT) reform", *Journal of Chinese Tax and Policy*, Vol. 3, Special, pp. 226–237.

Kato, T. and Long, C. (2006), "Executive turnover and firm performance in China", *The American Economic Review*, Vol. 96 No. 2, pp. 363–367.

Khan, M., Srinivasan, S., and Tan, L. (2017), "Institutional ownership and corporate tax avoidance: New evidence", *The Accounting Review*, Vol. 92 No. 2, pp. 101–122.

Kholbadalov, U. (2012), "The relationship of corporate tax avoidance, cost of debt and institutional ownership: Evidence from Malaysia", *Atlantic Review of Economics*, Vol. 2 No. 1, pp. 1–36.

Khurana, I. K. and Moser, W. J. (2013), "Institutional shareholders' investment horizons and tax avoidance", *The Journal of the American Taxation Association*, Vol. 35 No. 1, pp. 111–134.

Kim, C. and Zhang, L. (2016), "Corporate political connections and tax aggressiveness", *Contemporary Accounting Research*, Vol. 33 No. 1, pp. 78–114.

Klassen, K. (1997), "The impact of inside ownership concentration on the trade-off between financial and tax reporting", *The Accounting Review*, Vol. 72 No. 3, pp. 455–474.

Li, O. Z., Liu, H., and Ni, C. (2014), *Controlling shareholders' incentive and corporate tax avoidance – A natural experiment in China*, Available at SSRN: https://ssrncom.libproxy.wlu.ca/abstract=2401619 or http://dx.doi.org.libproxy.wlu.ca/10.2139/ssrn.2401619

Lin, K. Z., Mills, L. F., and Zhang, F. (2014), "Public versus private firm responses to the tax rate reduction in China", *Journal of American Taxation Association*, Vol. 36 No. 1, pp. 137–163.

Madzharova, B. (2012), *Intertemporal income shifting in expectation of lower corporate tax rates: The tax reforms in central and eastern Europe*, Working Paper, CERGE-EI Working Paper Series No 462.

Mindzak, J. and Zeng, T. (2016), *Why are pyramid-affiliated firms more tax aggressive?* Working Paper, Wilfrid Laurier University, Canada.

Roubi, R. R. and Richardson, A. W. (1998), "Managing discretionary accruals in response to reductions in corporate tax rates in Canada, Malaysia and Singapore", *The International Journal of Accounting*, Vol. 33 No. 44, pp. 455–467.

Salihu, I. A., Obid, S. N. S., and Annuar, H. A. (2014), *Government ownership and corporate tax avoidance: Empirical evidence from Malaysia*, Proceedings Book of ICETSR, Malaysia. Handbook on the Emerging Trends in Scientific Research. ISBN: 978-969-9347-16-0.

Scholes, M. S., Wilson, G. P., and Wolfson, M. A. (1992), "Firms' responses to anticipated reduction in tax rates: The Tax Reform Act of 1986", *Journal of Accounting Research*, Vol. 30, Supplement, pp. 161–191.

Shackelford, A. D. and Shevlin, T. (2001), "Empirical tax research in accounting", *Journal of Accounting and Economics*, Vol. 31 No. 2, pp. 321–387.

Shleifer, A. and Vishny, R. W. (1997), "A survey of corporate governance", *The Journal of Finance*, Vol. 62 No. 2, pp. 737–783.

Stoianoff, N. P. (2011), "The coming of age of enterprise taxation in China", *Journal of Chinese Tax and Policy*, Vol. 1 No. 1, pp. 2–12.

Wang, W. (2014), "Ownership concentration and corporate control in Chinese listed companies", *US-China Law Review*, Vol. 11 No. 1, pp. 57–93.

Wilson, R. J. (2009), "An examination of corporate tax shelter participants", *The Accounting Review*, Vol. 84 No. 3, pp. 969–999.

Wu, L., Wang, Y., Wei, L., and Gillis, P. (2012), "State ownership, tax status, and size effect of effective tax rate in China", *Accounting and Business Research*, Vol. 42 No. 2, pp. 1–18.

Zeng, T. (2010a), "Long term income tax liability for large corporations in China: 19982007", *Asian Review of Accounting*, Vol. 18 No. 3, pp. 180–196.

Zeng, T. (2010b), "Ownership concentration, state ownership and income tax reporting: Evidence from China's listed corporations", *Accounting Perspective*, Vol. 9 No. 4, pp. 271–289.

Zeng, T. (2011), "Institutional environment, inside ownership and effective tax rate", *NanKai Business Review International*, Vol. 2 No. 4, pp. 348–357.

Zeng, T. (2014), "Earning management around corporate tax rate cut: Evidence from China's 2007 Corporate tax Reform", *Asian Review of Accounting*, Vol. 22 No. 3, pp. 304–317.

Zhang, M., Ma, L., Zhang, B., and Yi, Z. (2016), "Pyramidal structure, political intervention and firms' tax burden: Evidence from China's local SOEs", *Journal of Corporate Finance*, Vol. 36 No. 1, pp. 15–25.

Zimmerman, J. (1983), "Taxes and firm size", *Journal of Accounting and Economics*, Vol. 5 No. 1, pp. 119–149.

14

INCOME TAX PLANNING AND EARNINGS MANAGEMENT

Additional evidence

Nanwei Hu, Qiang Cao, Lulu Zheng, Tingyong Zhong[1]

1. Introduction

Earnings management prevails among the listed companies in China as the stakeholders pay more attention to earnings information. This decreases the quality of listed companies' financial information, and earnings information cannot fairly reflect firms' financial status and operating results, which hurts the interests of information users. Thus it is important to study earnings management.

A new set of accounting standards was issued by the Ministry of Finance on February 15, 2006 (CAS2006), which requires the listed companies to use a balance sheet liability approach to conduct tax income accounting, and to introduce the concept of assets and liabilities tax and confirm deferred tax assets and deferred liabilities on the basis of "Asset-Liability View". There are significant differences in the concepts and methods of tax accounting between the balance sheet liability approach and the taxes payable methods or tax effect accounting. The new standards provide a new chance for managers to use it as one of the options in conducting earnings management strategies. The National People's Congress passed the "PRC Enterprise Income Tax Law" on March 16, 2007, and the law was implemented on January 1, 2008. Different earnings management strategies can yield different tax expenses, and the amount of income tax that needs to be paid in the current period will also vary. Besides, the amount of income tax that needs to be paid is closely related to firms' free cash flow. On one hand, the amount of income tax that needs to be paid in the current period is firms' cash outflow, which decrease the net amount of cash flow generated from the business activities and thus decrease the free cash flow. On the other hand, the level of free cash flow restricts the amount of income tax that needs to be paid and thus influences firms' choice of earnings management strategies, for example, when a firm has a high level of free cash flow, which means the cash that can be available to be used for income tax is sufficient, the firm won't care about the amount of income tax that needs to be paid in the current period. So because income tax cost is associated with earnings management, firms need to choose conforming earnings management and/or nonconforming earnings management.

The current studies on earnings management mostly focus on the cost, motivations, means and results of earnings management. There are few studies discussing the choice of earnings management strategies and the different purposes and motivations that affect the choice from the perspective of income taxes. We try to explore the choice of different earnings management strategies and the motivations that affect the choice from the perspective of the income tax. We not only investigate the effect of earnings management on income tax, but also the effect of different earnings management motivations on the choice of earnings management strategies.

By definition, companies that manage earnings in such a manner do not incur any current or deferred income tax costs related to the earnings management. We measure this type of pre-tax earnings management by our misstatement companies and find little evidence of such activity, consistent with companies having limited opportunities to engage in this type of earnings management. Accordingly, we focus on nonconforming earnings management that creates temporary book-tax differences and thus greater deferred tax expense. Hence, restatements of income tax accounts reveal the type of pre-tax earnings management (i.e., book-tax conforming or nonconforming) that managers employ. Based on this, we choose misstatement firms as our sample, which enable us to investigate the choice of conforming and nonconforming earnings management through measuring the differences of tax account between originally reported and restated financial statements, and to measure the amount of pre-tax earnings management more accurately. Restating financial results can presumably still reflect unacknowledged earnings management, nonetheless, we assume that restated amounts reflect strictly less earnings management than the amounts companies originally reported. Consistent with Erickson, Hanlon and Maydew (2004), we find that income-increasing conforming earnings management results in a downward restatement of current tax expense as well as pre-tax income. Consistent with Phillips, Pincus and Rego (2003), income-increasing nonconforming earnings management results in a downward restatement of deferred tax expense and pre-tax income. Restatement companies that managed pre-tax earnings upward in ways that create permanent book-tax differences would restate pre-tax income downward, but not restate either current or deferred tax expense. We also find that when the company has motivations to turn losses into gains and has motivations to avoid penalty cost associated with fraud being found, firms from more developed market areas are more likely to employ conforming earnings management strategies. State-owned firms are more likely to employ conforming earnings management strategies when they have a motivation to avoid penalty associated with fraud being found, while non-State-owned firms are more likely to do so when they have motivations to avoid reporting a loss.

2. The background of tax reform in China

2.1 The history of China's tax system development

It is a current multiple taxation system which consists of many taxes that enables China's tax system to function at different levels and fields. Since the "Open and Reform" policy began, China's tax system has improved and achieved great success through several reforms over the past 30 years. At the earlier stage of open and reform, the main breakthrough in the tax system reform was to set up a new system involving foreign trade that could adapt to open policies. Therefore, in 1983 and 1984, the central government conducted the reforms of those State-owned enterprises in terms of the change of tax in two steps respectively, which meant the replacement of profit delivery by taxes. In this way, the new relationship in distribution between the government and the enterprises has been firmly reset. In 1994, the most effective tax system reform was carried out, with the greatest significance in the largest fields and scales since PRC. It aims to set a new social marketing economy system, and to positively build a responding tax system in order to serve it. Since 2004, on the basis of the central idea of scientific development, to center on the perfection of the social marketing economy system and the building of a moderately prosperous

Table 14.1 the stage of tax reform in China

Stage	Span of Time	Main Points of Tax Reform
First Stage: Tax Reform in 1984	1984–1993	comprehensive industrial and commercial tax system reform, restoration and reconstruction of the tax law system
Second Stage: Tax Reform in 1994	1994–2003	the unification of the tax law, fair reasonable tax burden, simplify the tax system, and the reasonable separation of powers, establish a compatible with market economy system of the tax law
Third Stage: Tax Reform in 2004	2004–2012	Reform partially in tax system, the implementation of structural tax cuts, more specifications, complete tax law system is established
Fourth Stage: Tax Reform in 2016	2012-present	Reform from business tax to added-value tax, reduce the repeated tax and further reduce the enterprise tax, deepen the lateral structural reform of the supply

society in all respects, we gradually carried out the tax reforms in rural areas and perfected the tax system in goods and labors, the income tax system and the property tax system, and so on, which concludes a series of tax system reforms and export tax rebates. Since 2012, the business tax has been changed to added-value tax (VAT), which only taxes the added-value part of products or services, so that it reduces those repetitive taxes, aiming to speed up financial and tax system reforming, that relieves enterprises' taxes and motivates them, fostering industrial and consuming upgrading, offering new motivations and deepening the lateral structural reform of supply. It should be another great reform in the field of finance and the tax system, since tax-division reform in 1994. Through several reforms, at present, in China, we have 17 taxes, including: the added-value tax, the consumption tax, the enterprise income tax, the individual income tax, resource tax, the urban land use taxes, the property tax, the city maintenance and construction tax, the cultivated land usage tax, the land added-value tax, the vehicle purchase tax, the vehicle and vessel tax, the stamp tax, the deed tax, the tobacco taxes, the tariff and ship's tonnage dues. Among them, 15 taxes should be collected by the tax departments of the government. Tariffs and a tonnage tax are collected by the customs authorities. In addition, the imports added-value tax and the consumption tax should also be collected by the customs authorities on behalf of the government. Table 14.1 shows the main stage of tax reform in China.

2.2   China's current tax system

It consists of five main types of tax (1) *turnover tax*: added-value tax, consumption tax and tariff. (2) *income tax*: enterprise income tax, individual income tax. (3) *properties and behavior tax*: the property tax, vehicle tax, stamp tax, deed tax. (4) *resource tax*: resource tax, land added-value tax and urban land usage tax. (5) *special purpose tax*: urban maintenance and construction tax, vehicle purchase tax, cultivated land usage tax, tobacco taxes and vessel tonnage dues.

The above 17 tax laws and regulations form the tax substantive law system in China. Despite the 17 kinds of taxes in China's tax law and regulation system (including tonnage tax and tariff), not everyone should pay all taxes. Taxpayers only pay the corresponding tax according to the taxable behaviors in tax law. On the contrary, if the taxable behavior does not occur, they needn't pay the tax. Actually, there are about ten taxes that might be collected from those enterprises with a wide scope of business. In fact, most enterprises would pay six to eight taxes.

2.3   Enterprise income tax

In the early 20th century, China's income tax system was created and affected by income tax systems in European and American countries and Japan. Before and after 1910, the Qing dynasty government had drafted the articles of the income tax system, but finally it failed to be issued and carried out. In the Republic of China, the national government formulated the Income Tax Regulations on the basis of the constitution and promulgated it in 1914, but failed to do live up to it. In July 1936, the national government released the Provisional Regulations on Income Tax, which began on October 1, the first income tax in China's history. This is the first tax law in Chinese history.

In the 30 years before the founding of the People's Republic of China in 1949 and the reform and opening up in 1978, the income tax system of Chinese enterprises experienced a tortuous development. At the first national tax conference, held in November 1949, the national tax system was identified, including a tax on enterprise income. On January 30, 1950, the State Council of the people's central government of the People's Republic of China released the programmatic document: *The Principles and Implementation of National Tax System*. It set up 14 taxes, including industrial and commercial income tax and interest income tax. Interest income tax was first imposed in 1950. Since then, less and less tax has been collected. Therefore, it has been closed since 1959.During these 30 years, China has not developed an independent and unified enterprise income tax system.

Since the reform and opening-up policy, the construction of our enterprises' income tax system has entered a new stage. The third session of the fifth National People's Congress, held on September 10, 1980, passed China's first enterprise income tax law after the founding of the People's Republic of China: *Sino-foreign Joint Venture Enterprise Income Tax Law of the People's Republic of China*. On December 13, 1981, the fourth session of the fifth National People's Congress passed the income tax law of the foreign enterprise of the People's Republic of China, too. By this, a relatively complete set of foreign tax systems has been formed. On April 9, 1991, at the fourth session of the seventh National People's Congress, the two foreign enterprise income tax laws were merged. The government issued and released the implementation of the *Tax Law of Foreign-funded Enterprises and Foreign Enterprises Income Tax of the People's Republic of China*. Hereinafter it can be referred to as the *Tax Law of Foreign-funded Enterprises and Foreign Enterprises Income Tax*, and it was implemented on July 1. This marks the unification of the foreign enterprise income tax system.

The development of the income tax of the domestic enterprise

Between 1983 and 1984, China turned over 30 years of State-owned enterprises' profits system to the state enterprise income tax system, the reform of the State-owned enterprise "profit tax". On September 18, 1984, the State Council issued the draft of the *Regulations of the State-owned Enterprise Income Tax of the People's Republic of China* and the *Measures for the Tax Collection of State-owned Enterprises*. The publication and implementation of these two administrative regulations marks the establishment of the State-owned enterprise income tax system. In April 1985, the State Council issued the *Provisional Regulations on the Income Tax of Collective Enterprises of the People's Republic of China*. Collective enterprise income tax were levied on collective enterprises. In June 1988, the State Council issued the *Provisional Regulations on the Income Tax of the Private Enterprise of the People's Republic of China*. We imposed an income tax on private enterprises in urban and rural areas and also suspended business income tax. In December 1993, China made a big reform for domestic enterprise income tax system and formulated the *Provisional Regulations of the Enterprise Income Tax of the People's Republic of China*. Hereinafter it can be referred as the *Provisional Regulations of the Enterprise Income Tax*, and it came into force on January 1, 1994.

2.4 Jurisdiction of the state taxation of the enterprise income tax

The scope of separate taxation in 1995

The Scope of Administration of the Bureau of National Taxation System consists of a three tax system. First, it includes the income tax of the central departments and the corporation, industry association, the association's enterprises and institutions, social organizations, foundation and the above enterprises and institutions to set up (including money, physical objects, land use rights, intellectual property rights, investment in the form of the establishment of) budget, foreign enterprise income tax (including domestic and foreign income). Second, it includes the income tax of the financial insurance enterprise. That includes policy banks, commercial banks and their branches, cooperative banks, urban and rural credit cooperatives, urban and rural credit cooperative societies; insurance companies and their branches, insurance brokers and insurance agents; securities companies and their branches, securities trading centers, investment fund management companies, securities registration companies; trust and investment companies, finance companies and financial leasing companies and their branch offices, financing, financing center, financial futures companies, credit guarantee companies, pawn shops (company), such as credit card companies engaged in financing business enterprise income tax. Finally, it includes the income tax of State-owned enterprises of the armies (including the armed police force).

The Scope of Administration of the Bureau of Local Taxation System also contains three kinds of income tax: (1) the income tax of local State-owned enterprises and institutions at all levels, including local department or company, industry associations and community groups, affiliated enterprises and institutions and the establishment of the State-owned enterprise income tax; (2) collective enterprise income tax; and (3) the income tax of the private enterprise. The collection and management of joint enterprises and joint-stock enterprises shall be carried out in accordance with the relevant provisions of the Ministry of Finance and China's State Administration of Taxation.

Added scope of the enterprise income tax in 2002

First, regarding all original enterprises involving restructuring and transferring, absorbing to merger, even for the opening registration, the collection and management of the enterprise income tax is still conducted by the original collection and administration authority.

Second, the original domestic enterprise reorganization restructuring for foreign investment enterprises and enterprises with foreign investment and foreign enterprises income tax shall be levied according to regulations, regardless of the industrial and commercial registration. Enterprises with foreign investment and foreign enterprise income tax administrative authority shall determine the scope of the collection and management.

Last, the scope of administration of business units and social organizations shall be carried out in accordance with the provisions of the State Administration of Taxation, the eighth document, 2002, and the above-mentioned provisions.

Scope of the new enterprise income tax in 2009

In 2008, the taxpayer of the enterprise income tax, which is administered by the national tax bureau and the local tax bureau before the end of 2008, will not be adjusted. Regarding the enterprise that should pay the added-value tax in the new enterprise income tax taxpayer in

2009, the enterprise income tax shall be managed by the state tax bureau; the enterprise should pay business tax, and its enterprise income tax is managed by the local tax bureau. At the same time, the following rules are applied to the following new enterprise income tax administration in 2009: (1) the enterprise income tax, which is full of enterprise income tax, and the enterprises that pay business tax in the state tax bureau, shall be managed by the State Administration of Taxation; (2) bank (credit unions), the enterprise income tax of insurance company is managed by the state administration of taxation. Furthermore, the other kinds of financial companies of enterprise income tax should be managed by the local taxation bureaus; (3) the enterprise income tax of foreign investment enterprises and permanent representative offices of foreign enterprises are managed by the State Administration of Taxation.

The enterprise income tax during the period of 1994 to 2007 are as follows. The nominal tax rate for domestic enterprises was 33% and the actual tax burden was 25%. Of income tax to enterprises with foreign investment and foreign enterprises in China which established the institution engaged in production and management, the income of enterprise income tax payable (calculated on the taxable income amount) was 30%, and the real tax rate was 15%. The enterprise income tax during the period of 2008 to the present are as follows: the nominal tax rate for domestic enterprises was 25%. Of enterprise income tax of enterprises with foreign investment and foreign enterprises in China that established the institution engaged in production and management, the income of enterprise income tax payable, calculated on the taxable income amount, comes to a tax rate of 20%.

3. Prior research

Earlier literature focused on book-tax conforming upward earnings management, which increases both financial and taxable incomes and thus has current tax consequences (Scholes, Wilson and Woflson 1990, Matsunaga, Shevlin and Shores 1992, and Dhaliwal, Frankel and Trezevant 1994). That is, conforming earnings management includes any transaction that has the same impact on the current financial and taxable incomes. A common example of conforming earnings management is accelerating revenue recognition by recording receivables sooner than justifying and postponing inventory purchases under LIFO.

In contrast, a few studies focus on nonconforming upward earnings management, which increases financial accounting income with no current tax consequences (Mills and Newberry 2001; Joos, Pratt and Young 2003; Phillips, Pincus and Rego 2003; and Phillips, Pincus, Rego and Wan 2004). This type of earnings management includes transactions that accelerate revenue recognition or defer expense recognition for financial reporting purposes relative to tax purposes, such as aggressively recognizing unearned revenue, extending the useful lives of depreciable assets or reducing the provision for doubtful accounts for financial reporting purposes.

Previous studies conclude that firms will make a trade-off between increase financial incomes and decrease taxable incomes (Frank, Lynch and Rego 2009). This understanding is based on the consistence between accounting and tax rules, that is, firms need to pay high tax cost for increasing financial incomes. But with the book-tax differences, which tends to expand, and managers' discretion given by CAS 2006, firms are able to increase financial incomes without increasing taxable incomes, that is, pay little or no tax cost for increasing financial incomes.

The trade-off between the cost of financial report and income tax has been the interest of researchers. Based on A-shares manufacturing firms, Ye (2006) shows that the more earnings listed companies' managers manage, the higher the book-tax differences are, which means the listed companies accomplish earnings management via nonconforming earnings management to avoid income tax cost, but results also show that the avoidance is limited.

Prior literature considers a change in the national corporate income tax (CIT) rate as a strong firm incentive to manage earnings. Sundvik (2016) examines the link between two recent CIT reforms in Sweden and earnings management with a large dataset of private firms. The effects of tax rate cuts are estimated on aggregate measures as well as on decomposed measures of accrual-based earnings management. The results suggest that taxation clearly influences these firms in their high book-tax conformity setting. Downward earnings management is documented before the reduction in the CIT rate, consistent with research on public firms with lower book-tax conformity. Primarily accounts receivable is noted to drive these results. Weaker evidence is provided with the inventory and depreciation accrual vehicles. The tax effects are statistically and economically significant. Furthermore, the income-decreasing behavior prior to the CIT reforms is consistent over time.

De Simone (2016) tests whether adoption of IFRS by individual affiliates of multinational entities (MNEs) for unconsolidated financial reporting facilitates tax-motivated income shifting. He uses a dataset of European unconsolidated financial and ownership information over 2003–2012 and finds an increase in the arm's length range of book profits reported by potential IFRS benchmark firms following affiliate adoption of IFRS. He then estimates a statistically and economically significant 11.3%tax-motivated change in reported book pre-tax profits following affiliate IFRS adoption, relative to pre-adoption and non-adopter affiliate-years.

Sundvik (2017) investigates the link between earnings management and jurisdictional differences in book-tax conformity. He used a dataset of national reforms lowering the corporate tax rate to estimate the effect of conformity on private firm's earnings management behavior when a specific incentive to manage earnings downward exists. Total and discretionary accruals are used to measure earnings management and a continuous measure is used to assess the level of book-tax conformity. He finds that changes in the statutory tax rate affect firms in jurisdictions with high book-tax conformity more than firms in jurisdictions with less book-tax conformity. However, more overall earnings management is attributed to firms in low conformity jurisdictions. These findings contribute to the ongoing debate on the appropriate level of book-tax conformity.

The above studies examine the relationship between earnings and income tax and the balance of financial reporting and income tax costs, but few domestic researches reflect earnings management behavior by financial restatements, also few are based on the differences of income tax account between originally reported and restated financial statements to investigate firms' choice among different earnings management strategies and how manager's motivations and purposes influence this choice. Relative to previous studies, we estimate the choice of conforming earnings management and nonconforming earning management from the perspective of income tax and we use the changes in current and deferred tax expense disclosed in earnings restatements to measure conforming and nonconforming earnings management.

4. Illustration of book-tax difference

4.1 Treatment of book-tax differences

Figure 14.1 schematically illustrates the accounting processes of Corporate Income Tax under the balance sheet liability method. The balance sheet liability method means starting from the balance sheet, recognizing taxable temporary differences and deductible temporary differences by comparing difference between the book value that is determined in accordance with GAAP and

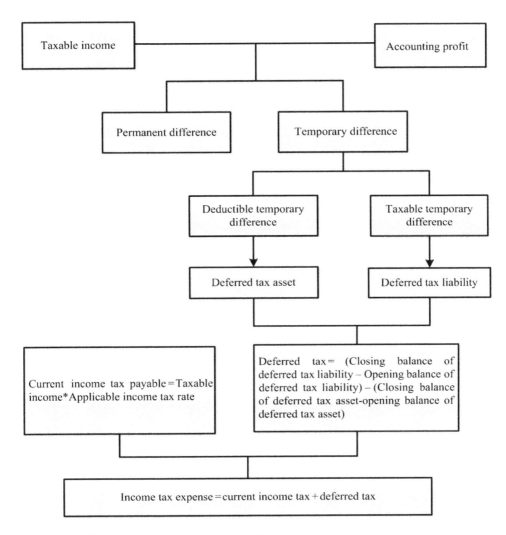

Figure 14.1 The accounting processes of corporate income tax

a tax basis that is determined according to the provisions of the Income Tax Law and then recognizing deferred income tax liabilities and deferred income tax assets and thus determining the income tax expense for each period. Shown in Figure 14.1, when companies engage in earnings management, managers can choose conforming earnings management strategies, strategies affect both accounting profit and taxable income and thus have effect on current income tax expense without having effect on deferred income tax expense, and they can also choose nonconforming earnings management strategies, strategies only affect accounting profit and don't affect taxable income and thus have effect on deferred income tax expense without having effect on current income tax expense. Of course, companies can adopt both kinds of earnings management strategies. The two earnings management strategies have different influences on current income tax expense. Thus, the company can decrease the current period's tax payable through choosing different earnings management.

4.2 *Earnings management strategies and book-tax differences*

With the steady progress in the reform process of CAS, companies get more opportunities to choose accounting policies and accounting estimates, these factors led to the differences between Chinese listed companies' accounting profits and taxable income. And this also result in the increase of managers' choice of earnings management strategies. This paper mainly discusses the relationship between the choice of different earnings management strategies, conforming earnings management strategies and nonconforming earnings management strategies and book-tax differences. We focus on earnings management bringing temporary differences, because companies rarely have the opportunity to engage in earnings management generating permanent differences. When companies engaged in conforming earnings management strategies, the book-tax differences will be generated, while when companies engaged in nonconforming earnings management strategies, the book-tax differences will not be generated. And the more nonconforming earnings management strategies companies engaged in, the greater the book-tax differences are. We illustrate the relationship between the two different earnings management strategies and book-tax temporary differences through the following example.

Assume that in the current year t and also in year $t + n$, both company X and company Y have RMB 1000 of "true" pre-tax book income. The company X engages in RMB 100 of earnings management through a conforming manner and thus originally reports RMB 1100 of pre-tax income in year t. While the company Y engages in RMB 100 of earnings management through a nonconforming manner and thus also originally reports RMB 1100 of pre-tax income in year t. As a result, the changes in the two companies' book-tax differences and income tax expenses before and after engaging in earnings management is as follows (the income tax rate is 25%):

Table 14.2 Illustration of earnings management and tax expenses

Panel A: After engaging in earnings management

	Company X	*Company Y*
Accounting profit	1100	1100
Taxable income	1100	1000
Current income tax payable	275	250
Book-tax differences	0	100
Deferred tax expenses	0	25

Panel B: Before engaging in earnings management

	Company X	*Company Y*
Accounting profit	1000	1000
Taxable income	1000	1000
Current income tax payable	250	250
Book-tax differences	0	0
Deferred tax expenses	0	0

Therefore, conforming earnings management will not cause book-tax differences, but it will affect taxable income, and thus this earnings management strategy only affects current income tax payable and has no effect on deferred income tax expense. On the contrary, nonconforming earnings management will cause book-tax differences, but it will not affect taxable income, and thus this earnings management strategy only affects deferred income tax expense and having no effect on current income tax payable.

4.3   Earnings management and income tax burden

In the capital market, the management of listed companies often engaged in earnings management consciously for the purpose of financing, contract or political control (Healy and Wahlen 1998). However, earnings management is not without cost, in addition to potential legal costs, one of the direct costs of earnings management is the income tax cost: when the management attempt to increase profits through earnings management, they often need to pay more income tax for the increasing profit. Therefore, in most cases, when companies increase profits through earnings management, the income tax burden will be affected. Compared to conforming earnings management, nonconforming earnings management can bring income tax benefit. Let us come back to the example above:

Assuming both company X and company Y reverse the temporary differences in the year $t + n$. Since company X performs earnings management in a conforming manner, company X would incur income tax costs of RMB 275 in year t (1100 times 25%) and RMB225 in year $t + n$ (900 times 25%). The present value of income tax costs would be $275 + [225 / (1+r)^n]$, where r is company's discount rate. Company Y performs earnings management in a nonconforming manner, company Y would incur income tax costs of RMB250 in year t (1000 × 25%) and RMB 250 in year $t + n$ (1000 × 25%) since nonconforming earnings management does not affect taxable income (in this case, RMB1000). The present value of income tax costs would be $250 + [250/ (1+r)^n]$, where r is the company's discount rate.

The income tax benefit from engaging in nonconforming versus conforming upward earnings management equals the present value of income tax costs under conforming earning management minus the present value under nonconforming earnings management. This amount is computed as:

$$\{275 + [225 / (1+r)^n] \} - \{250 + [250/ (1+r)^n]\} = 25 - [25/ (1+r)^n].$$

It can be seen that, the present value of income tax costs associated with nonconforming earning management is lower than that of income tax costs associated with conforming earning management, that is, compared to company X, company Y can bring income tax benefits. Thus, companies can achieve the purpose of reducing the income tax burden through the choice of conforming earning management and nonconforming earning management.

5.   Research design

5.1   Hypothesis

Book-tax conforming upward earnings management increases both financial and taxable incomes and thus has current tax consequences; nonconforming upward earnings management increases financial accounting income but has no current tax consequences. Compared to conforming upward earnings management, nonconforming earnings management can decrease current income tax expense and thus increase firms' cash flow, so firms prefer to manage earnings upward in a nonconforming manner to avoid income tax cost. We suppose managers' motivations and purposes influence the choice. When firms are facing punishment of the suspension or termination of the listing for three consecutive losses, firms will have a great incentive to manage earnings in order to turn losses into gains. Thus, when firms have motivations to turn losses into gains, firms can't wait to manage earnings to increase incomes and won't consider income tax cost too much. If they employ nonconforming earnings management which bring greater book-tax differences, it may increase the probability of being detected and earnings management behavior may also be found. Thus, we predict that in this motivation, listed companies will employ more conforming earnings management. Therefore, Hypothesis 1 is:

> *H1: When the firm has motivations to turn losses into gains, the firm prefers to employ more conforming earnings management strategies.*

It can be seen that, conforming earnings management don't generate book-tax difference, while nonconforming earning management generate book-tax difference and the greater the earnings management degree is, the greater the difference is. The book-tax difference tends to attract regulatory agencies' attention, as Frank, Lynch and Rego (2006) think it will attract the attention of the SEC, so the detection cost associated with nonconforming earnings management is greater than that with conforming. We think that the greater the detection cost associated with nonconforming earnings management is, the less the earnings firms manage in a nonconforming manner. And we use fraud as a proxy for detection cost, thus, when the firms engage in fraudulent activities (the detection cost is greater), they prefer to employ more conforming earnings management strategies. On the other hand, if firms engaging in fraudulent activities employ nonconforming earnings management bringing greater book-tax difference which is easy to attract regulatory agencies' attention, the fraud may be found. Therefore, the firms engaging in fraudulent activities will employ more conforming earnings management strategies to avoid penalty cost associated with fraud being found. Therefore, Hypothesis 2 is:

> *H2: When the firm has the motivation to avoid penalty cost associated with fraud being found, the firm prefers to employ more conforming earnings management strategies.*

5.2   Sample

Chinese listed companies began to implement CAS 2006 in 2007 and companies generally restate financial statements in the year following the misstatement period. Thus, we think that only restatements in 2008 and after 2008 can offer the data we need. Base on this, we identify misstatement firms (i.e., firms that restated their financial statements in a subsequent year) as the A-share listed company's report in Shanghai and Shenzhen Stock Exchanges from 2008 to 2010, the data comes from CSMAR. We first get 435 misstatement firms as a sample. The restatements corrected previous material misstatements of financial statement numbers caused by accounting irregularities. We manually collect the following variables from both the originally reported and restated financial statements: total assets, pre-tax net income and restated income, current tax expense, deferred tax expense from operations. Then we lose 266 firms without sufficient data. We finally get our misstatement sample consisting of 169 misstatement firms.

5.3 Model and variable definitions

Model

To investigate managers' motivations and purposes that impact the choice of conforming and nonconforming earnings management (H1 and H2), we estimate the following regression model:

$$NONCON_{EM} = \alpha_0 + \alpha_1 TLTG_i + \alpha_2 FRAUD_i + \alpha_3 LAG\_DTE_i + \alpha_4 REV\_ONLY_i$$
$$+ \alpha_5 EXP\_ONLY_i + \sum X_{it} + \varepsilon_{it} \tag{1}$$

Where:

NONCON_EM equals 1 if the firm employs nonconforming earnings management (nonconforming earnings management strategies, strategies only affect accounting profit but not affect taxable income and thus have effect on deferred income tax expense without having effect on current income tax expense, and 0 otherwise;

TLTG equals 1 if the firm turns losses into gains in year t, and 0 otherwise;

FRAUD equals 1 if the firm engages in fraudulent activities in year t, and 0 otherwise;

LAG_DTE equals deferred tax expense in year t−1, scaled by total assets at year-end t−2;

REV_ONLY equals 1 if the firm only restates revenue accounts in year t, and 0 otherwise;

EXP_ONLY equals 1 if the firm only restates expense accounts in year t, and 0 otherwise;

Year t is the year in which firm restates its financial statements. When firm restates multiple years' financial statements, year t is the first misstatement year.

Variable definitions

NONCON_EM, which is the dependent variable in Model (1), is used to measure the restatement firm employs nonconforming earnings management. Specially, if the firm only restates deferred income tax expense, we can judge that it employs nonconforming earnings management; if the firm only restates current income tax expense, we can judge that it employs conforming earnings management; if the firm not only restates deferred income tax expense, but also restates current income tax expense, we need to compare the relative amount of the differences of current and deferred tax expense account between originally reported and restated financial statements to judge which type of earnings management it is engaged in, and when the amount of difference in deferred tax expense is greater than that in current tax expense, we think the firm employs nonconforming earnings management.

TLTG, which is the independent variable in Model (1), is used to measure whether the restatement firm has the motivation to turn losses into gains in the year that the misstatement occurs. If the firm's pre-tax net income that disclosed in originally financial statement is positive but negative in restated financial statement, we can judge that the firm has the motivation to turn losses into gains.

FRAUD, which is the independent variable in Model (1), is used to measure whether the firm has the motivation to avoid penalty cost associated with fraud being found. If there are words "fraud", "fiction", "published by SFC or the tax authorities" or "special inspected or questioned by independent third party, such as SASAC, the Ministry of Finance, the Audit Committee, the independent directors" in all restatement firms' misstatement information, we think that the firm engages in fraud.

Consistent with H1 and H2, we believe the coefficients of a_1 and a_2 in Model (1) are negative, that is, the listed firms engage in more conforming earnings management.

Because there are likely different costs and benefits associated with different types of earnings management, we include two additional indicator variables in model (1), one for misstatements only involving revenue recognition (*REV_ONLY*) and the other for misstatement only involving expense recognition (*EXP_ONLY*). If there is a systematic relation between revenue and expense management, whether such earnings management is achieved via a conforming or nonconforming manner, our results could be biased. Thus, we introduce variables *REV_ONLY* and *EXP_ONLY* to control a possible link between earnings management type (conforming or nonconforming) and the type of account managed (revenue-only and expense-only) in our multivariate analysis.

Finally, we use several controls and fixed effects throughout our analysis because accounting research has identified numerous factors that influence earnings management (e.g., Teshima and Shuto 2008; Kin Wai, Baruch and Yeo 2007; Klein 2002). The most important factors are leverage and size. Controlling for leverage (*LEV*) is based on the assumption that managers are more likely to use discretion in accounting as they move closer to violating debt-covenant constraints (Sweeney 1994). The inclusion of firm size (*LNLAG_TA*) is justified by positive accounting theory, which indicates that large firms engage in more earnings management than do small firms due to reduced political costs (Watts and Zimmerman 1978). However, it is argued that these firms have fewer opportunities to engage in earnings management because they are more likely to be closely monitored (Jiambalvo, Rajgopal and Venkatachalam 2002). We also include *LAG_DTE*, deferred tax expense in the year prior to the misstatement period, to control for the prior year's nonconforming earnings management. Furthermore, we control for industry and year fixed effects.

6.   The empirical results

6.1   Descriptive statistics

Table 14.3 shows the descriptive statistics of *NONCON_EM* by *TLTG*, *FRAUD* classification. The descriptive statistics show that, on the one hand, the mean of *NONCON_EM* is less than 0.5 when the firm engages in fraudulent activities and turns losses into gains. Even in the presence

Table 14.3 Descriptive statistics of NONCON_EM

	NONCON-EM	
	Mean	Std.
TLTG=0	0.390	0.489
TLTG=1	0.090	0.302
FRAUD=0	0.400	0.491
FRAUD=1	0.300	0.463

Note: NONCON_EM, which represents nonconforming earnings management, equals 1 if the firm employs nonconforming earnings management, and 0 otherwise. TLTG, which represents turning losses into gains, equals 1 if the firm turns losses into gains in year t, and 0 otherwise. FRAUD, which represents fraudulent activities, equals 1 if the firm engages in fraudulent activities in year t, and 0 otherwise.

Table 14.4 Correlation matrix

	NONCON_ EM	TLTG	FRAUD	REV_ ONLY	LNLAG_ TA	EXP_ ONLY	LEV	LAG_ DTE
NONCON_EM	1							
TLTG	−0.060	1						
FRAUD	−0.0410	−0.0910	1					
REV_ONLY	0.1961	0.0240	0.312	1				
LNLAG_TA	−0.0270	−0.0610	0.0130	−0.021	1			
EXP_ONLY	−0.347	−0.0180	0.0440	−0.515★★★	0.0050	1		
LEV	−0.135	−0.142	−0.0510	−0.112	0.0440	0.0800	1	
LAG_DTE	0.0660	−0.0670	0.0480	−0.0860	−0.101	0.0410	0.185	1

of permanent differences (as already said the case is relatively less), we can also consider the mean of *NONCON_EM* is less than the mean of *CON_EM*. More importantly, on the other hand, when the *FRAUD* and *TLTG* varies from 0 to 1, the means of *NONCON_EM* are smaller. These all show that when the firm engages in fraudulent activities and turns losses into gains, the firm prefers to employ less nonconforming earnings management strategies. The two aspects indicate that when the firm has motivations to turn losses into gains and has the motivation to avoid penalty costs associated with fraud being found, the firm prefers to employ more conforming earnings management strategies.

Table 14.4 presents Pearson correlation test of the variables in the Model (1). The results show that *TLTG*, Lev, EXP_ONLY, LNLAG_TA and *FRAUD*, are negatively related to the dependent variable (*NONCON_EM*), which is consistent with the hypothesis. Moreover, the VIF test (which is not tabulated) shows that the variables we use in the regression have no serious multicollinearity issue.

6.2 Multivariate testing

Table 14.5 reports the results based on the Model (1). To be robust, we use three samples to test the hypotheses. We first run the regression based on the full sample and then the State-owned firms and non-State-owned firms which are defined according to the ownership. The results are listed from columns (1) to (3) in Table 14.5. The coefficients of *TLTG* is significantly negative at 5% from columns (1) to (3). The coefficient of TLTG in the non-state sample is the largest (the absolute value is 6.12) and in the state sample it is the smallest one (the absolute value is 0.458) which means the State-owned firms prefer more conforming earnings management strategies than non-State owned firms when they have the motivation to turn loss to gain. *FRAUD* also significantly negative at 5% from columns (1) to (3) respectively. However, the largest absolute value is in the State-owned firms and the smallest one in the non-State-owned firms, which means the former firms have less motivation to engage in the conforming earnings management strategies for the purpose of being punished for fraud. Our results are consistent with the results in Erickson, Hanlon and Maydew (2004), who document that their sample of firms with fraudulent financial reporting relied on significant amounts of conforming earnings management. In sum, these results show that when the firm has motivations to turn losses into gains, the firm prefers to employ more conforming earnings management strategies; when the

Table 14.5 Results of earnings management and restatement based on ownership

	(1)	(2)	(3)
	Full sample	*State-owned*	*Non-state owned*
TLTG	−0.517★★	−0.458★★	−0.612★★
	(−0.182)	(−0.216)	(−0.239)
FRAUD	−0.602★★	−0.793★★	−0.571★★
	(−0.214)	(−0.262)	(−0.244)
REV_ONLY	0.1589★	0.1293★★★	0.199★★
	(0.084)	(0.037)	(0.073)
EXP_ONLY	−0.515★★★	−0.481★★	−0.679★★
	(−0.141)	(−0.189)	(−0.302)
LEV	0.486★★★	0.321★	0.834★★
	(0.152)	(0.207)	(0.304)
LNLAG_TA	0.407★★★	0.326★★★	0.414★★★
	(0.0395)	(0.051)	(0.117)
LAG_DTE	−0.538★	−0.325★	−0.637★
	(−0.345)	(−0.208)	(−0.301)
Constant	−0.544★★★	−0.867★★★	−0.264★★★
	(0.021)	(0.056)	(0.081)
N	169	118	51
R-squares	0.396	0.402	0.774
F	10.312	10.039	10.335

Note: ★, ★★, ★★★ indicate the coefficient is significant at the levels of 10%, 5% and 1%. The values in the brackets indicate the standard error. *TLTG*, which represents turning losses into gains, equals 1 if the firm turns losses into gains in year t, and 0 otherwise. *FRAUD*, which represents fraudulent activities, equals 1 if the firm engages in fraudulent activities in year t, and 0 otherwise. *REV_ONLY*, control variable, equals 1 if the firm only restates revenue accounts in year t, and 0 otherwise. *EXP_ONLY*, control variable, equals 1 if the firm only restates expense accounts in year t, and 0 otherwise. LEV is defined as the liabilities in the end of year t−1 divided by total assets at year-end t−1. *LAG_DTE* equals deferred tax expense in year t−1, scaled by total assets at year-end t−2. *LAG_TA* equals logarithm of total assets at year-end t−1.

firm engages in fraudulent activities, the firm prefers to employ less nonconforming earnings management strategies.

As a robustness test, we further test the hypothesizes by separate the sample into high marketization and low marketization. We run the regressions based on the three samples and the results are reported in Table 14.6 Column (1) to Column (3). Again, both the coefficients of TLTG and FRAUD are significantly negative at 5% from Column (1) to (3). When the firms in the highly marketized provinces have the stronger motivation to turn loss into earnings than that in the low marketization provinces, the absolute value of the difference is 0.346 (which equals to 0.758–0.412). The fraud is significant at 1% through Columns (1) to (3), and firms in the high-marketization provinces are more possible to engineer fraud than those in the low marketization provinces.

Table 14.6 Results of earnings management and restatement based on marketization

	(1) Full sample	(2) High marketization	(3) Low marketization
TLTG	−0.517★★	−0.758★★	−0.412★★
	(−0.182)	(−0.316)	(−0.189)
FRAUD	−0.602★★	−0.871★★★	−0.509★★
	(−0.214)	(−0.215)	(−0.176)
REV_ONLY	0.1589★	0.193★★★	0.119★★
	(0.084)	(0.097)	(0.053)
EXP_ONLY	−0.515★★★	0.513★	0.389★★
	(−0.141)	(0.043)	(0.098)
LEV	0.486★★★	−0.659★★	−0.332★★
	(0.152)	(−0.321)	(−0.156)
LNLAG_TA	0.407★★★	0.567★	0.321★
	(0.0395)	(0.296)	(0.168)
LAG_DTE	−0.538★	−0.784★	−0.564★
	(−0.345)	(−0.401)	(−0.285)
Constant	−0.544★★★	−0.325★★★	−0.18★★★
	(0.021)	(0.039)	(0.002)
N	169	85	84
R-squares	0.396	0.425	0.650
F	10.312	0.738	1.643

Note: ★, ★★, ★★★ indicate the coefficient is significant at the level of 10%, 5% and 1%. The values in the brackets indicate the standard error. *TLTG*, which represents turning losses into gains, equals 1 if the firm turns losses into gains in year t, and 0 otherwise. *FRAUD*, which represents fraudulent activities, equals 1 if the firm engages in fraudulent activities in year t, and 0 otherwise. *REV_ONLY*, control variable, equals 1 if the firm only restates revenue accounts in year t, and 0 otherwise. *EXP_ONLY*, control variable, equals 1 if the firm only restates expense accounts in year t, and 0 otherwise. LEV is defined as the liabilities in the end of year t−1 divided by total assets at year-end t−1. *LAG_DTE* equals deferred tax expense in year t−1, scaled by total assets at year-end t−2. *LAG_TA* equals logarithm of total assets at year-end t−1.

7. Conclusions and recommendations

Based on the new set of accounting standards (CAS2006), we examine the choice of two types of earnings management confronted by publicly listed companies in China: book-tax conforming and book-tax nonconforming. We also examine how firm-specific motivations and purposes impact the choice among these earnings management strategies. Based on a sample of firms that restated their earnings (and thus had managed earnings), and using the changes in current and deferred tax expense account disclosed in originally and restated financial statements, we compare the relative amounts of changes in current and deferred tax expense to judge which type of earnings management a firm is engaged in, and find that when firms motivations to turn losses into gains and has the motivation to avoid penalty costs associated with fraud being found, they prefer to employ more conforming earnings management strategies. We also find that when the company has motivations to turn losses into gains and has motivations to avoid penalty costs associated with fraud being found, firms from more developed market areas are more likely to employ conforming earnings management strategies. State-owned firms are more likely to employ conforming earnings management strategies when they have a motivation to avoid penalty costs associated with fraud being found while non-State-owned firms are more likely to do so when they have motivations to avoid reporting a loss.

Our research provides new perspectives and theoretical evidence for exploring the listed companies' choice of conforming and nonconforming earnings management. Meanwhile, our results are helpful for regulators to strengthen the administration of listed companies' restatement. For instance, our results have implications for accounting standards. The regulators should learn from the relevant provisions of international accounting standards to improve and revise existing accounting standards and its core ideas should be to narrow options that firms are free to choose. In particular, the language and concept of accounting standards should be standardized; reduce the alternative accounting policies and methods; minimize management's accounting estimates and professional judgment; specify changing conditions of accounting policies and accounting estimates and corrections of accounting error. In addition, regulators might need to pay attention to implications for manager performance. Currently, managers' revenues consist of a basic salary and bonus in most enterprises and the basic salary and bonus are linked to managers' performance. It can be seen that managers' compensation not only incentivize managers to focus on financial performance, but also to induce earnings management activities. Therefore, optimizing the compensation mechanism is an effective method to prevent earnings management activities. On the one hand, companies need to combine long-term development with manager compensation; on the other hand, give managers the appropriate option awards to align the interests of managers and shareholders together, promoting managers to pay more attention to the firm's long-term development and thus weakening their incentives to manage earnings.

The limitation in our research is as follows. First, we mainly focus on the conforming and nonconforming earnings management when the listed companies restate their financial statements. However after the issue of CAS 2006, many listed companies still do not disclose income tax accounts, which restricts our sample. Second, without the acquisition of private companies' data, our empirical results may not be generalized to private firms. These issues demand future studies.

Note

1 The original version of the essay was published in *Journal of Industrial Engineering and Management* as: Hu, N., Cao, Q., and Zheng, L. (2015). Listed companies' income tax planning and earnings management: Based on China's capital market. *Journal of Industrial Engineering and Management*, 8(2), 417–434. The current version has been revised to incorporate more discussion of the income tax system in China, along with additional tests and results. The authors would like to thank OmniaScience for their permission to publish part of the paper mentioned above. The original paper was supported by grants from the National Natural Science Foundation of China (No.71302123) (No.71102126), Science Foundation of Ministry of Education of China (No. 13YJC790048) and the Specialized Research Fund for the Doctoral Program of Higher Education of China (Grant No. 20120023120015).

References

De Simone, L. 2016. Does a common set of accounting standards affect tax-motivated income shifting for multinational firms? *Journal of Accounting and Economics*, 61(1), 145–165.

Dhaliwal, D., Frankel, M., and Trezevant, R. (1994). The taxable and book income motivations for a LIFO layer liquidation, *Journal of Accounting Research*, 2, 278–289.

Erickson, M., Hanlon, M., and Maydew, E. (2004). How much will firms pay for earnings that do not exist? Evidence of taxes paid on allegedly fraudulent earnings, *The Accounting Review*, 79(2), 387–408.

Frank, M., Lynch, L., and Rego, S. (2006). *Does Aggressive Financial Reporting Accompany Aggressive Tax Reporting (and Vice Versa)?* Working paper, University of Virginia and Iowa.

Frank, M., Lynch, L., and Rego, S. (2009). Tax reporting aggressiveness and its relation to aggressive financial reporting, *The Accounting Review*, 2, 467–496.

Healy, P. M., and Wahlen, J. M. (1999). A review of the earnings management literature and its implications for standard setting. *Accounting Horizons*, 13(4), 365–383.

Jiambalvo, J., Rajgopal, S., and Venkatachalam, M. (2002). Institutional ownership and the extent to which stock prices reflect future earnings. *Contemporary Accounting Research*, 19(1), 117–145.

Joos, P., Pratt, J., and Young, S. D. (2003). Using deferred taxes to infer the quality of accruals. Working paper, *Massachusetts Institute of Technology*.

Kin Wai, L., Baruch, L., and Yeo, G. (2007). Organizational structure and earnings management. *Journal of Accounting, Auditing and Finance*, 22(2), 293–331.

Klein, A. (2002). Audit committee, board of director characteristics, and earnings management. *Journal of Accounting and Economics*, 33(3), 375–400.

Matsunaga, S., Shevlin, T., and Shores, D. (1992). Disqualifying dispositions of incentive stock options: Tax benefits versus financial reporting costs, *Journal of Accounting Research*, 30(Supplement), 37–68.

Mills, L., and Newberry, L. K. (2001). The influence of tax and nontax costs on book-tax reporting differences: Public and private firms, *Journal of the American Taxation Association*, 23(1), 1–19.

The Ministry of Finance. (2006). *Accounting Standards for Business Enterprises*. Beijing: Economic Science Press.

Phillips, J., Pincus, M., and Rego, S. (2003). Earnings management: New evidence based on deferred tax expense, *The Accounting Review*, 78(2), 491–521.

Phillips, J., Pincus, M., Rego, S., and Wan, H. (2004). Decomposing changes in deferred tax assets and liabilities to isolate earnings management activities, *The American Taxation Association*, 26(Supplement), 43–66.

Scholes, M., Wilson, P., and Woflson, M. (1990). Tax planning, regulatory capital planning, and financial reporting strategy for commercial banks, *The Review of Financial Studies*, 3(4), 625–650.

Sundvik, D. (2016). Earnings management around Swedish corporate income tax reforms. *International Journal of Accounting, Auditing and Performance Evaluation*, 12(3). www.inderscienceonline.com/doi/pdf/10.1504/IJAAPE.2016.077892

Sweeney, A. P. 1994. Debt-covenant violations and managers' accounting responses. *Journal of Accounting and Economics*, 17(3), 281–308.

Teshima, N., and Shuto, A. 2008. Managerial ownership and earnings management: Theory and empirical evidence from Japan. *Journal of International Financial Management and Accounting*, 19(2), 107–132.

Watts, R. L., and Zimmerman, J. L. 1978. Towards a positive theory of the determination of accounting standards. *The Accounting Review*, 53(1), 112–134.

Ye, K. T. (2006). Earnings management and payment of income tax: Research based on book-tax difference, *China Accounting Review*, 2, 205–223.

PART VI

Internal controls and corporate governance

15

INTERNAL CONTROL IN CHINA

Framework, practices and literature

Wang Dong, Yun Ke[1]

1. Introduction

Our purpose for this chapter is twofold. First, we want more scholars and practitioners outside of China to better understand internal control framework, practices, and its related research in China. Second, we hope that our review can motivate more studies on internal control using the unique institutional characteristics of a Chinese setting, such as non-financial reporting-related internal control deficiencies.

We first describe the development of internal control framework in China. Along with the economic growth in China, the demand for enterprise internal control also surges. To improve management expertise, the Chinese government and its agencies strive to promote the establishment of internal control framework and enhance the monitoring of firms' internal control. Several important milestones are: (1) the publication of two different *Guidelines for the Internal Control of Listed Companies* by Shanghai and Shenzhen Stock Exchanges, respectively, in 2006; (2) the joint issuance of *the Basic Internal Control Norms for Enterprises* (hereafter *Basic Norms*) by five government agencies in 2008 (see details in section 2); and (3) the issuance of three related guidelines, including *the Guidelines for the Application of Enterprise Internal Controls* (EICs), *the Guidelines for the Evaluation of EICs*, and *the Guidelines for the Auditing of EICs*, in 2010. The *Basic Norms* and the related three guidelines constitute the framework of internal control in China, which is referred to as Chinese "SOX act" (C-SOX). Unlike the SOX Act in the US, C-SOX is designed to reflect the role of internal control on enterprise management more comprehensively, not only on financial reporting.

Next, we discuss the policies on internal control disclosure in China, which is overall sophisticated. The regulation of internal control disclosure is through the exchanges and CSRC. The disclosure has voluntary, semi-mandatory, and mandatory components. The content of such disclosure includes firms' self-evaluation reports and auditor attestations on internal control effectiveness. The disclosure of internal control weakness includes financial reporting-related and non-financial reporting-related weaknesses. We provide some descriptive statistics of internal control disclosure in China.

Finally, we review literature on internal control in China. While early studies tend to use normative approach, recent literature is dominated by empirical research. Many of them focus on the determinants and economic consequences of internal control, including the impacts of internal control on financial reporting quality, auditing and corporate finance. In addition, Chinese scholars developed new and innovative index, based on the framework, to measure internal control quality.

The chapter proceeds as follows. In Section 2, we describe the development of internal control framework in china. Section 3 introduces the policies on internal control disclosure. We then provide some basic descriptive statistics of internal control in China enterprises in Section 4. Normative research on internal control in China is discussed in Section 5, followed by a literature review on empirical research in Section 6. We conclude in Section 7.

2. The development of an internal control framework

Since its economic reform started in 1978, China has experienced strong and prolonged economic growth, becoming the second largest economy in the world. While the growth was largely due to the huge development of Chinese enterprises, the practice of business management, including internal control, in Chinese enterprises still significantly lags behind their peers in Western countries. Prior to 2006, companies mainly relied on internal accounting control, which makes it difficult for them to grow business and adapt to the changes in external business environments and business risks. To improve management expertise in Chinese enterprises, the government and its regulatory agencies actively promoted the development of an internal control framework. Starting in 2006, several agencies strived to establish a unified and authoritative internal control framework, which was expected to be structured and systematic. By 2010, such a framework was eventually established. We review the timeline and some key events below (see Table 15.1).

On June 5, 2006, Shanghai Stock Exchange (hereafter SSE) first issued the *Guidelines of Shanghai Stock Exchange for the Internal Control of Listed Companies*. Three months later, Shenzhen Stock Exchange (hereafter SZSE) also issued the *Guidelines of Shenzhen Stock Exchange for the Internal Control of Listed Companies* on September 28. These two guidelines were developed based on two publications by the Committee of Sponsoring Organizations of Treadway Commission (COSO), *Enterprise Risk Management – Integrated Framework*[2] and *Internal Control – Integrated Framework*,[3] respectively. Between the issuances of two guidelines, on July 15, 2006, the Ministry of Finance (MOF), the State-owned Assets Supervision and Administration Commission (SASAC), the China Securities Regulatory Commission (CSRC), the China National Audit Office (CNAO), the China Banking Regulatory Commission (CBRC) and the China Insurance Regulatory Commission (CIRC) jointly founded the Commission of Enterprise Internal Control Standard, whose objective is to develop a complete set of generally accepted guidelines on internal control.

Table 15.1 Key events on the development of internal control framework

Time	Event
June 5, 2006	SSE issued "the Guidelines of Shanghai Stock Exchange for the Internal Control of Listed Companies".
July 15, 2006	The Commission of Enterprise Internal Control Standard was founded.
September 28, 2006	SZSE issued "the Guidelines of Shenzhen Stock Exchange for the Internal Control of Listed Companies".
June 28, 2008	The Basic Internal Control Norms for Enterprises was issued.
April 26, 2010	The Guidelines for the Application of Enterprise Internal Controls (EICs), the Guidelines for the Evaluation of EICs, and the Guidelines for the Auditing of EICs were issued.

On June 28, 2008, the *Basic Internal Control Norms for Enterprises* was issued jointly by five agencies, including the MOF, CSRC, CNAO, CBRC and CIRC. Article 3 of *Basic Norms* clearly points out that internal control

> refers to a process through which an entity's board of directors, management and other personnel operate to achieve the objectives of internal control. The objectives of internal control are to ensure, to a reasonable extent, the compliance with applicable laws and regulations, the security of assets and the reliability of financial reporting of an enterprise, improve the business effectiveness and efficiency and help the enterprise realize its development strategy.

While the definition is consistent with that in *Internal Control – Integrated Framework*, the objectives are more comprehensive by combining the contents from both *Internal Control – Integrated Framework* and *Enterprise Risk Management – Integrated Framework*. Specifically, *Basic Norms* adopts the five elements from *Internal Control – Integrated Framework* – internal environment, risk evaluation, control activities, information and communication and internal monitoring – and interprets these five elements in great detail. Toward this end, *Basic Norms* established a complete internal control framework.

To help listed companies implement *Basic Norms* effectively, the five agencies further issued three related guidelines on April 26, 2010: the *Guidelines for the Application of* EICs, the *Guidelines for the Evaluation of EICs*, and the *Guidelines for the Auditing of EICs* (hereafter *Enterprise Internal Control Guidelines*). Together, these guidelines can help companies build an internal control system that is based on the principles and five elements of internal control. *The Application Guidelines* are constituted of 18 sets of detailed guidelines, which can be categorized into three different types: internal environment, control activities and control tools[4] (see Table 15.2). They

Table 15.2 The application guidelines of enterprise internal control

Types of Guidance	Details
Guidelines on internal environment	No 1 – Organizational structure
	No 2 – Development strategy
	No 3 – Human resources
	No 4 – Social responsibility
	No 5 – Organization culture
Guidelines on control activities	No 6 – Capital management
	No 7 – Procurement
	No 8 – Asset management
	No 9 – Sales
	No 10 – R&D
	No 11 – Project management
	No 12 – Guarantee business
	No 13 – Outsourcing
	No 14 – Financial reporting
Guidelines on control tools	No 15 – Budgeting
	No 15 – Contract management
	N0 17 – Internal communication
	No 18 – Information system

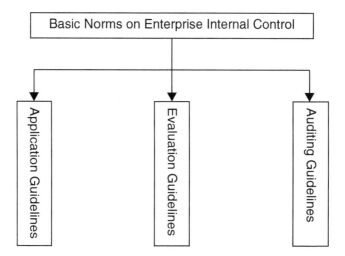

Figure 15.1 Internal control system in China (Chinese SOX)

basically cover various items at enterprise, business and reporting levels. The *Evaluation Guidelines* help companies conduct self-evaluation on the effectiveness of internal control. Finally, the *Auditing Guidelines* advise CPAs and accounting firms on how to conduct business related to the auditing of internal control. While the three guidelines are independent of each other, they are interconnected to a certain degree and become an integrated system.

Basic Norms and the set of guidelines constitute the framework of internal control for Chinese enterprises, which is also called the Chinese "SOX act" (see Figure 15.1). However, different from that of the SOX Act in the US, the framework of internal control in China reflects the role of internal control on enterprise management more comprehensively. Beyond its effect on financial reporting, the framework provides a fundamental and authoritative guidance on internal control, which not only helps companies improve management expertise and risk management, but also supports the sustainable development of capital market. This was due to the fact that Chinese enterprises significantly lagged behind companies in Western countries due to weak institutional development. Thus, Chinese government attempted to use the opportunity of internal control development to improve companies' management expertise. For example, to promote companies' strategic development and to encourage them to optimize governance, management and operation, organizational structure was included as No. 1 in the Application Guidelines.

3. Policies on the disclosure of internal control in China

The disclosure of internal control is a key component of internal control monitoring and practice. Therefore, it has long been an important topic of academic study. In China, public companies' disclosure is mainly regulated by the policies established by the exchanges and CSRC, including the *Guidelines of SSE*, the *Guidelines of SZSE*, *Basic Norms* and related notices.

We first discuss the disclosure requirement in the Shanghai Stock Exchange (SSE). On June 5, 2006, SSE issued the *Guidelines on the Internal Control of Listed Companies*, requiring all listed companies to disclose self-evaluation reports of internal control effectiveness and auditor attestations at the time of filing an annual report.[5] However, considering the time constraint and the implementation cost, SSE removed the mandatory disclosure requirement in a follow-up announcement: *Year 2006 Notice of the Shanghai Stock Exchange on Effectively Preparing Listed Companies' Annual Reports*. While *Year 2006 Notice* only required companies to elaborate the implementation and completion of internal control system in the "Major Issues" section of annual reports, it did encourage listed companies to voluntarily disclose self-evaluation report and auditor's attestation of internal control. Two years later, *Year 2008 Notice* required listed firms to explain the implementation and completion of internal control system in the "Corporate Governance" section. Companies in the SSE Corporate Governance Sample, firms cross-listed overseas and financial firms must disclose the Board of Directors' self-evaluation report on internal control. While the attestation of internal control was still not mandatory, the *Notice* urged listed companies to get auditing firms to attest to the effectiveness of internal control. *Year 2011 Notice* further required cross-listed companies to disclose both self-evaluation reports and auditor's attestations, and encouraged firms in internal control pilot programs (see discussion below about CSRC's disclosure requirement) to voluntarily disclose these two reports. Other companies should disclose their proposed plans of implementation and completion of internal control system in their 2011 annual reports.

We next turn to the disclosure requirement in Shenzhen Exchange. Companies listed on SZSE include those on Main Board, on Small and Medium Enterprise Board and on Growth Enterprise Board.[6] SZSE had different disclosure requirements for companies listed on Main Board and Small and Medium Enterprise Board. Similar to SSE, companies listed on the Main Board are required to disclose self-evaluation reports and auditor attestations under SZSE guidelines issued on September 28, 2006. In its follow-up notice, *Year 2007 Notice on Effectively Preparing Listed Companies' Annual Report*, issued in December, 2007, SZSE required these companies to disclose self-evaluation reports and encouraged companies to get auditors to attest to their internal control effectiveness.[7] On December 31, 2008, SZSE announced *Year 2008 Notice of Effectively Disclosing Annual Reports of Listed Companies*, which further required all firms listed on Main Board to disclose self-evaluation reports in a separated report along with annual reports, and continued to encourage voluntary disclosure of auditor attestations. Three years later, *Year 2011 Notice on Effectively Disclosing Annual Reports of Listed Companies* ruled that dual-listed companies (having both A-share and H-share) and companies in internal control pilot program should follow the requirements in *Basic Norms* to disclose self-evaluation reports and auditor attestations.

Companies listed on Small and Medium Enterprise Board are subject to the *Guidelines for Internal Auditing of Listed Companies on the Small and Medium-size Enterprise Board* issued by SZSE on December 26, 2007. The Guidelines required that firms must have auditor attestations on the effectiveness of internal control at least once for every two years, and disclose both self-evaluation reports and auditor attestations along with annual reports. *Year 2007 Notice of Effectively Preparing Annual Reports of Listed Companies on the Small and Medium-size Enterprise Board* also encouraged firms to disclose annual internal control self-evaluation reports following the Guidelines. *Year 2008 Notice* further required that auditing committees must follow *Basic Norms* and the Guidelines for Internal Control Auditing to disclose annual self-evaluation reports. In addition, self-evaluation reports must be evaluated by the Board of Directors, and attested to by the Board of Supervisors, independent directors or recommender (if applicable). Starting in 2008, auditor attestations must be disclosed at least once every other year. Also, self-evaluation reports and auditor attestations (if applicable) must be disclosed along with annual reports.

Besides regulations by two exchanges, at a higher level, the disclosure of internal control is monitored by CSRC based on *Basic Norms* issued in 2008. Article 46 in *Basic Norms* required companies to periodically self-evaluate internal control effectiveness and disclose self-evaluation reports. According to *Notice on Issuing the Basic Internal Control Norms for Enterprises*, listed companies should conduct self-evaluations and disclose self-evaluation reports, and, if possible, have auditors to attest to their internal control effectiveness. In 2010, the aforementioned five agencies jointly issued related guidelines. According to *Notice on Issuing the Enterprise Internal Control Guidelines*, cross-listed companies must start following the *Enterprise Internal Control Guidelines* on January 1, 2011. Companies listed on Main Board of SSE and SZSE should start on January 1, 2012. Companies listed on Small and Medium-size Board and Growth Enterprise Board should start at an appropriate time. The *Notice* also encouraged non-listed large and medium-size companies to voluntarily implement these guidelines. Moreover, *the Notice* required those listed companies, who were subject to *Basic Norms* and *Enterprise Internal Control Guidelines*, to conduct self-evaluations, disclose self-evaluation reports, have auditors to attest to their internal control effectiveness and issue auditor attestations. In order to completely implement *Basic Norms* and related guidelines, the CSRC issued *Notice of Effectively Implement Listed Companies Internal Control Pilot Program* on February 14, 2011, which not only requires 68 cross-listed companies to implement internal control systems, but also to select another 216 companies into internal control pilot programs, conditional on their willingness and on a CSRC recommendation. In 2012, the MOF and CSRC issued *Notice on the Implementation of Internal Control System by Companies Listed on the Main Board under Different Categories and Groups*. The notice required listed companies on the Main Board to disclose both internal control self-evaluation reports prepared by the Board of Directors and auditor attestations issued by CPA firms, along with annual reports. Listed companies should implement this in the following order: State-owned companies in 2012, large-size non-State-owned companies in 2013, and other companies in 2014. Issued by the MOF and CSRC in 2014, *the Preparation Rules for Information Disclosure by Listed Companies No. 21 – General Provisions on Financial Reports* further emphasized the content of evaluation reports. Most importantly, Article 15 in *the Rules* stated that companies should differentiate financial reporting internal controls from non-financial reporting internal controls, and separately disclose standards of material weakness, significant deficiency and general control deficiency.

To summarize, the disclosure of internal control for Chinese public companies is regulated in two tiers: the stock exchanges and the CSRC. On the level of stock exchanges, there are differences between SSE and SZSE regulations. There also exist differences among the requirements of disclosure (e.g. self-evaluation reports and auditor attestations): voluntary disclosure, semi-voluntary and mandatory disclosure. Moreover, there are multiple methods to disclose information related to internal control. For example, the disclosure can be made in annual reports (e.g. in the Corporate Governance or Other Issue section), in self-evaluation reports issued by the Board of Directors or in auditor attestations. In addition to the disclosure of internal control weakness related to financial reporting, non-financial reporting-related internal control deficiencies are also required to be disclosed in China. Due to the complexity of the disclosure regulations in China, researchers have to be cautious of when examining firms' internal control quality or analyzing incentives of disclosure decisions. For example, when applying signaling theory to study firms' decisions on whether or not to disclose their internal control information, if researchers fail to use voluntary disclosure companies as the treatment group, the result will be biased, or even meaningless. Another possible problem is that researchers may fail to distinguish between mandatory and voluntary disclosure companies. Furthermore, because the Chinese disclosure regulation system does not define legal liabilities, companies' cost of violation is relatively low. If researchers adopt signaling theory to build their hypotheses, they should assess if the presumptions still hold. Nevertheless, the unique internal control institutional setting in China provides ample opportunities to conduct studies related to internal control.

4. Descriptive statistics of internal control in Chinese enterprises

To illustrate the development of internal control in Chinese listed companies, we analyze the disclosure of self-evaluation report and auditor attestation of all SSE and SZSE listed companies from 2007 to 2015. We obtained the data from the China Stock Market Trading Database (CSMAR). The database covers internal control information on companies listed on the Main Board, the Small and Medium Enterprise Boards and the Growth Enterprise Board starting from 2007.

Table 15.3 shows total number of listed companies, the percentage of companies that disclose self-evaluation, and the percentage of companies that disclose auditor attestations. Prior to 2007, the disclosure of internal control, including self-evaluation and/or auditor attestations, was voluntary. In 2007, among 1,549 public companies, only 10.9% disclosed their self-evaluation of internal control, and even fewer companies (5.3%) disclosed auditor attestations. Following the announcement and implementation of SSE and SZSE Guidelines, the *Basic Norms* and subsequent notices, mandatory disclosure requirements have been applied to a broader range of companies. Some companies, while not required, also chose to voluntarily disclose information related to internal control, as more companies started to realize the importance of internal control and actively develop internal control systems. Thus, the percentage of companies disclosing self-evaluation reports increased steadily from 50.8% in 2009 to 94.4% in 2015, and the percentage of companies disclosed auditor attestations rose from 21.8% in 2009 to 79.4% in 2015.

In particular, the percentage of companies disclosing their self-evaluation jumped from 10.9% in 2007 to 45.5% in 2008. This is because SSE required listed companies on the SSE Corporate Governance Board, cross-listed companies and financial companies to disclose self-evaluation reports. Meanwhile, SZSE also required listed companies on the Main Board to disclose self-evaluation report using a separated report. However, as SSE and SZSE did not mandatorily require the disclosure of auditor attestations, the magnitude of increase in attestation disclosure is not as high as self-evaluation.

Another noticeable jump happened in 2012 when the MOF and CSRC issued the *Notice on the Implementation of Internal Control System by Companies Listed on the Main Board*. The *2012 Notice* required State-owned listed companies to fully implement internal control system and disclose both self-evaluation reports and auditor attestations. The requirement was subsequently extended to large-size non-State-owned companies in 2013, and other companies in 2014. As a result, Table 15.3 shows that in 2012 the percentage of companies disclosing self-evaluations exceeded 90%, and the percentage of companies disclosing auditor attestations also exceeded 60%.

Table 15.3 Self-evaluation and auditor attestation of internal control

Year	Number of companies	Disclose of self-evaluation	Disclose of auditor attestation
2007	1549	0.109	0.053
2008	1603	0.455	0.091
2009	1752	0.508	0.218
2010	2107	0.746	0.297
2011	2341	0.789	0.425
2012	2470	0.902	0.606
2013	2515	0.929	0.711
2014	2631	0.981	0.770
2015	2823	0.944	0.794

Table 15.4 Internal control effectiveness and weakness

Year	Number of companies disclosing self-evaluation	Self-evaluated as effective	Material weakness	Significant deficiency	General deficiency
2007	169	1.000	0.000	0.000	0.000
2008	730	1.000	0.000	0.000	0.000
2009	890	1.000	0.000	0.000	0.001
2010	1571	0.998	0.001	0.001	0.011
2011	1847	0.998	0.002	0.009	0.070
2012	2227	0.996	0.004	0.016	0.230
2013	2337	0.996	0.012	0.020	0.186
2014	2580	0.992	0.014	0.021	0.201
2015	2665	0.995	0.012	0.021	0.334

Table 15.5 Auditor attestation of internal control

Year	Number of companies disclosing attestation	Unqualified opinion	unqualified opinion with explanatory notes	qualified opinion	adverse opinion	disclaimer opinion
2007	82	80	2	0	0	0
2008	146	145	1	0	0	0
2009	382	381	1	0	0	0
2010	625	624	0	0	1	0
2011	995	989	4	1	1	0
2012	1496	1471	20	0	5	0
2013	1788	1736	36	2	13	1
2014	2026	1947	55	1	20	3
2015	2241	2132	90	1	18	0

Next, we further analyze internal control effectiveness and weakness disclosed in self-evaluation reports. Table 15.4 shows that the number of companies disclosing self-evaluations increased from 169 in 2007 to 2,665 in 2015. Within those firms, more than 99% of companies reported that they had effective internal control systems. Only about 1% observations disclosed that they had material internal control weakness. Around 2% had significant deficiency, while the percentage with general deficiency was higher. The material weakness and significant deficiency is reported in many instances. For example, in debt-covenant management, some companies fail to structure effective covenants, which results in failure to collect receivables on time. In capital management, some companies misclassify bank accounts, failing to include some account balances into financial reports, or failing to conduct account reconciliation on schedule. In asset management, a few companies ineffectively manage fixed assets, inventory or other assets, or not properly conduct impairment assessment.

Finally, we examine auditor attestation. As shown in Table 15.5, the number of companies disclosing auditor attestation of internal control increased rapidly from 82 companies in 2007 to 2,241 in 2015. Most auditors of the attestation service issue standard unqualified opinions on the effectiveness of internal control. While the incidence of other opinions, including unqualified opinions with explanatory notes, qualified opinions, adverse opinions and disclaimer opinions, were relatively small, we do see an increasing trend. One possible explanation is that firms that are subject to mandatory disclosure in earlier periods had better internal control quality. With the expansion of mandatory disclosure requirements, more firms with lower quality were required to disclose auditor attestations containing non-standard unqualified opinions, which led to the trend observed above.

5. Normative research on internal control in China

Chinese scholars used to study internal control with normative approaches by analyzing its underlying theory and application in China. Early studies examine the evolution of internal control, ranging from internal check, internal control system to internal control structure (Xu, Zhu, and Xu, 1992; Zhu and Xu, 1996; Liu and Chen, 2000). Later on, the internal control integrated framework of COSO was introduced into China (Liu and Chen, 2000; Wu, Chen, and Shao, 2000a, b). Building on COSO's framework, some researchers developed new frameworks. For example, Gu and Zhang (2003) proposed a three-dimensional system of internal control, arguing that enterprise internal control is mainly influenced by institutional control, marketing control and cultural control. Other researchers examine internal control from different research angles, including control theory (Wu, Chen, and Shao, 2000a), system theory and new institutional economics (Liu and Zhang, 2002), value creation orientation (Li, 2007) and on the switch from the power restriction concept to information aspects (Yang, 2006a). The literature on internal control also develops a breadth of research topics. These topics include the nature and objective of internal control (Yang, 2006b; Xie, 2009), internal control environment (Chen, Liu, and Yu, 2005; Pan and Zheng, 2008), the monitoring and evaluation of internal control (Chen and Zhang, 2008; Han, Guo, and Chen, 2009), internal control and auditing (Chen, Li, Lin, and Wu, 2001; Fang, 2002; Yuan, 2008), the informationization of internal control (Wang, 2008, 2009; Luo and Zhang, 2008; Wu, Lin, and Sun, 2009), the efficiency of internal control (Lin and Xu, 2009; Xu and Wang, 2013), the evolution of internal control theory (Shi, 2008), disclosure of internal control information (Zhang, Qian, and Li, 2003; Li, He, and Ma, 2003; Yang and Chen, 2009), government internal control (Liu and Wang, 2008) and commercial bank internal control (Qu, Li, Yang, and Ye, 2009; He, 2009).

6. Empirical research on internal control in China

Benefiting from internal control theory built on normative approach and the increasing disclosure of internal control information, empirical research on internal control quickly emerges in recent years. These studies can be broadly categorized into two streams: one is on determinants of internal control disclosure and its quality, and the other is on the economic consequences of internal control effectiveness.

Determinants of internal control disclosure and quality

Several studies examine the impact of institutional environment, firm characteristics, and management background on internal control. Liu, Luo, He, and Chen (2012) suggest that both state ownership and institutional environment have great impacts on internal control quality. Specifically, State-owned enterprises controlled by central government have higher internal control quality than those controlled by local governments, but their internal control quality is similar to that of non-State-owned emprises. In addition, they find that the development of provincial institutional environment has a positive effect on internal control quality. Fang and Dai (2012) demonstrate that mitigating agency cost and signaling are two key incentives for managers to voluntarily disclose audit attestations of internal control and increase the quality of voluntary disclosure.

With regard to firm characteristics, Tian, Qi, and Li (2010) indicate that firms with more complex operations, greater sales growth and auditor resignations are more likely to report internal control deficiencies, whereas those with high quality auditors are less likely to report internal control deficiencies. Fang, Sun, and Jin (2009) investigate the factors that affect voluntary disclosure of internal control information, and find that voluntary disclosure is positively related to cross-listing, Big 4 CPA firms, firm size, ROA, board independence, size of the board of supervisors and the existence of audit committees, whereas it is negatively related to audit opinion. Lin and Rao (2009) find that firms with higher internal control quality are more likely to disclose auditor attestations of internal control, signaling their real value. Specifically, firms with more resources available for internal control, rapid growth and an internal audit department are more likely to disclose auditor's internal control reports voluntarily; consequently, those in a weak financial condition and with misconduct are less likely to disclose.

Managers' characteristics also matter in internal control quality. Chi, Yang, and Zou (2014) find that internal control quality is associated with managers' characteristics, including age, gender, education, tenure and work experience. Zhao and Xu (2013) indicate that managers with greater power are less likely to disclose the existing internal control deficiency. Lu, Wang, and Fu (2014) find that CEOs with excessive monetary payment and equity incentives are more likely to enhance the effectiveness of internal control.

Besides the aforementioned studies, a few other studies describe and analyze the information of internal control in great details. For example, Huang (2008) focuses on Chinese listed banks' annual reports from 2001 to 2006 and analyzes information related to internal control. She finds many inconsistencies in the disclosure of internal control information and suggests several ways to correct the problem. Zhang, Qian, and Li (2003) look at A-share ST companies' internal control in 2001 and 2002. They find that while overall the disclosure improved in 2002, many inconsistencies still exist in some companies, and companies tend to report good news and withhold bad news.

Internal control and financial reporting quality

On the relationship between internal control quality and financial reporting quality, the results are mixed. Both Zhang (2008) and Wang and Zhang (2010) find that accruals quality actually decreases when the quality of internal control increases. Zhang, Wang, and Zhang (2010) and Lei, Wu, and Sun (2013), however, show that firms with internal control attestations have higher earnings quality than those without. Tian, Li, and Qi (2011) find that there is no significant association between disclosure of audit attestations on internal control and accrual quality, which suggests that audit attestations on internal control in China are not always credible. However, both Dong and Chen (2011) and Fang and Jin (2011) find that internal control quality is positively associated with accrual quality and earnings responses coefficients, suggesting that high quality internal control improves financial information quality. Fan, Zhang, and Liu (2013) find that high quality internal control can reduce accrual earnings management but not real earnings management. Liu and Liu (2014) find that firms with internal control deficiency usually employ extraordinary income to manage earnings, whereas those without deficiency usually employ investment income and asset impairment to manage earnings. In addition, Wu (2009) investigates the association between internal control and earnings quality from the perspective of value relevance. He finds that the positive relation between disclosure of internal control and value relevance of accounting information only exists when there is independent auditor attestation. Without auditors' attestations, internal control disclosure does not increase the value relevance of accounting information, as investors question the credibility of disclosure.

Internal control and auditors' behavior

On the relation between internal control and auditing, Yang and Hu (2010) find that auditors are less likely to detect earnings management for clients with high quality internal control, which suggests a substitution relation between audit and internal control. However, this substitution relation is moderated by audit fees. Zhang, Zhang, and Yang (2011) examine the relation between internal control and audit fees. They find that good corporate governance can increase the effectiveness of internal control and auditors subsequently lower audit fees for firms with higher internal control quality. Zhang (2010) shows that firms with unqualified audit opinions tend to have shorter auditing lag. However, when these firms conduct their first attestation of internal control, there is no further delay in auditing. Zhang and He (2013) demonstrate that types of internal control audit opinions affect individual investors' confidence in unqualified audit opinions on financial statement, suggesting that the extent of internal control disclosure and the attestation are informative for investors in forecasting misreporting. In addition, Zhang (2012) investigates the determinants of audit fees related to internal control and indicates that the internal control attestation fee is positively related to firm size, transaction complexity and audit firm reputation.

Internal control and corporate finance

A few studies focus on how internal control affects corporate finance and investment activity. Yang, Zhang, and Chen (2014) find that acquirer firms with high quality internal control achieve better performance and less bankruptcy risk in the subsequent years after M&A, indicating that internal control can enhance acquirers' integration ability and performance. Thus it provides valuable empirical evidence for the role of internal control on operational activities. Li, Lin, and Lu (2011) indicate that firms with high quality internal control invest more efficiently than those with low quality. Internal control can also reduce agency cost (Yang, Wang, and Cao, 2010). For example, Lu, Liu, and Xu (2011) find that internal control can increase executive pay-performance sensitivity because high quality internal control plays an import role in reducing managers' self-interest behavior. Yang, Lin, and Wang (2009) demonstrate that internal control can constrain the largest shareholder from tunneling. Fang and Chen (2015) find that high quality internal control can effectively reduce both idiosyncratic risk and systematic risk, and explain how internal control fulfills a risk management function. Li (2013) suggests that internal control improve investor relations management. Cheng, Yang, and Yao (2013) find that high quality internal control mitigates corporate financing constraints, and that the quality of internal control is more important for non-bank connected firms than for bank connected firms in reducing information asymmetry and decreasing financing constraints. Li and Chen (2012) shed light on the consequences of internal control from the perspective of tax. They find that improving internal control quality significantly reduces effective tax rates. Mao and Meng (2013) find that internal control can reduce litigation risk, which supports internal control objectives on the compliance with applicable laws and regulations (COSO, 1992).

Innovation on the measure of internal control quality

Most of the studies measure the quality of internal control using companies' self-evaluations and auditors' attestations. For example, the widely used dichotomous indicator variable to measure internal control quality is whether companies have internal control weakness. Due to the lack of high quality data on internal control effectiveness in China, scholars attempt to construct their own and more comprehensive indexes to measure the quality of public companies' internal control (Zhou, Hu, Lin, and Liu, 2013). To date, the most influential internal control indexes in China are Xiamen University's internal control index (XMU index) developed by Chen, Dong, Han, and Zhou (2017) and the DIB index constructed by Shenzhen Dibo Enterprise Risk Management Technology Development Ltd.[8] Both indexes are built on *Basic Norms*, the *Guidelines of Enterprise Internal Controls, Internal Control – Integrated Framework*, and *Enterprise Risk Management – Integrated Framework*. However, their designing principles differ considerably. The XMU index is based on the evaluation of five elements, internal environment, risk assessment, control activity, information and communication and internal monitoring, to measure the quality of internal control (for details, please see Chen, Dong, Han, and Zhou, 2017). BID index, however, uses internal control compliance, reporting, assets safety, operation and strategy to evaluate internal control (for details, see Wang, Jiang, Hu, Zhao, and Lin, 2011). More importantly, XMU index can be decomposed intro five sub-indices to separately evaluate five elements of internal control.

The development of internal control index enables scholars to conduct research at the level of five elements and explore their different effects on internal control. Separating the XMU index into five sub-indices for five elements of internal control, Chen, Dong, Han, and Zhou (2017) show that control environment, control activities and information and communication play an important role in mitigating earnings management. In addition, they find that the control environment has a positive impact on earnings response coefficient (ERC) in the short-window, whereas information and communication has a positive impact on ERC in the long-window. Chen, Chan, Dong, and Zhang (2017) employ the five XMU sub-indices to explore the effect of internal control on stock price crash risk. They find that control environment, information and communication and monitoring are negatively related to future stock price crash risk, whereas both risk measures and control activities have no significant effect on future stock prices crash risk.

This series of research based on internal control indexes contributes to accounting literature in at least two ways. First, these papers create a comprehensive evaluation system on internal control, which can transform qualitative information into quantitative and comprehensive indexes. These indexes overcome the deficiency of dichotomous measures (e.g. whether or not internal control weakness exists) pervasively used in prior literature and generate further insights. Second, Chinese researchers conduct the leading works to explore the role of each element of internal control on internal control. Their findings suggest that five elements of internal control exert different impacts and are important in explaining the mechanisms through which internal control works. Meanwhile, this series of research also has significant influence on accounting practices, including investors, enterprises and regulators.

7. Conclusions

We review the internal control framework in China and its related research in this chapter. To enhance enterprise management expertise and promote sustainable economic growth, the Chinese government along with its agencies established its own internal control framework based on *Basic Norms* and three related guidelines. The disclosure of internal control in China is also evolving, which provides excellent research opportunities to scholars. While prior research, including both normative and empirical, conducted by Chinese scholars largely contributes to our understanding of the determinants and consequences of internal control in China, we believe more studies can be done in this relatively new research field.

Notes

1 Wang Dong acknowledges financial support from the National Natural Science Foundation of China (Grant Numbers NSFC-71302060 and NSFC-71332008).
2 Committee of Sponsoring Organizations of Treadway Commission. (2004). *Enterprise Risk Management – Integrated Framework*.
3 Committee of Sponsoring Organizations of Treadway Commission. (1992). *Internal Control – Integrated Framework*.
4 Control tools typically involve enterprise business activities and management, emphasizing the property of tools.
5 Article 32 states that the board of directors should disclose the self-evaluation of internal control and its attestation by an auditing firm along with an annual report.
6 As the Main Board and the Small and Medium Enterprise Board were established earlier, we mainly focus on disclosure requirement related to companies listed on these two Boards. The Growth Enterprise Board was created at the end of 2009. Due to its short history, we do not discuss it in this essay.
7 Notice 2007 stated that self-evaluation can either be included in the Corporate Governance section of the annual report or reported separately along with the annual report. For companies reporting self-evaluation in the annual report, the *Notice* specified the content and format of self-evaluation, which is similar to the requirement for a standalone report required by subsequent notices. Thus, self-evaluation of internal control disclosed in the annual report is equivalent to a standalone self-evaluation report.
8 Refer to website: www.dibcn.com

References

Chen, Hanwen, Wang Dong, Hongling Han, Nan Zhou. (2017). A Comprehensive and Quantitative Internal Control Index: Construction, Validation, and Impact. *Review of Quantitative Finance and Accounting*, 49(2): 337–377.
Chen, Hanwen, Shuhua Li, Zhiyi Lin, Qiankui Wu. 2001. *Security Market and Accounting Regulation (in Chinese)*. China Financial and Economic Publishing House, Beijing.
Chen, Hanwen, Qiliang Liu, Jinsong Yu. 2005. Nation, Ownership Structure, Trust, and Corporate Governance. *Management World (in Chinese)*, 8: 134–142.
Chen, Hanwen, Yixia Zhang. 2008. The Effectiveness of Internal Control and Its Evaluation Methods. *Auditing Research (in Chinese)*, 3: 48–54.
Chen, Jun, Kam C. Chan, Wang Dong, Feida Zhang. (2017). Internal Control and Stock Price Crash Risk: Evidence From China. *European Accounting Review*, 26(1): 125–152.
Cheng, Xiaoke, Chengcheng Yang, Lijie Yao. 2013. Internal Control, Bank Connection and Financing Constraints. *Auditing Research (in Chinese)*, 5: 80–86.
Chi, Guohua, Jin Yang, Wei Zou. 2014. The Influence of Management Background Characteristics on Internal Control Quality. *Accounting Research (in Chinese)*, 11: 67–74.
Committee of Sponsoring Organizations of the Treadway Commission (COSO). 1992. *Internal Control-Integrated Framework*. Jersey City, NJ: AICPA.
Dong, Wang, Hanwen Chen. 2011. Internal Control, Accruals Quality and Earnings Response: Empirical Evidence of Chinese A-share Listed Companies in 2009. *Auditing Research (in Chinese)*, 4: 68–78.
Fan, Jinghua, Yaman Zhang, Qiliang Liu. 2013. Internal Control, Auditor Industry Expertise, Accrual and Real Earnings Management. *Accounting Research (in Chinese)*, 4(81): 88–96.
Fang, Hongxing. 2002. Internal Control Audit and Organization Efficiency. *Accounting Research (in Chinese)*, 6: 58–64.
Fang, Hongxing, Zuohua Chen. 2015. Can High Quality Internal Control Effectively Respond to Idiosyncratic Risk and Systematic Risk? *Accounting Research (in Chinese)*, 4: 70–77.
Fang, Hongxing, Jiemin Dai. 2012. Companies' Incentives, Auditors' Reputation and Voluntary Internal Control Audit Reporting. *Accounting Research (in Chinese)*, 2: 87–95.

Fang, Hongxing, Yuna Jin. 2011. Can High Quality Internal Control Reduce Earnings Management? *Accounting Research (in Chinese)*, 8: 53–60.

Fang, Hongxing, He Sun, Yunyun Jin. 2009. Corporate Characteristics, External Audit, and Voluntary Disclosure of Internal Control Information. *Accounting Research (in Chinese)*, 10: 44–52.

Gu, Qi, Xiangzhou Zhang. 2003. Three Dimensional System of Internal Control. *Accounting Research (in Chinese)*, 11: 10–13.

Han, Hongling, Yanmin Guo, Hanwen Chen. 2009. The Applicative Development of Monitoring Component in Internal Control: A Risk-oriented Model and Its Implication for Chinese Companies. *Accounting Research (in Chinese)*, 8: 73–79.

He, Yu. 2009. Occputational Fraud, Internal Control and Internal Auditing. *Auditing Research (in Chinese)*, 2: 91–96.

Huang, Qiumin. 2008. The Analysis of the Internal Control Information Disclosure by Listed Banks. *Auditing Research (in Chinese)*, 1: 82–89.

Lei, Ying, Jinayou Wu, Hong Sun. 2013. Internal Control, Impact of Internal Control Audit on Earnings Quality. *Accounting Research (in Chinese)*, 11: 75–81.

Li, Minghui, Hai He, Xikui Ma. 2003. Analysis of Internal Control Information Disclosure in China. *Auditing Research (in Chinese)*, 1: 38–43.

Li, Wanfu, Huili Chen. 2012. Internal Control and Corporate Effective Tax Rate. *Journal of Financial Research (in Chinese)*, 9: 195–206.

Li, Wanfu, Bin Lin, Song Lu. 2011. The Role Played by the Internal Control in Companies' Investment. *Management World (in Chinese)*, 2: 81–99.

Li, Xinhe. 2007. Internal Control From Financial Statement Oriented to Value Oriented. *Accounting Research (in Chinese)*, 4: 54–60.

Li, Zhibin. 2013. Internal Control and Investor Relations Management in China. *Accounting Research (in Chinese)*, 12: 72–78.

Lin, Bin, Jing Rao. 2009. Why Do Listed Companies Disclose the Auditor's Internal Control Reports Voluntarily? *Accounting Research (in Chinese)*, 2: 45–52.

Lin, Zhonggao, Hong Xu. 2009. A Study on Division of Labor, Allocation of Control Power and Efficiency of Internal Control. *Accounting Research (in Chinese)*, 3: 64–71.

Liu, Minghui, Yixia Zhang. 2002. Analysis of Internal Control From Economic Perspective. *Accounting Research (in Chinese)*, 8: 54–56.

Liu, Qiliang, Le Luo, Weifeng He, Hanwen Chen. 2012. State Ownership, the Institutional Environment, and Internal Control Quality? *Accounting Research (in Chinese)*, 3: 52–61.

Liu, Xingjian, Zhao Liu. 2014. The Influence of Internal Control on Fair Value and Earnings Management. *Auditing Research (in Chinese)*, 2: 59–66.

Liu, Yuting, Hong Wang. 2008. Evolution and Practices of Internal Control in Governance Agency in USA. *Accounting Research (in Chinese)*, 3: 3–10.

Liu, Zongliu, Hanwen Chen. 2000. *Enterprise Internal Control: Theory, Practice, and Case (in Chinese)*. China Financial and Economic Publishing House, Beijing.

Lu, Dong, Yunchen Wang, Peng Fu. 2014. Do CEO Incentives Improve the Effectiveness of Internal Control? *Accounting Research (in Chinese)*, 6(6): 66–72.

Lu, Rui, Jianhua Liu, Ning Xu. 2011. Internal Control, Property Right and Executive Pay-performance Sensitivity. *Accounting Research (in Chinese)*, 10: 42–48.

Luo, Liangbin, Bai Zhang. 2008. Research on Internal Control in Informationization Process. *Accounting Research (in Chinese)*, 5: 69–75.

Mao, Xinshu, Jie Meng. 2013. Internal Control and Litigation Risk. *Management World (in Chinese)*, 11: 155–165.

Pan, Yan, Xianping Zheng. 2008. Construct Internal Control Theory: Discussion on Basic Assumption. *Accounting Research (in Chinese)*, 2: 63–67.

Qu, Xu, Ming Li, Dan Yang, Jianming Ye. 2009. Research on the Material Weakness Disclosure in Internal Control of Listed Banks. *Accounting Research (in Chinese)*, 4: 38–46.

Shi, Xianwang. 2008. The Vicissitude and the Enlightening Guidance of the Internal Control Theory. *Auditing Research (in Chinese)*, 6: 79–83.

Tian, Gaoliang, Liuchuang Li, Baolei Qi. 2011. Audit Report on Internal Control: The Dishonest Signal and Its Discrimination. *Nankai Business Review (in Chinese)*, 14(5): 109–117.

Tian, Gaoliang, Baolei Qi, Liuchuang Li. 2010. Determinants of Discovery and Reporting of Internal Control Deficiencies Over Financial Reporting. *Nankai Business Review (in Chinese)*, 13(4): 134–141.

Wang, Hailin. 2008. Research on Enterprise Internal Control Mode Based on IT. *Accounting Research (in Chinese)*, 11: 63–68.

Wang, Hailin. 2009. Research on IC-CMM Model of Internal Control Capability Evaluation. *Accounting Research (in Chinese)*, 10: 53–59.

Wang, Hong, Zhanhua Jiang, Weimin Hu, Lisheng Zhao, Bin Lin. 2011. Research on Internal Control Index of China Public Company. *Accounting Research (in Chinese)*, 12: 20–24.

Wang, Meiying, Weihua Zhang. 2010. Accrual Quality and Voluntary Disclosure of Internal Control Attestation. Proceeding of *the 5th Five-School Accounting Youth Scholar Forum*. School of Management, Xiamen University: 134–142.

Wu, Shuipeng, Hanwen Chen, Xiandi Shao. 2000a. The Development and Enlightenment of Internal Control Theory. *Accounting Research (in Chinese)*, 9: 43–48.

Wu, Shuipeng, Hanwen Chen, Xiandi Shao. 2000b. On the Improvement of Internal Control in China. *Accounting Research (in Chinese)*, 9: 43–48.

Wu, Yantai, Bin Lin, Ye Sun. 2009. Research on the Risk Management of Information System Internal Control Based on Life Cycle. *Accounting Research (in Chinese)*, 6: 87–92.

Wu, Yibing. 2009. Internal Control Disclosure Audit, ERC and Cost of Equity Capital. *Economic Management Journal (in Chinese)*, 9: 64–69.

Xie, Zhihua. 2009. The Nature and Structure of Internal Control. *Accounting Research (in Chinese)*, 12: 70–75.

Xu, Xibing, Yonghai Wang. 2013. Incomplete Contract, Enterprise Capability and Internal Control. *Auditing Research (in Chinese)*, 6: 102–107.

Xu, Zhendan, Rongen Zhu, Jianxin Xu. 1992. *Internal Control Theory (in Chinese)*. Liaoning People Publication, Shenyang.

Yang, Daoguang, Chuancai Zhang, Hanwen Chen. 2014. Internal Control, Integration Ability and Performance in Merger and Acquisition. *Auditing Research (in Chinese)*, 3: 43–50.

Yang, Deming, Ting Hu. 2010. Internal Control, Earnings Management and Audit Opinions. *Auditing Research (in Chinese)*, 5: 90–97.

Yang, Demeng, Bin Lin, Yanchao Wang. 2009. Internal Control, Audit Quality and Large Shareholder Tunneling. *Auditing Research (in Chinese)*, 5: 74–81.

Yang, Xiongsheng. 2006a. The Barriers Facing Internal Control Research and the Solutions. *Accounting Research (in Chinese)*, 2: 53–59.

Yang, Xiongsheng. 2006b. The Nature and Objection of Internal Control. *Accounting Research (in Chinese)*, 11: 45–52.

Yang, Youhong, Lingyun Chen. 2009. Research on Internal Control Self-assessment of Public Listed Companies in Shanghai Stock Exchange in 2007. *Accounting Research (in Chinese)*, 6: 58–64.

Yang, Yufeng, Huoxin Wang, Qiong Cao. 2010. The Correlation Study on Internal Control Information Disclosure Quality and Agency Cost. *Auditing Research (in Chinese)*, 1: 82–88.

Yuan, Min. 2008. Internal Control Audit of Listed Company: Issues and Improvement – Evidence From 2007 Annual Reports. *Auditing Research (in Chinese)*, 5: 90–96.

Zhang, Guoqing. 2008. Internal Control and Earnings Quality. *Economic Management Journal (in Chinese)*, 3: 112–119.

Zhang, Guoqing. 2010. The Economic Consequences of Voluntary Internal Control Audit: Empirical Study Based on Audit Delay. *Economic Management Journal (in Chinese)*, 6: 105–112.

Zhang, Jixun, Yanan He. 2013. The Type of Internal Control Audit Opinion and Individual Investors' Confidence in Unqualified Audit Opinion on Financial Statement. *Auditing Research (in Chinese)*, 4: 93–100.

Zhang, Limin, Hua Qian, Minyi Li. 2003. The Current Situation and Improvement of the Internal Control Information Disclosure – Evidence From Analysis Based on Chinese ST Public Companies. *Auditing Research (in Chinese)*, 5: 10–15.

Zhang, Longping, Junzhi Wang, Jun Zhang. 2010. Study of the Effect of Assurance of Internal Control on Accounting Earnings Quality. *Auditing Research (in Chinese)*, 2: 83–90.

Zhang, Wangfeng, Zhaoguo Zhang, Qingxiang Yang. 2011. Study on the Internal Control and Audit Pricing. *Auditing Research (in Chinese)*, 5: 65–72.

Zhang, Yixia. 2012. Factors Influencing Audit Fees of Internal Control Over Financial Reporting: Empirical Research Based on Chinese Companies Listed in the USA. *Auditing Research (in Chinese)*, 12: 70–77.

Zhao, Xi, Ningning Xu. 2013. Managerial Power, Opportunism Motivation and Internal Control Deficiency Information Disclosure. *Auditing Research (in Chinese)*, 4: 68–78.

Zhou, Shouhua, Weimin Hu, Bin Lin, Chunli Liu. 2013. Research on Internal Control of Chinese Listed Companies in 2012. *Accounting Research (in Chinese)*, 7: 3–12.

Zhu, Rongen, Jianxin Xu. 1996. *Modern Enterprise Internal Control System (in Chinese)*. Chinese Audit Publication, Beijing.

16

CASH FLOW MANIPULATION, AUDIT OPINION AND INTERNAL CONTROL – EVIDENCE FROM CHINA

Haiyan Jiang, Huiting Guo, Grant Samkin

1. Introduction

The extant literature on audit opinion is fruitful and has identified a number of determinants of modified audit opinions, including Big N affiliation (e.g., Francis and Yu, 2009), audit firm industry specialization (e.g., Mayhew and Wilkins, 2003), audit firm and audit partner tenure (e.g., Carey and Simnett, 2006), non-audit fees (Habib, 2012), audit report lag (e.g., Ireland, 2003) and client specific variables such as firm size, leverage, profitability and default status.[1] Accrual earnings management is also identified as a common trigger for non-standard audit opinions (Butler, Leone, and Willenborg, 2004; Johl, Jubb, and Houghton, 2007). In addition to accruals management, the recent cash flow management (CFM hereafter) literature finds that firms also manipulate their cash flow information (Lee, 2012; Zang, 2012). This challenges the traditional belief that cash is free from manipulation and can thus be used to gauge the credibility of earnings (Wild, Subramanyam, and Hasley, 2004). Despite this evidence, the monitoring function of auditors on CFM remains under-researched. Thus, it would be an interesting research question whether auditors maintain the same degree of vigilance over cash flow manipulation when compared to accrual management, and are likely to issue a modified audit opinion on client firms who present cash flow irregularities.

CFM is an accounting irregularity designed to mislead users' perceptions of a firm's cash flow position (Lee, 2012). When mangers undertake discretionary CFM, for example, accelerating collections from customers or delaying payments to suppliers, their intention is often unobservable by outsiders. CFM is therefore illusive and difficult to verify. CFM differs from accrual earnings management in that the latter has no direct cash flow implications (e.g., manipulation occurs through change to allowances and provisions). CFM also differs from real earnings management (REM hereafter). REM is employed by managers to manipulate the timing or structure of real operations during the year to meet certain earnings targets using actions such as postponing investment in research and development or overproduction (Roychowdhury, 2006). While some REM activities, such as delaying investment in research and development and cutting discretionary expenses, have cash flow consequences, other activities, such as the timing of sales, do not (Roychowdhury, 2006). There is a paucity of direct evidence on auditor's monitoring on CFM, although recent evidence on auditors' role in REM has important implication.

Recent studies use US data to document auditor's reaction to clients' REM activities. These studies find evidence on higher audit fees to compensate for increased audit effort and perceived business risk (Greiner, Kohlbeck, and Smith, 2017); increased likelihood of auditor resignation from clients conducting REM activities (Kim and Park, 2014); and increased discomfort with clients' engaging with REM activities (Commerford, Hermanson, Houston, and Peters, 2016). In line with these studies, our study investigates the effectiveness of auditor's monitoring, measured as the likelihood of issuing MAOs, on client firms' cash irregularities as measured by abnormal cash flows.[2]

Our empirical investigation uses Chinese data for several reasons. First, compared the extent of CFM conducted by Chinese listed firms to those the US, CFM behavior around zero and zero changes in cash flow are more prevalent in the Chinese than in the US market (Zhang, 2009). Second, it is unclear from prior research whether auditors' monitoring effect on CFM exists in China. Research suggests that audit quality is comparatively less satisfactory and is often compromised in firms with controlling owners (higher degree of ownership concentration). For example, Liu, Su, and Wei (2010) contend that in relationship-based economies like China, auditors are often selected by controlling shareholders to defend them against regulatory investigations in the event of reporting irregularities. Lin and Liu (2010) demonstrate that firms with weak corporate governance, as measured by ownership concentration and CEO-chairman duality, are more likely to switch to a low quality auditor to mask financial reporting opacity. Chan, Lin, and Wong (2010) report that in institutionally weak regions, audit collusion is likely to occur between local State-owned enterprises (SOEs hereafter) and local auditors, as evidenced by auditors' propensity to issue fewer modified audit reports.

In recent years, China has issued a series of accounting and auditing regulations which has resulted in a noticeable enhancement in audit quality (Gillis, 2014). However, it is unclear whether this improvement is reflected in auditors' detecting cash flow manipulation conducted by clients. Using a large sample of listed firms for the period 2007 to 2015, we find that CFM is positively related to MAO in firms with weak internal control but is not related to MAO in firms with strong internal control. We also find that in the absence of good internal control, Top10 auditors show a stronger likelihood of issuing modified audit opinion on client firms suspected of cash flow manipulation than non-top ten auditors. Finally, the analysis reveals that the auditors of SOEs are more likely to issue modified audit opinion for clients firms' cash flow manipulation than non-SOEs' auditors in firms with weak internal control.

This study contributes to literature in several ways. First, to the best of our knowledge, our study is the first to examine the association between CFM and MAOs. The positive effect of CFM on MAOs in firms with weak internal control identifies CFM as an additional audit risk factor which increases the likelihood of non-standard audit opinion. Second, since the underlying intention of CFM is hard to verify, abnormal cash flow can be either a result of justifiable operational decision or an intentional misrepresentation. Our findings demonstrate that auditors do not place the same risk factors on CFM increasing their likelihood of issuing MAOs monotonically, but only penalize CFM of those clients with weak internal control and SOE clients where agency problems are severe. In addition, we highlight the difference between top ten and non-top ten auditors in their propensity to issue MAOs on cash flow irregularities for clients with weak internal controls.

The remainder of the paper proceeds as follows. Section 2 reviews relevant literature and develops testable hypotheses. Section 3 describes sample selection procedures and the research design. Section 4 presents descriptive statistics, correlation analysis and main test results, and Section 5 concludes.

2. Literature review and hypotheses development

Cash flow information is important for investors to assess firms' financial health and verify the credibility of accruals. As a result there has been a significant increase in demand by investors for management and financial analyst cash flow forecasts (Call, Chen, and Tong, 2009; Defond and Hung, 2007). The reason for this is that a large disparity between cash flow from operating activities (CFO hereafter) and earnings is considered to be a "red flag" of earnings quality based on the belief that cash is more "real" than earnings (Dyckman, Magee, and Pfeiffer, 2011; Wild et al., 2004). The traditional belief that CFO is a true reflection of cash inflows and outflows of a firm and is relatively free from managerial manipulation, which is incorrect. Cash flows can be subject to managerial manipulation if incentives are present. Both anecdotal evidence and academic research reports incidences of cash flow misreporting. Lee (2012) reports that managers tend to inflate CFO when firms (1) are financially distressed; (2) have their long-term credit rating near the investment/non-investment grade cutoff; (3) are followed by analysts making CFO forecasts; and (4) have stock returns being highly associated with CFO. Lee (2012) illustrates how managers are able to manipulate CFO by mis-classifying items on cash flow statements★★★★,[3] by accelerating collections from customers, or delaying payments to suppliers. Although these actions increase CFO without altering bottom-line earnings, they significantly affect investors' perceptions and expectation of cash flows (Lee, 2012). While the CFM literature has explored when, why and how firms manage CFO, little evidence is provided on how auditors' react to managers' manipulation of cash flows.

Until recently the audit literature focused exclusively on the auditors' monitoring role in constraining accrual earnings management (e.g., Butler et al., 2004; Johl et al., 2007) rather than on REM. However, the limited literature on the association between audit quality and REM is inconclusive. On one hand, Chi, Lisic, and Pevzner (2011) reports a positive effect of high quality audit, as proxied by city-level industry specialists, on REM. The reason for this is that firms shift accrual earnings management to REM techniques in the presence of stringent monitoring from high quality auditors. However, Zang (2012) finds insignificant relationship between a firm's use of top eight auditors and REM.

On the other hand, recent research provides some evidence on auditor's monitoring on REM evidenced by increased auditor discomfort, increased audit fees due to increased audit effort and perceived audit risks, and high likelihood of auditor resignation (Commerford et al., 2016; Greiner et al., 2017; Kim and Park, 2014). Specifically, Kim and Park (2014) demonstrate that in order to avoid high litigation risk, there is a high likelihood of auditor resignation when clients undertake REM activities. They also find clients' shift to a low quality auditor after high quality auditor's resignation due to REM. Commerford et al. (2016) investigate whether firms' real earnings management causes auditor discomfort. Based on 20 in-depth interviews, they find that auditors are not only aware of, but also actively identify REM through formalized protocols including analytical procedures, discussions with management, or their knowledge of the business. Interviewed auditors believe that REM indicates managers' desire to conduct accrual earnings management or accounting fraud. Auditors respond to the discomfort caused by clients' REM, by increasing scepticism, adjusting audit procedures and risk assessments, and in extreme cases, resigning from an engagement. Additionally, Greiner et al. (2017) find that aggressive income-increasing REM is positively associated with both current and future audit fees due to auditors' increased effort and perceived risk. However, little is known about auditor's monitoring role when client firms conduct CFM, which captures only cash flow manipulation.

Zhang (2009) examines cash flow manipulation in China and finds mangers' undertaking CFM to: (1) report a positive cash flow; (2) avoid a decrease in cash flow from last year's balance;

and (3) achieve positive cash flow surprises in the presence of analyst cash flow forecasts. The first two reasons for undertaking CFM are more prevalent in China than in the US. Zhang (2009) also reveals that in a Chinese context, CFM includes the misclassification between cash flow from financing or investing activities and cash flow from operating activities, selling receivables, transferring in and out of trading securities, and altering the timing of transactions. Examining Chinse listed firms' accounting restatements over the period of 2001 to 2011, Jiang, Habib, and Zhou (2015) find that accrual earnings manipulation increases the likelihood of earnings-related restatement, while a high quality audit reduces the likelihood of earnings-related restatement. However, Jiang et al. (2015) fail to identify auditors' mitigating effects on cash flow restatements associated with cash flow manipulation. These findings suggest that Chinese auditors may not impose the same level of scrutiny on the Statement of Cash Flow as they do on the Income Statement.

Auditors form audit opinions after their assessment of client business, control risks and audit evidence about management assertions (Felix and Kinney, 1982; Rittenberg, Johnstone, and Gramling, 2012). The most common form of audit opinion is the "standard unqualified" audit opinion. However, where auditors are unable to provide a standard clean opinion, they provide qualified, adverse, or disclaimer opinions (Rittenberg et al., 2012). A substantial volume of academic research has identified the likely reasons why auditors' provide qualified reports. For example, Gissel, Robertson, and Stefaniak (2010) provide a comprehensive literature review on the formation and consequences of auditors' going concern opinions. A meta-analysis by Habib (2013) on the modified audit report literature reveals that Big N afffiliation and audit report lags are positively related, whereas the negative effect of non-audit fees on MAOs is found only in non-US studies. Firm-specific factors including size, leverage and profitability are major determinants of auditors' MAOs decisions (Habib, 2013).

Fruitful research has identified determinants of MAOs that are unique to China. Using 180 MAOs and 13341 clean opinons from 1995 to 1997, Chen, Chen, and Su (2001) find that listed Chinese firms who manipulate earnings to meet profitability thresholds are likely to receive MAOs. In a later study, Chen, Su, and Wang (2005) find that the percentage of MAOs issued by Chinese auditors is similar to countries with more mature stock markets. Jiang, Lee, and Yue (2010) find that auditors are more likely to provide qualified audit opinions for those audit clients with large intercorporate loans. This finding is confirmed by Habib, Jiang, and Zhou (2015), which reports that Chinese auditors charged high levels of audit fees to their clients who had extensive intercorporate loans with related parties. Chan et al. (2010) find that in institutionally weak regions of China, local auditors are more likely than non-local auditors to issue standard unqualified opinions to listed companies controlled by local governments when compared to local auditors in institutionally strong regions. Furthermore, companies in institutionally weak regions can successfully engage in opinion shopping and switch to local auditors after receiving a qualified opinion. Recently, Dhaliwal, Liu, Xie, and Zhang (2014) reveal that auditors in China are more likely to issue MAOs to clients who receive negative press coverage due to the perceived litigation risk. They also find that such a positive relation did not exist in a low litigation risk period (2001–2004) and was only observable in a high litigation risk period (2006–2009) after a reform in auditors' responsibilities in 2005.

The audit market in China is competitive due to the active participation of small- and mid-sized audit firms (Simunic and Wu, 2009; Habib and Jiang, 2015). Although the Chinese supplementary market is dominated by the Big 4 firms, they have lower concentration when compared to their counterparts in developed countries.[4] During the period from 2007 to 2014, the Big 4 audit firms only accounted for 21% of the Chinese market, implying a dominance of local audit firms. Although prior literature suggests that audit quality of the Big 4 firms is higher than that of their non-Big 4 counterparts in the US (Becker, Defond, Jiambalvo, and Subra-manyam, 1998), the empirical evidence on the Big 4's audit quality in China is inconclusive. Chen and Zhang (2010) fail to find evidence that international reputable auditors outperform their local Chinese auditors with regard to IFRS compliance. Liu and Lu (2007) suggest that in China, the Big 4 may have lower audit quality in some years or when audit quality is measured with client conservatism. Habib, Jiang, and Zhou's (2013) find that the Chinese stock markets do not assign incremental premium on earnings and earnings components for firms audited by Big 4 auditors.

Audit regulation in China has undergone major changes since the mid-1990s. The first set of Chinese independent auditing standards became effective on January 1, 1996. New standards modeled after the International Standards on Auditing issued by the International Federation of Accountants (IFAC) were issued. The new standards provide auditors with detailed audit-ing procedures, including audit planning procedures, sampling guidelines, standards of audit evidence and clear guidance for audit opinion formulation (Defond, Wong, and Li, 2000). DeFond et al. (2000) report that the frequency of modified audit opinions increased substan-tially after the adoption of the first batch of auditing standards, suggesting an increase in audit quality. However, they also note that the increase in modified reports is followed by a decline in market share among larger auditors who have the greatest incentive to issue modified reports. Since these reforms companies have experiences a significant increase in trading volume and price volatility, a decrease in earnings management and a decrease in stock price synchronicity (Sami and Zhou, 2008). This suggests that the implementation of new auditing standards in 1996 has improved the information environment. During 1997–1998, Chinese government undertook further reforms and introduced policies to disaffiliate auditors from their previously associated government agencies, sponsors, universities or research institutions.[5] To examine the effectiveness of the reform, Gul et al. (2009) show that the likelihood of receiving qualified audit opinions significantly increases after the disaffiliation program. This is not only true for companies previously audited by affiliated auditors, but also for companies previously audited by non-affiliated auditors.

Further reforms occurred in 2004 when China's State-owned Assets Supervision and Admin-istration Commission of the State Council (SASAC) issued two rules in an attempt to improve the audit quality in State-owned enterprises controlled by the central government (CSOEs). These rules mandate that SASAC assign auditors for CSOEs and that the CSOEs retain auditors for at least two years and not more than five years. In the context of this regulatory change, Chi, Lisic, Long, and Wang (2013) find that relative to non-SOEs, CSOEs' audit quality, proxied by a reverse measure of discretionary accruals, has improved. This result is most pronounced for CSOEs' that appointed new auditors in the post regulatory regime. In 2005, China amended its Securities Law. For the first time, auditors would become jointly and severally liable with issuers for losses resulting from shareholders relying on audited financial statements that prove to be false, misleading, or containing major omissions. Taken together, although early audit research in China generally find sub-optimal audit quality when compared to their counterparts in more developed economies, recent regulations and reforms, and mergers have improved auditor inde-pendence and audit quality.

We examine the audit monitoring of CFM conditional on the quality of firms' internal controls. Auditors are required to assess client's internal controls in both the US (PCAOB, 2007) and China (MOF, 2010). The audit engagement starts with a thorough evaluation of a client's internal controls, which then provides the basis for planning the audit procedures. As there are potentially more risks associated with clients with material internal control weaknesses, auditors are more inclined to issue going concern opinions so as to protect themselves from increased legal lability (Carcello and Palmrose, 1994). Using a sample of financially distressed US firms that issued internal control reports under SOX Section 404 in 2004 and 2005, Jiang, Rupley, and Wu (2010) find that they are more likely to receive going concern audit opinions. In addition, weak internal controls facilitate opportunistic behaviors and reduce the reliability of financial reporting. Clients with weak internal controls are therefore more likely to resort to opportunistic reporting to conceal distressed financial situations and impend bankruptcy (Jiang et al., 2010). We argue that internal control weakness also exacerbates client's financial constraint resulting in strong motives of opportunistic CFM, because internal control deficiencies are associated with a higher cost of capital (Ashbaugh-Skaife, Collins, and Lafond, 2009) and negative credit ratings (Jonas, Rosenberg, and Gale, 2006). In this case, the propensity for auditors to issue MAOs for these clients would be high. Taken together, we conjecture that auditors in China are more likely to issue MAOs for client firms with weak internal controls, as they are prone to conduct CFM opportunistically. The hypothesis is formulated as follows:

> *H1: Ceteris Paribus, auditors are more likely to issue MAOs for client firms conducting CFM and with weak systems of internal control.*

The Chinese audit market is dominated by the top ten auditors comprising the Big 4 international firms and six top-tier local firms ranked on the basis of audit revenues. Audit quality of the top ten is considerably better than the remainder of the local audit firms (Defond et al., 2000). Market-based incentives coupled with regulatory requirements meant that from 1999, audit firms in China have merged to form larger firms (Chan and Wu, 2011). In their study, Chan and Wu (2011) find that auditor independence as measured by the change in auditors' propensity to issue MAOs has increased significantly around multi-license mergers between two (or more) audit firms. Chinese audit firms realize the benefits of the economies of scale arising from audit firm mergers in that top ten audit firms significantly reduce audit hours after merger (Gong, Li, Lin, and Wu, 2016). The effect is more pronounced when client firms are more complex. In addition, using a sample of Chinese A-share firms from 1998 to 2012, Ye, Xue, and Yang (2016) find that client firms' financial reporting comparability is significantly increased after mergers. We therefore posit a differential effect of top ten vs. non-top ten audit firms in their likelihood of issuing MAOs for clients who conduct CFM and have weak internal control, leading to the following hypothesis:

> *H2: Ceteris Paribus, top ten auditors are more likely to issue MAOs than non-Top 10 auditors for client firms conducting CFM and with weak systems of internal control.*

3. Sample and methodology

3.1 Sample and data

We extract financial data from the CSMAR for all listed A-shares from 2007 to 2015. To be included in the sample, a firm must have all financial statement data required for computing the research variables, audit opinion and auditor-related variables for each sample year. We exclude firms in the financial service industry (industry code J) to maintain homogeneous interpretations of various accounting variables (e.g., accounting accruals, debt obligations) across the sample firms in different industries. We also delete the observations with negative book values of equity. To alleviate concerns over potential problems arising from the existence of extreme observations, we delete observations that fall within the top and bottom 1% of the annual empirical distributions of the major research variables. After applying the above selection criteria and data requirements, we obtain 15,515 samples that we use for estimating the regression analyses. The sample selection is presented in Panel A of Table 16.1. Panel B of Table 16.1 shows the industry distribution of the sample observations. Machinery, equipment and instrument (Petroleum, chemical, rubber, papermaking, printing, medicine) contributes about 35% (17%) of sample observations.

Table 16.1 Sample selection and industry distribution

Panel A: Sample selection

Description	Observations
Number of firm-year observations in non-financial industries year t during 2007–2015	19890
Less:	
Observations in a year with negative assets, loans, sale revenues and other abnormal negative value	(973)
Observations issued less than three years	(2543)
Observations in a year with other abnormal value	(876)
Preliminary sample during 2007–2015	15498

Panel B: Industry distribution of observations

	Industry Description	Observations	% of sample
1	Farming, forestry, animal husbandry and fishery	238	1.54%
2	Mining and quarrying	406	2.62%
3	Food and beverage	573	3.70%
4	Textile, clothing, fur	471	3.04%
5	Petroleum, chemical, rubber, plastic, papermaking, printing, medicine	2642	17.05%
6	Machinery, equipment, instrument	5436	35.08%
7	Other manufacturing	253	1.63%
8	Production and supply of power, gas, water	588	3.79%
9	Construction	353	2.28%
10	Wholesale and retail trades	1008	6.50%
11	Transportation, storage	596	3.85%
12	Hotel industry	72	0.46%
13	Information technology industry	1210	7.81%
14	Real estate	836	5.39%
15	commercial service industry	156	1.01%
16	Special technical services industry	38	0.25%
17	Public facility, environmental governance industry	100	0.65%
18	Social services	30	0.19%
19	Education industry	9	0.06%
20	Health care industry	14	0.09%
21	Transmitting, culture industry	121	0.78%
22	Integrated	348	2.25%
	Total	15498	100%

3.2 *Empirical models*

Equation (1) is designed to test H1.

$$Logit(MAO) = \beta_0 + \beta_1 CFM + \beta_2 IC + \beta_3 CFM \star IC + \sum_{k=4}^{16} \beta_k X + \varepsilon \tag{1}$$

MAO denotes a modified audit opinion on a firm's financial statement, and cash flow manipulation (CFM) is the variable of interest, measured as abnormal cash flow following Roychowdhury (2006). For all variables, firm and year subscripts are omitted for brevity. The strength of internal control (IC) is measured using the internal control index developed by Shenzhen Dibo Internal Control Database. The index evaluates the company's overall internal control efficiency at the aggregate level, rather than its internal control of financial reporting only. The index is a construction of firm-specific internal control strength scores in relation to five aspects of internal control including internal control strategies, operation efficiency, reporting quality, legal compliance, and asset safety. The Dibo internal control dataset is widely used in research into internal controls of Chinese listed firms (e.g., (Shu, Wang, Zhao, and Zheng, 2015).[6] As our H1 is based on the general monitoring function of effective internal controls, we believe that an aggregate internal control score constructed by the Dibo database is appropriate for the research question.

We also control for a set of variables identified by prior studies that affect auditors' MAOs, including discretionary accruals (DA) measured using Kothari, Leone, and Wasley (2005)'s model, auditor fee (AFE), high quality auditor (Top10), lag of audit report date (ALAG), firm size (SIZE), cash coverage ratio (CCR), return on assets (ROA), ownership concentration (HERF), profit dummy (PFT), profit dummy in last year (LAGPFT), duality of manager and CEO (DUAL), and Tobin's Q (Q). The variable definitions used in the study are detailed in the Appendix. The regression analyses also control for industry and year fixed effects. The standard errors are adjusted for heteroscedasticity and possible correlation among the residuals within firm clusters, in estimating all regressions (Gow, Ormazabal, and Taylor, 2010; Petersen, 2009).

Equation (1) is tested to examine whether the effect of CFM on MAOs is conditional on client firm's internal controls. The second approach we use to test H1 is to partition our sample observations into two sub-samples including strong vs. weak internal control groups based on the median of internal control scores of sample observations. We then test Equation (2) for each sub-sample to identify whether there is significant difference on the coefficients on CFM between the two sub-samples. Equation (2) is a simple variation from Equation (1) excluding internal control strength (IC) and the interactive term, CFM★IC.

$$Logit(MAO) = \beta_0 + \beta_1 CFM + \sum_{k=2}^{14} \beta_k X + \varepsilon \tag{2}$$

Our H2 posits that top ten auditors are more likely to issue MAOs for CFM for those clients who have weak internal controls. To test this hypothesis, we focus on firms with weak internal controls. We divide the sample observations with weak internal control (IC < median of IC) into top ten vs. non-top ten sub-sample groups based on whether or not a firm's annual report is audited by a top ten firm. Then, we estimate a trimmed Equation (1) excluding top ten, internal control strength (IC) and the interactive term, CFM★IC, for top ten vs. non-top ten auditor sub-sample groups respectively. Then, we compare the coefficients on CFM between these two sub-sample groups. We expect a more profound positive effect on CFM for firms audited by top tens than those audited by non-top ten if H2 is supported.

4. Empirical results

4.1 Descriptive statistics and correlation

Table 16.2 provides descriptive statistics used for estimating the regression in Equation (1). The mean of MAO is 0.036, suggesting that most audit opinions are clean and reasonably distributed. With respect to the CFM variables, the mean and median values for absolute abnormal CFO are 0.012 and 0.068 respectively. Approximately 52% of our sample observations are audited by top ten auditors, while in 18% of observations, CEOs also serve as board chairman (DUAL). SOEs (SOE) account for 65.8% of sample observations. To prevent our results from being distorted by extreme outliers, we winsorized continuous variables at the 1% and 99% percentiles.

Table 16.2 Panel B presents Pearson's correlation matrix of variables used in Equation (1). All the correlation coefficients significant at less than the 1% level are detailed in bold, while the one significant at less than the 5% level is shown in italics. We can see that the relationship between MAO and CFM are positive indicating a positive association between MAO and CFM. MAO is negatively correlated with IC (correlation coefficient −0.191), suggesting a lower likelihood of MAOs for firms having strong internal controls. CFM is also negatively associated with IC (correlation coefficient −0.080), which is in accordance with the notion that strong internal controls curb accounting irregularities.

4.2 Multivariate results

We test a baseline regression where the interactive term, CFM*IC, is excluded from Equation (1). The result of the baseline regression is presented in Column 1 of Table 16.3. It suggests that CFM is not related to MAOs significantly for the pooled sample observations. The result indicates that auditors do not perceive CFM homogeneously, and the consequence of a MAO is conditional on other mechanisms. Our H1 proposes internal control as the contextual factors, and thereby Equation (1) also examines this proposition. The results of Equation (1) are presented in Columns (2) of Table 16.3. The effect of CFM on MAO is positive and significant (coefficient 2.270, t statistic 4.808, p<0.01), suggesting that auditors are more likely to issue MAOs in the presence of CFM without considering the strength of internal controls. Internal controls (IC) are negatively associated with MAO (coefficient −0.003, t statistic −13.792, p<0.01), which agrees with literature that auditors' likelihood of issuing MAOs reduces with an increase in the strength of clients' internal controls. The negative coefficient on the interactive term, CFM*IC, suggests a mitigating effect of internal control strength on the likelihood of receiving MAOs in firms with cash flow irregularities (coefficient −0.087, t statistic −3.936, p<0.01). The results therefore support the proposition that the effect of CFM on MAOs is conditional on the strength of internal controls. The signs of coefficients of control variables are consistent with MAO literature in general. For instance, auditors show higher likelihood of issuing MAOs for clients with more discretionary accruals (DA), audit report lag (ALAG) and higher growth rate (Q), while they show a lower propensity to issue MAOs for larger clients (SIZE), better accounting performance (ROA), and firms with positive earnings in the current and previous year (PFT and LAGPFT).

In order to test whether auditors are more likely to issue MAOs for client firms conducting CFM and showing weak internal controls (H1), we conduct a sub-sample analysis using Equation (2). The results are reported in Columns (3) and (4) of Table 16.3. For firms with strong internal controls in column (3), CFM is insignificantly associated with the issue of MAOs (coefficient

Table 16.2 Descriptive statistics and correlation matrix

Panel A: Descriptive statistics

variable	min	p25	mean	media	p75	max	sd
MAO	0.000	0.000	0.037	0.000	0.000	1.000	0.188
CFM	0.001	0.032	0.121	0.068	0.136	1.085	0.168
IC	0.000	6.435	6.310	6.520	6.569	6.903	1.102
DA	0.000	0.021	0.072	0.048	0.092	0.424	0.078
AFE	3.664	13.082	13.538	13.430	13.845	23.744	0.759
Top10	0.000	0.000	0.521	1.000	1.000	1.000	0.500
ALAG	2.079	4.357	4.500	4.477	4.673	10.622	0.612
SIZE	19.268	21.027	21.966	21.802	22.726	25.738	1.294
CCR	−0.647	0.002	0.182	0.111	0.287	1.706	0.352
ROA	−0.175	0.010	0.036	0.031	0.062	0.227	0.058
HERF	0.000	0.006	0.095	0.051	0.152	0.492	0.113
PFT	0.000	1.000	0.895	1.000	1.000	1.000	0.307
LAGPFT	0.000	1.000	0.906	1.000	1.000	1.000	0.291
DUAL	0.000	0.000	0.181	0.000	0.000	1.000	0.385
Q	0.163	0.856	2.158	1.556	2.691	12.027	2.038
SOE	0.000	0.000	0.658	1.000	1.000	1.000	0.474

(*Continued*)

Table 16.2 (Continued)

Panel B: Correlation matrix

	MAO(1)	CFM(2)	IC(3)	DA(4)	AFE(5)	Top10(6)	ALAG(7)	SIZE(8)	CCR(9)	ROA(10)	HERF(11)	PFIT(12)	LAGPFIT(13)	DUAL(14)	Q(15)
(1)	1														
(2)	*0.02*	1													
(3)	−0.191	−0.080	1												
(4)	0.043	0.299	−0.033	1											
(5)	−0.037	−0.024	*0.018*	*−0.049*	1										
(6)	−0.021	−0.022	*0.018*	−0.036	0.237	1									
(7)	0.038	*0.003*	*−0.012*	*0.010*	*0.016*	*−0.006*	1								
(8)	−0.109	−0.045	0.072	*0.005*	0.472	0.088	*0.005*	1							
(9)	−0.060	*−0.003*	0.070	−0.067	*−0.020*	0.034	−0.021	−0.045	1						
(10)	−0.133	0.078	0.116	0.053	*−0.003*	0.039	−0.046	0.036	0.383	1					
(11)	−0.033	*−0.007*	*0.003*	−0.056	0.271	0.087	*0.001*	0.216	*0.026*	*0.001*	1				
(12)	−0.203	0.038	0.219	*−0.010*	0.021	0.023	−0.061	0.091	0.131	0.397	*0.010*	1			
(13)	−0.174	*−0.018*	0.202	−0.041	0.027	0.033	*−0.019*	0.092	0.087	0.181	0.039	0.153	1		
(14)	−0.004	*0.007*	*−0.011*	*0.003*	−0.077	*0.003*	*−0.007*	−0.106	*−0.006*	*0.004*	−0.085	*0.005*	*0.005*	1	
(15)	0.083	*0.017*	−0.041	0.054	−0.197	*−0.005*	−0.041	−0.363	0.183	0.218	−0.081	*−0.005*	−0.045	0.074	1

Note: Correlation analysis is based on CFM observations (15498); The correlation matrix is for the variables used in Equation (1); Pearson's correlation coefficients are provided; bold and italics numbers represent significance at the 1% and 5%.

Table 16.3 The effect of cash flow irregularity and internal control on modified audit opinion – H1 testing

$$Logit(MAO) = \beta_0 + \beta_1 CFM + \beta_2 IC + \beta_3 CFM \star IC + \sum_{k=4}^{16} \beta_k X + \varepsilon \qquad (1)$$

$$Logit(MAO) = \beta_0 + \beta_1 CFM + \sum_{k=2}^{14} \beta_k X + \varepsilon \qquad (2)$$

Variables	(1)	(2)	(3)	(4)
	Baseline model	Eq. (1)	Sub-sample analysis – Eq. (2)	
			Strong IC control	Weak IC control
Intercept	4.458★★	4.443★★	1.791	2.094
	(2.525)	(2.510)	(0.504)	(1.078)
CFM	0.364	2.270★★★	−0.654	0.786★★
	(1.177)	(4.808)	(−0.849)	(2.406)
IC	−0.003★★★	− 0.003★★★		
	(−14.143)	(−13.792)		
CFM★IC		−0.087★★★		
		(−3.936)		
DA	1.355★★	1.385★★	3.375★★★	1.061★
	(2.433)	(2.481)	(2.685)	(1.772)
AFE	0.113	0.122	−0.020	0.144
	(1.130)	(1.218)	(−0.143)	(1.238)
Top10	−0.000	0.011	0.100	−0.028
	(−0.001)	(0.085)	(0.399)	(−0.209)
ALAG	0.162★★★	0.157★★★	0.032	0.159★★
	(2.985)	(2.891)	(0.213)	(2.530)
SIZE	−0.295★★★	−0.303★★★	−0.224★	−0.259★★★
	(−4.739)	(−4.857)	(−1.903)	(−3.712)
CCR	−0.260	−0.260	−0.106	−0.327★
	(−1.595)	(−1.568)	(−0.276)	(−1.822)
ROA	−3.375★★★	−3.280★★★	−8.638★★★	−2.334★★
	(−3.659)	(−3.597)	(−3.252)	(−2.488)
HERF	−0.151	−0.074	0.824	−0.654
	(−0.218)	(−0.107)	(0.818)	(−0.810)
PFT	−0.905★★★	−0.909★★★	−0.445	−1.093★★★
	(−7.191)	(−7.318)	(−1.095)	(−9.284)
LAGPFT	−0.893★★★	−0.874★★★	−1.127★★★	−1.126★★★
	(−8.088)	(−7.900)	(−4.044)	(−10.411)
DUAL	−0.175	−0.178	0.013	−0.195
	(−1.039)	(−1.059)	(0.040)	(−1.066)
Q	0.096★★★	0.096★★★	0.124★★	0.102★★★
	(3.966)	(3.969)	(2.239)	(3.997)
Industry FE	Yes	Yes	Yes	Yes
Year FE	Yes	Yes	Yes	Yes
N	15498	15498	7779	7719
pseudo R^2	0.207	0.210	0.186	0.155

Note: ★★★, ★★, and ★ represent significance at the 1%, 5% and 10% levels.

All variables are defined in Appendix.

−0.654, t statistic −0.849), whereas the effect of CFM is positive and significant for firm-years with weak internal controls as shown in column (4) (coefficient 0.786, t statistic 2.406, p<0.05). This lends direct support to H1.

The results of the test of H2 are presented in Columns (1) and (2) of Table 16.4. Only observations with weak internal control are used here. Column (1) shows the regression result

Table 16.4 Sub-sample analyses: top ten vs. non-top ten; SOE vs. non-SOE in firms with weak internal control

Variables	(1)	(2)	(3)	(4)
	Sub-sample analysis − H2 testing		Additional analysis	
	Top Ten	Non-Top Ten	SOE	Non-SOE
Intercept	1.365	1.418	1.546	1.826
	(0.460)	(0.503)	(0.671)	(0.572)
CFM	1.154**	0.492	0.897**	0.868
	(2.510)	(1.126)	(2.513)	(1.218)
DA	0.920	1.208	0.725	1.482
	(0.996)	(1.481)	(1.023)	(1.257)
Top10			0.028	−0.099
			(0.174)	(−0.496)
AFE	0.097	0.251	0.149	0.158
	(0.650)	(1.243)	(1.002)	(0.851)
ALAG	0.259**	0.134*	0.206***	0.055
	(2.378)	(1.682)	(3.063)	(0.509)
SIZE	−0.246**	−0.278***	−0.229***	−0.271**
	(−2.469)	(−3.030)	(−2.791)	(−2.082)
CCR	−0.315	−0.424*	−0.502**	0.162
	(−1.297)	(−1.686)	(−2.281)	(0.482)
ROA	−3.325**	−1.845	−1.022	−5.874***
	(−2.303)	(−1.551)	(−0.917)	(−3.310)
HERF	0.815	−1.834	−0.871	−0.727
	(0.825)	(−1.324)	(−0.893)	(−0.457)
PFT	−1.140***	−1.036***	−1.081***	−1.093***
	(−6.248)	(−6.644)	(−8.025)	(−4.424)
LAGPFT	−1.151***	−1.116***	−1.171***	−1.126***
	(−6.983)	(−7.719)	(−8.641)	(−5.590)
DUAL	−0.514*	0.023	−0.267	−0.116
	(−1.859)	(0.098)	(−1.261)	(−0.391)
Q	0.151***	0.067*	0.094***	0.098**
	(4.344)	(1.902)	(3.120)	(2.107)
Industry FE	Yes	Yes	Yes	Yes
Year FE	Yes	Yes	Yes	Yes
N	3842	3877	4920	2799
pseudo R^2	0.172	0.158	0.151	0.195

Note: ***, **, and * represent significance at the 1%, 5% and 10% levels.

All variables are defined in Appendix.

for firm-year observations with top ten auditors, and Column (2) shows the regression result for firm-year observations audited by non-top ten auditors. The coefficient on CFM is significant and positive in Column (1) for the top ten sub-sample (coefficient 1.154, t statistic 2.510, p<0.05), but is not significant in Column (2) for the non-top ten sub-sample (coefficient 0.492, t statistic 1.126). Therefore, when irregularities exist in clients' CFO, top ten audit firms are more likely to issue MAOs than non-top ten audit firms.

Although no formal hypothesis is formulated, we extend our analysis to test whether SOEs' auditors are more likely to issue MAOs than auditors of non-SOEs client firms conducting CFM and having weak internal control. Prior studies suggest the severity of agency problems between government and minority shareholder in Chinese SOEs (e.g., Habib and Jiang, 2015). In addition, the quality of SOE accounting information is inferior (Piotroski and Wong, 2012). For this reason, we would expect a greater likelihood for auditors of SOEs to issue MAOs associated with cash flow irregularities than non-SOEs auditors. The sub-sample analysis is presented in Columns (3) and (4) of Table 16.4, which shows a positive (insignificant) coefficient on CFM for SOE (non-SOE) sub-sample. The results support the conjecture that auditors of SOEs are more likely to issue MAOs than non-SOEs auditors, suggesting that auditors of SOEs' are more concerned with accounting information quality than non-SOE auditors.

5.   Conclusion

This study investigates the likelihood of auditors issuing a modified audit opinion on a client firm's cash flow irregularities, and whether auditor takes into account the client firm's internal control strength. Our findings suggest that auditors are likely to issue MAOs on CFM to clients with weak internal rather than strong internal controls. Furthermore, when clients' internal controls are weak, top ten auditors show greater likelihood of issuing MAOs to clients suspected of CFM when compared to non-top ten auditors. Auditors of SOEs are more likely to issue MAOs for cash flow irregularity than those of non-SOEs. The findings shed light on the effectiveness of auditor monitoring on CFM in China suggesting the strength of internal control as an essential factors affecting audit opinions when judgment about the reliability of clients' cash flow information is needed.

The paper contributes to both audit and earnings management literature in the following ways. We extend the audit opinion literature through our examination of auditor's reporting decision on clients' cash flow irregularities. Although recent studies in the US provide evidence of auditors' awareness of REM, auditors' reporting decision on abnormal cash flow is unclear. Our findings also add to CFM literature showing that auditors' perception of and reaction to CFM vary with the strength of the client's internal controls and the presence of government control. Thus, the findings provide confidence in audit reporting in a country where audit industry has undergone major regulatory reforms to improve audit quality. As other emerging or transitional economies also share similar characteristics to China (e.g., strong economic growth, low level of investor protection, etc.), our findings should have implications for these emerging economies.

Appendix
VARIABLES DEFINITION AND MEASUREMENT

Main Variables	Definitions	Measurements
MAO	Modified audit opinion	A dummy variable coded 0 for clear opinion, or 1 for modified opinion
CFM	Cash flow manipulation	Cash flow management, measured as the absolute value of unexpected cash flow from operations (CFO) followed Roychowdhury (2006): $$\frac{CFO_{jt}}{A_{j,t-1}} = \alpha_1 \frac{1}{A_{j,t-1}} + \alpha_2 \frac{Sales_{jt}}{A_{j,t-1}} + \alpha_3 \frac{\Delta Sales_{jt}}{A_{j,t-1}} + \varepsilon_{jt}$$
IC	Internal control strength index	Internal control index developed by Shenzhen Dibo Internal Control Database, which evaluates the company's overall internal control efficiency. The data are extracted from Dibo internal control and risk management database (www.ic-erm.com/).
Control variables		
DA	Earnings management	Absolute discretionary accruals estimated using Kothari et al. (2005)'s model. $$\frac{TA_t}{A_{t-1}} = \alpha_1 \frac{1}{A_{t-1}} + \alpha_2 \frac{\Delta S_t - \Delta AR_t}{A_{t-1}} + \alpha_3 \frac{PPE_t}{A_{t-1}} + \alpha_4 ROA_{t-1} + \varepsilon_t$$
AFE	Audit fees	Natural logarithm of audit fees (in million) paid by a firm in year t
Top10	Auditor quality	An indicator variable set to equal one if a firm is audited by one of the top ten auditors in year t, and zero otherwise. Top ten auditors are identified by a ranking of audit firms' audit revenue per year.
ALAG	Audit report lag	Natural logarithm of the number of calendar days between fiscal year-end and auditor signature date (from Audit Analytics database)
SIZE	Firm size	Natural logarithm of total assets (AT)
CCR	Cash coverage ratio	The ratio measures the amount of cash available to pay for a borrower's interest expense. To calculate the cash coverage ratio, we take the earnings before interest and taxes (EBIT) from the income statement, and add back to it all non-cash expenses included in EBIT (such as depreciation and amortization), and divide by the interest expense.

Main Variables	Definitions	Measurements
ROA	Return on assets	Income before extraordinary items (IB)/total assets
HERF	Herfindahl_10	Ownership concentration measuring the sum of the squares of the top ten shareholders' holding
PFT	Profit or not of this year	An indicator variable set to equal 1 if a firm reports positive income before extraordinary items (IB) in year t, and 0 otherwise
LAGPFT	Profit or not of last year	An indicator variable set to equal 1 if a firm reports positive income before extraordinary items (IB) in year $t - 1$, and 0 otherwise
DUAL	CEO and chairman duality	Dummy variable taking value of 1 if CEO and chairman are the same, otherwise 0
Q	Tobin's Q	The Q ratio is calculated as the market value of a company divided by the replacement value of the firm's assets.
SOE	State control	Whether largest shareholder is the government

Notes

1. Please refer to Habib (2013) for a comprehensive review on audit opinion literature.
2. The cash flow management literature uses the terms cash flow irregularity, abnormal cash flow, cash flow manipulation and cash flow management interchangeably. The measure is estimated using a cash flow model explained later in this paper.
3. Misclassifying cash flow items among categories of operating activities, investing activities and financing activities does not increase total amount of cash flow and earnings, but it manipulates the impression of investors through financial statement misrepresentation (e.g., McVay, 2006).
4. Audit regulation in China requires audit firms to carry out audits in the statutory and supplementary audit market. Publicly listed companies that only issue domestic shares (A-shares) are required to undertake a statutory audit by any qualified audit firm to verify whether the statements are prepared in accordance with the Chinese GAAP. Companies that offer B-shares to foreign investments are required to undergo a supplementary audit to assure whether their Financial Statements follows International Financial Reporting Standards (IFRS). The statutory audit market has low entrance barriers and is highly competitive. China's regulatory preference for large foreign auditors means that the supplementary market is dominated by the Big 4 firms.
5. Prior to the privatization of the Chinese economy, most accounting and auditing firms were affiliated to government agencies, government-sponsored bodies or universities and research institutions. The affiliated relationship between those governmental organizations and firms created serious threat to auditor independence, assisted managerial misconduct and spurred a serial of corporate scandals in the early 1990s (Gul, Sami, and Zhou, 2009).
6. The alternative internal control measure used by several Chinese researchers is an index constructed by Chen, Dong, Han, and Zhou (2017) and was commissioned by Xiamen University, China. However, the index only covers the period from 2007 to 2010.

References

Ashbaugh-Skaife, H., Collins, D. W., William, Jr., R. K., and Lafond, R. (2009). The effect of SOX internal control deficiencies on firm risk and cost of equity. *Journal of Accounting Research*, 47(1), 1–43.

Becker, C. L., Defond, M. L., Jiambalvo, J., and Subramanyam, K. (1998). The effect of audit quality on earnings management. *Contemporary Accounting Research*, 15(1), 1–24.

Butler, M., Leone, A. J., and Willenborg, M. (2004). An empirical analysis of auditor reporting and its association with abnormal accruals. *Journal of Accounting and Economics*, 37(1), 139–165.

Call, A., Chen, S., and Tong, Y. H. (2009). Are analysts' earnings forecasts more accurate when accompanied by cash flow forecasts? *Review of Accounting Studies*, 14, 358–391.

Carcello, J. V., and Palmrose, Z. V. (1994). Auditor litigation and modified reporting on bankrupt clients. *Journal of Accounting Research*, 32(Suppl.), 1–30.

Carey, P., and Simnett, R. (2006). Audit partner tenure and audit quality. *The Accounting Review*, 81(3), 653–676.

Chan, K. H., Lin, K. Z., and Wong, B. (2010). The impact of government ownership and institutions on the reporting behavior of local auditors in China. *Journal of International Accounting Research*, 9(2), 1.

Chan, K. H., and Wu, D. (2011). Aggregate quasi rents and auditor independence: Evidence from audit firm mergers in China. *Contemporary Accounting Research*, 28(1), 175–213.

Chen, H., Dong, W., Han, H., and Zhou, N. (2017). A comprehensive and quantitative internal control index: Construction, validation, and impact. *Review of Quantitative Finance and Accounting*, 49(2), 337–377.

Chen, J. J., and Zhang, H. (2010). The impact of regulatory enforcement and audit upon IFRS compliance – Evidence from China. *European Accounting Review*, 19(4), 665–692.

Chen, J. P., Chen, S., and Su, X. (2001). Profitability regulation, earnings management, and modified audit opinions: Evidence from China. *Auditing: A Journal of Practice and Theory*, 20(2), 9–30.

Chen, S., Su, X., and Wang, Z. (2005). An analysis of auditing environment and modified audit opinions in China: Underlying reasons and lessons. *International Journal of Auditing*, 9(3), 165–185.

Chi, W., Lisic, L. L., Long, X., and Wang, K. (2013). Do regulations limiting management influence over auditors improve audit quality? Evidence from China. *Journal of Accounting and Public Policy*, 32, 176–187.

Chi, W., Lisic, L. L., and Pevzner, M. (2011). Is enhanced audit quality associated with greater real earnings management? *Accounting Horizon*, 25(2), 315–335.

Commerford, B. P., Hermanson, D. R., Houston, R. W., and Peters, M. F. (2016). Real earnings management: A threat to auditor comfort? *Auditing: A Journal of Practice and Theory*, 35(4), 39–56.

Defond, M. L., and Hung, M. (2007). Investor protection and analysts' cash flow forecasts around the world. *Review of Accounting Studies*, 12, 377–419.

DeFond, M. L., Wong, T. J., and Li, S. H. (2000). The impact of improved auditor independence on audit market concentration in China. *Journal of Accounting and Economics*, 28(3), 269–305.

Dhaliwal, D. S., Liu, Q., Xie, H., and Zhang, J. (2014). *Negative press coverage, litigation risk, and audit opinions in China*. Working Paper. University of Arizona.

Dyckman, T., Magee, R., and Pfeiffer, G. (2011). *Financial accounting*. Illinois: Cambridge Business Publishers.

Felix, W. L., and Kinney, W. R. (1982). Research in the auditor's opinion formulation process: State of the art. *The Accounting Review*, 622(2), 247–271.

Francis, J. R., and Yu, M. D. (2009). Big 4 office size and audit quality. *The Accounting Review*, 84(5), 1521–1552.

Gillis, P. (2014). *The big four and the development of the accounting profession in China*. West Yorkshire, England: Emerald Group Publishing Limited.

Gissel, J., Robertson, J., and Stefaniak, C. M. (2010). Formation and consequences of going concern opinions: A review of the literature. *Journal of Accounting Literature*, 29(59–141).

Gong, Q., Li, O. Z., Lin, Y., and Wu, L. (2016). On the benefits of audit market consolidation: Evidence from merged audit firms. *The Accounting Review*, 91(2), 463–488.

Gow, I. D., Ormazabal, G., and Taylor, D. J. (2010). Correcting for cross-sectional and time-series dependence in accounting research. *The Accounting Review*, 85(2), 483–512.

Greiner, A., Kohlbeck, M. J., and Smith, T. J. (2017). The relationship between aggressive real earnings management and current and future audit fees. *Auditing: A Journal of Practice and Theory*, 36(1), 85–107.

Gul, F. A., Sami, H., and Zhou, H. (2009). Auditor disaffiliation program in China and auditor independence. *Auditing: A Journal of Practice and Theory*, 28(1), 29–51.

Habib, A. (2012). Non-audit service fees and financial reporting quality: A meta-analysis. *Abacus*, 48(2), 214–248.

Habib, A. (2013). A meta-analysis of the determinants of modified audit opinion decisions. *Managerial Auditing Journal*, 28(3), 184–216.

Habib, A., & Jiang, H. (2015). Corporate governance and financial reporting quality in China: A survey of recent evidence. *Journal of International Accounting, Auditing and Taxation*, 24(1), 29–45.

Habib, A., Jiang, H., and Zhou, D. (2013). Audit quality and market pricing of earnings and earnings components in China. *Asian Review of Accounting*, 22(1), 20–34.

Habib, A., Jiang, H., and Zhou, D. (2015). Related-party transactions and audit fees: Evidence from China. *Journal of International Accounting Research*, 14(1), 59.

Ireland, J. C. (2003). An empirical investigation of determinants of audit reports in the UK. *Journal of Business Finance and Accounting*, 30(7/8), 975–1015.

Jiang, G., Lee, C. M. C., and Yue, H. (2010). Tunneling through intercorporate loans: The China experience. *Journal of Financial Economics*, 98(1), 1–20.

Jiang, H., Habib, A., and Zhou, D. (2015). Accounting restatements and audit quality in China. *Advances in Accounting*, 21(1), 125–135.

Jiang, W., Rupley, K. H., and Wu, J. (2010). Internal control deficiencies and the issuance of going concern opinions. *Research in Accounting Regulation*, 22(1), 40–46.

Johl, S., Jubb, C. A., and Houghton, K. A. (2007). Earnings management and the audit opinion: Evidence from Malaysia. *Managerial Auditing Journal*, 22(7), 688–715.

Jonas, G., Rosenberg, A., and Gale, M. (2006). *The second year of section 404 reporting on internal control*. New York: Moody's Investors Service.

Kim, Y., and Park, M. (2014). Real activities manipulation and auditors' client-retention decisions. *The Accounting Review*, 89(1), 367–401.

Kothari, S. P., Leone, A. J., and Wasley, C. E. (2005). Performance matched discretionary accrual measures. *Journal of Accounting and Economics*, 39(1), 163–197.

Lee, L. F. (2012). Incentives to inflate reported cash from operations using classification and timing. *The Accounting Review*, 87(1), 1–33.

Lin, Z. J., and Liu, M. (2010). The determinants of auditor switching from the perspective of corporate governance in China. *Advances in Accounting*, 26(1), 117–127.

Liu, F., Su, X., and Wei, M. (2010). *The insurance effect of auditing in a regulated and low litigation risk market: An empirical analysis of Big 4 clients in China*. Working Paper. Sun Yat-sen University, China.

Liu, Q., and Lu, Z. (2007). Corporate governance and earnings management in the Chinese listed companies: A tunneling perspective. *Journal of Corporate Finance*, 13(5), 881–906. http://dx.doi.org/10.1016/j.jcorpfin.2007.07.003

Mayhew, B. W., and Wilkins, M. S. (2003). Audit firm industry specialization as a differentiation strategy: Evidence from fees charged to firms going public. *Auditing: A Journal of Practice and Theory*, 22(1), 33–52.

Ministry of Finance (MOF) (2010). *Enterprise internal control auditing guideline*. Beijing, China.

Petersen, M. (2009). Estimating standard errors in finance panel data sets: Comparing approaches. *Review of Financial Studies*, 22, 435–480.

Piotroski, J. D., and Wong, T. J. (2012). Institutions and information environment of Chinese listed firms. In J. Fan and R. Morck (Eds.), *Capitalizing China* (pp. 201–248). Chicago, USA: National Bureau of Economic Research and University of Chicago Press.

Public Company Accounting Oversight Board (PCAOB), 2007. Auditing standard no. 5: An audit of internal control over financial reporting that is integrated with an audit of financial statements. Washington, DC. USA.

Rittenberg, L. E., Johnstone, K. M., and Gramling, A. A. (2012). *Auditing: A business risk approach* (8th ed.). Mason: South-Western CENGAGE Learning.

Roychowdhury, S. (2006). Earnings management through real activities manipulation. *Journal of Accounting and Economics*, 42(3), 335–370.

Sami, H., and Zhou, H. (2008). Do auditing standards improve the accounting disclosure and information environment of public companies? Evidence from the emerging markets in China. *The International Journal of Accounting*, 43(2), 139–169.

Shu, W., Wang, Z., Zhao, C., and Zheng, Y. (2015). *Internal control and corruption: Evidence from Chinese state-owned enterprises*. Working Paper. Xi'an University of Finance and Economics.

Simunic, D. A., and Wu, X. (2009). China-related research in auditing: A review and directions for future research. *China Journal of Accounting Research*, 2(2), 1–25.

Wild, J., Subramanyam, K. R., and Hasley, R. (2004). *Financial statement analysis*. New York: McGraw/Irwin.

Ye, F., Xue, S., and Yang, C. (2016). Does financial reporting comparability improve after accounting firm mergers? Evidence from Chinese listed companies. *China Journal of Accounting Studies*, 4(4), 475–493.

Zang, A. Y. (2012). Evidence on the trade-off between real activities manipulation and accrual-based earnings management. *The Accounting Review*, 87(2), 675–703.

Zhang, R. (2009). Cash flow management in the Chinese stock market: An empirical assessment with comparison to the U.S. market. *Frontiers of Business Research in China*, 3(2), 301–322.

INDEX

Note: Page numbers in *italic* indicate a figure and page numbers in **bold** indicate a table on the corresponding page.

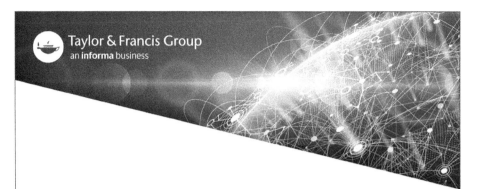

For Product Safety Concerns and Information please contact our EU
representative GPSR@taylorandfrancis.com
Taylor & Francis Verlag GmbH, Kaufingerstraße 24, 80331 München, Germany

www.ingramcontent.com/pod-product-compliance
Ingram Content Group UK Ltd.
Pitfield, Milton Keynes, MK11 3LW, UK
UKHW011454240425
457818UK00021B/821